THE NUCLEAR CAGE

THE NUCLEAR CAGE

CAGE

A Sociology of the Arms Race

Lester R. Kurtz

University of Texas at Austin

With the assistance of
Robert D. Benford and Jennifer E. Turpin

Prentice Hall
Englewood Cliffs, New Jersey 07632

Library of Congress Cataloging-in-Publication Data

KURTZ, LESTER R.
  The nuclear cage.

  Bibliography: p. 294.
  Includes index.
  1. Nuclear weapons.   2. Arms race—History—20th
century.   I. Benford, Robert D.   II. Turpin, Jennifer E.
III. Title.
U264.K87 1988   355'.0217   87-19296
ISBN 0-13-625369-5

Cover illustration: Sarah Beth Asher
Cover design: Bruce Kenselaar
Manufacturing buyer: Raymond Keating

 © 1988 by Prentice-Hall, Inc.
A Division of Simon & Schuster
Englewood Cliffs, New Jersey 07632

Printed in the United States of America
10 9 8 7 6 5 4 3 2 1

ISBN 0-13-625369-5

Prentice-Hall International (UK) Limited, *London*
Prentice-Hall of Australia Pty. Limited, *Sydney*
Prentice-Hall Canada Inc., *Toronto*
Prentice-Hall Hispanoamericana, S.A., *Mexico*
Prentice-Hall of India Private Limited, *New Delhi*
Prentice-Hall of Japan, Inc., *Tokyo*
Simon & Schuster Asia Pte. Ltd., *Singapore*
Editora Prentice-Hall do Brasil, Ltda., *Rio de Janeiro*

Acknowledgment is gratefully made for permission to use material from the
following sources:

page 45: From *Death in Life: Survivors of Hiroshima*, by Robert Jay Lifton.
Copyright © 1967 by Robert Jay Lifton. Reprinted by permission of
Basic Books, Inc., Publisher, and by Deborah Rogers Ltd.
page 55: Max Weber, 1958, *The Protestant Ethic and the Spirit of Capitalism*,
Totowa, NJ: Charles Scribner. Epigraph reprinted by permission of
Allen & Unwin Ltd.

*These acknowledgments are continued on page 322, which constitutes an extension of the
copyright page.*

To my students
and my students' students

Contents

Prologue: A Tale of a Wall   **xi**
Acknowledgments   **xv**

PART ONE   A NUCLEAR WEAPONS PRIMER

CHAPTER ONE
Nuclear Weapons and the Nuclear Arms Race   **1**

CHAPTER TWO
Nuclear War: Past and Present   **21**

CHAPTER THREE
Nuclear War and the Future   **41**

PART TWO   THE SOURCES OF THE ARMS RACE

CHAPTER FOUR
Reciprocity, Bureaucracy, and Ritual   55
Lester R. Kurtz, John Dillard, and Robert D. Benford

CHAPTER FIVE
The Social Psychology of Warfare   77
Lester R. Kurtz and Jennifer E. Turpin

CHAPTER SIX
Economic and Social Roots of the Arms Race   90

PART THREE   COPING WITH THE NUCLEAR THREAT

CHAPTER SEVEN
Alternative Strategies for National Security   107

CHAPTER EIGHT
Deterrence Policies and Assumptions   127

CHAPTER NINE
Civil Defense and Crisis Relocation   145

CHAPTER TEN
"Star Wars": The Strategic Defense Initiative   158

PART FOUR   PREVENTING THE HOLOCAUST

CHAPTER ELEVEN
Superpower Relations   **180**

CHAPTER TWELVE
Arms Control and Disarmament   **204**

CHAPTER THIRTEEN
The Church and the Bomb   **219**

CHAPTER FOURTEEN
The Nuclear Disarmament Movement   **237**
Robert D. Benford

CHAPTER FIFTEEN
Visions of a New World Order   **266**

APPENDIX A
The Methods of Nonviolent Action   **278**

APPENDIX B
Nuclear Arms Control Treaties and Options   **283**

Notes   **286**

Bibliography   **294**

Index   **323**

Prologue: A Tale of a Wall

For whatever reason, we humans have always been careful about establishing our boundaries. We have been great wall-builders throughout history, protecting ourselves against enemies of all sorts, both human and nonhuman. Thus great walls and fences, residues of past civilizations, dot the landscape. The Great Wall of China, Hadrian's Wall, and the castle and city walls of medieval Europe are symbols of ingenuity in this type of defense.

Castle and city walls threatened to become obsolete, however, with the invention of the cannon, which seemed to ignore such barriers. More sophisticated fortifications thus emerged. A competition between sides for better fortifications followed, and concern about "wall gaps" arose. If the enemy had better "walls," the cry arose to modernize one's own defenses.

As civilization "advanced," additional walls became ineffective. Airplanes made it possible to fly over enemy walls and submarines enabled people to sneak under them. Tanks provided troops with mobile walls that allowed soldiers to move into enemy territory.

Finally, toward the end of World War II, the wall to end all walls was built: the *nuclear* wall. Once constructed it was a wall that was both physical and psychological, both visible and invisible. It was most sophisticated, but also quite primitive. The nuclear wall worked by silently projecting that ancient territorial message: "Cross this line, and I'll blow your head off!"

The nuclear wall is small, mobile, and devastating; it is dynamic and ever-changing. It proved extremely successful in actual use—the only time the wall was activated, it blew up two cities. The country that first built a nuclear wall very quickly began expanding it in several directions, building it higher, and increasing the danger that it posed to any intruders. Other countries soon began building the wall, too, and before long the wall encircled the entire globe in a mutual system of threats.

People in different parts of the globe constantly watched what others were doing to the nuclear wall, and when advances were made in one area, efforts were doubled on the other side of the planet. When new building methods were devised on one side, they were duplicated and improved upon on the other side. When a new stockade or guard tower was added in one section, workers in another section frantically constructed something similar. Wall experts were constantly modernizing the wall, and they became so caught up in the details of design and construction that they seldom stood back to see what they had created. What they did not realize was that it was not really a wall at all. Despite the original intentions of its creators, it had made walls obsolete. All that was left was the threat of a kind of aggression against which all defense, even retaliation, would produce ruin without victory if ever carried out.

One major problem of the nuclear fortress was that it was therefore very dangerous, and many people were convinced that some day—perhaps accidentally—it would explode and destroy much of the planet. Because it was so complex, very few people actually understood how it worked. Consequently, it seemed to take on magical powers. For the most part, although people feared it, they simply went about their everyday business and ignored it. Like all other barriers, however, the nuclear wall not only shuts your enemy *out*, it shuts you *in*. The wall thus became a cage—a *nuclear cage*—within which all of humanity was soon trapped. It ceased to provide the defense for which it was built; in fact, rather than making people feel secure, it created what was called a "balance of terror."

Nobody really cared much for the cage, although many people profited monetarily from its construction, and some, at least in the beginning, felt more secure because of it. Moreover, few people were willing to give it up, because of the apparent power it had, and people were less frightened about a potential catastrophe with the wall than they were of what would happen if they eliminated it.

The two major nuclear countries in the world now spend a major portion of their national wealth on their nuclear cages. The basic structure has been in place for some time, but the wall experts are constantly coming up with new ideas, and the wall is constantly changed.

This book tells the story of the nuclear cage—why we became trapped in it, what it might mean, and how we might free ourselves from it. It tells the tale of many attempts to get rid of the nuclear cage and the proposals people are currently putting forth to end the threat it poses to all humanity. It also recounts the tale of the structures and deceits that keep the cage in place. Although written from a sociological perspective, it draws on a wide variety of academic disciplines to provide an overview of what may be the most important social problem the human race has ever faced.

A NOTE ON OBJECTIVITY

When discussing such a controversial subject as the nuclear arms race, an important first step is to examine the assumptions of those who are providing information about the topic. That is a major theme of this book, and a good sociological rule of thumb. Different people have quite diverse perceptions of the problem, in large part because of their personal interests; there are no disinterested parties on the issue of the nuclear arms race, because every individual has something at stake. In the words of the old aphorism, "Where you stand depends on where you sit." You can expect, for example, that a university professor will have a different perspective from an Air Force general, whose ideas will differ from those of a member of Congress or a military contractor. Each will approach the issue from his or her own point of view and will interpret the same facts in different ways. Ironically, nationality often plays a less important role than occupation in molding opinions about the arms race: It is likely that a Soviet and an American general will have more in common on this issue than a U.S. general and a U.S. Catholic bishop. It is remarkable how easily we can rationalize almost any position we hold, bending the truth to fit our definition of the situation.

It is also important to examine one's own assumptions, to try to figure out why we think the way we do about a particular topic. Therefore, it is important that I be candid from the beginning about where I stand on the problem of the nuclear threat.

That we are trapped in a nuclear cage is the first assumption of this book. It is a cage that we have constructed, so it is possible for us to change the situation, but the cage is something that encompasses *everybody* and it is not easily altered. The metaphor of the nuclear cage is adapted from sociologist Max Weber's metaphor of the "iron cage," which he used to describe the nature of bureaucratic institutions. Ironically, when bureaucracies are created for a particular purpose, they seem to take on a life of their own and operate somewhat independently of their creators. Furthermore, they often subvert the very purposes for which they were created.

A second assumption found in this book, therefore, is that the nuclear cage is undesirable; in fact, it is disastrous. The military institutions built up around nuclear arsenals dangerously subvert the security they were supposed to provide, despite the good intentions of many individuals within them. The approach here is a *critique* of the nuclear arms race. In that sense, it is a case study in the sociology of knowledge. The purpose of this book is not only to report some of the knowledge we have about nuclear weapons and their implications but also to analyze that knowledge from a critical sociological perspective. I believe that is an appropriate role for social scientists to play when approaching any topic, although some would disagree.

Third, I assume that pure objectivity about the nuclear arms race is impossible. Objectivity refers to knowing something "in and of itself," without biases or perspectives. As Immanuel Kant pointed out, it is impossible for humans to have that kind of knowledge about any phenomenon. That does not mean, however, that one should not strive for objectivity. I will try to present some balance in this book, despite its critical tone, because it is important to understand *all* sides (there are not just two) of the issue.

If we are to understand the nuclear threat with any objectivity whatsoever, we must do more than simply master the facts and figures. Simply to know how many warheads each of the superpowers has, or any other of the thousands of bits of information one might obtain, is not to know the nuclear threat objectively. Nuclear war means death. More than death, it means the potential annihilation of life as we know it. In order to understand what nuclear war is, we must feel as well as think; we must think the unthinkable, and use our imaginations to come to grips with the possible extinction of human life.

I invite you to maintain an open mind and to enter these troubled waters in an earnest search. I do not pretend to have the answers to the problems raised here; some of the answers have probably not even been invented yet. I do feel that a way out of the nuclear cage can be found, but only if we all keep looking for it. My purpose in writing this book is to make a small contribution to an ongoing process, and to challenge others to join the struggle.

Acknowledgments

Scholars often appear to work alone, but it is the community that makes even the most individual efforts possible. That is very much the case with the work that resulted in this book; the stimulation and assistance of an extended community were indispensable. This work is dedicated to my students because they provided what Max Weber called the "value relevance" that was the driving force behind it. For five years I have been encouraged by the interest and seriousness with which the hundreds of students who have taken my course on the nuclear arms race have grappled with the difficult issues of this book. Lively debates and ongoing challenges in the classroom have been among the most valuable learning experiences in my search for an understanding of this baffling topic.

The dedication is also directed to my students' students, with a hope for the future that flies in the face of what I consider the most probable future of humanity. We now confront a difficult struggle in our attempts to escape the nuclear cage, but my students inspire an optimism that may be irrational, but is nonetheless genuine.

Special thanks go to the two students who have played a key role in the writing of this book: Robert D. Benford and Jennifer E. Turpin. Hours of conversations and concrete assistance from them has made it possible. Others who have made exceptional contributions are John Dillard, Sam

Marullo, Louis Kriesberg, John Stockwell, and John Bandy. Sarah Beth Asher illustrated the book and provided many helpful suggestions.

A long list of friends and colleagues made significant contributions to portions of the manuscript, either directly or indirectly. Among them are Joe R. Feagin, Peter Rutland, Steven Dubin, Louis Zurcher, Randy Hodson, Carol Heimer, Art Stinchcombe, Morris Janowitz, Ira Chernus, Joel Sherzer, Nancy Bell, and Gregory Urban. Finally, my friends in United Campuses to Prevent Nuclear War (UCAM) played an important role by supporting and inspiring me to write the book, especially Sanford Gottlieb, Tina Clarke, Lisbeth Gronlund, Sam McFarland, Peter Stein, April Moore, Wayne Bryan, and Nick and Joan Cominos.

Beverly LeSuer's careful editing resulted in many helpful suggestions and changes. Encouragement from Prentice Hall's Bill Webber was invaluable, as was financial support from the University Research Institute at the University of Texas at Austin.

CHAPTER ONE

Nuclear Weapons and the Nuclear Arms Race

NUCLEAR WEAPONS AND HOW THEY WORK

One of the difficulties encountered by people wishing to participate in policy debates about the nuclear cage is that the debates are often highly technical and the experts sometimes resent public discussions about the issue. If we are to act as if we live in a democracy, we must familiarize ourselves with the basic properties of nuclear weapons and the limited knowledge available about what might happen should a nuclear war occur.

A Clear and Present Danger

President Kennedy, in his inaugural address, spoke of the nuclear sword of Damocles hanging over our heads. What is remarkable is that twenty-five years later, that sword is still there—larger and more precarious, but it manages to remain in the air.

Apocalyptic pronouncements are always suspect, especially in cautious academic circles, and they are often proven incorrect. And yet, the impending danger of a nuclear holocaust is a central fact of life in the modern world, and predictions of its coming run across the entire political spectrum. From the Peace through Strength slogan of right wing efforts to justify a massive military buildup, to the most ardent disarmament activist, the tale of impending doom is a frequent argument.

Most of us do not like to think about the nuclear cage and its implications, let alone to dwell on them. And yet, that is precisely what we must do if we are to solve what may be the most urgent social issue of our time. We must analyze and study the threat it presents; we must weigh the facts and the various interpretations of them. Then we must act. The analytical part of our duty is the challenge of this book, and especially of this first chapter.

Although the unlocking of the secret of nuclear weapons was a difficult and complex process, it is relatively easy for someone with the proper technical background to build such a weapon—provided he or she can obtain the fuel for it. Fortunately, this fuel is not easy to obtain. The explosion of even the most primitive atomic weapon could have devastating consequences.

Nuclear Weapons and Their Effects

There are two kinds of nuclear explosions: fission and fusion. Nuclear fission takes place within atomic bombs and nuclear power plants; it involves the fission, or breaking apart, of the nucleus of a uranium-235 atom, caused by impact with a neutron (see Figure 1.1). The energy that is given off by the fission of a nucleus and the liberating of neutrons creates the famous chain reaction that occurs within a tiny fraction of a second, un-

Figure 1.1 Nuclear fission.

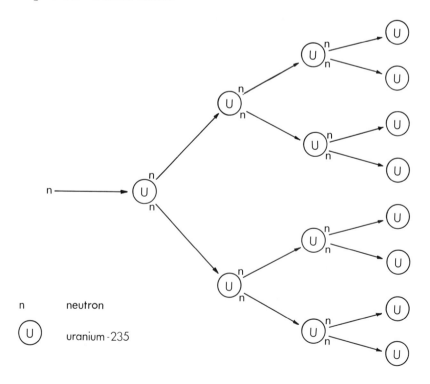

n   neutron

Ⓤ   uranium-235

leashing an astonishing blast. Nuclear fusion, on the other hand, takes place in hydrogen bombs. It requires the fusion, or bringing together, of the nuclei of two heavy isotopes of hydrogen, deuterium and tritium (see Figure 1.2). Under very high temperatures and pressures, the fusion of these hydrogen isotopes forms helium and releases tremendous energy.

The hydrogen bomb, or thermonuclear weapon, is really two bombs in one: It uses both fission and fusion (see Figure 1.3). First, a plutonium bomb (at the top) is set off by chemical explosives (left) creating a *fission* chain reaction (center) which, in turn, releases radiation that reflects off of the outer walls of uranium (right). The radiation then bombards the container of fusion materials, causing it to collapse and produce the high temperatures and pressures required for the fusion of deuterium and tritium. The *fusion* explosion in turn sets off a fission chain reaction in the uranium in the container and outer walls. The entire process takes only a millionth of a second and unleashes a violent series of consequences.

Recent work in nuclear technology is directed at developing a third generation of nuclear weapons—very accurate, small weapons such as the X-ray laser. (The first generation is fission bombs; the second generation, hydrogen bombs.)

Put simply, a nuclear weapon has three basic effects: thermal (heat) radiation, a blast wave, and nuclear radiation. Scientists who study weapons effects often discuss the effects of a 1-megaton (MT) bomb, which is equivalent to 1 million metric tons of TNT. The Hiroshima bomb was much smaller, approximately 14 kilotons (KT), or 14,000 tons of TNT.

Such vast amounts of explosives are difficult to envision. It was esti-

Figure 1.2 Fusion reaction.

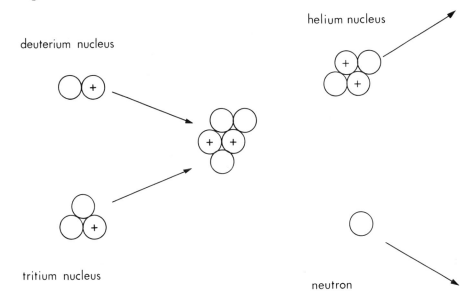

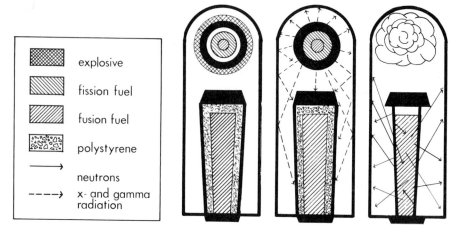

Legend:

explosive	
fission fuel	
fusion fuel	
polystyrene	
→	neutrons
----→	x- and gamma radiation

Figure 1.3 The hydrogen bomb.

mated, for example, that the truck that exploded in the U.S. Marine compound in Beirut in 1983 contained about half a ton of explosives. A kiloton would be equal to two thousand of those trucks of explosives, all detonated together in a fraction of a second. A megaton would be approximately two million of them.

A 1-megaton nuclear explosion could melt 1.6 million tons of ice and turn it into steam, almost instantaneously. An estimated total of 3 million tons of explosives were used in all of World War II, but a single MX missile carries warheads with a total of 5 million tons of explosives. A nuclear warhead little more than a yard high can have an explosive equivalent of 1 million tons of TNT; that amount of TNT would fill a freight train 300 miles long (see Tsipis 1983:44; cf. Glasstone and Dolan 1977).

Thermal effects. When a nuclear explosion occurs, enormous amounts of heat are released, producing a fireball that is similar in heat intensity to the sun, tens of millions of degrees Fahrenheit. It is smaller, of course, but it is also not 93 million miles away. A 1-megaton blast lasts ten seconds and creates a fireball that continues to expand for nine minutes until it is three miles in diameter.

The bright flash of light suddenly illuminates the landscape; anyone glancing at the fireball with unprotected eyes is immediately blinded. Not only human eyes are affected; all animal life is subjected to the same danger. Once the fireball touches the ground, it evaporates almost everything: steel, rock, concrete, and people.

Blast effects. About 50 percent of the energy yield of a nuclear blast is in the form of blast effects. A shock wave moves out in all directions from the point of detonation, moving at about the speed of sound. The blast wave from a 1-megaton explosion crushes all but the strongest structures to a distance of about 1.7 miles from ground zero (the spot on earth directly beneath the detonation). Most factories and commercial buildings collapse; small wood-frame and brick residences shatter, and the debris flies through the air at enormous speeds. The blast wave is a traveling wall of pressurized air, and its strength is measured in terms of overpressures. The blast wave diminishes gradually as it moves out from the point of detonation, so that the farther it moves from the explosion, the smaller the overpressures it creates.

When the human body is subjected to high overpressures, it is immediately squeezed inward from all directions. It is more likely, however, that persons within a few miles of ground zero will be killed or injured by being thrown through the air or hit by flying debris. At 17 psi (pounds per square inch) of overpressure, the winds would throw people at a speed of 60 miles per hour until they hit a solid object. Even at 5 psi of overpressure, a windowpane would shatter and its pieces would hurl through the air at 120 miles per hour (see Tsipis 1983:53ff.).

Radiation effects.   Finally, for those far enough away from the fireball and blast wave to escape immediate death, there is the danger of immediate radiation and, even more deadly, radioactive fallout. The neutrons and gamma rays emitted briefly during the detonation are a very powerful form of ionizing radiation, which is so called because it removes electrons from the atoms that form cell molecules in body tissues. Such radiation damages or destroys molecules and cells, until, at high enough levels, it causes radiation sickness.

However, even more radiation danger is associated with the familiar mushroom cloud. The cloud is initially created by the condensation of water from the intense temperatures of the fireball, and it sucks up dust and debris as it rises into the air (especially after a ground burst). Longer lived radioactive byproducts are then dispersed over a wide area through contaminated dust and rain that fall out of the mushroom cloud downwind from ground zero.

The amount of damage caused by radiation depends upon the dose (the amount of radiation entering the body) and the period of exposure. The same amount of radiation (measured in roentgen units, or rem) received during one or two days would lead to death within one or two weeks, whereas if received over a period of months, it might cause genetic damage or cancer but not create the symptoms of radiation sickness.

After exposure to about 100 rem the body no longer makes white blood cells, reducing one's ability to fight infection (similar to the effect of AIDS). Approximately 150 rem cause hair loss and nausea, while 200 rem would create severe radiation sickness and sometimes death. Almost all victims die after exposure to 600 rem. Recent studies suggest that lethal doses may even be much lower, perhaps only 150 rem. Furthermore, the early symptoms of radiation sickness are indistinguishable from those created by panic, and diagnosis is almost impossible even by trained medical personnel.

Some of the effects of fallout come much later. A fifteen-year-old girl who was one kilometer from ground zero in Hiroshima spent a year in the hospital recovering from radiation sickness. Fourteen years later, she gave birth to a baby girl who was deformed and died shortly after birth.

Moreover, the effects of radioactive fallout can be widespread, as the 1986 nuclear power plant accident at Chernobyl demonstrated. Within two weeks, radioactive rain was falling throughout the Northern Hemisphere, and dangerous levels of radioactivity (according to government officials) were found among the Soviet Union's more immediate neighboring countries.

Thus, even in a limited attack on the United States of 10,000 to 20,000 MT, directed toward military targets rather than cities, the entire country would receive lethal fallout.

Other effects.   In addition to blast, heat, and nuclear radiation effects, a number of other effects are created by the detonation of a nuclear bomb, such as the electromagnetic pulse (EMP) set off by the explosion. During the blast, gamma rays strip atoms in the atmosphere of some of their electrons—much as lightning does, but on a vastly greater scale. The EMP moves outward in all directions ahead of the blast wave, traveling much faster and affecting a much larger area. It is likely that a single high-altitude burst over the midwest would bathe the entire United States in an EMP that would create a total electric blackout, eliminate communications, damage solid-state circuits in computers, trip switches in relay stations, shut down generating plants, and much more.

Another effect is the occurrence of massive fires, which dramatically increase the lethal area of nuclear weapons effects. All flammable material within about six miles of a 1-megaton ground burst would probably ignite. Firestorms would be fed by broken gas lines, fuel storage tanks, and industrial materials. We do not know how long such firestorms would continue to burn, but temperatures could reach thousands of degrees. Such fires would burn up oxygen and asphyxiate people in shelters, as happened during the firestorms in Dresden during World War II.

In short, just as the fission or fusion process sets off a chain reaction on a microscopic scale, so the detonation of large numbers of nuclear weapons would set off a chain reaction on a macroscopic (global) scale, resulting in a catastrophe that exceeds the imagination (see Chapter Three). In addition to there being millions of deaths, survivors would face social, economic, and political collapse. And no outsiders would arrive to help, as they did in Hiroshima.

The more we learn about the effects of nuclear war, the worse it appears it would be. In a major exchange (for example, 10,000 MT) the ozone layer would be partially destroyed, and it would take thirty years for ozone levels to return to normal. Every unprotected eye on the planet, human and nonhuman alike, would be blinded. The blast wave would be followed by winds reaching hundreds of miles per hour. The dust and smoke generated by explosions and fires would be thrown into the atmosphere and envelop the earth, preventing normal levels of sunlight from reaching the earth's surface. Land temperatures might plunge to 13 degrees below zero Fahrenheit, stay below freezing for months, and destroy most plant and animal life on the planet. Human survivors would likely starve to death in a twilight, radioactive gloom—a "nuclear winter"—that would last for months (Turco et al. 1983; Ehrlich et al. 1983).

What is being done to prevent such a catastrophe from happening? Each superpower is frantically adding to its nuclear arsenal in an effort to intimidate the other into not using the weapons it possesses. The world now has almost 50,000 nuclear warheads, about 97 percent of them in the United States and the Soviet Union (Sivard 1985:12).

NUCLEAR ARSENALS

Until recently, discussions about new weapons systems usually concerned developments in *delivery* systems. Although no typology is hard-and-fast, weapons systems are often divided into three categories: strategic, theater, and tactical, as shown in Table 1.1.

Table 1.1   Types of Weapons Systems

Strategic nuclear weapons: long-range delivery systems that can reach an adversary's homeland
   1. *Intercontinental ballistic missiles (ICBMs)*: usually defined as having a range greater than 5,500 kilometers
   2. *Submarine-launched ballistic missiles (SLBMs)*
   3. *Intercontinental bombers*

Theater nuclear forces: deployed to wage war in a particular region, such as the European theater
   1. *Intermediate-range ballistic missiles*: range of 2,200–5,500 kilometers
   2. *Ground-launched cruise missiles*: range of 2,400 kilometers

Tactical nuclear weapons: for use on the battlefield
   1. *Land-based warheads*: short-range artillery rounds, Lance missiles, atomic land mines
   2. *Naval Warheads*: aerial bombs, depth bombs, Terrier missiles, Asroc antisubmarine weapon missiles, Subroc antisubmarine missiles

---

Much emphasis is placed on strategic nuclear weapons, which can travel the distance between the United States and the Soviet Union. Both superpowers have a triad of strategic forces: Intercontinental ballistic missiles (ICBMs), submarine-launched ballistic missiles (SLBMs), and strategic bombers.[1]

The American Strategic Triad

Strategic bombers. The bomber leg of the U.S. triad currently relies primarily on the B-52 Stratofortress. The B-52H and B-52G models carry up to 20 nuclear short-range attack missiles (SRAMs) and 4 nuclear gravity bombs. There are currently 167 B-52G and 96 B-52H operational bombers in the U.S. arsenal, with almost 3,250 weapons. In addition, 98 B-52Gs carry 12 air-launched cruise missiles (ALCMs).

A second strategic bomber is the FB-111A, which can fly more than twice the speed of sound at altitudes over 60,000 feet, carrying 6 nuclear SRAMs, 6 nuclear bombs, or conventional weapons. The United States has about 61 FB-111s (with 366 weapons), all of which have Terrain Following Radar, which allows them to fly at very low altitudes to avoid detection by radar.

The newest bomber in the U.S. arsenal is the controversial B-1, which became operational in 1986. Each B-1 bomber is expected to cost between $200 million and $300 million. The B-1 is scheduled to replace the B-52 until the new radar-evading stealth bombers (or advanced technology bombers—ATBs) are produced in the early 1990s. Each B-1 can carry 32 nuclear missiles or cruise missiles, or 115,000 pounds of conventional bombs.

ICBMs. Intercontinental ballistic missiles comprise the land-based leg of the triad, with 1,024 Minuteman and Titan missiles. ICBMs are deployed in "hardened" cement silos that are designed to protect them from all nuclear explosions except those that make a direct hit on the silo. The silos are guarded by two-officer duty crews on alert twenty-four hours a day.

Until the United States began dismantling ICBMs in 1982 (to stay within the limits of the SALT agreements), it had 52 Titan II missiles, first deployed in 1959, each of which carries a single warhead with a yield of about 9 megatons. The Minuteman III, which was used to replace the Titans, has three multiple independently targetable reentry vehicles (MIRVs), each with a yield of 170 kilotons. As shown in Figure 1.4, each of the three warheads can hit a separate target.

The most recent ICBM development in the American arsenal is the Missile Experimental—usually known as the MX, although officially renamed the Peacekeeper. The MX is a very large, extremely accurate missile that carries 10 MIRVs of 350 kilotons each. With a reported accuracy of about 300 feet, it has a first-strike capability.

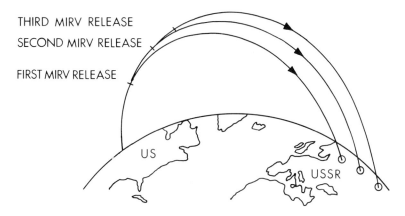

THIRD MIRV RELEASE

SECOND MIRV RELEASE

FIRST MIRV RELEASE

US

USSR

Figure 1.4   Multiple independently targetable reentry vehicles.

Submarine-based missiles.   Most of the American SLBMs are on Poseidon submarines. There are 31 Poseidon submarines still operational; each carries 16 missiles, with 10 to 14 MIRVs on each missile, for a total of up to 224 warheads. Just one Poseidon submarine carries more explosive power than all of the firepower used by all sides in World War II; it could, by itself, destroy the largest cities in the USSR, effectively eliminating it as a functioning society.

Nevertheless, the Poseidon is being replaced by the new Trident submarine. There are now 6 Trident submarines, each of which carries 24 Trident missiles, with 8 to 10 MIRVs of 100 kilotons each. At least 20 Tridents are planned by the turn of the century, and in 1989 the Navy will begin deploying new, highly accurate Trident II/D-5 missiles.

The United States has 37 nuclear submarines with 5,728 warheads, 1,024 ICBMs[2] armed with 2,124 warheads, and a fleet of 324 bombers with about 3,614 bombs. Any one leg of the triad is capable of destroying the Soviet Union; with a total of an equivalent of over 73,000 Hiroshima bombs, the United States has more than 18 times the amount of explosives required to destroy the Soviet Union.

The Soviet Nuclear Arsenal

On the other side of the planet stands a similar threat: the Soviet Union's arsenal, based primarily on ICBMs.

Soviet ICBMs.   Although the United States has concentrated on building smaller, more accurate nuclear weapons, the Soviet Union (until very recently) has emphasized larger, more powerful weapons, which cannot be delivered with as much accuracy.[3] The older SS-9 missile, which has now been replaced with newer weapons, was able to carry either a huge 25-megaton warhead (Mod-2) or three 4 to 5 megaton warheads (Mod-4).

The Soviets have about 308 SS-18 missiles, most of which have 10 warheads, but some of which are single-warhead missiles, for a total of about 2,990 warheads.

Soviet bombers.   Soviet long-range bombers include the Tu-95 (code named the Bear) and the Mya-4 (code named the Bison). They became operational in 1956 and the Soviets today have a total of about 170 of them. Whereas the Bear is a propeller-driven bomber, the Bison is a four-jet bomber. Another bomber in the Soviet arsenal is the Backfire, which has a medium range of about 3,000 nautical miles. The Soviets have 130 Backfire aircraft. Because of its short range, the Backfire is not an intercontinental bomber unless it is refueled in flight.

Soviet submarines.   The Soviets have two classes of submarines: the Delta class and the Yankee class. (The Yankee class Soviet submarines are nuclear powered.) The Soviets probably have 656 missiles with single warheads,[4] and another 268 missiles that carry 3 to 9 warheads each, totalling about 1,522 warheads. All together, the Soviets have approximately 2,178 warheads on SLBMs.

The Soviet arsenal provides the equivalent of 114,000 Hiroshimas, an overkill of more than 28 times the amount of explosive power needed to destroy the United States. The attentive reader will immediately ask the question: If the Soviets can destroy the United States 28 times, and the Americans can destroy the Soviet Union 18 times, does that mean that the United States is behind in the arms race?

WHO IS WINNING THE ARMS RACE?

There has been a great deal of discussion throughout the arms race about who is ahead and who is behind, but many experts claim that such questions are meaningless once a certain level of destruction is reached. In the 1980s both superpowers have the ability to destroy the other side many times over. It is not necessary to be an expert to question the debate over superiority and inferiority that fills the newspapers. So, what is all of the fuss about?

A major concern since the late 1970s has been the so-called window of vulnerability. Essentially, the argument was that American ICBMs would be threatened by Soviet missiles by the mid-1980s. If the Soviets were suddenly to attack without warning, what would happen? Because some Soviet missiles will probably not hit their targets as planned, hundreds of American ICBMs may in fact survive; but let us suppose, for the moment, that the worst possible case comes true. A study conducted by the Congressional Budget Office concluded that such a surprise attack by the Soviets would leave the United States with a force of 400 land-based missiles, about 25 submarines, and about 100 bombers. In short, the United States would be left with approximately 6,000 hydrogen bombs, for an equivalent of 36,000 Hiroshima bombs. Since just one Poseidon submarine could destroy the Soviet Union as a functioning society, the question of the American ability to retaliate seems rather foolish. Six thousand thermonuclear weapons could probably destroy the Soviet Union nine times over.

This example demonstrates a major problem with the bean-counting aspect of nuclear policy: Because of the specialization of the arms race, people who are concerned with one matter, for example, with the survivability of ICBMs, tend to focus on their particular part of the puzzle and ignore other key elements of the overall picture.

Soviet and American Comparisons

But what about claims that the United States is behind the Soviet Union in important areas of weapons development? In one sense, they are true, but only because the two superpowers have followed slightly different strategies in developing their nuclear forces. These different strategies are due to deliberate choices made by each country related to their technological capabilities. The American arsenal is more diversified than the Soviet arsenal. As shown in Figure 1.5, about half of the American arsenal is based on SLBMs, 19 percent on ICBMs, and 31 percent on bombers. The Soviets, on the other hand, have 68 percent of their warheads on ICBMs, 24 percent on SLBMs, and only 8 percent on bombers. The Soviet Union, with limited port facilities for submarines, was the first country to develop ICBMs and made land-based missile development the major priority of its system.

Observe how easily the figures can be manipulated because of the different strengths of the American and Soviet programs. Soviet leaders

Figure 1.5 Diversification of strategic triads.

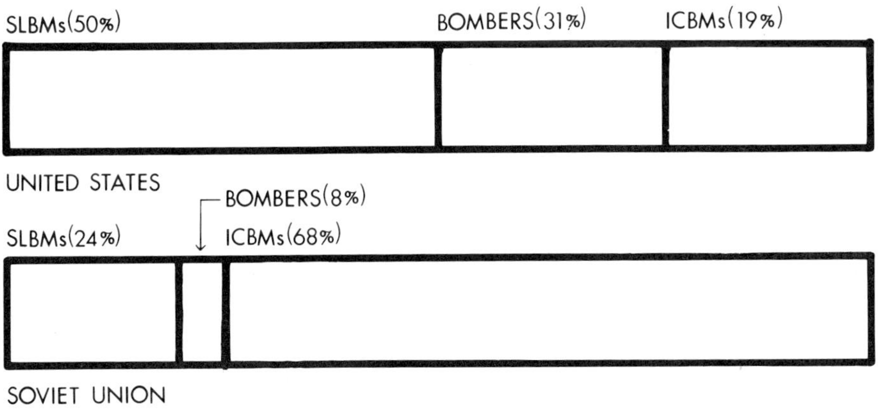

SLBMs(50%)   BOMBERS(31%)   ICBMs(19%)

UNITED STATES

BOMBERS(8%)
SLBMs(24%)   ICBMs(68%)

SOVIET UNION

or increased defense spending can point to American superiority rines or bombers and conveniently ignore the ICBMs. Similarly, by looking only at ICBMs, American officials can make a convincing case for Soviet superiority. As an example, note how much attention is paid to ICBMs in public debate about nuclear weapons in the United States.

A second major difference concerns the trade-off between accuracy of delivery systems and the size of nuclear weapons. It is much easier to deliver a small nuclear warhead to a specific target than a larger one. Consequently, American planners have opted for the smaller weapons and have led in weapons accuracy, but have lagged behind in total explosive power and what is called throw-weight. If one looks only at accuracy, the Americans are ahead in the arms race; if throw-weight is emphasized, the Soviets are superior.

A final area of potential misunderstanding about the strategic balance is the number of missile launchers as opposed to the warheads on the launchers. The United States has converted its arsenal to carry MIRV warheads more rapidly than the Soviet Union has, so that whereas the Soviets have more missile launchers, the Americans have more warheads (see Table 1.2).

In conclusion, each side has some advantages and some disadvantages. The Soviets excel in the number of launchers, but the Americans have more warheads; U.S. weapons have greater accuracy, but the Soviet weapons have more throw-weight. In the final analysis, since both arsenals are so destructive, such comparisons have little meaning except as political tools to justify new weapons.

Superpower Military Budgets

Similar conclusions can be drawn about military expenditures, although there is much controversy about how to calculate them, especially the Soviet expenditures. In the 1960s the Soviet Union began outspending the United States militarily, according to the U.S. Central Intelligence Agency (CIA). At the time, however, the U.S. arsenal was far superior to that of the

Table 1.2 U.S.–Soviet Strategic Nuclear Forces, July 1985

	United States			Soviet Union		
	Launchers	Warheads	%	Launchers	Warheads	%
ICBMs	1,024	2,124	19	1,398	6,286	68
SLBMs	640	5,728	50	924	2,178	24
Bombers	324	3,614	31	170	780	8
Total	1,988	11,466	100	2,492	9,244	100

Source: Data taken from *The Defense Monitor* 14(6).

Soviets, who had to spend more just to gain equality with the United States. Because we do not actually know how much the Soviets spend, the estimates vary widely. A Soviet arms escalation was used as a justification for the Reagan administration buildup of the 1980s, but as shown in Table 1.3, the allegations (on the U.S. side) of a spending gap are quite suspect. Whereas the U.S. Joint Chiefs of Staff (1980) estimated that the Soviets were outspending the United States, the independent estimates by Sivard (1984) show exactly the opposite.

According to most estimates NATO spending far exceeds Warsaw Pact budgets. (Note, however, that the Joint Chiefs ignore this comparison.) It is easy to see why NATO spending is so much greater: Whereas American allies include Great Britain, West Germany, and France, Soviet allies include Czechoslovakia, Poland, Bulgaria, and other Eastern European countries. Even East Germany, which has a relatively strong economy, is no match for the NATO powers, so most of the Warsaw Pact military burden is shouldered by the USSR. Because the annual Soviet gross national product (GNP) is only about half that of the United States, the Soviet Union spends about twice as large a proportion of its annual production as does the United States.

Furthermore, there are some serious problems with intelligence estimates of Soviet expenditures because of the methods by which they are made. Also, approximately 20 percent of Soviet military efforts do not threaten the United States or Western Europe, but are directed toward China. A report by the CIA in the fall of 1983 admitted that there were serious problems with previous estimates of Soviet expenditures. According to the CIA, "We estimate what it would cost to build the actual Soviet weapons and equipment in the United States at prevailing dollar prices for materials and labor (including overhead and profit)" (Adams 1984: 22). Because wage and material costs in the USSR are a fraction of what they are in the United States, estimates of Soviet spending are drastically higher than actual costs.

Table 1.3 Military Defense Expenditures in 1980

	U.S.	USSR	NATO	Warsaw Pact
I. Joint Chiefs of Staff (1980) estimate: 1980 expenditures				
(Billions of U.S. $)	ca.160	230	(No NATO–Warsaw Pact comparisons)	
II. Sivard estimates: 1980 expenditures (Sivard 1984)				
Total outlay				
(Billions of U.S. $)	144	130	256	147
Percent of GNP	5.6	10.7	4.5	8.5
Per capita (U.S.$)	632	490	330	391

The CIA further reported that Soviet military costs "have leveled off since 1976" and only increased at an annual rate of about 2 percent through 1981, and probably in 1982. More importantly, Soviet "procurement of military hardware—the largest category of defense spending—was almost flat in 1976-81" (Smith 1983: 1).

Whatever happened in the arms race in the 1960s and 1970s, one thing is certain: It is making a dramatic leap forward in the 1980s. This is happening in two areas: with increases in expenditures and with a new generation of nuclear weapons.

The Escalation of Military Spending

During the first half of this decade, the United States was engaged in the largest peacetime buildup in the history of the country. Military budgets for 1982–89 were projected to total an estimated $2.6 trillion in only eight years, more than the United States had spent in the preceding thirty-five years ($2.6 trillion, not accounting for inflation).[5] Initiated by the Carter administration, and dramatically accelerated by President Reagan, the buildup from 1980 to 1983 was 6 percent greater than the 1965–68 Vietnam War buildup. Arms procurement alone grew by over 90 percent (in constant dollars) from 1980 to 1983, as opposed to an approximate 60 percent increase during the Vietnam mobilization (Figure 1.6).

Figure 1.6   Vietnam War vs. the Reagan buildup.

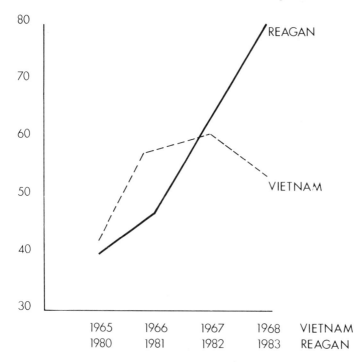

Military expansion involves a massive transfer of government funds to defense spending and now costs about $300 billion per year. Some of the major weapons systems are remarkably expensive; the Center for Defense Information estimates, for example, that the Trident submarine program will cost about $31–39 billion, the Trident II missile program will cost almost $38 billion, the B-1B bomber about $40 billion, and the Stealth bomber $40–50 billion. Research and development funding have increased by 300 percent in a five-year period, and the amount of money spent on overall military expenses is absolutely staggering. The administration's proposed military budget for 1987 was about $38 million per hour, or more than half a million dollars per minute.

Military spending in the 1980s buildup was oriented primarily toward arms procurement, with that part of the budget almost doubling between 1980 and 1985.[6] Congress faced a clear tradeoff between military and social programs. United Campuses to Prevent Nuclear War (UCAM), which engages in peace education and lobbying, was quick to point out the direct effect military spending proposals in the 1986 budget would have on students. The administration's proposal would drop one million students from the Guaranteed Student Loan Program and cut student aid overall by $2.3 billion, while adding exactly the same amount to the Strategic Defense Initiative (Star Wars) research program.

In short, the increased expenditures in the military budget are being used to finance the creation of a new generation of weapons that is altering the face of the arms race.

A New Generation of Counterforce Weapons

The most recent generation of American weapons delivery systems constitutes a new phase of the arms race. Such new weapons as cruise missiles, the MX, and the Trident II/D-5 (with a satellite guidance system) add up to the development of an ability to attack the enemy's military forces—missile silos, command and control centers, bomber bases, submarine ports, storage facilities, and so forth (Aldridge 1983a). Strategic policies that involve the use of weapons for that purpose are called *counterforce* strategies (as opposed to *countervalue* strategies, which emphasize the targeting of population centers).

Counterforce strategies are sometimes used interchangeably with the notion of a first strike as an effort to disarm the enemy. A first-strike capability is the notion of counterforce taken to its extreme and requires extremely accurate weapons that can destroy missiles before they are launched, disrupt communication, etc. Although counterforce and first-strike strategies have been secretly discussed in strategic circles at least since the mid-1950s,[7] it has only been in recent years (as the technologies for counterforce attacks have become increasingly sophisticated) that they have become matters of widespread public discussion. Inflammatory rhetoric about fighting and prevailing in a nuclear war, from the early days of the Reagan administration, and about the deployment of ground-launched cruise missiles (GLCMs) and Pershing II ballistic missiles in Europe have heightened concern that the nuclear threshold is becoming blurred.

These new-generation weapons have four important characteristics: precision, a short warning time, mobility, and survivability.

Precision.   Precision is the most important characteristic of the new weapons; that is what makes them counterforce weapons. The cruise missile is an excellent example of this wave of the future. It is a pilotless kamikaze jet plane that flies within the atmosphere, rather than following a high arc like a ballistic missile. It requires continuous power and has its own guidance system. It can thus make frequent adjustments in course to counteract deviations caused by such things as the weather.

Cruise missiles are nothing new; they were used by the Germans in World War II (the buzz bomb). These were crude, unreliable, and inaccurate weapons, however. The new cruise missiles are different primarily because they have (1) microelectronic devices that allow an on-board computerized guidance system to update the location and adjust course, and (2) small, efficient jet engines.

The cruise missile has a high-tech guidance system called TERCOM (terrain contour matching), which "reads" the varying altitudes of the territory over which the missile flies. Digital maps are first prepared with the help of satellite photos and stored in the computer on board. The maps are divided into squares and identified by numbers in order to inform the guidance system of the altitudes of the terrain along the intended course. The guidance system then matches the altitudes of the actual terrain over which the missile is flying with those on the maps and adjusts the missile's course en route so that it comes within a few feet of its target.

Although the system has been plagued with difficulties in tests, and we do not actually know what would happen if the missiles were sent toward targets in the Soviet Union,[8] cruise missiles have an estimated precision of 100–300 feet, depending on the size of the warhead. This figure refers to the circle of equal probability, or circular error probable (CEP), which is based on performance in tests. If several missiles are fired at a target and a circle drawn around the points at which half of them land, the radius of that circle is the CEP of that missile system. This does not mean that the missiles would necessarily hit the target, however, because CEP does not account for the bias of the system—that is, the distance between the target and the center of the circle (Tsipis 1983:139–46).

Despite technical problems, the fact remains that the new-generation weapons, such as the cruise missile, are designed with increasing precision, so that they can have counterforce or first-strike capabilities. Two new developments in guidance systems are also planned to increase the precision of the MX and Trident II/D-5 missiles. A global positioning system of navigational satellites (called NAVSTAR) will enable on-board guidance systems on the missiles to determine their exact position. Then a Mark-500 maneuvering reentry vehicle (MARV) will allow for course adjustments as the missile zeros in on its target. With these two features, the MX might be able to fly 7,000 nautical miles and have a CEP of only 100 feet.

Short warning time. A second feature of the new weapons is their short warning time. It is not an entirely new feature, because SLBMs might hit their targets within six to ten minutes, but it is now combined with the vastly increased number of such weapons and their greater precision.

The new Pershing II missiles, for example, fly at 6,000 miles per hour, for an officially stated range of 1,000 miles. They can hit targets inside the Soviet Union from their Western European bases but may not be able to reach Moscow.[9] From launch to impact, a Pershing II missile would take only five to eight minutes, and with its small CEP it is best suited for a surprise counterforce attack. The cruise missile, which flies under radar following the contour of the land, could possibly even reach its target undetected.

Some critics contend that one danger of such threats is that the Soviet Union might feel compelled to go to a launch-on-warning system; that is, as soon as its warning system indicated an incoming attack, its missiles would be launched in order to avoid being destroyed (the "use them or lose them" syndrome). The problem with that strategy is that the warning systems are simply not reliable. The U.S. system, for example, experienced at least 147 false alarms and malfunctions during an eighteen-month period between 1979 and 1980. It is likely that the Soviet system is even less reliable, so the adoption of a launch-on-warning system by the Soviets would dramatically increase the possibilities of an accidental nuclear war.

Neither the machines that launch and guide nuclear weapons nor the humans who program and control them are capable of performing their tasks without error. As Dumas (1980:20) states: "We have created a world in which perfection is required if a disaster beyond history is to be permanently avoided. But in the world of human beings perfection is unattainable." He documents a number of problems, from malfunctioning equipment to problems of drug abuse among military personnel. According to a Department of Defense study, approximately five thousand people were removed annually from the nuclear weapons programs from 1975 to 1977 for such problems as alcohol and drug abuse, negligence, or "significant physical, mental or character trait, or aberrant behavior, medically substantiated as prejudicial to reliable performance" (ibid.:16).

Since 1945 there have been an estimated 30 major and 250 minor nuclear accidents in the United States alone (Beres 1979b). The combination of nuclear proliferation and shortened warning time could result in an increase in the number of accidents and could increase the probability of an accidental nuclear war.

Mobility and survivability. With the exception of the MX, the new weapons systems are remarkably mobile, especially the cruise missiles. The GLCM is only about 20 feet long and can be carried on the back of a truck capable of launching four missiles. It is small enough to store in a garage, although this is not advisable. It is remarkably versatile—in addition to GLCMs, there are sea-launched (SLCM) and air-launched (ALCM) cruise missiles. Submarines can fire them from torpedo tubes, and surface ships can serve as launching pads. Since airplanes can launch cruise missiles before reaching enemy territory, some experts argue that we no longer need bombers (the Air Force does not like the idea, however). ALCMs could even be carried in modified commercial airliners like Boeing 747s or DC-10s. The Pentagon currently has plans to build 4,068 SLCMs, 1,787 ALCMs, and 656 GLCMs.[10]

Because of their small size and mobility, and their ability to carry either nuclear or conventional weapons, the proliferation of thousands of cruise missiles will create a situation in which arms control agreements will become almost impossible to verify. Whereas, until now, all major weapons systems have been verifiable, cruise missiles add a formidable obstacle to the arms control process.

One of the most highly touted aspects of the new generation of weapons is their survivability. That is, many of the new weapons, because of their mobility, would be quite difficult to locate and might therefore survive an attack by enemy forces. There are efforts on both sides—especially the Soviet Union—to develop mobile ICBMs as well, although the United States abandoned an effort to deploy the MX in a mobile "race track" mode. Because submarines are extremely difficult (if not impossible) to detect in any reliable fashion, they are a continuing priority in the U.S. weapons program. And of course, because cruise missiles are so small and mobile, they are also difficult to locate.

And Now, . . . Space Weapons

One final aspect of the current escalation must be mentioned, but will be discussed in more detail in Chapter Ten: the militarization of space. It is almost as if, having filled the entire globe with the nuclear cage, we are now seeking new territories of conquest. Of course, space is already a major arena for military activity; over 75 percent of the American space program, for example, is dedicated to military purposes. The Soviets have made almost no effort to separate the military and civilian aspects of their space program. Furthermore, almost all current U.S. military operations are somehow dependent upon satellites, from spying to communications to new guidance systems for counterforce weapons (Aldridge 1983a:211-26).

Such matters are only a beginning, however, with increased efforts of late to develop antisatellite weapons and perhaps even a space-based antiballistic missile system, despite the international agreements that currently prohibit it.

SUMMARY

This chapter reviewed the nature of nuclear weapons and what happens when they are used, the current state of the nuclear arms race, and the direction in which it is proceeding. There are two kinds of nuclear explosions: fission and fusion. Thermonuclear weapons (hydrogen bombs) use a fission explosion as a trigger to set off a fusion process, which in turn creates another fission chain reaction. A third major type of nuclear weapon—the nuclear-powered (or X-ray) laser—is now being developed.

Upon detonation nuclear weapons have three primary effects: thermal (heat) radiation, a blast wave, and nuclear radiation. The sizes of nuclear blasts are measured in kilotons, equivalent to one thousand tons of TNT, and megatons, equal to one million tons of TNT. A single 3-megaton bomb would be the equivalent of all of the explosives used in World War II. The detonation of large numbers of nuclear weapons would set off a chain reaction of effects on a global scale, including an electromagnetic pulse, massive fires, partial destruction of the ozone layer, and a nuclear winter that might destroy the ecosphere and most life on the planet.

The world now has about 50,000 nuclear weapons—most owned by the two superpowers—in three broad categories: (1) strategic, or long-range weapons; (2) theater, or intermediate-range weapons; and (3) tactical nuclear weapons for use on the battlefield. Strategic nuclear weapons can be delivered by intercontinental bombers, land-based missiles (ICBMs), or submarine-launched missiles (SLBMs). The American triad of weapons systems is diversified for flexibility and survivability; 68 percent of the Soviet weapons are on ICBMs.

In assessing the arms race, we argued that there is an essential equivalence or approximate "parity" in the superpowers' forces. Whereas the Soviets excel in the number of launchers, the Americans have more warheads; the Soviet weapons have more throw-weight and yield, but the U.S. weapons have greater accuracy. Exact estimates of the strength of the arsenals are somewhat meaningless, however, because the destructive capabilities of both sides are so great.

Estimates of Soviet spending on the arms race vary so widely that it is difficult to know whether the Soviet Union is spending more or less than the United States. It is clear, however, that the NATO alliance spends more annually than the Warsaw Pact, and that is the most significant comparison. Whereas the CIA estimates that Soviet arms spending has leveled off, the United States has been engaged in the largest peacetime buildup in history, with a total projected budget of $2.6 trillion from 1982 to 1989. The Soviets are likely to respond with their own buildup.

A dangerous new generation of weapons are being built that have great enough accuracy to carry out counterforce strikes—that is, attacks against military targets and even missile silos. The new weapons shorten warning time, which dramatically increases the possibility of an accidental war. For example, the Pershing II missile takes five to eight minutes from launch to impact; cruise missiles are designed to fly under radar and may provide no warning whatsoever.

Finally, the new weapons are designed to be highly mobile in order to survive attack. Because of the small size and mobility of these weapons, verifiable arms control agreements will be almost impossible to attain sometime in the near future, locking us even more tightly into the nuclear cage. And as if that were not enough, the arms race in space closes the cage over our heads.

CHAPTER TWO

Nuclear War: Past and Present

HIROSHIMA AND NAGASAKI

On the sixth of August 1945, the first experimental use of nuclear weapons against people was carried out in Hiroshima, Japan. On that clear August day, an American plane (the *Enola Gay*) flew over the city, dropped a lone bomb named Little Boy, and an explosion lit Hiroshima.

Public statements by President Truman and other U.S. officials asserted that the bombings of Hiroshima and Nagasaki saved 500,000 to one million American lives. Those public arguments were probably a deliberate lie, although many people continue to believe them. A series of top-secret documents have come to light showing that U.S. intelligence estimates of the costs of an invasion—which was not scheduled until the following March (1946)—would have been more on the order of 40,000 American servicemen dead (Mohr 1985e:7). A briefing paper delivered to the president on 18 June 1945 said that the planned American invasion of the Tokyo plain "should be relatively inexpensive" (ibid.).

Gar Alperovitz (1985a) claims that the president ruled out two other options: to assure the Japanese that the United States would not remove the Japanese emperor (the major Japanese objection to surrender), and "simply to await the expected Soviet declaration of war—which, United

States intelligence advised, appeared likely to end the conflict on its own" (Alperovitz 1985b:E21). A number of documents (including Truman's diaries, lost until 1978) make it clear that Truman and others were convinced that a Soviet declaration of war against Japan would force a Japanese surrender.

Several high-level U.S. officials were opposed to the bombing. In addition to the scientists who signed a petition to that effect, General Eisenhower was appalled that the bomb would be used against a city: "It wasn't necessary to hit them with that awful thing," he said. The chairman of the Joint Chiefs of Staff, Admiral William D. Leahy, said: "The use of this barbarous weapon at Hiroshima and Nagasaki was of no material assistance in our war against Japan. The Japanese were already defeated and ready to surrender" (ibid.).

The real target of the bombing was the Soviet Union. Secretary of State Byrnes was reportedly convinced that "demonstrating the bomb would make Russia more manageable" (ibid.). The "Soviet enemy" factor can be traced back even earlier, however: General Leslie Groves claimed that after a few weeks as director of the Manhattan Project he became convinced that "Russia was our enemy and . . . the project was conducted on that basis" (Powers 1984b:138).

Whatever the rationale for the bombing of Hiroshima, that was when we first learned what an atomic bomb would do to a city. According to the Committee for the Compilation of Materials on Damage Caused by the Atomic Bombs in Hiroshima and Nagasaki, it created a fireball 18,000 feet in diameter. Near the center, people became nothing; within nine seconds, 100,000 people were killed or fatally injured. Two hours later, drops of black rain the size of marbles began to fall on the city. Ninety percent of all the doctors in Hiroshima were killed or disabled (see Table 2.1) and all hos-

Table 2.1 Number of Medical Personnel Killed or Injured in Hiroshima

Profession	Number of Casualties	Percentage of Total Profession
Physicians	270	90
Dentists	132	86
Pharmacists	112	80
Nurses	1,650	93

Source: The Committee for the Compilation of Materials on Damage Caused by the Atomic Bombs in Hiroshima and Nagasaki, 1981, *Hiroshima and Nagasaki: The Physical, Medical, and Social Effects of the Atomic Bombings*, Trans. Eisei Ishikawa and David L. Swain, Tokyo: Iwanami Shoten, p. 379. Reprinted with permission.

pitals were destroyed. Shadows of Hiroshima's citizens were burned onto sidewalks and on the sides of buildings. Patterns of victims' clothes were burned into their skin. Four to five thousand children were orphaned (Committee 1981:435).

On the twelfth day after Hiroshima was bombed, after Nagasaki had been bombed and the war had ended, the survivors' wounds began to open. On the fourteenth day, hair began to fall from the heads of Little Boy's victims. Skin came off in patches; there was vomiting, diarrhea, bleeding from the gums, and nausea.

As discussed in Schell (1982:42), "physical collapse brought emotional and spiritual collapse with it. The survivors were, on the whole, listless and stupefied." In his *Hiroshima Diary*, Dr. Michihiko Hachiya (1955) writes:

> Those who were able walked silently toward the suburbs in the distant hills, their spirits broken, their initiative gone. When asked whence they had come, they pointed to the city and said, "That way," and when asked where they were going, pointed away from the city and said, "This way." They were so broken and confused that they moved and behaved like automatons.

Because of the confusion surrounding Hiroshima after the bombing, it is impossible to know exactly how many people were directly affected. Estimates of the number of people killed vary widely (see Table 2.2). The Japanese Committee (1981:367) estimates that about 130,000 people (110,000 civilians) died within three months and that another 60,000 to 70,000 people were killed in Nagasaki.

Not only did the bombing affect the estimated 350,000 people present in Hiroshima at the time of the bombing; it also greatly affected thousands of others not present when the bomb exploded, such as early entrants into the city looking for relatives and friends, relief workers, and people outside Hiroshima who became victims of radioactive fallout (ibid.:353).

The entire social fabric of Hiroshima was destroyed with one bomb in a matter of minutes. As the Committee (ibid.:354) reports, "In an instant, all key functions of prefectural and municipal agencies, all means of defense, relief, medical care, police protection, and firefighting, were destroyed or thrown into confusion." One history professor reflected, "I saw that Hiroshima had disappeared."

In Hiroshima, we get a glimpse of what happens in a nuclear war. However, what happened there was a small fraction of what would occur if a nuclear war were to begin today, so that although much can be learned by looking at Hiroshima and Nagasaki data, such knowledge can also be somewhat misleading. Lifton (1985b:5) suggests that although the contrast between the bombing of Japan and today's potential nuclear holocaust is enormous, "We need Hiroshima and Nagasaki for a very specific purpose: to give substance to our terror." The history of our knowledge about nuclear weapons effects is the story of an ever-darkening picture.

Table 2.2 Main Estimates of A-Bomb Deaths Including Missing Persons*

Source	Dead	Missing	Total
Hiroshima			
Hiroshima Prefecture, Governor's report, 20 August 1945	32,959	9,591	42,550
Hiroshima Prefecture, public health section report, 25 August 1945	46,185	17,429	63,614
Hiroshima Prefecture, police department report, 30 November 1945	78,150	13,983	92,133
Hiroshima City, "Official Report," 8 March 1946	47,185	17,425	64,610
Hiroshima City, survey section report, 10 August 1946	118,661	3,677 (fate unknown)	122,338†
Joint Japan–United States survey report, 1951	64,602	—	64,602
Japan Council against A- and H-bombs: "White Paper on A-bomb Damages," 1961	119,000–133,000 (32,900 military personnel not included)	—	(151,900–165,900)
Nagasaki			
Nagasaki Prefecture, report, 31 August 1945	19,748	1,924	21,672
Nagasaki Prefecture, external affairs section, 23 October 1945	23,753	1,924	25,677
Private estimate by Motosaburō Masuyama, January 1946 survey	29,398–37,507	—	29,398–37,507
British Mission report‡	39,500	—	39,500
Nagasaki City, A-bomb Records Preservation Committee, 1949	73,884	—	73,884
Joint Japan–United States survey report, 1951	29,570–37,997 –39,214	—	29,570–39,214
Joint Japan–United States survey report, 1956	39,000	—	39,000

*All estimates are of civilian deaths (military personnel excluded) except for the last column under Hiroshima.

†Estimated one year after the bombing.

‡The British Mission participated in the United States Strategic Bombing Survey but compiled an independent report, which is thought to have been done prior to 1947.

Source: The Committee for the Compilation of Materials on Damage Caused by the Atomic Bombs in Hiroshima and Nagasaki, 1981, *Hiroshima and Nagasaki: The Physical, Medical, and Social Effects of the Atomic Bombings*, Trans. Eisei Ishikawa and David L. Swain, Tokyo: Iwanami Shoten, p. 364. Reprinted with permission.

SINCE HIROSHIMA

No major scientific studies, or new discoveries since 1945, suggest that nu-clear war would not be as bad as we have expected it to be. On the contrary, every new study, each revelation, presents us with information suggesting that a nuclear war would be more staggering than we had ever imagined. Here are a few examples.

Blast Effects

Dr. Kistiakowsky, one of the scientists working on the Manhattan Project, estimated the power of the explosion of the first atomic bomb before it was tested in Alamogordo, New Mexico, in July 1945. His calculations were off by a factor of 200—the test was much more powerful than he had antic-ipated. In fact, the new bomb was so much more powerful than anything known before it that even those who had developed it were in awe of its power.

Radiation Effects

Although there was some knowledge of nuclear radiation, the scientists who developed the bomb were somewhat naive about its effects, and our understanding of its deadly properties was a long time in coming. When the first bomb was exploded in the desert, some of the sand at the Trinity site was fused into pretty radioactive crystals of glass. Some of the scientists took them as souvenirs; one even had a necklace made out of them for his wife! Apparently they either downplayed the hazard or did not realize that nuclear radiation could enter the body and slowly burn internal organs, causing radiation sickness that could lead to death in a few weeks for some, and to cancers and death several years later for many others.

Then came the bombings of Hiroshima and Nagasaki, and the first victims of radiation sickness. Even then, "scientists who developed the atomic bomb [denied] Japanese propaganda claims that delayed radioactiv-ity could have caused deaths" (Lundberg 1985:660).

The first test of a large (ca. 15 megaton) thermonuclear bomb—the Bravo test of 1 March 1954 in the Marshall Islands—resulted in the unex-pected exposure of those living near the test site (see Lindop and Rotblat 1981:138ff.). About 20,000 square kilometers were contaminated with le-thal doses of radiation, but the islanders were not evacuated until three days later, by which time some had received up to 200 rads. (A single rad is a dosage of absorbed radiation equal to the absorption of 100 ergs of en-ergy per gram of material.) More than twenty years later, in 1979, the northern islands of the Rongelap Atoll were still declared too radioactive to visit (Johnson 1980:24).

There is still much to be learned about the health consequences of prolonged exposure to radiation. Recent analyses of Hiroshima data suggest that earlier estimates of radiation effects on Hiroshima victims should be at least doubled (Leaning 1982:102).

Electromagnetic Pulse

Seventeen years after the Trinity tests, the United States detonated a 1.4-megaton hydrogen bomb (in July 1962) above Johnson Island in the Pacific. Eight hundred miles away in Hawaii street lights failed, burglar alarms went off, and circuit breakers popped open in power lines. The physicists were baffled. They had stumbled upon the electromagnetic pulse (EMP) that is created by nuclear explosions. As they subsequently discovered, the pulse moves out in all directions from the detonation, causing damage to solid-state circuits and electrical equipment. Even after the EMP was understood, however, its implications were denied. It was only in 1981 (almost twenty years later) that the Joint Chiefs of Staff (1981) spelled out these implications in their posture statement.

Partial Destruction of the Ozone Layer

The surprise of the 1970s was that a nuclear explosion releases nitrogen oxides, which rise up 50,000 to 70,000 feet and eat up a portion of the ozone layer surrounding the earth's atmosphere. That layer filters out some of the ultraviolet rays coming from the sun—like a good suntan lotion. (It is ultraviolet rays that cause sunburn.) Without the protective layer, not only would the sun cause severe burns, but all unprotected eyes on the planet would be blinded. Humans might wear protective goggles (as do people observing nuclear weapons tests), but we cannot expect dogs and cats, wildlife, and insects to do the same.

One study by the National Research Council of the National Academy of Sciences (1975) estimated that a 10,000-megaton nuclear exchange (with several thousand nuclear explosions) would result in a 70 percent reduction in the ozone layer in the Northern Hemisphere and a 40 percent reduction in the Southern Hemisphere. It would take the ozone layer about thirty years to recover from such damage, and in the meantime, the fragile network of life on the planet could possibly break down: Bees could not pollinate flowers, and all sorts of wildlife and farm animals would be unable to survive. Major links in the food chain would be destroyed.

Nuclear Winter

The most shocking study of the potential consequences of a nuclear war was not undertaken until the 1980s, almost forty years after Hiroshima. Pieces of the puzzle slowly began to come together, as researchers drew on data from such seemingly unrelated topics as dust storms on Mars, the environmental impact of volcanic eruptions, and the hypothesis that mass extinctions of animals were caused by clouds of dust from the impact of asteroids or comets.

When the *Mariner 9* space probe arrived at Mars, it observed a dust storm in progress; the upper atmosphere was warmer than usual, and the lower atmosphere colder. Scientists concluded that airborne dust was absorbing much of the incoming sunlight, preventing it from reaching the planet's surface. Consequently, the upper Martian atmosphere was heated by the sunlight but surface temperatures cooled. Atmospheric scientist Owen Toon noted that there were some parallels between the environmental effects of dust storms on Mars and those of volcanic eruptions on earth. Then, Mount St. Helen's erupted and a town near it was plunged into darkness because of the cloud of particles thrown into the air.

In the meantime, Paul Crutzen and John Birks published an article in the Swedish journal *Ambio* (1982) pointing out that a nuclear exchange would ignite forest fires and that cities would burn, sending tons of smoke up into the atmosphere. No one had thought about the smoke!

A group of scientists began pulling these disparate threads together, and examined them using a computer model designed to predict the atmospheric consequences of volcanic eruptions. In an article in *Science* published in December 1983, Richard Turco, Owen Toon, Thomas Ackerman, James Pollack, and Carl Sagan (called TTAPS from the authors' last initials) reported the results of their computer simulations, which predicted that a nuclear war would cause thousands of tons of dust and smoke to rise into the atmosphere. Blocking the sun's rays from reaching the planet's surface, this cloud of dust would move around the globe, causing surface temperatures (except around the coastlines, where the effect would not be as dramatic) to plunge to 13 degrees below zero Fahrenheit. It would be too dark for plants to carry out photosynthesis, and virtually all crops and farm animals would be destroyed. Any human survivors of a nuclear war would die from starvation in a long, dark, cold, radioactive nuclear winter.

The report stunned even the Pentagon officials who are accustomed to the horror stories about nuclear war. Although the theory has been debated, few scientists dispute its validity. The major remaining question is how many nuclear explosions it would take to create the nuclear winter effect. Turco et al. (1983) began with a baseline exchange of 5,000 megatons, with only about 20 percent hitting urban or industrial targets.[1] Taking into account factors previously unaccounted for, the TTAPS computer models also suggest additional problems that could be much more severe than previously anticipated, notably, the amount of radioactive fallout, nitrogen oxides, and toxic gases.

A number of other scenarios were tested with computer simulations, including one astounding possibility: A nuclear winter might be triggered by a 100-megaton attack on cities (with one thousand 100-kiloton warheads). Such an exchange represents only about 1 percent of the world's nuclear arsenals.

A panel of biologists used the TTAPS models to estimate the long-term biological effects of a nuclear war (Ehrlich et al. 1983:1293) and concluded:

> Subfreezing temperatures, low light levels, and high doses of ionizing and ultraviolet radiation extending for many months after a large-scale nuclear war could destroy the biological support systems of civilization, at least in the Northern Hemisphere. Productivity in natural and agricultural ecosystems could be severely restricted for a year or more. Postwar survivors would face starvation as well as freezing conditions in the dark and be exposed to near-lethal doses of radiation. If, as now seems possible, the Southern Hemisphere were affected also, global disruption of the biosphere could ensue. In any event, there would be severe consequences, even in the areas not affected directly, because of the interdependence of the world economy. In either case, the extinction of a large fraction of the Earth's animals, plants, and microorganisms seems possible. The population size of *Homo sapiens* conceivably could be reduced to prehistoric levels or below, an extinction of the human species itself cannot be excluded.

If true, the nuclear winter phenomenon calls into question all nuclear warfighting plans. As Powers (1984a:55) puts it:

> In a sense, the bad news about nuclear winter is *so* bad that it might even be taken as grounds for a perverse optimism. If we finally admit that we can't fight a nuclear war without destroying ourselves—*really* destroying ourselves—then perhaps the time has come to quit preparing to fight one. . . .
>
> It's an either/or proposition: either we stick to the plan and court ecological catastrophe, or we get rid of the plan and try to think of something else to do with the 9,500 strategic nuclear warheads in the American arsenal.

Dr. Lewis Thomas, chancellor of the Memorial Sloan-Kettering Cancer Center, contends that the discovery of nuclear winter "may turn out, in a world lucky enough to continue its history, to have been the most important research finding in the long history of science" (Peterson 1984:xiii).

Major environmental and atmospheric studies of nuclear effects have just emerged in the last decade. The social sciences have yet to provide anything comparable that would help us understand the effects of a nuclear war (or the arms race itself) on social life. A recent study by Kurt Finsterbusch (1985) found that there were only four articles on the nuclear arms race, out of about sixty-five hundred total, in the three major sociology journals since 1945.[2] In fact, the most thorough explorations of the social impact of a nuclear war have been done by a chemist, Arthur M. Katz (1982). Thus, the human effects are even more unknown than the environmental effects, though obviously just as significant (certainly to us!).

Jonathan Schell, in his eloquent book *The Fate of the Earth* (1982), provides a metaphor for understanding those costs. He talks about the "Second Death," which refers to the annihilation of the human species (cf. Lifton et al. 1984). (The first death is individual death—the knowledge of individual mortality, told in the Genesis story of the Garden of Eden.) Just as knowledge of our own mortality casts a shadow back on our personal life, affecting how we organize our life, so the knowledge of the nuclear threat casts a shadow back on our social and political life and affects how we organize it.

THE NUCLEAR COLD WAR: DESTRUCTION WITHOUT DETONATION

Even though not a single nuclear weapon has been exploded in war in the past forty years, there are nonetheless contemporary victims of nuclear war—a nuclear cold war. It is what Victor Sidel, past president of the American Public Health Association, calls destruction without detonation. It is likely that the very existence of nuclear weapons (not to mention a spiraling arms race, international conflict, and loose talk about winning a nuclear war) has subtle, pervasive, and hidden psychological and social costs. In an effort to assess the price paid for the stockpiling of nuclear weapons, I will look at four interrelated areas: the distribution of economic resources, the effect of the bomb on children, the social construction of evil, and the domestic political implications of the nuclear arms race.

The Distribution of Economic Resources

While the nations of the world spend $2 billion per day on the military, thousands of people are starving to death; millions more are living on the verge of starvation. Every second, somewhere in the world, a child dies or is permanently scarred by the diseases of poverty; in that same second we spend $23,000 on our militaries.

No country has a monopoly on massive military spending; it is a global problem that most people, including many ardent supporters of the military, would gladly eliminate, if only they could find a way to stop the upward spiral. As Ruth Leger Sivard (1983:23) observes:

> The military competition for superiority in arms has no counterpart on the social side. National leaders compete fiercely for military preeminence. Unfortunately, there is no evidence of a race among nations for top rank in social goals, in insuring satisfactory living standards, the best education for their children, accessible health care for all.

President Eisenhower (1953:419) recognized the enormity of the problem when he spoke before the American Society of Newspaper Editors, 16 April 1953, contending,

> Every gun that is made, every warship launched, every rocket fired signifies, in the final sense, a theft from those who hunger and are not fed, those who are cold and are not clothed. This world in arms is not spending money alone. It is spending the sweat of its laborers, the genius of its scientists, the hopes of

its children. . . . This is not a way of life at all in any true sense. Under the cloud of threatening war, it is humanity hanging from a cross of iron.

In the post–World War II era, the superpowers have created what C. Wright Mills calls a permanent war economy. He argues that "to a considerable extent, militarism has become an end in itself and economic policy a means of it" (Mills [1958] 1976:57). The militarization of the economy, which occurred during the Second World War, has been perpetuated by the economic elites and institutions that benefit from it, the ritualistic momentum of the military-industrial complex, and the threat of nuclear annihilation.

In the Soviet Union, an ongoing economic crisis is fueled by enormous military budgets that divert scarce resources from an economy in which many basic consumer goods are scarce. Many economists argue that there is a direct link between the massive transfer of funds to military spending and key problems in the American economy as well.

Because the effects of military spending on the U.S. economy are more easily documented than those in the Soviet case, they will be examined here in some detail (although it is important to keep in mind that similar effects occur in many countries). Seymour Melman, an economist at Columbia University, and William W. Winpisinger, president of the International Association of Machinists and Aerospace Workers, argued in congressional hearings in 1982 that there is a direct link between

1. the rapid escalation of military budgets and deterioration of the U.S. economy;
2. the capital- and technology-intensive demands of the Pentagon's new war systems and the declining competitiveness of U.S. industry;
3. military expenditures and decreasing U.S. employment; and
4. the $1.6 trillion demand for military expenditures and the prospect of ever-enlarging federal deficits and further inflation.

Economist Lloyd Dumas contends that despite the mistaken impression that "military spending stimulates production, creates employment, and generally brings prosperity" (1984:172), it actually contributes to economic decay and has had devastating effects on the American economy for a number of reasons. He observes (ibid.:173) that

> military-oriented production . . . does not add to the supply of consumer goods or to the supply of producer goods, and so contributes to neither the present nor future material standard of living. Resources put to this use can then be said to have been diverted, i.e., channeled away from ordinary contributive use. They are not, in and of themselves, adding to material well-being.

Resources that are used unproductively will eventually be a drain on an economy, whether it is capitalist or socialist (Galbraith 1981). In the

United States, those costs have emerged primarily in the form of high inflation and high unemployment because of deteriorating productivity. During the Vietnam military buildup, for example, politicians made the decision to pay for the increased military spending by allowing inflation to spiral, rather than by increasing taxes (a move that is always politically unpopular), and a similar strategy is being followed in the 1980s.

Military spending has negative effects on a nation's economy in a number of other ways. For example, the U.S. international economic position has been directly affected by the outflow of dollars for defense expenditures abroad, helping to create a negative balance of payments in international trade. During the 1969–70 period, the United States had a $35 billion balance-of-payments deficit. During the same period, total direct defense expenditures (net after military sales abroad) were more than $30 billion. Hence, "U.S. military expenditures abroad accounted for 86.6 percent of the entire U.S. balance-of-payments deficit during that period" (Dumas 1984:179).

Furthermore, a large proportion of the country's scientific and engineering resources are channeled into military research, diverting them from civilian technological development. An estimated one-third to one-half of American scientific and engineering personnel are devoting their talents to military research.

It is no coincidence, Dumas further claims, that the two countries most responsible for making inroads into U.S. technological development are West Germany and Japan, which (from 1961 to 1975) spent an average of about 20 percent and 4 percent respectively, of their government R&D expenditures on defense and space, compared to a U.S. average of about 70 percent between 1961 and 1977 (ibid.:185). For every $100 available for domestic capital formation, $46 is spent on the military in the United States, in contrast to only $14 in West Germany and $3.70 in Japan (Melman 1983).

Dumas (1984:189) argues that the collapse of technological innovation, and therefore productivity growth in the United States, "is a direct, inevitable, though long-term result of the decades-long diversion of a large fraction of the nation's critical scientific and engineering effort from productive civilian-oriented technological development." Such innovation is crucial to offset rising costs of production (since machine labor, for example, is often much more efficient than human labor), so that American industry has become less and less competitive in relation to foreign competition. Major U.S. companies have also moved their production facilities to other countries, resulting in increased domestic unemployment and a worsening balance of trade.

In short, the militarization of the American economy has resulted in what Melman calls "profits without production" in two senses: First, many of the nation's resources are diverted from civilian to military production, which is not useful in the conventional sense. Second, that diversion undermines American inventiveness and productivity, thereby increasing the flight of U.S.-owned production to locations outside the United States.

The American public—far from benefiting economically from military spending—is thus subjected to rising prices and unemployment as a result of the burgeoning military budget. Although one sector of the economy certainly benefits from massive military spending, other sectors suffer. Excessive military spending is thus both a national and a global problem. The consequences, although difficult to estimate, are clearly staggering, because of the enormous sums of money involved.

Tarzie Vittachi, deputy executive director of the United Nations International Children's Emergency Fund (UNICEF), estimates that if only "one percent of U.S. military aid were allocated to foreign aid for the next 20 years, every basic need—food, shelter, and education—of every child in the world could be provided" (Bean 1983).

Children and the Nuclear Threat

During recent years, in light of extensive public discussion and media coverage of the topic, a number of scholars have begun to investigate the question of what it means for children to grow up under the shadow of the bomb. In a review of that literature, Stuart Reifel (1984:80) concludes that "the research we have on children and the threat of nuclear war paints a bleak picture. Growing up with the possibility of nuclear destruction may be more significant than anyone had imagined."

A number of studies (see Beardslee and Mack 1982, 1983; Schwebel 1964, 1965; Escalona 1964; Chivian et al. 1985) suggest that children first become aware of the nuclear threat in early childhood. Despite limitations of the data, some important discoveries were made by Escalona (1964) in a survey of children (ages four to adolescence). When asked what the world would be like when they were grown, more than 70 percent spontaneously singled out a destructive nuclear war as a likely possibility. Escalona concluded that an uncertainty about the future, because of fears about a nuclear war, exerts a "corrosive and malignant influence" on the development even of normal children.

In 1978, child psychiatrists John Mack and William Beardslee of Harvard began studying attitudes of children and adolescents toward the prospect of nuclear war. Although they had not expected that young people would know much about the issue, they were startled by the intensity of the fears revealed by the study (Yudkin 1984:18; Beardslee and Mack 1982). Beardslee and Mack concluded that "children are deeply disturbed about the threats of nuclear war and the risks of nuclear power," despite the fact that they "also recognize possible benefits from nuclear power and nuclear weapons" (1982:88-89). Their strongest finding is that children show "a general unquiet or uneasiness about the future and about the present nature of nuclear weapons and nuclear power." Furthermore, there is considerable uncertainty and fear about nuclear war and the possibilities of surviving one (ibid.:89).

A comparative study of Soviet and American children (Chivian et al. 1985) reveals both similarities and differences in their attitudes about nuclear war and its potential effects (see Table 2.3). Whereas the Soviet children were more pessimistic about surviving a nuclear war, more U.S. children thought it likely to happen in their lifetime. Among children in both countries, however, there was a remarkable uncertainty and pessimism about the future. Lifton contends that the potential of annihilation results in a "sense of radical futurelessness" that influences such things as increased divorce, "significant impairment of the parent-child bond," and the growth of religious fundamentalism (Goodman 1985:12).

Not all psychologists and psychiatrists agree with him; Harvard psychologist Robert Coles (1985; Butterfield 1984) believes that many reports about children's fears of a holocaust are "sentimental balderdash." As a consequence of the early studies, a few efforts to do more research into the problem have emerged. At the same time, a rapidly growing nuclear education movement has sparked considerable controversy in a few cities.[3] Although much more is to be learned, it is clear that growing up under the shadow of the bomb has profound potential consequences on future generations, without a shot being fired.

Table 2.3 Soviet and American Children on Nuclear War

Response	Question A*		Question B		Question C		Question D	
	U.S.	USSR	U.S.	USSR	U.S.	USSR	U.S.	USSR
1. Definitely not	2.5%	24.9%	11.9%	45.1%	11.9%	54.3%	4.5%	2.0%
2. Probably not	14.4%	28.3%	29.4%	35.5%	25.9%	22.5%	10.0%	0.7%
3. Uncertain	44.8%	33.8%	40.8%	16.4%	39.8%	15.4%	19.9%	4.8%
4. Probably yes	28.9%	9.2%	11.4%	2.4%	16.9%	3.1%	39.3%	16.7%
5. Definitely yes	9.5%	3.4%	5.0%	0.3%	5.0%	3.8%	25.9%	75.1%
Mean rating	3.30	2.38	2.67	1.77	2.77	1.78	3.73	4.63
t	−10.33†		−10.50†		−10.28†		10.10†	

*A = Do you think that nuclear war between the USSR and the U.S. will occur within your lifetime?
  B = Do you think that you and your family could survive a nuclear war?
  C = Do you think the Soviet Union and the United States could survive a nuclear war? (American sample asked only about U.S. survival.)
  D = Do you think it is possible to prevent a nuclear war between the USSR and U.S.?
  †*p*<.001.

Source: Chivian et al., 1985, "Soviet Children and the Threat of Nuclear War: A Preliminary Study," *American Journal of Orthopsychiatry* (October): 497. Reprinted with permission from the *American Journal of Orthopsychiatry* and the author. Copyright © 1985 by the American Orthopsychiatric Association, Inc.

The Social Construction of Evil

One of the difficulties of maintaining a nuclear weapons program is the process of justifying it, both to the general public and—especially for individuals involved in actual development and construction of the weapons—to oneself. It is difficult to imagine a justification for stockpiling weapons of such destructive power if they exist as a defense against a benign enemy. On the contrary, perhaps the only conceivable reason for stockpiling such weapons is as a defense against an obviously monstrous enemy who is bent on destruction.

It is easier, of course, if the enemy has nuclear weapons as well, which is what has happened in the relationship between the superpowers. Erich Fromm points out that humans often engage in a pathological mechanism of projection. Although projection is easily recognized in individuals, it is more difficult to see when carried out by whole societies and their leaders. The result of such thinking is that "the enemy appears as the embodiment of all evil because all evil that I feel in myself is projected on to him. Logically, after this has happened, I consider myself as the embodiment of all good since the evil has been transferred to the other side" (Fromm 1961:22).

As a consequence, there is a great deal of projection and mirroring in American and Soviet images of each other. "Projection is mixed with paranoid thinking," producing "a dangerously explosive pathological mixture, which prevents sane and anticipatory thinking" (ibid.:23). The only reason for our continued construction of nuclear weapons, citizens of both countries exclaim, is because we are forced to engage in an arms race with our enemy, who is also making these horrible weapons. What choice do we have but to defend ourselves by keeping up with them?

As Nikita Khrushchev reported in his memoirs (Khrushchev 1971–74), the most common rationale for continued military expenditures is to keep up with the adversary. If one country has a certain kind of weapon, the other feels compelled to reciprocate. A major aspect of the social construction of evil is an exaggeration, on both sides, of the evil character of the opposition.

The litanies of denunciation are familiar to us: In the USSR, Americans and capitalists are depicted as the source of all suffering in the world. In the United States, communism is believed to be the instigator of unrest and war throughout the globe. By making such charges, people in each superpower are likely to see their own vices in the faces of the enemy and to assume that they themselves are virtuous.[4] However, it becomes nearly impossible to interpret an adversary's actions objectively when an entire society feels justified in its behavior because of its image of the enemy. Frank (1982:6) suggests that

> the image of the enemy as malevolent and untrustworthy leads to progressive restriction of communication until virtually the only messages that get

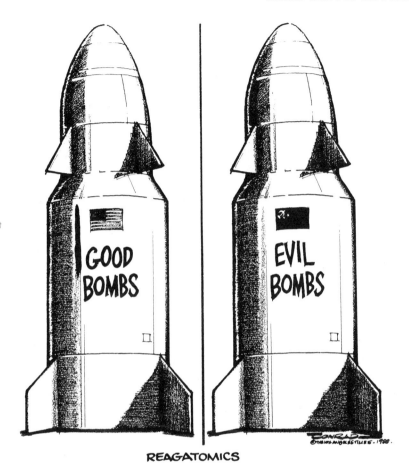

REAGATOMICS

through are those that reinforce the image, resulting in further restrictions—an ominous, vicious circle. This accompanying fear and hate create emotional tension. This facilitates oversimplification of thought, one feature of which is the *strain to consistency*. Since the enemy by definition is bad, *all* its actions are interpreted as motivated by malevolence.

The social construction of evil operates in a dialectical fashion as both cause and consequence of the nuclear arms race. It becomes an integral part of the nuclear cage: Once the image of the enemy is constructed with a diabolical face, then all subsequent actions of the adversary are interpreted through that cognitive screen.

As Jerome Frank (1982:6) suggests, the malevolent image of the enemy impedes the resolution of conflicts, thus becoming an additional source of the arms race itself. First, it creates a self-fulfilling prophecy by causing enemies to acquire the evil characteristics they attribute to each other. In combatting what they perceive to be the other's warlikeness and treachery, each side becomes more warlike and treacherous itself. As a result, the enemy image nations form of each other more or less corresponds to reality. Although the behavior of an enemy may be motivated by fear more than by aggressiveness, the nation that fails to recognize an enemy as treacherous and warlike would not long survive.

This evil image construction thus restricts communication and empathy, providing a deep-seated psychological source of war. Individuals living on the other side are often dehumanized and seen as faceless, immoral subhumans.

An interesting example of how the social construction of evil works and of its impact on international relations is seen in a comparison made by James Wall (1983) of two airline tragedies. The first occurred on 21 February 1973. A Libyan Airlines 727 was on a routine flight between Tripoli and Cairo when it encountered some difficulties with vision because of a sandstorm. Four jet fighters soon appeared around the plane, but the captain assumed they were Egyptian and calmly assured his 113 passengers that there was nothing to worry about. They were not Egyptian; the Libyan passenger jet had strayed over the Israeli-occupied Sinai Peninsula and was being intercepted by Israeli planes. After bobbing and weaving around the airliner, trying to force it to land, two of the fighters unleased a deadly burst of 20-mm cannon fire that ripped into the 727's wing and fuselage.

The death toll was 108. Prime Minister Golda Meir expressed deep regret over the loss of life, but pointed out that the pilot had not responded to repeated warnings. Three days later Defense Minister Moshe Dayan acknowledged an "error of judgment" but noted that the aircraft was 100 miles inside occupied territory.

Time magazine (5 March 1973) called the attack an incident, referring to it in an overall roundup of Middle Eastern events. The story suggested in rather mild language that the "Sinai incident" was a breach of international decency. After their initial 5 March reports, neither *Time* nor *Newsweek* carried any other stories on the tragedy.

Wall (1983:835) alleges that the reaction to the downing of Korean Air Lines Flight 007, on the other hand, was "due more to an anticommunist crusade than to authentic anger and grief over the death of 269 civilians." Following the tragedy, a barrage of criticism from U.S. officials was carried on the front pages of American newspapers for days and weeks. Despite the fact that the CIA became convinced that the Soviets actually mistook the airliner for a spy plane, the tragedy became the focus of countless articles, books (see Hirsch 1986; Dallin 1984; Clubb 1984; cf. Sayle 1985), and even annual memorial services (see Haberman 1984).

In the one instance, when an ally's careless behavior resulted in the death of 108 people, the incident was interpreted in a nonjudgmental light as an unfortunate mistake that did not reflect negatively on the nation responsible. In the other, the image of evil constructed about the enemy resulted in the continued denunciation of the tragedy, which was subsequently taken as confirming evidence of the evil nature of the adversary.

The social construction of evil in the nuclear age is a complex process in which a variety of factors come together to exacerbate a cold war and the division of the world into two blocs, each of which rests under the alleged protection of a nuclear umbrella. In that context, perceptions are filtered through preconceived notions by each side about the other, and each side is blinded to its own faults and the other's virtues.

Domestic Political Implications

Another example of destruction without detonation is the serious domestic political consequences of the nuclear arms race, notably, the erosion of the democratic process. Princeton political scientist Richard A. Falk (1984c:194) maintains that

> the existence of nuclear weapons, even without any occurrence of nuclear war, interferes with democratic governance in fundamental ways. In other words, we don't have to wait for Armageddon to begin paying the price, as measured by the quality of democracy, for a system of international security constructed around the central imagery of nuclear deterrence.

The most obvious means by which democratic governance is undermined by nuclear weapons is through the walls of secrecy that have grown up around nuclear policy issues. Whereas secrecy has always been an instrument of governance in the United States, as Doyle Carson (1982:34) points out, it has usually been temporary and confined to a period of crisis. In the nuclear age, however, "Secrecy, once invoked, has lingered. This has created a public tendency to expect and accept secrecy, certainly in government military operations and to some extent even in civilian aspects of life." It has led to what Edward Shils (1956) has called the torments of secrecy.

Secrecy is inherently antidemocratic, and information is a vital source of power. The purpose of withholding information is to prevent outsiders from obtaining data that would give them power. Secrecy is also an inherent characteristic of bureaucratic organization. The military is a veritable paradigm of institutional secret-keeping, as information gathering and withholding is central to almost every aspect of warfighting. In the nuclear age, the success or failure of major conflicts between the superpowers is not measured in terms of lives or territory won or lost in actual battles but in the abstract accounting of force capabilities and *potential* warfighting scenarios. Consequently, chronic secrecy has emerged because of the necessity to manipulate information for a variety of audiences: the nation's adversaries and allies, other branches of the government and military, the public, and one's own superiors in the bureaucracy.

The secrecy surrounding nuclear weapons at the time of Hiroshima was not an exception, but the rule. Harold Nieberg (1964) outlines four phases of America's nuclear secrecy:

1. *Manhattan District Project*: During World War II, the intent was to develop nuclear weapons before the Germans and without their knowledge, and, at the same time, to prevent the development of these nuclear weapons by either allies or enemies of the United States.
2. *1946–53*: An effort was made to prevent or delay the Soviet Union's development of nuclear weapons.
3. *1953–60*: The purpose of secrecy during this phase was to prevent nations other than the Soviet Union from developing nuclear weapons.
4. *1960–on*: Secrecy during this phase remained about the same as before, but with an emphasis on non-nuclear military options. This was done in order to free the United States from relying entirely on nuclear force to resolve its international conflicts.

Carson (1982:38ff.) suggests that the policy of chronic secrecy has a number of potential adverse consequences. First, it supports or enhances the denial mechanism so frequently associated with the nuclear threat. Second, the revelation of previously kept secrets tends to result in outrage and distrust of the government, thereby generally undermining its legitimacy.

Secrecy also impairs the ability to accurately perceive the enemy, resulting in under- or overestimations of the adversary's military capacity and power. Furthermore, once an extensive institutional apparatus for the protection of secrets has emerged, it tends to grow and take on a life of its own. Finally, Carson argues, secrecy impairs the democratic process, which relies on an informed public.

The existence of nuclear weapons, as Falk (1984c:195ff.) and Mandelbaum (1981:183) point out, results in an unprecedented delegation of decision-making power to the president. As Falk puts it,

> The actuality of nuclear weapons is such, with its requirement of constant readiness, as to defy the moral constitutional expectation that the President must have the unchallenged authority to make battlefield decisions in wartime, an authority conceived of as pertaining only to that special circumstance of emergency and national unity that is presumed to exist during a properly declared war. (Falk 1984c:196)

Such powers are usually reserved for divine right prerogatives, which are ordinarily capable of only limited damage; but with the advent of nuclear weapons, the presidential prerogative appropriates continuous authority for almost unlimited destruction. Because of the tremendous power of the weapons and of those who control them, nuclear policy becomes

> in many ways the decisive undertaking of national political leadership, the one upon which . . . all else hinges. If that undertaking is perceived by a substantial fragment of the citizenry as a criminal enterprise, then it will be impossible for political leaders to achieve legitimate authority. Deception, se-

crecy, and coercion will become increasingly indispensable instruments of governance, not to handle anti-social deviants, but to prevent citizens of the highest moral authority from challenging the absolutism of the state. (ibid.:200)

Finally, however, Falk observes that the erosion of democracy by nuclearism has paradoxically stimulated a revitalization of democratic forces in some states, as can be seen in the European grass-roots movement to return the power of government to its citizens.

SUMMARY

The ever-darkening picture of what a nuclear war would be like has been examined in this chapter, as well as how the arms race causes destruction without detonation. It is hard to envision worse destruction than that caused by the explosion of one small bomb each on Hiroshima and Nagasaki in 1945. Each city essentially disappeared in an instant; hundreds of thousands were killed or wounded, and the entire social fabric of those cities was ripped to shreds. But the story does get worse.

Each decade since 1945 has had its own surprises in terms of previously undiscovered effects of nuclear weapons. Dr. Kistiakowsky's original estimates of the *blast effects* of the first atomic bomb were off by a factor of 200. Next, the scientists who built the bomb were not aware of the extreme lethality of the *radiation effects* of atomic explosions. Recent reexaminations of these radiation effects on the victims of Hiroshima and Nagasaki suggest that earlier estimates of lethality should be doubled. Then it was only in 1962 that we discovered the *electromagnetic pulse* that is created by an atomic explosion.

In the 1970s, scientists discovered that the nitrogen oxides released from a major nuclear exchange could lead to a *destruction of the ozone layer*, resulting in the possible death of the planet's fragile ecosystem. Even that frightening realization pales, however, in light of the surprise of the 1980s: the *nuclear winter* effect. The TTAPS studies, based on computer models of volcanoes and dust storms that occurred on Earth and Mars, suggest that a nuclear exchange would throw thousands of tons of dust and smoke into the atmosphere. Temperatures would probably plunge well below zero Fahrenheit and virtually destroy food supplies, so that survivors from a nuclear war would likely die from starvation in a long, dark, cold, radioactive nuclear winter. The scientists discovered, astonishingly, that it might take as little as 1 percent of the world's current nuclear arsenals, targeted on cities, to create a nuclear winter, calling into question the concept of nuclear warfighting.

Just as we are becoming increasingly knowledgeable about the dramatic potential effects of a nuclear war, our awareness of the costs of the arms race itself is growing. The very existence of nuclear weapons, and the threat of a nuclear holocaust, has subtle, pervasive, and hidden psychological and social costs. This destruction without detonation is visible in (1) the way economic resources are distributed, (2) the effect of the bomb on children, (3) the social construction of evil, and (4) the domestic political implications of the nuclear arms race.

Military spending around the globe currently averages about $2 billion a day, while thousands of people die of starvation in the same period. While almost nobody *in principle* favors such spending, the world's population appears trapped in a nuclear cage that drains scarce resources from more productive activities. Moreover, a number of economists have linked rapidly escalating military budgets to inflation and economic deterioration.

The arms race also diverts valuable human resources. For instance, an estimated one-third to one-half of America's scientists and engineers are engaged in military research, and an average of 70 percent of the federal research and development expenditures from 1961 to 1977 were spent on defense and space.

Recent studies have shown that the psychological effect of an impending nuclear holocaust on children is substantial. Children list nuclear war as one of their greatest worries, and evidence suggests that those fears create a remarkable uncertainty and pessimism among children and adolescents about the future.

A third cost of the arms race is the social construction of evil: those images of the enemy that result in projection and paranoid thinking, which in turn prevent an objective evaluation of adversaries. The evil aspects of opponents are exaggerated on both sides and affect the way in which all information about them is filtered, until communication and empathy are restricted and the international political arena is poisoned.

Finally, the nuclear weapons race creates serious domestic political problems—specifically, the erosion of the democratic process. The walls of secrecy that have grown up around nuclear policy issues inhibit democratic discussion and undermine the legitimacy of the government. Thus, the shadow of the bomb falls back across the organization of social, political, economic, and even family life, creating profound, yet subtle, effects.

All this came to pass without the firing of a single nuclear weapon at an enemy's territory since World War II. But what of the future? That is the question we will consider in Chapter Three.

CHAPTER THREE

Nuclear War and the Future

A plane crashes in Dallas or Chicago or New Orleans, and hundreds are killed. Millions of Americans are riveted to their television sets for hours, watching Cable News Network, perhaps crying with the families and survivors, becoming nauseous with the rescue workers who sift through the rubble. One man is shot and killed while traveling through a city in a motorcade and millions mourn. A shuttle explodes in mid-air and the entire nation gasps. When human tragedy strikes, it affects not only the direct victims but a wide network of individuals and institutions.

Human life, like all life on earth, is highly interdependent. At the level of the organism, all parts of the body are interrelated. As we all know from personal experience, the human body is a finely tuned system that can be upset rather easily. A backache can affect one's entire disposition. An increase of 4 or 5 percent in body temperature and the world appears a very different place. Make a slight adjustment in the chemical balance of the body and remarkable changes take place (in many states, a driver is legally drunk when his or her blood has an alcohol content of only one-tenth of 1 percent).

There are some parallels between the bodily system and social systems. A conflict in one's family, or a tragedy caused by the death of a

friend, causes people to lose their ability to concentrate at work. Affect one part of a social network, and the whole system is affected.

We now live in a global socioeconomic system, so that events in one part of the world often have a direct effect elsewhere. The nuclear power plant accident at Chernobyl caused grain prices to rise dramatically in Chicago. Because of the complexity of the social system, we are not always aware of how changes within it affect us. As Arthur Katz (1982:5) observes, previous estimates of the consequences of a nuclear war tend to understate its impact because they focus only on physical measures of destruction and fail to account for the interactive effects of one part of society on another.

Because the potential effects of a nuclear war are so staggering, one runs out of ordinary adjectives in attempting to describe them. Such attempts are even more suspect in light of the increased public awareness of the horrors of nuclear war in recent years. Furthermore, the nuclear winter studies make most previous discussions of the aftermath of a nuclear war read like a child's bedtime story.

However, two recent trends make it imperative that social scientists attempt such descriptions: First, U.S. government officials continue to minimize the effects of a nuclear war. The most dramatic example is the thinking of Thomas K. Jones, deputy under secretary of defense for research and engineering, Strategic and Theater Nuclear Forces, who claims that more than 90 percent of the American population might survive a nuclear war (Scheer 1982:21). Although met with suspicion by many, such images of nuclear war have led to a revival of civil defense programs, this time in the form of crisis relocation plans (see Chapter Nine). Second, policymakers are taking seriously the possibility of a limited nuclear war, as evidenced by a recent shift in strategic thinking toward nuclear warfighting plans and counterforce weapons. Both these lines of thought require an examination of what might happen not only in a major nuclear exchange but even in a more limited conflict.

Therefore, the following discussion focuses on how some of the dimensions of a limited nuclear attack would affect the biological, psychological, institutional, and social aspects of human life. This point will be obvious: Talk of 90 percent survival rates after a nuclear war is absurd.

A LIMITED NUCLEAR WAR

For purposes of illustration, I will focus on some effects of a limited nuclear war—a counterforce attack by the Soviet Union on U.S. strategic targets, such as ICBM silos, Strategic Air Command (SAC) bases, and nuclear-powered ballistic missile submarine bases. Whether a nuclear war can be limited to counterforce attacks is highly questionable (see Chapter Eight), but I will ignore that for the moment to focus attention on what a limited nuclear attack on the United States might mean.

Biological Effects

Despite the important knowledge to be gained from the bombings of Hiroshima and Nagasaki, they "do not serve as precedents for any probable nuclear war scenario" (Geiger 1981:173). Both explosions were very small compared to those of contemporary nuclear weapons—a 1-megaton weapon would have the explosive equivalent of seventy simultaneous Hiroshima explosions. Moreover, each of those early bombings was a single, isolated event, whereas the bombing of Moscow today might include warheads for each of the sixty military targets identified there in the U.S. Strategic Integrated Operation Plan (SIOP). Thus, when the term *limited nuclear war* is used, it does not refer to a small tragedy such as the bombing of Hiroshima or Nagasaki. Because a counterforce attack would target not cities but silos and bases, the immediate impact on civilians would depend largely on the amount of fallout and whether it reached major populated areas. One could expect fallout to be considerable after a counterforce attack, since surface bursts are most effective in destroying military targets. In a typical attack in March, the fallout would reach Chicago, whereas it probably would not in winter (Katz 1982:43). Weather and season would have an effect on the distance and direction in which fallout would travel.

Fatalities alone do not provide an accurate picture (ibid.:45). One must also take into account those injured and those affected by the deaths and injuries of others. The Office of Technology Assessment (OTA) estimates that if injuries were added to fatalities, a limited nuclear war might yield 6 to 32 million immediate casualties.

Because much is unknown about the effects of radiation or the extent and intensity of fallout after a nuclear war (Leaning 1982:101ff.), it is difficult to make accurate estimates. It may be possible to shelter people in areas peripheral to a limited attack, but those areas might be hazardous for several months.

In addition to the 6 to 32 million immediate casualties, many effects of the attack, such as radiation-induced cancers, would not be felt until much later (Finch 1981; Lindop and Rotblat 1981; Committee 1981). At the very least,

> the incidence of malignancies, congenital malformations, and genetic mutations will increase significantly and will certainly alter longevity and quality of life, but will probably not have dramatic consequences for overall population growth. If the population survives, leukemia induction will begin to be expressed within 5 years after the exposure, but solid tumor excess will not be seen until 10 to 40 years after the event. (Leaning 1982:103)

The medical implications of even a limited nuclear war are staggering. Katz (1982:62ff.) estimates that if 50 percent of the survivors injured in a counterforce attack required hospitalization, and if all hospitals and medical personnel remained operative, there would be one bed for every fifteen to thirty patients. Of course, even without an attack on population centers, a substantial portion of the doctors and nurses of the region would be killed or injured, hospitals would be contaminated, and the entire infrastructure of the medical establishment in the region would be badly damaged or paralyzed.

The situation is made even more bleak by the almost certain spread of infectious diseases and epidemics caused by reduced resistance to disease, the presence of millions of corpses (both human and animal), malnutrition, the breakdown of sanitary systems, and an exuberant overgrowth of insects (Leaning 1982:105). Possible infectious diseases include "viral and bacterial diarrheas, hepatitis, pneumonia, diphtheria, whooping cough, tuberculosis, cholera, malaria, plague, smallpox, and typhoid fever" (ibid.). New epidemic diseases may appear to which the survivors have no immunities, vaccines, or antibiotics. Historical studies suggest that it takes a population about 120 to 150 years to stabilize their responses to the onslaught of such diseases (ibid.:106; Neill 1976). Communicable diseases alone might claim the lives of 20 to 25 percent of the survivors within one year (Leaning 1982:106; Abrams 1981).

Another biological effect of a nuclear war would be widespread famine. Even before the nuclear winter studies (which predicted that eventually the entire world's food supply could be endangered), it was clear that a counterforce attack would produce unparalleled damage to the nation's food supplies. U.S. ICBM silos are located primarily in the Great Plains, where 80 percent of the nation's food is produced. Contamination would limit the amount of productive land, and crops would suffer direct radiation damage if the attack occurred in late spring or early summer (Katz 1982:51).

Farm animals are little more resistant to radiation than humans, and because they are less likely to be sheltered, they would be exposed to high levels of radiation. In a typical winter attack, more than 40 percent of the cattle and 60 percent of the hogs raised in the United States would be in the most seriously affected states (ibid.:57). Furthermore, food distribution might be impossible. The Northeast produces only two-thirteenths of its own food (Leaning 1982:103).

Even recovery of the agricultural industry would be doubtful. Shortages or complete lack of such pivotal resources as refrigeration, pesticides, heavy machinery, and irrigation is a near certainty. The loss of fertilizer alone might result in a 50 percent decrease in major crop yields (ibid.:104-5). Furthermore,

> regardless of what extent a remnant of skilled farmers may survive the attack, the majority of the population will have had little experience with farming. People will be disoriented, hungry, perhaps ill from radiation and disease. The work required to prepare and plant fields may be beyond the capability of many.
>
> Questions about soil and seed contamination, when people are very hungry, will most probably be dismissed, and some crops may be planted with little regard for radioactivity. (ibid.:105)

Moreover, an attack on the American breadbasket would cause worldwide food shortages, because the United States exports 70 percent of its wheat, 20 percent of its corn, and 40 percent of its soybean production (Katz 1982:61).

However, if the limited nuclear attack would trigger a nuclear winter, the entire previous discussion would be far too conservative.

Psychological Effects

> I spent three months in the hospital because of extreme weakness. . . . Everybody in the farming area where we lived knew where I was. . . . My children were treated very unkindly at school. Other children would taunt them and cry out: "Son of a patient of the A-Bomb Hospital." They said these things because they thought I was definitely going to die.
>
> —a Nagasaki engineer quoted by
> Robert Jay Lifton, *Death in Life*

Our first clues to the psychological effects of a nuclear war come from Lifton's (1968) study of the Hibakusha (the survivors of the atomic bombings of Japan). Lifton finds parallels between the Hibakusha and survivors of the Nazi persecutions, the plagues of the Middle Ages, and other extreme historical experiences (1968:479).

Five recurring themes emerged in Lifton's interviews with survivors: the death imprint; death guilt; psychic numbing; counterfeit nurturance and contagion; and formulation, which is the survivor's effort to rebuild his or her internal and external world. The death imprint, Lifton observes, is the basis for all survivor themes. It comes from the immediate "jarring awareness of the fact of death" (ibid.:481) and creates a heightened sense of vulnerability and grotesqueness. It is an indelible image imprinted on the psyche of the survivor, as revealed in the extraordinary sense of immediacy of the bombing that remained in the Hibakushas' memories years after the event. Because of the enormity and suddenness of the disaster, Hiroshima survivors experienced an inability to accomplish the work of mourning that ordinarily accompanies disaster.

One consequence of the death imprint is a lingering sense of guilt. This guilt may be the result of the "survivor's unconscious sense of an organic social balance which makes him feel that his survival was purchased at the cost of another's" (ibid.:489). The survivor's major defense against both the death imprint and guilt is psychic numbing, which "comes to characterize the entire life style of the survivor" (ibid.:500). It is a psychic closing-off and withdrawal in which the survivor undergoes "a reversible form of symbolic death in order to avoid a permanent physical or psychic death." It suppresses the survivor's rage and may linger unresolved for years.

The survivor's personal relationships are dominated by counterfeit nurturance and a perception of others' fear of contagion. Feelings of weakness and a lack of autonomy contribute to an unconscious identification with the aggressor as "an attempt to share the power by which one feels threatened. For the survivor, this means power over death itself" (ibid.). Some Hibakushas ally themselves with America and even with the bomb itself. "The survivor feels drawn into permanent union with the force that killed so many others," so that the death guilt is unintentionally intensified, as is the victim's sense that his or her own life is counterfeit.

Such feelings are fed by the isolation that springs from a tendency by nonvictims to view the Hibakusha as contagious carriers of death (ibid.:516ff.). The Hibakusha became outcasts in Japanese society. As one victim put it,

> There is the phrase, "A-bomb outcast community [*genbaku buraku*]." This comes from the inferiority complex—physical, mental, social, economic— which *hibakusha* have, so that when people hear the word [Hibakusha], they don't feel very good, but rather feel as though they are looked down upon. (ibid.:169–70)

Survivors of the bombings are often recognizable because of the stigmata that distinguishes them from others—especially the keloid, or whitish-yellow area of overgrown scar tissue that disfigures hands and especially faces.

Finally, "the dropping of the atomic bomb in Hiroshima annihilated a general sense of life's coherence as much as it did human bodies," so that survivors must engage in the anguish of formulation normally associated with a grieving process (ibid.:525). New relationships must be formed and the inner world must be reconstructed. Such a quest may involve scape-goating or the search for a sense of world order in which one's suffering is acknowledged and reparations are made. It may include a reconstruction of the past (before the bombing) as a golden age in which the dead are ide-alized. An effort to construct images of mastery compensates somewhat for the Hibakusha's vulnerability; the survivor "must call forth life-affirming elements from his own past even as he molds these into a new formulation" (ibid.:538).

The sudden violence inflicted on the network of social relationships by the atomic bomb also imposed psychological costs upon the survivors of Hiroshima. Behind the cold statistics of casualty estimates are the people for whom the dead and injured were formerly a source of support, warmth, and meaning.

Retrospective studies of disasters have shown that in extreme situa-tions, given sufficient stress, everyone will develop symptoms whether they have a disease or not (Leaning 1982:107), and many of the symptoms of panic are identical to those of radiation sickness. Moreover, the enormity of the loss would take some time to soak in.

Institutional and Social Costs

It is impossible to predict the consequences of the destruction of the social fabric of a major portion of the United States. In addition to the break-down of family and friendship networks, which would leave many people floundering, every social institution would be destroyed. Imagine the American public surviving without banks and supermarkets, not to men-tion football and television!

Just as the fission or fusion in a bomb sets off a chain reaction at a microscopic level, so the destruction caused by a nuclear attack triggers a chain reaction of social consequences in a society. The family structures of the victims would be the most immediately devastated sector of society. In central Hiroshima, 84.2 percent of the households lost at least one mem-ber.

> The massive human damage caused by atomic bombs is not a matter of mere numbers: the lives of breadwinners along with wives, the aged, youth, chil-dren, and babies are swept away without distinction, or they are left maimed

for life. Whole families are wiped out, while others are deprived of key members. The normal bonds of family life are so ruptured that innumerable households are doomed to serious breakdown, if not to total disintegration. (Committee 1981:370)

A counterforce attack on the United States would destroy the family structure of middle America. Because of the high geographical mobility of American families,[1] many people throughout the country who would not be directly affected by the bombing would still lose family members. For those families in which there were survivors, the sense of grief, vulnerability, and depression would lead to psychic numbing and a breakdown of many support groups. Everyone would sustain major emotional and financial losses. In many families, the breadwinner would be killed.

There would be major gaps in every aspect of the social order. Functioning schools would be without sufficient teachers. Classes might meet in makeshift facilities, and they would be crowded with refugee students who had lost families and friends. Churches, civic groups, businesses—literally every major social institution—would be devastated.

A limited counterforce attack on American ICBM silos and bases, whether in winter or March, might affect approximately one-third of the country's manufacturing capacity (see Table 3.1; Katz 1982:48ff.). Although such measures are imprecise, clearly the loss of the institutional base on which manufacturing facilities are built would hamper any effort

Table 3.1 National Economic Activity Potentially Disrupted by Fallout[a]

SIC	Economic Categories Affected	March	Winter
28	Chemicals and allied products[b]	25	30
283	Drugs[b]	30	25
33	Primary metal industries[b]	30	35
331	Blast furnaces, steel works, and killing and finishing mills[b]	35	45
34	Fabricated metal products[b]	40	40
346	Metal forgings and stampings[b]	50	40
361	Electrical distribution products[b]	20	40
	Total MVA (1977)[c] for affected states	30	30

[a]Rounded to nearest 5 percent.

[b]Bureau of Census, 1972 Census of Manufacturers, Department of Commerce (Washington, D.C.: Government Printing Office).

[c]Bureau of Census, 1977 Census of Manufacturing, Department of Commerce (Washington, D.C.: Government Printing Office). MVA refers to manufacturing value added, a measure of manufacturing capacity.

Source: Reprinted with permission from Arthur Katz, 1982, *Life After Nuclear War*, Copyright © 1982 by Ballinger Publishing Company, p. 48.

to make use even of plants *not* destroyed by the bombing, or of factories that are contaminated with radioactive fallout.

Following major bombing raids, Japanese workers during World War II "disengaged themselves from production and became very interested in their own self-preservation" (Katz 1982:49). Furthermore, the interdependent nature of the economy ensures that industrial bottlenecking would occur, as disruptive losses in a key industry would affect many other industries as well. This effect is seen when auto workers go on strike—an entire chain of workers is affected, from the steel industry, through the parts and machinery suppliers, to the showroom salespeople, to the people who run retail shops that service the workers. The entire national economy would be devastated by the destruction of high-risk areas, and the effect would be felt worldwide. As someone once remarked, when the U.S. economy sneezes, the rest of the world catches cold.

A breakdown of the social order would be accompanied by an effort to impose totalitarian rule, with internal migration control, medical triage, and the elimination of civil rights, that is, the very things the weapons allegedly preserve. In Hiroshima, "crime was virtually uncontrolled immediately after the bomb. With order established, the crime rate apparently remained high, reaching a peak around 1950 and 1951" (Lifton 1968:264–65). With shortages of food and other consumer goods, and a breakdown of community services, widespread theft and riots might occur, followed by a police state. Consumer items might even be reserved for law enforcement officials.[2]

NUCLEAR PROLIFERATION AND THE INCREASING THREAT OF WAR

But surely, it will never happen. We have gone without a major world war for more than forty years now. Why should we expect a nuclear war to break out in the near future? There are several good reasons to anticipate such an unthinkable occurrence. First, the new generation weapons now being developed by the superpowers heighten the possibility of an accidental war because of their shortened warning times and increased reliance upon computers.

Second, the spread of nuclear weapons to countries and groups beyond the current nuclear powers increases the chances of a nuclear war simply by increasing the number of decisionmakers involved. In fact, the dangers posed by threats on the horizon may be more ominous than the existing superpowers' arms race. Roger Molander and Robbie Nichols (1985:vii) argue that

> there is a second arms race, masked by the big one, that is becoming even more dangerous—to Americans, Soviets, and the planet—than the superpow-

ers' arms race. Just think ahead fifteen or twenty years and imagine what countries might have the bomb. . . . There are a number of likely candidates: India, Israel, South Africa probably already have the bomb. Pakistan, Argentina, Brazil, Iraq, Libya, South Korea, and Taiwan may not be far behind.

And then there's a third arms race more hidden than the second one. . . . But the players in this third race—terrorists or madmen—do not even fit our categories of thought about security: they have no borders to secure. Will deterrence work at all for outlaw nations or terrorist gangs or madmen who have no stake in the status quo? What could possibly deter them?

It seems very likely that a number of other nations, if not terrorist groups or isolated individuals, will eventually get the bomb; and this eventuality may be just around the corner. Although we have been lucky thus far, there has been a steady growth in the number of nuclear powers—with two new members of the nuclear club each decade—and there are many signs that a dramatic increase in proliferation is just around the corner. Not only is the nuclear genie out of the bottle, but it is well within the reach of many.

Building the Bomb: Getting Easier All the Time

Designing a bomb is not a difficult task, as one Princeton University physics major demonstrated in 1977. He ordered $15 worth of U.S. government documents, obtained through the Freedom of Information Act, and designed a bomb that would cost $2,000 and weigh only 125 pounds.

It would not be so easy, of course, to obtain the fuel for a nuclear weapon, although there are many reports of plutonium that is unaccounted for. That does not mean it is impossible, however. Ground Zero (1982:226) summarizes the scenario a country might follow.

1. Purchase a nuclear reactor either for research or power production from the United States, Canada, France, Germany, or one of the other half dozen nations that have the capability to build such reactors and are often eager to sell them.
2. Acquire fuel for the reactor from a fuel supplier nation like the United States or France.
3. Secretly process or refine the fuel to separate weapons-grade fissionable materials. . . .
4. Use the fissionable material to assemble the weapon—the easiest part.

In fact, one provision of the Nonproliferation treaty (NPT) requires countries possessing nuclear technology to sell nuclear power and research reactors to those nations that do not have them.

Because of recent advances in fuel reprocessing and enrichment technology, it is becoming simpler all the time to produce weapons-grade fuel from a reactor. A nuclear power plant generating 500 million watts of electricity produces about 100 pounds of plutonium-239 in two years, which would fuel ten to twelve bombs (ibid.:227). A group of Princeton physicists recently estimated that by 1984 enough plutonium had been separated from reactor fuel to produce 7,500 small nuclear weapons. That number might rise to 49,000 weapons by the year 2000 (Sivard 1985:19, 44). The nuclear power industry is almost dead in the United States, especially since Chernobyl, and construction on new nuclear plants has stopped (except for some already under construction). Consequently, there is increasing pressure for the industry to sell its expensive technology to other countries.

There is considerable debate over the potential dangers posed by these developments. Lewis Dunn (1986:330) claims that the chance of a nuclear confrontation between some of the emerging nuclear nations is much higher than between the superpowers, because of shared borders, territorial disputes, historical hostilities, and so forth:

> Regardless of these leaders' intentions, flash points for conflict among these new nuclear powers abound. The festering civil war in Lebanon involving Christians, Palestinians, Syrians, and Israelis; border clashes between Libya and Egypt; a renewal of the Iraq-Iran war; a new incident between the Koreas; and unrest in Baluchistan or Kashmir are all potential tripwires. And the risk of unintended escalation will be considerable. . . . Once under way, limited confrontations or low-level clashes could spill over quickly into vital national territory and threaten critical national interests, perhaps even survival.

Dunn also points to other problems, from the potential technical deficiencies of new nuclear forces produced on a shoestring budget and with a potential lack of safeguards, to the possibility of a nuclear coup d'état.

K. Subrahmanyam (1986:345) counters that such fears have been exaggerated. "Those who try to frighten the world with the idea of nuclear bombs in the hands of irresponsible Third World rulers should ponder the equal risks of these weapons in the control of the developed nations," in which leaders have delegated the authority to use nuclear weapons to others and have made threats to other nations. Furthermore, he insists, "There is no reason to believe that the leadership of any developing country is likely to be more rash in resorting to the weapons than the leadership in the industrialized countries" (ibid.).

Probably the most effective way the superpowers can act to stop horizontal proliferation (the spread of nuclear weapons to other countries) is to stop their own vertical proliferation, that is, the growth of their existing arsenals. It is difficult for the United States and the Soviet Union to oppose a nuclear buildup by other countries when their own arms race continues to spiral, and many nonnuclear countries are resentful of the double standard.

NUCLEAR WAR AND THE SOCIOLOGY OF KNOWLEDGE

The underlying question raised by this chapter is: How do we know so little when we know so much? There are two striking aspects of that question which must be considered: First, despite the impressive body of scientific knowledge that created the nuclear cage, knowledge about the effects of nuclear weapons and of a potential nuclear war have only emerged slowly through the decades. Why, then, did it take so long for us to gain the knowledge we now have? Second (and relatedly), why have we been unable to find a way out of the nuclear cage? Given the virtual consensus that nobody wants a nuclear war, why is it that we have found no way to extricate ourselves from the shadow of the bomb?

One way to address these questions is to draw upon the sociology of knowledge tradition, the central thesis of which is that "thought has an existential basis insofar as it is not immanently determined and insofar as one or another of its aspects can be derived from extra-cognitive factors" (Merton 1968:516). In other words, definitions of knowledge and understandings of what is known are only loosely related to reality itself. In some ways, the sociology of knowledge goes back to the Greeks, who understood the problematic nature of human knowledge. Plato, for example, claimed that what we think we see in the world is merely a set of shadows reflected on a cave wall.

How, then, do we know what we know? There are many theories about how knowledge is constructed, but most sociologists agree that it is somehow related to the class or status positions of those who claim to have the truth. Given that premise, I would like to examine a number of possible reasons for the knowledge dilemmas associated with the nuclear cage.

One obvious reason for our slow pace in learning about what we have created is the ever-present dilemma of human ignorance. We simply do not know what makes the universe tick. The most important discoveries of the twentieth century concern our gradual understanding of the complex interconnectedness of life on the planet, as recognized in the past two decades. Only after the concept of the ecosystem emerged, and some of its properties were understood, did people make the connections between the interaction of various parts of that system and how damage to one part affects all others. It was only in the 1980s that the damage to the ecosystem caused by the bombings of Hiroshima and Nagasaki was realized. The problem is most clearly seen in the nuclear winter studies of this decade: It was not until atmospheric scientists began looking at the effects of smoke and dust on the atmosphere—and then on surface temperatures—that someone thought about the potential consequences of the massive fires that would be ignited by nuclear explosions (see Turco et al. 1983; Ehrlich et al. 1983).

A second reason for our lack of knowledge about nuclear war is our resistance to learning, in part a result of psychological defense mechanisms such as psychic numbing. Denial is typically the first reaction of someone who is told that he or she has cancer (family and friends often have the same response).

Another cause of the resistance is that we manage to ignore information that contradicts our prevailing understandings of a phenomenon. We construct a definition of the situation, as William I. Thomas puts it, which is used to filter out data that seem irrelevant. Whenever we try to interpret something, we are required to synthesize many pieces of information and fit them together in a coherent manner, in order to fashion an opinion. For a topic as complex as nuclear war, conflicting data prevent our building a simple picture without choosing some information as relevant and discarding some as unnecessary or untrue.

This construction of reality is not done by individuals in isolation but is a collective, social process. We rely upon those whom we trust to process information for us, so that we tend to agree with some people and disagree with others not only on the basis of the information itself, but on whether we feel positively tied with the individual presenting a particular interpretation. We tend to overlook contradictions in interpretations made by our allies and friends, and focus on the faults in definitions made by our enemies.

A third, and related, reason for our lack of knowledge is that our prejudices are institutionalized. Max Weber wrote of an "elective affinity" that exists between certain ideas and the interests of the people who hold them. It is simply more convenient—especially if one's job or political position is involved—to believe some versions of reality and to discount others. Most of us have a keen ability to rationalize our positions, so that we can actually become convinced that black is white and white is black, if it is in our interest to do so.

There is a more somber side of institutionalized prejudices, however: The history of the nuclear age is also a history of lies and deceptions on the part of governments and militaries to mislead the public. There are few things that seem more susceptible to rationalizations and deceit than the field of national security. Few of us believe that lying is *always* immoral. Consider the following classic scenario. You are at a friend's house and your friend is in another room. Someone (other than a police officer) arrives at the door, brandishes a gun, and demands to know if your friend is at home. Your immediate reaction would probably be to claim that he or she was not there, and you would feel justified in lying. Those who are convinced that a certain nuclear policy is, in fact, best for the country, and that it is essential to national security, therefore may have little difficulty justifying the use of deception to prevent what they would perceive as a disaster. Usually one deception leads to another, until a web of lies has been woven. If any one lie is discovered, the others may be called into question as well, so that new lies have to be invented to conceal the old ones.

In the final analysis, and at a certain level, all of us suspect that reassurances from government officials about the potential effects of a nuclear war do not quite ring true. Most of us have the same sense about nuclear war as that developed by Dr. George Kistiakowsky, one of the scientists on the Manhattan Project who helped build the first A-bomb tested at Alamogordo. As revealed in an article by Thomas Powers (1982) about that first test of the Trinity device, Kistiakowsky watched from the top of the command bunker about five and a half miles from where the bomb detonated.

> The shock wave buffeted him severely. Even wearing dark glasses and with his back to the explosion, the intense light reflected from the surrounding mountains blinded him for a few moments. It was then that he saw what he had helped build.
>
> The following day he was back in Los Alamos, already at work on the device that would destroy Nagasaki three weeks later. At lunchtime . . . he was joined by William Laurence, a reporter from the *New York Times.* Laurence asked for his reaction to the Trinity test. Kistiakowsky said, "I am sure that at the end of the world—in the last millisecond of the earth's existence—the last human will see what we saw."

CHAPTER FOUR

Reciprocity, Bureaucracy, and Ritual

Lester R. Kurtz, John Dillard, and Robert D. Benford

No one knows who will live in this cage in the future, or whether at the end of this tremendous development entirely new prophets will arise, or there will be a great rebirth of old ideas and ideals, or, if neither, mechanized petrification, embellished with a sort of convulsive self-importance. For of the last stage of this cultural development, it might well be truly said: "Specialists without spirit, sensualists without heart; this nullity imagines that it has attained a level of civilization never before achieved."

—Max Weber, *The Protestant Ethic and the Spirit of Capitalism*

People and governments of this present age have not yet learned how to create and cultivate great military establishments . . . without becoming the servants rather than the masters of that which they have created.

—George Kennan, *The Nuclear Delusion*

What is it that created the nuclear cage in the first place, and what caused the arms race to escalate to such heights? Many argue that fear is the culprit. Fear of the Nazis, Japanese, and Soviets motivated Americans to build atomic weapons. Fear is certainly a factor, but it is not an adequate explanation of the nuclear cage that threatens us with annihilation.

Fear provides motivation for the arms race; it does not provide direction. It helps to fuel the arms race but does not determine the course it takes. Fear *could* motivate people to avoid an arms race and to negotiate treaties. Certainly people negotiate out of fear, for example, out of concern that a continued arms race will be calamitous, or at least expensive. Why do some people, at some times, choose to negotiate, and others, at other times, decide to build new and more weapons?

Another motivation involved is hope—the hope for military victory or military superiority. The search for an elusive technical fix is motivated by hope: a belief that research may result in the ultimate weapon. The weapon to end all weapons, like "the war to end all wars" (World War I), would make either deterrence or conquest certain, once and for all.

The fundamental sociological insight into behavior is that it is *structured*; individuals make decisions within a social context. This does not mean that people have no freedom of choice, but rather that they seldom exercise the freedom they do have.

Any decision—to build a weapon or not, to negotiate or not—is influenced by the context within which it is made. All decisions are preconditioned by social structures and by the momentum set in motion by previous decisions. They are made on a stage that sets parameters for the decision-making process. This is why the metaphor of the nuclear cage also applies to the preconditioning dilemma by which humankind has inadvertently trapped itself into the nuclear arms race. In examining this preconditioning process, we will discuss three sociological concepts: reciprocity, bureaucracy, and ritual.

RECIPROCITY

Reciprocity may be defined as an exchange between two parties that results from a feeling of obligation by one party to return any good or harm received from the other (see Mauss [1925] 1954; Gouldner 1960). When we receive a gift, we try to find some way of returning the favor; it is apparently a universal norm of human behavior. Deciding how to reciprocate is not always easy. You cannot simply pull out your wallet when receiving a gift and say, "Here, let me repay you. How much did it cost?" Nor can you usually offer the giver the same gift in return.[1] You must be much more subtle. First, you decide how much the gift is worth, and what sort of relationship you wish to have with the giver. You may take into account a number of factors: the cash value of the gift, how appropriate it is, and what it may have meant for the person to give it to you (for example, its sentimental value).

Deciding how to reciprocate also involves assessing the difference in value between initiating an exchange and simply returning a favor. When one person in a relationship gives the first gift to pass between the parties, there is a value in the initiation itself (perhaps a risk that the gift will not be appreciated) that is difficult to repay.

If both parties feel satisfied with an exchange, a balance is struck and the two parties come to terms. Each has given the other what was expected, so the exchange is designated as balanced reciprocity. There is, however, often an imbalance in exchanges, so that one side or the other feels wronged—this is known as negative reciprocity.

In other contexts, a recipient may be unable to repay, as in the case of a child who is given food, clothing, and shelter. Here a generalized reciprocity emerges (Sahlins 1965:147; Levi-Strauss [1949] 1969) in which recipients are not asked to reciprocate measure for measure. When a child is given gifts by an adult, the giver may expect little more than a smile or a hug. The giver may be repaying others for unreciprocated favors. Thus, through generalized reciprocity, the weak and unproductive are cared for despite their failure to contribute materially (Gouldner 1960:178).[2]

When something is given without payment, how do the parties involved decide if the exchange is a generalized reciprocity exchange (which has positive connotations and sustains relationships) or a negative reciprocity exchange (which might lead to conflict)? For the most part, generalized reciprocity occurs within social boundaries; that is, the exchanging parties are within the same family or social network. Negative reciprocity is an impersonal form of exchange (Sahlins 1965:148) that rarely appears within tightly knit social groups. It is more likely to emerge during interactions between strangers. In Western cultures, it is immoral to cheat or maim others within the household, among relatives and neighbors, or in one's own political or geographic grouping. Outside this we-group, the "other" may be dealt with harshly and without moral qualms, especially in a war. To kill the other during wartime is more likely to win one medals than moral recriminations.

Not only are there different forms of reciprocity (generalized, balanced, and negative), but those forms may have different contents as well. Within each form of exchange, the content may be either benevolent or harmful. (The form of an exchange, of course, may cause a shift in the content of exchange; for example, when there is negative reciprocity, in which parties feel cheated, subsequent exchanges may be harmful rather than benevolent.)

Definition of an exchange as generalized, balanced, or negative, and of its content as beneficial or harmful, is highly subjective and varies from culture to culture. It is possible that a gift intended as a beneficial, generalized exchange may be perceived by the recipient as harmful and negative. Or, a gift that is actually intended to place someone under the giver's control (e.g., a lavish gift by a boss to his or her secretary) may be masked by rhetoric that claims the gift is simply a means of reciprocating for something already given.

In the exchange of harm for harm, the initiation factor may be even more important than in the benevolent exchange, because it is likely to lead to a strong perception of imbalance in the relationship. Often a person who receives one blow feels justified in returning several blows in order to even the score. Whenever there is an imbalance of reciprocity, there is a built-in escalation process. That is the dynamic factor in the reciprocity process.

The Escalation of Reciprocity

When people who have been injured respond by escalating the conflict, they feel justified in doing so because they were not the aggressors. This value is often institutionalized in societies, taking the status of a norm or law (e.g., justifiable homicide). Such rationalization spurred the change in the name of the U.S. Department of War to the Defense Department in 1947 (see Chomsky 1982:18). The latter implies that when the United States engages in military spending, it is simply responding to threats made by adversaries.

One apt example of how reciprocity works in the arms race can be found in Nikita Khrushchev's account of a conversation which he had with President Eisenhower (Khrushchev 1970:519–20).

> I remember a conversation I once had with President Eisenhower when I was a guest at his dacha at Camp David. We went for walks together and had some useful informal talks.
>
> During one of these talks, he asked, "Tell me, Mr. Khrushchev, how do you decide the question of funds for military expenses?" Then, before I had a chance to say anything, he said, "Perhaps first I should tell you how it is with us."
>
> "Well, how is it with you?"
>
> He smiled, and I smiled back at him. I had a feeling what he was going to say. "It's like this. My military leaders come to me and say, 'Mr. President, we need such and such a sum for such and such a program.' I say, 'Sorry, we don't have the funds.' They say, 'We have reliable information that the Soviet Union has already allocated funds for their own such program. Therefore if we don't get the funds we need, we'll fall behind the Soviet Union.' So I give in. That's how they wring money out of me. They keep grabbing for more and I keep giving it to them. Now tell me, how is it with you?"
>
> "It's just the same. Some people from our military department come and say, 'Comrade Khrushchev, look at this! The Americans are developing such and such a system. We could develop the same system, but it would cost such and such.' I tell them there's no money; it's all been allotted already. So they say, 'If we don't get the money we need and if there's a war, then the enemy will have superiority over us.' So we discuss it some more, and I end up by giving them the money they ask for."
>
> "Yes," he said, "that's what I thought. You know, we really should come to some sort of an agreement in order to stop this fruitless, really wasteful rivalry."

In large part, the upward spiral of the arms race can be attributed to the ability of the superpowers to justify their escalations by pointing to similar activities "on the other side."

Reciprocity of the Superpowers

The nuclear arms race has evolved primarily around the two major actors, the United States and the Soviet Union, which together own 97 percent of the nuclear weapons in the world today. Because the exchange between these two parties is primarily an impersonal one, which exists outside the boundaries of their respective in-groups, pressure exists to make it a negative one. There is a widely held belief in the United States, the Soviet Union, and many other countries that the international scene is a "devil take the hindmost" affair. It is assumed that in a shrinking world (with no new frontiers), international power politics must necessarily be a zero-sum game. Thus, imbalanced exchanges are rarely defined as generalized reciprocity, or as exchanges that promise long-term benefits.

The United States was clearly the initiator in the series of exchanges that constitute the nuclear arms race. It was the first country to develop atomic weapons, the only country ever to use them, and the first to make the major improvements in those weapons (see Table 4.1).

The American nuclear weapons program was immediately perceived as a negative, harmful exchange (and not without reason) by the Soviet Union.[3] The escalation of a reciprocal process is extremely difficult to stop. It is often easier for the initiator of a process to stop it, and in the case of the nuclear arms race it might be simpler for the United States than the Soviet Union to do so, since the United States tends to be the clear leader in most new steps of the race. Of course, one might argue that the Americans were merely reciprocating when they built the first bomb; they were responding to acts of aggression by the Germans and the Japanese. Of course, the Germans and Japanese were also provoked, so that one moves back historically through a series of reciprocal provocations.

History is quite clear in what happens as such escalations occur. The fairly consistent record thus far shows that reciprocal processes continue to escalate until one country or alliance defeats another in war. Traditionally, the process ends when one side's strength is exhausted and the military effort collapses. However, as Jonathan Schell (1982:190) points out, "In nuclear 'war' no one's strength fails until *both* sides have been annihilated."[4] Rear Admiral Gene R. La Rocque has suggested, for example, that Poseidon submarines, submerged far below the ocean, could continue lobbing missiles at the Soviet Union three months after a nuclear conflict had begun. By that time, there might be no Soviet Union to speak of; the weapons would merely explode over the rubble. There is no winner in a nuclear war, so war itself is called into question by the creation of nuclear weapons.

Table 4.1   Reciprocity in Weapons Developments

	Year Achieved[a]	
Technological Advance	U.S.	USSR
Nuclear chain reaction	*1942*	1946
Atomic bomb	*1945*	1949
Intercontinental bomber	*1948*	1954
Thermonuclear explosion	*1952*	1953
Hydrogen bomb test	*1954*	1955
Nuclear-powered submarine	1955	1955
Test of submarine-launched missile	1959	*1955*
Test of ICBM	1958	*1957*
Operational ICBM	*1959*	1960
Photoreconnaissance from satellite	*1959*	1962
Submarine-launched ballistic missile	*1960*	1968
Solid-fuel ICBM	*1962*	1968
Multiple warhead (MIRV)	*1966*	1968
Test of MIRV	*1968*	1974
Operational MIRV	*1970*	1975
Antiballistic missile (ABM)	1972	*1968*
Cruise missile	1982	?
Neutron bomb	1983	?

[a]The year a particular advance was first achieved is italicized under the respective country that led the escalation.

Sources: Morrison (1983:16); Ground Zero (1982:62–72); Forsberg (1982:53); York (1970); Sivard (1984:14).

We do not know how long the escalating spiral of the current arms race might continue without the outbreak of a nuclear war. Some people argue that nuclear war will never happen, that nuclear weapons will never be used, but such a position may be naive and idealistic. There is certainly no historical precedent for such a hope, and given the nature of reciprocity, it would seem unlikely. Rather than preventing war, nuclear deterrence—the well-named "balance of terror"—might simply be postponing it.

BUREAUCRACY

The concept of reciprocity gives some insight into the social psychological aspects of the arms race (see Chapter Five), but the arms race is more complex than the simple exchange between two superpowers. Reciprocal processes are institutionalized in an elaborate social structure of international politics, domestic politics, and the military-industrial complexes within the various nations involved. The nuclear arms race is deeply rooted in the structure of the modern world. It is not simply the Soviets and the Americans (or even the Warsaw Pact allies and the NATO allies) who are engaged in this convoluted reciprocity. Within each country, competition exists among the various branches of the services and different industries who vie for contracts (see Chapter Six). Also, within each service or corporation, different branches or divisions engage in competition and collusion.

One cannot fully understand why the arms race continues without examining the way in which it is institutionalized. Since the arms race is carried out within institutions, sociological studies of bureaucracy can help us understand why the race continues. A bureaucracy is a stable, formal organization of roles and functions with a clear division of labor, based upon the principle of positional hierarchy and codified rules of procedure (see Weber 1968:26–30). Several features of bureaucracy are relevant to a study of the arms race, and we shall discuss them under three broad categories: the general principles of bureaucratic operation, the structure of personal careers, and the authority of experts.

General Principles of Operation

Just as the term democracy means rule by the people, bureaucracy literally refers to rule by the bureau. That is, a bureaucracy is technically run not by individuals but by a set of procedures that everyone in the organization is supposed to follow. Even those at the top of the hierarchy are bound by the rules of the organization, most of which are clearly specified and written down (although people at the top obviously have more say in writing the rules than those at the bottom). Such rules often serve to restrict freedoms and certainly constrain choices.

One of the most notable students of bureaucracy, German sociologist Max Weber, suggested that such organizations seem to take on a life of their own once they are created. He referred to bureaucracy as an iron cage.[5] Weber noted that there is considerable irony in the bureaucratic form of organization, which was initially created to help people overcome the whims of dictators, autocrats, irrationality, and the uncontrollable forces of nature. Most German philosophers (and much of modern thought) equate human freedom with rationality and reason. Bureaucracies are, in some ways, the most rational of institutions, and yet they have many unintended consequences. Although designed to provide people with *more* control over their lives, formal organizations are complex structures that are often beyond the control even of those who are ostensibly in charge, resulting in less freedom rather than more.

Consequently, bureaucracies are one of those things we do not seem able to live with or without. We all experience a great deal of ambivalence toward them; we rely upon them and hate them at the same time. It is hard to imagine a university, for example, without bureaucratic organization: What would it be like if there were no course schedules that specify when and where classes will meet? On the other hand, most individuals have little positive to say about the university's bureaucracy when they are filling out forms, standing in long lines, or coping with its restrictions.

The military probably comes closer than any other institution to Weber's ideal type of bureaucracy: It has a strict hierarchy of authority, a rational organization of labor, codified rules of procedure and written documents, specialized training with official duties, and impersonal decision-making. People working within a bureaucracy are expected to separate their personal affairs from those of the office or position they hold.

Stability.   Because of their tightly structured nature, bureaucracies tend to be quite stable over time. Arthur Stinchcombe (1972) has noted, in fact, that many structural characteristics of a given bureaucracy are related to the time at which it was founded. He compares, for example, the types of workers employed by industries created before the growth of factories to those in industries initiated in the early nineteenth century, the railroad age, and the modern period. Industries emerging in different periods vary in percentage of different kinds of workers: unpaid family members, self-employed and paid family members, clerical workers, and professionals. The later industries (e.g., petroleum and aircraft) tend to employ a higher proportion of professionals, whereas the earlier industries (e.g., agriculture and retail trade) have more unpaid and paid family workers and self-employed workers.

Organizations thus have characteristics that tend to persist over time. This tendency has several implications for our understanding of the arms race: First, military institutions are among the oldest organizations, and many of the early traditions persist from generation to generation. Militaries are created to fight and win wars; it is remarkable how much of what Thucydides describes of the organization and rituals of the Peloponnesian War would be applicable to today's military. Strict hierarchical organization and authoritarianism, the structured mobilization of violence, the segregation of the sexes, and the social and ideological mechanisms for exacting great sacrifices from its members have been characteristic of military organizations for centuries (see Lang 1972:53ff.).

On the other hand, there is something unique about the organizational structure of the modern military. It consists of a complex interplay between modern industrial bureaucracy, the decisionmaking bodies of government, and the military itself. This structure was formed during the two world wars of this century for the purpose of massive mobilization of a major proportion of the world's resources for conflict. Many of the characteristics of the military of the 1980s can no doubt be traced back to the growth of the military machine in those wars: its massive size, its reliance on sophisticated technologies and the industrial infrastructure that produces them, and its ability to engage in activities of mass destruction that dwarf all previous war-fighting efforts.

Despite the fact that the development of nuclear weapons may very well have made the entire military tradition antiquated, because conventional notions of fighting and winning wars are so questionable, military institutions continue to operate as if the general pattern has not changed. The major shift has been not so much in terms of style, but of scope. The massive scope of the contemporary military complex is made possible by the economic infrastructure of modern industrial societies.[6]

Because of the way bureaucracies are organized, they tend automatically to expand their influence and diversify their functions. James Thompson's (1967) study of formal organizations concludes that they have a built-in tendency to expand in order to account for contingencies at their boundaries. Bureaucrats attempt to gain rational control over everything that affects their tasks, and they are frustrated by events and activities that occur outside their organization and consequently outside their jurisdiction. This is seen in military weapons acquisitions, for example. As Dörfer (1984:xv) points out,

> The weapons acquisition process is characterized by internal and external uncertainties. A high proportion of the internal acquisition process involves research and development activities whose outcomes are considered to be highly unpredictable and the external environment can change suddenly and unpredictably in terms of technology, enemy plans, and defense policies.

One common way to alleviate the problem of uncertainty in an organization's environment is to expand the institution so that it encompasses the problem areas. For example, automobile manufacturers, in order to prevent irregularities in the marketing of their cars, will require everyone who sells their new cars to have dealership franchises that follow the rules established by the larger corporation. In order to prevent excessive price fluctuations in the raw materials and component parts required for car production, they might buy up companies that supply those raw materials and parts.

Diversification.   A related characteristic of modern bureaucracies is diversification. Because the intention of every business enterprise is to show an annual profit, a corporation that specializes in a product for which the market is declining or fluctuating may acquire companies that make other products, in order to protect its own profit-making activities. As General Hoover testified before a congressional committee, the weapons establishment is like a large corporation that develops an investment strategy with various product lines (e.g., the theater nuclear product line) and is concerned with corporate survival (DeWitt 1983:29). The military-industrial complex has been greatly enlarged through the efforts of bureaucrats in government and industry to protect their organizational territory and expand its influence and control.

In a study of health and welfare organizations, Michael Aiken and Jerald Hage found that "organizations with many joint programs are more complex organizations, that is, they are more highly professionalized and have more diversified occupational structures" (1972:381). Apparently, as organizations develop joint programs with other institutions, they encounter a need to increase specialization and diversification. They also become more innovative. Aiken and Hage suggest that "the degree of complexity gives rise not only to joint programs, but also to new programs" (ibid.:385). A dialectical process thus emerges in the military establishment: Increased diversity enables innovations such as new weapons programs, which in turn stimulate diversification. Thus, both the internal process of a major bureaucratic organization and its relationships with other key organizations help to stimulate continual growth.

Another finding by Aiken and Hage is that increased complexity also leads to the decentralization of decisionmaking in organizations. In the military establishment, although there are individuals in charge of specialized parts of the military-industrial complex, nobody can really control the entire bureaucratic apparatus that comprises it. As the chairman of the Joint Chiefs of Staff said of the Pentagon on the "CBS Evening News" (5 February 1985), "It's difficult to find out who's in charge. Everybody's in charge of everything and nobody's in charge of anything." William Stringfellow (1984:25) argues that the Pentagon victimizes everybody, "not only ordinary folk, but presidents as well."

Within the military-industrial complex (which will be examined in more detail in Chapter Six) there is a need for cooperation and specialization, as a number of very complex production projects are juggled among several bureaucracies. The highly technical nature of the military industry results in the proliferation of specialized divisions, shops, research labs, and production facilities. The efforts to coordinate all of these projects give rise to administrative branches and large staffs that specialize in orchestrating the reciprocal exchanges among various sectors of the complex (see Levine and White 1972). In most large organizations, staff members are assigned explicitly to the task of managing interorganizational relations. One of the key actors, as Charles Perrow (1970:123) points out, is the purchasing agent:

> In one case which I observed, the company was obliged to hire, during summer vacations, the incompetent and disruptive college-going son of a purchasing agent in a large firm. . . . Gifts, football tickets, expensive entertainment at key clubs, and call girls are all part of this relationship. A great deal is at stake for the supply firm, and these costs are only a tiny fraction of the total volume of business.

One consequence of the diversification and specialization of the military establishment is the redundancy created by interservice rivalry. General David Jones, former chairman of the Joint Chiefs of Staff, claims that military decisions are made in terms of individual services, by people "who are going back to their services for promotion and [the decisions] serve service ends, not the United States" (Louis Goldman 1984:55).[7] The result of interservice rivalry can be seen most clearly in the fight for resources among various legs of the strategic triad. Goldman insists that "there is probably no better example of the trading off of special interests to the detriment of the common good than blind adherence to the Triad policy" (ibid.).

Secrecy. One final characteristic of the general principles of bureaucratic operation is secrecy, which is found in virtually every bureaucracy. Information is often a source of power, from the most mundane secrets in an office, such as where the extra pens and correction fluid are kept, to secrets about new weapons contracts. People in various departments of an organization protect their territory by keeping secrets and by divulging them only to certain people at opportune times. Although secrets are cautiously guarded in any bureaucracy, such behavior is even more prevalent in the military and in defense industries, where secrets are maintained on the basis of national security.

Sometimes secrecy on military issues is so extreme that even those who would be expected to know the secrets do not. The Soviet negotiators at the SALT talks, for example, reportedly had to be informed discreetly by American negotiators about their own weapons systems, because the Soviet military had not given them the information their discussions required. Similarly, Vice President Harry Truman was not informed about the Manhattan Project until two weeks after he became president. People who work on weapons development and construction, as well as the war planners, operate in a context of high secrecy that insulates them from the outside world. However, such secrecy also makes it difficult for them to test assumptions about their work against the ideas of others not dependent upon the institution for their livelihood.

The Structure of Personal Careers

Because of the way bureaucratic institutions are structured, individuals who work in the military-industrial complex expand the arms race by simply pursuing their own careers. In day-to-day decisionmaking, in order to justify their job responsibilities, they must provide reports and strategies of action that enhance their own status as well as that of their superiors and the institutions for which they work. That requirement, combined with the push for advancement (so central in American culture), creates pressure for bureaucratic expansion and is one of the key social mechanisms of the nuclear cage. The decisionmaking process is structured so that those who benefit directly from the upward spiral are precisely those consulted on the advisability of new weapons projects.

The military, in this respect, is like any other bureaucracy except in its task, which is to provide rational war plans and to mobilize people and technology to prepare for war. People who work as military strategists and for military contractors must be prepared to (1) develop winning scenarios, (2) insulate themselves from the implications of what would happen if their weapons were actually used, and (3) become involved in worst-case analyses when estimating how to respond to the adversary's capabilities. Cooperation in these tasks leads to a final hard-to-resist outcome—career security and organizational expansion.

Development of winning scenarios.   Suppose you are a military strategist given responsibility to develop scenarios for a new weapons system or a battle plan. As Stringfellow (1984:25) suggests, technocrats cannot calculate failure—they must succeed, or at least declare they have. What would happen if you wrote a report predicting that your side would lose the battle? You would probably lose your job. That is one reason why military manuals, such as the *Combat Leader's Field Guide*, provide instructions on how to respond optimistically to nuclear attacks. Soldiers are told to seek cover (in a ditch, foxhole, etc.) when nuclear weapons are exploded on the battlefield and to prepare to advance (Table 4.2).

An interesting example of the importance of winning scenarios is the development of civil defense planning as part of the overall nuclear policies of the United States and the Soviet Union. As Leaning (1982:95) contends,

> What is perhaps most significant about civil defense planning, and the policy that flows from it, is that the government bureaucracies are taking these plans most seriously and seem to be using them . . . as part of government military strategy. Key officials in the Federal Emergency Management Agency (FEMA) now advocate civil defense planning as a viable means of protecting the U.S. population from attack. T. K. Jones, former advisor on Soviet affairs for Boeing and now Deputy Under Secretary of Defense for Strategic and Nuclear Forces, was recently quoted as saying that the United States would recover fully from an all-out war in just 2 to 4 years, given an adequate civil defense program.

Insulation from the implications of weapons use.   Weapons specialists and strategic planners cannot allow themselves to dwell on what would happen if the weapons and plans they design were actually used. Like medical professionals in a hospital emergency room, military planners and weapons producers must insulate themselves from the horror and the human suffering inherent in their work. Military institutions themselves operate as

Table 4.2 Protective Measures Against Nuclear Explosions

Before	If ALERT is sounded, follow unit SOP. If warned before detonation, pick strongest shelter you can find. Underground shelters, deep foxholes, tanks and personnel carriers give good protection.
During TAKE COVER	If you see a BRILLIANT LIGHT, brighter than sunlight, DIVE FAST to put something (dirt, tree, a wall) between you and the detonation. FALL FLAT on the ground if you cannot reach shelter. CLOSE EYES and keep head covered. Protect face and hands. Stay until blast effect is over or until heavy material has stopped falling.
After STAY CALM	Reform your unit. Establish contact with subordinate, adjacent and higher units. Be ready for orders and instructions. Your life and your unit depend on you doing the right thing at the right time.
CONTINUE MISSION	The nuclear burst is only part of the enemy's plan. If you are in a forward area, be prepared for an enemy attack after the detonation. Be prepared to attack following a friendly detonation on enemy positions.
MONITOR AREA	Have unit monitor check area for residual nuclear radiation. If nuclear radiation is detected, report this to your commander. . . .

Source: Combat Leader's Field Guide, 1980, Ninth edition, Harrisburg, Pa.: Stackpole Books, p. 177. Reprinted with permission.

"total institutions" that are segregated from society at large and therefore exert unusual power over their members (see Zurcher 1965).

Roger Molander, a former weapons targeter for the Pentagon, recalls what happened to him one Saturday when a colleague's wife came into his office

> to find me sticking different-colored pins—representing different-sized weapons—into a map of the Soviet Union. Add a pink pin for Minsk—another 200,000 dead. My colleague's wife was horrified. But when the pin went into Minsk or Moscow, I didn't see people working or children playing. I assumed that someone above me in the system thought about those things. I just stuck in the pin. (Molander 1982:D5)

Thus, the division of labor within a bureaucratic organization can help personnel manage to remain ignorant of the implications of their work (see Peattie 1986).

The inherent moral problems in the structure of bureaucratic organization, with its instrumental orientation, are best exemplified by the Nazi concentration camps. In his interviews with people who worked at the camps, Lifton (1984:121) found that, as one Nazi doctor put it, "The word 'ethics' was never used in Auschwitz. . . . We just asked what worked."

Henry T. Nash, who worked as an analyst in the Political and Economics Section of the Air Targets Division, recalls that his responsibility was to nominate targets for the Bombing Encyclopedia (the official Secret Air Force catalogue of targets).

> While I worked at selecting and justifying political targets, fellow analysts in other offices were busy identifying different types of strategic targets—petroleum depots, airfields, or industrial centers. Each of us made nominations for the integrated Air Force strategic target list and we each hoped that our targets would be chosen for a DOD strategic plan of nuclear attack designed to bring about a rapid, unconditional surrender of Soviet forces. (Nash 1980:22)

Within the context of his office, according to Nash, such matters as having one's targets chosen were important signs of distinction to those who worked there. The highest compliment was to be accepted for top security clearances. "Being cleared," Nash recalls, "represented a flattering experience sharpened by the quality of selectivity, not unlike the feeling accompanying acceptance by a fraternity or country club" (ibid.:24).

Such procedures are built into the bureaucratic structure of the military-industrial complex and naturally discourage critical thinking or open questioning. Bureaucracies seem to promote formal rather than substantive rationality (Weber 1968), that is, the kind of thinking that emphasizes efficiency rather than moral or contextual considerations. For example, the formal rational question of "How do we build better bombs?" is asked, rather than the substantive rational issue of "Should we be building bombs?" While the neglect of such substantive questions may be a problem endemic to all bureaucracies, it would seem to be even more acute within the military, given the context of a total institution and the discomfort of the military in considering its underlying assumptions. Furthermore, because bureaucracies within the military-industrial complex are total institutions, exits are not as easily undertaken as they are in other bureaucratic contexts.

Worst-case analyses.   Military planners also engage in what is called worst-case analysis. Their work is highly speculative; they must try to reciprocate not only what the adversary has done, but what it *might* do. Consequently, they develop worst-case scenarios to show that their own side can win in spite of the worst possible developments by the enemy. They are thus technically able to protect themselves against miscalculations about the enemy's progress, so that their own particular corner of the war-making business does not find itself in an inferior situation. This means that new weapons developments are undertaken not only to overcome actual threats but to prepare for the worst possible potential threats. Few planners deal in likely or probable situations.

It should be emphasized that individual workers in military industries are, for the most part, conscientious, moral people simply trying to do their jobs. However, the structure of their situation forces them into working on projects that many of them might question, but which they have accepted as inevitable. Furthermore, because such activities occur in highly structured bureaucratic institutions, individuals are ordinarily not expected to take responsibility for the broader implications of their actions; they are simply doing what is required of them by their supervisors. The overall result, of course, may be corporate activities that individuals would ordinarily consider unethical.

Some people decide that building nuclear weapons is immoral; they quit their jobs and look for other work. Bishop Matthiesen, the Roman Catholic bishop of Amarillo, Texas, where—at the Pantex plant—all nuclear weapons in the United States are assembled, recently made a statement to the effect that he believed the making of nuclear weapons is unacceptable within the teachings of the Christian tradition (National Conference of Catholic Bishops 1983). As a result, several people who work at the plant have gone through a great deal of soul-searching about their jobs and are faced with tremendous pressures, such as the need to support their families and problems in finding other work.

Those few individuals who feel compelled to quit military jobs for reasons of conscience may find leaving their jobs difficult for other reasons, often because of the challenging, lucrative, and professionally rewarding nature of their work. "It was far and away the best job I ever had," recalled Ronald Coleman, who left his engineering job with the Air Force (Day 1981:27). "I didn't look at it in human terms. To me, it was just a problem—and I was happy that someone could come at me with a problem and I could give them a satisfactory answer" (ibid.:28).

Career security and organizational expansion. Another aspect of the career structure of a bureaucracy is salient to our understanding of the arms race: Workers in military bureaucracies are encouraged to support the growth of their sectors of the military-industrial complex. Continuous expansion and the development of new responsibilities are considered desirable because they help increase job security and promotion chances. As Peter Blau (1963:24) observes, the development of new programs is in the interests of most organizational officials, who are rewarded by their superiors for thinking up new tasks that would bring more resources to the organization and benefit those who work there. Consequently, it is in the interests of the experts to make recommendations that will expand the scope of their own bureaucratic niches and possibly of the entire military-industrial complex.

Officials who are successful at one job within the military-industrial complex may be able to find other jobs as well because of what is called the revolving door between different parts of the "iron triangle": the military, Congress, and military contractors. Military officers, for example, often have excellent post-military career opportunities within defense industries because of their knowledge and contacts.

The Authority of Experts

A final aspect of bureaucracy that is relevant to our study is the authority of the experts. At the core of bureaucratic organization is a division of labor based upon the specialized training of experts who fill the offices of the institution. Historically, weapons experts have always been among the most powerful experts in any society. In the current, highly technological weapons race, the role of the expert becomes even more significant. Current weapons technologies are so complicated that not only average citizens, but even congressional representatives and senators, cannot understand them. Because weapons specialists can talk about these highly speculative matters in a convincing fashion, decisionmakers often find themselves dependent upon them.

This very situation is often exploited by the experts themselves, because it gives them more control over the process and increases their job security and prestige. National security issues thus become concealed through a "mystification of technique" process that prohibits democratic discussion and makes citizens and members of Congress dependent upon the experts. The myriad of statistical and technical reports that emerge can be manipulated to give the impression that one thing is happening when something altogether different may be going on. It is not always deliberate deception; the experts are usually just operating within the structure provided for them. Many of the experts like the authority given to them, and some would like to see nuclear policy decisions made outside the democratic process altogether. Edward Luttwak, a long-time Pentagon consultant, has proposed that a new constitutional amendment establish a fourth branch of the American government—a Nuclear Supreme Council—that would make all decisions regarding nuclear weapons. "Our system of government," he argues, "which was built to cope with ordinary problems, which is run by ordinary men in a rather ordinary way, is now supposed to control nuclear weapons, which are none of these things" ("A Complex" 1982:29).

A major consequence of organizational expansion is the trend toward a centralization of institutions within the military-industrial complex and the concentration of power in the hands of a small elite (see Mills 1959).

RITUAL

A third sociological concept, ritual, illuminates the symbolic aspects of the arms race.[8] Although this idea is not part of the conventional analysis of the arms race, it is key to understanding the arms race as an emotional expression of the human need for security.

A ritual is a regularly repeated, traditional, and carefully prescribed set of behaviors that symbolizes a value or belief. Rituals consist of actions that are symbolic expressions of sentiments (Radcliffe-Brown 1977). They are what Georg Simmel (1971) refers to as "social forms," that is, ways of organizing behavior that has certain characteristics. There are social forms in the same way that there are, for example, geometric forms, such as circles, squares, or rectangles. If we study a geometric form, we can discover a number of properties it will always have, regardless of its *content*. For example, the area of a circle is always the square of the length of the radius times 3.1416 (πr^2), regardless of size. When we look at ritual as a social form, we can expect different kinds of rituals to exhibit similar characteristics. For example, despite very different contents, such apparently different rituals as a rain dance and a Christian worship service present certain formal similarities. Each involves regularly repeated behaviors as a way of symbolizing the relevant values and beliefs of its participants.

Four characteristics of rituals that help us understand the arms race include the following: (1) they provide solutions to problems; (2) they are rooted in experience; (3) they involve the identification of evil and the marking of boundaries; and (4) they reify social processes—that is, they make social structures appear unchangeable and natural when in fact they are artificial, change frequently over time, and are different in different cultures.

Solutions to Problems

Rituals provide solutions to problems on a number of levels, one of the most important being that they relieve social and psychological tensions that arise when people are confronted with crises, uncontrollable forces, or the unknown. They do so by allowing people to focus their energies on details of the ritual rather than on the broader, unanswerable aspects of the problem.

A funeral ritual provides a good example. When someone dies, his or her close friends and relatives feel a deep sense of grief and personal crisis. Those affected by the death need both an ability to respond in some way to the death (what to do, what to say, etc.) and answers to broader questions of meaning (e.g., What is life all about? What happens after death?). Funerals provide formulas for both. The various prescribed activities constituting a funeral provide people with time-tested, appropriate responses, and link them to broader world views. Making arrangements for the funeral, such as finding the clergy who will perform the ceremony, acquiring flowers, the casket, food and transportation for guests, and so forth, allows people to focus on specific ritual details and to avoid dwelling on the more unsettling aspects of the death.

The nuclear arms race is full of ritual details, such as the so-called bean counting by which people attempt to compare the total number of warheads, total megatonnages, and throw-weights in the superpower arsenals. Notice how often conversations of nuclear arms advocates about nuclear weapons shift to bean counting or to ritual denunciations of the Soviet Union and its aggression. Such focus on ritual detail provides a veneer of rationality to the most irrational actions and gives an appearance of control in a crisis where there is none.

Experiential Bases of Ritual

Although rituals are rooted in experience and appear to be verifiable, they cannot be verified. Whether they are perceived as effective depends instead upon whether people believe in them. Negative evidence that appears to discount a ritual can be explained away by the participant who has faith in the ritual. If the desired effect of a ritual is not produced, believers attribute its failure to an improper performance or to the possibility that an opponent performed the ritual more effectively. Because rituals are time-tested formulas demonstrated by wise sages or ancestors, people can always recall instances in which the ritual worked. There are many times when it has rained after a rain dance has been performed; on the other hand, when rain does not come, people can blame the failure on flaws in the rain dance performance.

Because rituals are rooted in experience and are firmly believed by at least some participants, they provide historical solutions that are considered appropriate long after the conditions in which they were developed have disappeared, a phenomenon referred to by William F. Ogburn as cultural lag (see Ogburn 1922). Ceremonial sequences of the arms race are thus carried over from prenuclear military rituals in which better arms and a more prepared military force could usually insure victory. Although in a nuclear war there would be no winners in any conventional sense of the term, people continue to act as if who can overkill their enemy the most number of times will make a difference. This focus on ritual detail provides a sense of rationality and security where there is no sensible basis for such.

Ritual Denunciations of Evil

Because rituals are symbols of values and beliefs, they remind people of those values and of their enemies, who ostensibly do not share those values and beliefs. Ritual behavior is an integral part of the social construction of evil (see Chapter Two). Every major ritual provides or implies a theory of evil that becomes a key to problem solving: an "evil" force or "evil" group of people is identified as responsible for the crisis and then denounced. The social construction of evil thus requires the creation of an image of the enemy that can be disseminated through the popular culture by the media, jokes, folktales, and official pronouncements.

Not only are external enemies—those outside the group or society— identified, but internal enemies are labeled as well (Kurtz 1986). External enemies are beyond the immediate control of a society and its leaders; of-ten little more can be done about them than to denounce them. Internal enemies are another story, however. Because they are within the jurisdic-tion of the group or society denouncing them, more direct action can be taken against them. Furthermore, internal enemies can often be linked to external enemies and thereby labeled as traitors. Thus, by taking action against them, one is thought to be affecting the external enemy as well. In the 1950s, for example, some Americans were concerned about the growth of international communism. Because they had little influence or control over communism outside the United States, they focused their efforts (in the McCarthy hearings and elsewhere) on condemning alleged communists within the country. Similarly, in the 1980s Freeze activists were at first said to be helping the enemy.

Reification of Social Processes

The term "reification" means the treatment of an abstraction as substan-tially existing, or as a concrete material object. A thousand claims of deter-rence are belied by the fact that weapons technology strives ever more suc-cessfully for first-strike arsenals. Similarly, first-strike arsenals are reifications in light of even a limited deterrence, or the pyrrhic victory of a nuclear winter. There consequently exists an abstract notion of defense, and also one of war, neither of which is possible. Yet, institutions responsi-ble for these matters are charged to keep real what has passed into myth and nightmare.

When people do not feel secure with current defenses, arms experts are called to the Congress and the Kremlin and asked to explain what can be done to improve the weapons. But if weapons cannot be used because their effects would be hideously absurd, how can they possibly be made more threatening? Instead, the very concept of security through arms is being clung to by institutions whose sacrosanct nature would collapse if the abstract plan of nuclear war were ever fully realized.

When we realize that social structures and institutions are themselves held together by abstract definitions and concepts, we see how reification can make concrete and unchangeable what was originally formed and di-rected by evolving human thought. Once out of the control of the minds that formed and maintained them, social structures and institutions come to be labeled sacrosanct. Built-in sanctions apply to those who refuse to participate in the trend toward unreality. An increased reliance is also placed on ritual experts who guide the arms race ceremony. Ironically, reliance upon experts is especially strong (in any ritual) when the rituals are *not* working. Since public criticism is usually directed toward the performance rather than the ritual itself, people turn ever more to the experts for advice on how to improve what is already misguided (see Kurtz 1986). Thus, a social process—the acquirement of weapons—becomes more concrete and real than what it produces. It is linked to political aims and political careers, and never suffers from an examination of its underlying assumptions, except by relatively powerless outsiders. It is interesting to note, however, that some of the most vocal and influential critics of the current arms race are former ritual experts, such as Rear Admiral La Rocque, former Deputy Director of the CIA Herbert Scoville, and former Secretary of Defense Robert McNamara, as well as former CIA Director William Colby and former National Security Advisor McGeorge Bundy.[9]

Ritual Elements of the Nuclear Arms Race

As with any ritual, there is an overall ceremony to the nuclear arms race, with a number of rites nested within it (just as rites at a worship service include praying, scripture reading, etc.). First, public displays of weapons and periodic official pronouncements about weapons programs are ritually performed. The parades of weapons in Red Square and the exhibitions of weapons and open houses at American military bases are accompanied by recitations of facts and figures about the arms race by government spokespersons. Just as it is easy to see that the Soviets' May Day Parade is a regularly repeated, traditional set of behaviors designed to symbolize a value or belief system, it is also possible to view a Defense Department press conference as a litany.

Second, mock battles, war games, and computer simulations provide rehearsals that offer a sense of security however false. They reassure the participant that we can respond effectively in the event of an enemy attack.

Third, there are ritualized approaches to defining nuclear strategy and policy, most clearly seen in the language used to describe war plans and security gaps, and in the bean counting discussed earlier. The term "gap" has been replaced by "window of vulnerability," but the ritual of nervous concern over a phantom danger (while ignoring the true one) is just as great.

Fourth, the research and development, testing, building, and deployment of nuclear weapons are traditional, regularly repeated behaviors that symbolize values and beliefs. Such rituals especially symbolize the logic of deterrence (the idea that enemies will not attack because of the danger of doing so); the sacredness of national interests (the idea that nuclear weapons are worth the potential risk involved); and the efficacy of military responses to security threats.

The civil defense planning and drills carried out by government agencies are a fifth ritual element of the arms race. They provide the participant with the conviction that something can be done.

Even arms control negotiations become ritualized activity by allowing the superpowers to foster the impression that they are peace-loving and serious about arms control while they continue their weapons build-up. The negotiations offer them a chance to feel that they are doing *something* about a race that is out of control, or, conversely, to justify escalation when progress is not achieved.

Finally, ritual denunciation of the enemy through the social construction of evil is an important component of the overall ritual. If all *our* efforts fail, we can always feel good because it is *"their* fault."

Although our comments about the arms race ritual have a decidedly negative tone, we should make it clear that we are criticizing the *content* of the ritual and not the idea of ritual itself.[10] Many critics of the arms race advocate the creation of new, less destructive rituals that would enable people to respond to the crisis in a manner other than simply building more weapons.

SUMMARY

An explanation for the continued escalation of the arms race requires a multilevel analysis. We have suggested three sociological concepts— reciprocity, bureaucracy, and ritual—as ways of framing a study of the manner in which decisions to escalate the arms race are preconditioned.

Reciprocity is an exchange between two parties that results from the feeling of obligation by one party to repay a good or harm received. When someone receives a gift, he or she feels obliged to somehow repay the giver. When a person is harmed by someone else, he or she feels justified in harming the offender. Such exchanges can be generalized, balanced, or negative, and can have beneficial or harmful contents.

Reciprocity has a built-in escalation factor. The person who receives one blow often feels justified in returning several blows in order to even things up. Thus, a conflict takes on a life of its own and is extremely difficult to end. Most of the escalation in the nuclear arms race is justified in exactly this way, on the basis of reciprocating for past, and even potential, actions by adversaries. The nuclear arms race was initiated by the United States, and the Soviet Union quickly reciprocated.

Historically, weapons escalations have not ended until one side's strength was exhausted in a war. In a nuclear war, however, there would be no winners. Thus there is a real danger that the nuclear arms race might not be stopped until everyone is annihilated in a nuclear war.

The nuclear arms race is fostered in bureaucratic institutions, that is, in stable, formal organizations of roles and functions with a clear division of labor, based upon the principle of office hierarchy and regulated by codified rules of procedure. Bureaucracy literally means rule by the bureau. Max Weber called it an iron cage, which is beyond the control of even those who are supposed to be in charge, despite the fact that bureaucracies were originally designed to give people rational control over their lives.

Bureaucracies have tendencies to expand, diversify, and provide for the maintenance of secrecy, all of which foster an escalation of the arms race. Formal organizations in the military-industrial complex are structured in such a way that when individuals merely pursue their own careers, they expand the arms race. They do this by developing winning-case scenarios and worst-case analyses while, at the same time, insulating themselves from the implications of what would happen if their plans were carried out and their weapons used.

Specialized experts are the major force within a bureaucracy, and they naturally tend to engage in a "mystification of technique" that enhances their control of their own careers and businesses. At the same time, they monopolize the decisionmaking process by making ordinary citizens, and even members of Congress, feel as though they do not sufficiently understand such complicated matters as nuclear weapons to have any substantial democratic input in the policy of the arms race.

Finally, we compared the nuclear arms race to a ritual, that is, a regularly repeated, traditional, and carefully prescribed set of behaviors that symbolizes a value or a belief. Rituals (1) provide solutions to problems, (2) are rooted in experience, (3) involve the identification of evil and the marking of boundaries, and (4) reify social processes. In fact, many aspects of the arms race are rituals: the stockpiling of weapons, mock battles, public displays, civil defense drills, and denunciations of the enemy, to name a few.

In subsequent chapters of this book, we will rely upon the concepts of reciprocity, bureaucracy, and ritual to provide a framework for the analysis of a variety of aspects of the nuclear arms race and to evaluate proposed solutions for the prevention of a nuclear holocaust. In doing so, we will draw upon research in several social science traditions.

CHAPTER FIVE

The Social Psychology of Warfare

Lester R. Kurtz and Jennifer E. Turpin

> Technically and intellectually we are living in an atomic
> age; emotionally we are still living in the Stone Age. We feel
> superior to the Aztecs who on a feast day sacrificed 20,000
> men to their gods, in the belief this would keep the universe
> in its proper course. We sacrifice millions of men for
> various goals that *we* think are noble and we justify the
> slaughter. But the facts are the same, only the rationaliza-
> tions are different.
>
> —Erich Fromm, *May Man Prevail?*

Our discussion of reciprocity, bureaucracy, and ritual suggests that the reasons for the arms race are complex. No single explanation will suffice—we
have to look at the arms race from a number of perspectives and levels.

In this chapter we examine the social psychology of the nuclear cage
at several levels: human instinct and motivation, interpersonal interaction,
group dynamics, and international relations. The dynamics of each level
are somewhat different, although what happens at one level affects all others. Individual instincts and motivations, for example, affect international
relations, and vice versa. Because properties emerge at higher levels of
analysis that are not present at lower levels, it is helpful to begin a
discussion of the social psychology of warfare with the individual and move
upward to increasingly complex social structures.

INDIVIDUAL MOTIVATIONS AND INSTINCTS

When people discuss the nuclear threat, someone inevitably says: "I certainly want world peace, but I know it's an unrealistic goal. Throughout history there have been wars, and people are just basically violent, aggressive, and hostile." Aggression, fear, and hostility are deeply rooted psychological factors that play a major role in the maintenance and building of the nuclear cage. As Rogers et al. (1982:v) point out,

> The nuclear arms race aggravates some ominous features of human behavior: the inability to adjust perceived reality to actual reality rapidly enough when the latter abruptly changes; the propensity to resort to violence when frustrated or frightened; blind obedience; and the primitivizing effect of emotions on thought and on images of the enemy, with special reference to deterrence.

That is only one side of human nature, however. Although history is filled with bloody wars, it is also the story of generations of people loving and caring for one another. The question is, why do human beings sometimes love one another and at other times fight and kill each other? A combination of factors—social, biological, and psychological—come into play. Aggressive human instincts provide motivation for the arms race, but they are not sufficient in and of themselves; they must be channeled by cultural norms and values and interpreted by individuals.

It was not until 1945 that human culture provided the milieu that

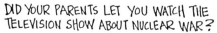

made the creation of nuclear weapons possible. Since the first nuclear weapons were built, they were exploded only in one war, by one country. Why is it that nuclear weapons have not been used on humans since World War II? Why do Americans feel threatened by Soviet weapons but not by British and French weapons? Why did Americans once think the Chinese nuclear arsenal was dangerous, but fear it no longer? Why do the Soviets feel threatened by everyone's nuclear weapons? For the answers to such questions, we must examine the complex relationship between instincts and motivations, as well as the sociocultural factors that give them shape and influence their outcome when people choose to act.

Jerome Frank (1982:3) suggests that three biologically and phylogenetically rooted aspects of human behavior are involved in building and maintaining the nuclear cage: the tendency "to resort to violence when frustrated or frightened, submission to authority, and the priority of group needs over those of the individual." There is little consensus, however, about the relationship between such tendencies and human war-making (see Fromm 1973).

Violence: Instinctive or Learned?

There is much debate as to whether violent human behavior is biologically based or learned. Some, like Konrad Lorenz, Robert Ardrey, and Desmond Morris, argue that aggression is instinctive in both animals and humans. Lorenz notes, however, that deliberate cruelty is distinctively human.[1] Others, like behaviorist B. F. Skinner, argue that aggression, like all human behavior, is learned and is a product of social and cultural conditioning.

Sigmund Freud ([1921] 1959, [1923] 1960) contended that aggressive, violent behavior is a result of the interaction between instinctive and environmental influences. His theory of the personality suggests that there are conflicting forces within an individual's unconscious: drives and instincts (the id), on the one hand, and internalized social values (the superego), on the other. Thus, drives and instincts are countered by the superego, which demands socially acceptable behavior. In Freud's theory, a third aspect of the personality, the ego, attempts to accommodate these competing internal forces.

What Freud failed to recognize is that there are conflicting demands even within the superego (commonly called the conscience). Catholic workers at the Pantex plant in Amarillo, Texas, for example, are faced with such conflicting demands. They have been told by their bishop that nuclear weapons are incompatible with Christian teachings, but they also belive strongly that defense work is patriotic, that they can take pride in providing for their families, and that they should work conscientiously. When the plant opened, Amarillo was well on the way to becoming a ghost town; there were very few jobs, and the Pantex plant was appreciated (see Mojtabai 1986).

Whatever drives and instincts humans may have toward violent behavior are channeled into different kinds of activity in different cultures and subcultures. Lifton (1985c:16) concludes from his study of Nazi doctors at concentration camps that "over the course of committing evil acts, an ordinary person becomes something different." A process emerges that he calls doubling, in which "a new self takes shape that adapts to the evil environment, and the evil acts become part of that self." An individual's social context thus preconditions the decisions that he or she will make in an attempt to reconcile instinctual drives with the demands of social norms.

According to Collins (1974), the nature of violent human behavior has changed over time. In modern industrial societies there has been a decline of highly personalistic ferociousness such as torture and dismemberment, but there has been an increase in *impersonal* violence, an institutionalized destructiveness with the callousness and impersonalization peculiar to established bureaucratic forms of government, business, and industry. Collins (ibid.) points to two examples of the kind of depersonalized cruelty found in industrial societies—the Nazi death camps, and high-altitude bombing. In both instances, individuals need not be personally hostile toward the victims of their violence; they are simply carrying out orders given by their superiors. As C. Wright Mills (1959:4) puts it, "Everywhere in the underdeveloped world, ancient ways of life are broken up and vague expectations become urgent demands. Everywhere in the overdeveloped world, the means of authority and violence become total in scope and bureaucratic in form."

Human violence probably does have some biological basis, but that predisposition alone cannot explain the nuclear arms race. First, it is only one side of complex human nature, which can be altruistic as well as cruel. Second, the direction in which violence is channeled is socially determined and varies widely from culture to culture.

Leahey and Lewin (1977) argue that warfare in human society emerged at the same time as the beginning of settled agriculture ten thousand years ago. Frank (1982:3–4), who emphasizes biological factors, nevertheless argues that although

> programs of violence are imbedded in the human central nervous system, there is no direct link between them and complex social behaviors such as waging war. Innate patterns of scratching, biting, hitting, and kicking have nothing to do with launching a nuclear missile. Waging war must be learned afresh by every generation.

Submission to Authority

Other deeply ingrained patterns of human behavior that may be biologically or genetically based include submission to authority and a readiness by individuals to sacrifice for the good of the group (ibid.:4ff). The extent to which humans are willing to submit even to unjust authority has been demonstrated by the shocking experiments carried out by Yale psychologist Stanley Milgram (1974). About two-thirds of the subjects in his study administered what they were told were painful, possibly lethal shocks to a stranger (who was part of the experiment and did not actually receive the shocks). When subjects were asked to throw a master switch that allowed others to participate, over 90 percent agreed to do so.

Milgram found that the subjects were more prone to administer painful shocks when their victims were farther away from them. It was easier, in this way, for the subjects to "deny" or put the reality of the victim out of their minds (what Milgram called denial and narrowing of the cognitive field). One implication of this study is that depersonalization of an enemy may make it easier to harm a person if the victim is distant.

According to Frank (1982:4), the Milgram experiments are "uncomfortably analogous to the circumstances under which a nuclear missile would be launched." When a Polaris submarine commander was asked what it was like to have responsibility for his submarine's destructive power, he replied, "I've never given it any thought, but if we have to hit, we'll hit and there won't be a second's hesitation" (ibid.).

Similar results emerged in a study by Haney, Banks, and Zimbardo (1973), who set up a mock prison to examine responses to roles of authority. Subjects in the experiment were randomly assigned roles as guards or prisoners. The results were so dramatic that the experiment was prematurely ended. Guards assumed an "active initiative" role, in contrast to the prisoners, who became passive. The researchers concluded that "the use of power was self-aggrandizing and self-perpetuating." The prisoners meanwhile developed a series of coping strategies to deal with the arbitrary control, eventually leading to a pathological "passivity, dependence, and flattened affect."

Risk-Taking

Risk-taking is another important psychological issue significant at a number of stages in the nuclear dilemma, from policy debates to choices about whether to fire nuclear weapons. Despite a veneer of rationality, real-life choices are made within the context of imperfect information, biases of risk assessment, and nonrational factors. At best, individuals use "bounded rationality" (Simon 1955), which is limited by the social environment (cf. Douglas and Wildavsky 1982).

Under conditions of uncertainty, people make decisions in incremental stages (see Kahneman and Tversky 1979). What happened in the previous stage serves as a boundary behind which one need not look for making the next decision. A classic analogy is the frog in a petri dish. Apparently, if a frog is put into very hot water, it will jump out immediately. If it is sitting in a petri dish of cool water, however, and the temperature is gradually increased, it will not notice the small increments and may remain until it is killed by the heat.

Conventional risk theory suggests that people are "risk averse"; they tend to avoid taking risks and prefer certainty to uncertainty. Douglas and Wildavsky contend, however, that this is true only of positive prospects, not negative ones:

> One of the oldest and most accepted generalizations in decision theory is that people are generally risk averse. Given the choice between a 90 percent chance of winning 3,000 and a 45 percent chance of winning 6,000, the majority go for the best probability and half the gain. . . . By what is called the reflection effect, the usual choices between sums and probabilities go into reverse when the sums concern prospects of losing. Think about it—you do the same: would you choose the certain loss of 3,000 or take some low probability of losing 6,000? If you are like everyone else, you would not choose the certain loss but hope that the probability would work out so that you do not lose anything at all. But in that case you have chosen a risk against a certainty. (1982:79)

Because of the importance of social groups in shielding individuals from external threats and providing psychological security, socially constructed norms have a formidable impact on opinion formation. Most people have a strong impulse to submit to extreme demands made by authorities. In order to understand why individuals think in such a fashion, we have to turn our attention to the levels of interpersonal interaction and group dynamics.

INTERPERSONAL INTERACTION

Instinctually motivated drives are channeled by structural conditions and shaped by ongoing processes of reciprocity (see Chapter Four). At the same time, individuals make decisions about behavior based on the requirements of the social roles they play in everyday life. They are taught these expectations through a process called socialization, during which they are given positive or negative cues by people with whom they are interacting.

Interaction (whether on the job, in the home, or in any other social setting) is carried out by what George Herbert Mead (1934) calls taking the role of the other. When we are interacting with someone, we try to take their point of view in order to predict how our actions or words will affect them. This important human ability to be reflexive makes it possible for us to anticipate potential responses and reciprocal interactions, and to make decisions about how to foster a desired impression (see Goffman 1959).

We thus form alliances on the basis of these interactions and share what W. I. Thomas (1966) calls definitions of the situation. We usually define a situation on the basis of how we think our friends and allies will see it, and in opposition to how our enemies will. Because we are always faced with more information than we can process, we are selective in what we pay attention to, even in the most mundane tasks. A person walking down the street, for example, cannot pay close attention to *everything* along the route, but only that which is defined as important. He or she may be vaguely aware of many other things at the same time, but most items in our environment are simply background; we focus selectively on what fits within our definition of the situation.

Interesting problems arise when others are defined as an enemy. We are faced with conflicting moral demands of cooperation and conflict, an ambivalence for which we must seek some psychological resolution. For example, a norm to "love your enemy" contradicts norms that require destroying an enemy who is defined as a threat.

Lines of action are built up and institutionalized, so that they influence decisionmaking processes from minute choices of day-to-day life to decisions at the Pentagon about new weapons programs, to debate about bills before Congress, and to deliberations at the White House on foreign policy. Such decisions are preconditioned by previous sets of choices, and people become locked into patterns of ritual behavior that keep the flow of events moving in the same direction. This does not mean that people cannot make choices outside the alternatives as they are structured; however, such action is rare indeed. Because of the social nature of decisionmaking processes, we need to look not simply at the individual or person-to-person level but at the dynamics of social groups as well.

GROUP DYNAMICS

Social groups take on lives of their own, especially within bureaucratic structures, and are developed out of ongoing personal interactions. New decisions are always made on the basis of past experience. That is how we predict the way people will respond to us when we "take the role of the other" and decide how to act in a situation.

The tendency of social groups is to move toward a consensus. Conflicts among friends and co-workers make life difficult, so people attempt to avoid confrontations and to increase group solidarity. Participants thus try to avoid saying or doing things that will create conflict. By taking the role of the others, they can adjust their behavior in accordance with group norms.

Studies of small groups suggest that the greater a group's cohesiveness, the more power it has to bring about conformity to its norms and to gain acceptance of its goals (Cartwright 1968). Highly cohesive groups provide a sense of security to group members, serving to reduce anxiety and heighten self-esteem. Because individuals become dependent upon the group, they are willing to sacrifice personal opinions that deviate from group norms. Consequently, most groups engage in what Irving Janis calls groupthink, that is, "a deterioration of mental efficiency, reality testing, and moral judgment that results from in-group pressures" (1972:9). People who belong to policymaking groups are subject to the same pressures—members will join forces against a "deviant" in order to preserve unanimity; nonconformists are eased out of the group.

Groupthink, Janis contends, has eight identifiable symptoms (ibid.:197–98):

1. An illusion of invulnerability, shared by most or all the members, which creates excessive optimism and encourages taking extreme risks;
2. Collective efforts to rationalize in order to discount warnings which might lead the members to reconsider their assumptions before they recommit themselves to their past policy decisions;
3. An unquestioned belief in the group's inherent morality, inclining the members to ignore the ethical or moral consequences of their decisions;
4. Stereotyped views of enemy leaders as too evil to warrant genuine attempts to negotiate, or as too weak and stupid to counter whatever risky attempts are made to defeat their purposes;
5. Direct pressure on any member who expresses strong arguments against any of the group's stereotypes, illusions, or commitments, making clear that this type of dissent is contrary to what is expected of all loyal members;
6. Self-censorship of deviations from apparent group consensus, reflecting each member's inclination to minimize to himself the importance of his doubts and counterarguments;
7. A shared illusion of unanimity concerning judgments conforming to the majority view (partly resulting from self-censorship of deviations, augmented by the false assumption that silence means consent);
8. The emergence of self-appointed mindguards—members who protect the group from adverse information that might shatter their shared complacency about the effectiveness and morality of their decisions.

One consequence of groupthink is that information is filtered as it moves up along communications channels in a bureaucracy. It is very difficult for people at the top (e.g., the president of the United States or the general secretary of the Soviet Communist Party) to receive accurate information. Individuals are hesitant to pass on any information to their superiors that contradicts the prevailing consensus.

An example of how that process works is the controversy provoked in May 1986 over President Reagan's appeal for military aid to the U.S.-backed rebels (the contras) fighting to overthrow the Sandinista government in Nicaragua. Although the White House's own polls indicated little public support for the aid, members of the White House staff failed to tell the president. As one anonymous White House official told the *New York Times* (1986), the president's aides "are not about to stick up their heads to the President and say, 'Don't do it,' because the fact is, he wants to do it."

A nation's nuclear policies constitute a social definition of the situation with regard to the nuclear cage that is constructed out of an ongoing dialectical process. Individual psychological, interactional, and group dynamics factors all affect one another, resulting in a larger overall picture or set of pictures. That definition contains the assumptions and guidelines on which people act. It is based not on empirical reality, but on a social consensus about that reality and is shaped by groupthink, interactional pressure, and socially constructed illusions.

INTERNATIONAL RELATIONS

International relations are motivated and structured by institutionalized reciprocity and have social psychological dynamics similar to interpersonal group interactions. Definitions made within small groups of policymakers affect international relations by setting off chain reactions that diffuse throughout the world community.

Imagine, for example, that a decision is made by a small group of policymakers in Washington or Moscow about the need for a new weapon. Groupthink pushes members of that group toward a consensus, and the decision is passed up along the hierarchy of the governmental bureaucracy, with similar processes operating at each level. Furthermore, a decision in one nation will probably evoke a similar response from another country. If a group of individuals in Moscow decides that an evacuation plan should be established for relocating citizens from major cities in times of escalating international tension, they may be able to convince their superiors that the plan is necessary. Soon the plan will be discussed by the Soviets' counterparts in Washington, who will formulate a response to the Soviet plan. Members of the group who express discontent about the decision may be expected to change their opinion, keep silent, or resign.

Thus, international relations are motivated by the fears and instincts that affect individual decisionmakers and are shaped by reciprocity, interpersonal interactions, and groupthink. Two aspects of that process are especially salient: First, a series of illusions are woven around attitudes toward nuclear weapons and their use, and second, the social construction of evil is used to legitimize escalations.

Nuclear Illusions

Nowhere is the potential for illusion more dangerous than within the nuclear cage. There is no way to test the key assumptions behind strategic theories: Can a nuclear war be kept limited? Will a nation under nuclear attack retaliate? Will missiles traveling thousands of miles over the north pole hit their targets? Will a nuclear war destroy the fragile ecosystem of the planet? These are all empirical questions best left untested. Because nuclear war is an abstract and speculative topic, even the most accurate imagining is bound to be far removed from the actual reality.

Lifton suggests that a series of nuclear illusions have emerged because of "the quality of fear . . . [that nuclear weapons] inspire, their special mystery, their relationship to the infinite, and our sense of profound helplessness before them" (Lifton 1982:13–22). To respond to those perceptions, Lifton argues, people have developed a series of illusions.

The overriding deception, and the basis of most false assumptions about the bomb, is the *illusion of limit and control*. According to Lifton, the assumption that a "preplanned combination of bold, limited nuclear action and . . . more or less *unlimited* nuclear threat can enable us to *control* the situation and keep it *limited* . . . defies virtually all psychological experience" (ibid.:16–17).

An *illusion of foreknowledge* suggests that survivors of an attack would be strengthened by more knowledge about nuclear weapons effects. This illusion is based on a mistaken comparison between nuclear war and natural disasters in which knowledge about the characteristics of the disaster does help people survive. In a nuclear war, however, knowledge of nuclear weapons effects will (at best) simply prolong one's agony.

Relatedly, the *illusions of preparation* and *protection* delude people into thinking that plans are being made to protect them from the effects of a nuclear attack. Belief in the importance of foreknowledge has led to elaborate evacuation and shelter plans. Lifton insists that this fantasy is a product of *social madness* in which psychologically "normal" people can "collude in forms of thought structure that are unreal in the extreme."

A fifth illusion is that of *stoic behavior under nuclear attack*. Lifton and Erikson (1982) contend, on the basis of behavior by the Hiroshima survivors, that survivors would be characterized by a psychic numbing so extreme that the mind would essentially be shut down altogether. The illusion of stoic behavior leads to an *illusion of recovery*, which could become a reality only if there were outsiders who would come in to help, as there were in the first nuclear war.

Finally, Lifton claims, there is an *illusion of rationality* surrounding nuclear issues. There is a certain rationality involved in nuclear strategies, but it is the logic of madness. Although the various elements of a "systems rationality" may make sense in relationship to one another, they are not founded on reality, and one illusion simply leads to others. Because the nuclear cage is a consequence of a collective rather than a personal madness, it is even more dangerous. There is no way to check the reality of the illusions and recognize the fallacies that underlie them. Advocates of nuclear warfighting plans, for example, are clinically sane and appear to be normal, Lifton argues, but are engaged in pathological behavior.

The social psychology of the nuclear cage reveals a web of complex social processes that are subject to illusions, false assumptions, and groupthink, which prevent people from grounding their attitudes and policies in reality. Consequently, it is extremely important, as suggested in the

Prologue, to scrutinize the basic assumptions of any position on the nuclear cage, including images of the enemy as evil.

The Social Construction of Evil

> Yes, let us pray for the salvation of all of those who live in that totalitarian darkness—pray they will discover the joy of knowing God. But until they do, let us be aware that while they preach the supremacy of the state, declare its omnipotence over individual man, and predict its eventual domination of all peoples on the Earth, they are the focus of evil in the modern world.
>
> —Ronald Reagan in remarks to the National Association of Evangelicals, Orlando, Florida, 8 March 1983

> Today in Washington, together with morality, elementary norms of decency are being trampled and disrespect shown not only for statesmen and states, but also for the United Nations Organization. . . .
>   All who raise today their voice against the senseless arms race and in defense of peace can be sure that the policy of the Soviet Union, of other socialist countries, is directed at attaining precisely these aims. The U.S.S.R. wants to live in peace with all countries, including the United States. It does not nurture aggressive plans, does not impose the arms race on anyone, does not impose its social order on anyone.
>
> —Yuri Andropov statement, 28 September 1983

In order to justify the stockpiling of nuclear weapons, the nuclear powers create images of their enemies that depict them as monstrous. Thus the rhetoric of the nuclear states (especially the superpowers) involves mirroring and projection, as each scrambles to justify its own behavior on the basis of the perceived malevolence of the adversary. The other side has a vast arsenal of weapons of mass destruction, so it is necessary to defend oneself by obtaining a comparable capability. Hence, the well-named balance of terror emerges as both a consequence and a cause of the nuclear arms race.

These images of evil are deeply rooted in the national psyche and are perpetuated in stereotypical presentations in the mass media, popular humor, and daily interpretations of international events. Evidence is filtered through this cognitive screen, so that contradictions are ignored and confirmations highlighted. Whereas the other side is evil and acts with malicious intent, our side is good and acts out of benevolence. With both sides thinking this way, both can claim their own nuclear weapons are only built for defensive purposes.

Regardless of how evil individuals and nations are, however, they are never totally evil or totally good. One of the great surprises of the trial of Nazi death camp official Adolf Eichmann was his many positive personal attributes. As Hannah Arendt (1977:25–26) writes,

> Half a dozen psychiatrists had certified him as "normal"—"More normal, at any rate, than I am after having examined him," one of them was said to have exclaimed, while another had found that his whole psychological outlook, his attitude toward his wife and children, mother and father, brothers, sisters, and friends, was "not only normal but most desirable."

The fact that people or countries who do evil things can also do good creates cognitive dissonance and an ambivalence in any thoughtful person's mind. A common means of resolving the ambivalence is to *depersonalize* one's enemies, to deny that they are fully human. The tactic is particularly effective in a modern bureaucratic setting that separates the person from the office and its tasks.

Henry Nash (1980:22) recalls the following about his work in the Air Targets Division:

> Our office behavior was no different from that of men and women who might work for a bank or insurance company. What enabled us calmly to plan to incinerate vast numbers of unknown human beings without any sense of moral revulsion? . . . The Cold War made selecting targets for attack in the Soviet Union seem respectable.

The individual who targets Soviet or American cities with nuclear warheads is probably not motivated by personal animosity but by the requirements of his or her work within the context of a conflict with a depersonalized enemy. Such depersonalization is the social psychological basis of the military-industrial complex and much strategic policymaking. It also provides an ideological rationale for actions that we might not be able to take (or even to plan) against warm, friendly human beings.

Finally, social psychological factors that have little to do with the arms race or international conflicts come into play; the most significant of these is the push for profits (see Chapter Six).

SUMMARY

No single explanation of the arms race is sufficient; a number of perspectives must be examined. This chapter explored the social psychology of the nuclear cage at the levels of instinct and motivation, interpersonal interaction, group psychology, and international relations.

Human beings seem to have drives and instincts for violent behavior, although there is much debate about the nature of such factors. Instincts are channeled into different kinds of activity in different cultures and subcultures. The social context *preconditions* the decisions that people make in reconciling instinctual drives with the demands of social norms.

Deeply engrained patterns in human behavior that may be biologically or genetically based include submission to authority and a readiness by the individual to sacrifice for the good of the group. People make decisions about their behavior on the basis of general cultural norms and values, and the requirements of their everyday roles.

Individuals form alliances on the basis of interactions and share "definitions of the situation" that are then used to screen out information contradictory to those definitions. Members of social groups move beyond this toward groupthink, which inhibits rational thoughts and results in the silencing or expulsion of individuals with differing opinions.

International relations are conditioned by the motivations, reciprocal interactions, and group dynamics that affect smaller arenas of action and are replete with socially constructed nuclear war illusions, including illusions of limit and control, of foreknowledge, of preparation and protection, of stoic behavior under attack, of recovery, and of rationality.

Finally, people engage in a social construction of evil that dehumanizes the enemy and legitimizes attitudes and actions toward others that would ordinarily not be allowed. The perception that leaders of other countries are monsters and our leaders are virtuous enables people to rationalize destructive behavior.

CHAPTER SIX

Economic and Social Roots of the Arms Race

A billion here, and a billion there, and pretty soon you're talking about real money.

—Senator Everett Dirksen

The conjunction of an immense military establishment and a large arms industry is new in the American experience. The total influence—economic, political, even spiritual—is felt in every city, every state house, every office of the Federal government. We recognize the imperative need for this development. Yet we must not fail to comprehend its grave implications. Our toil, resources, and livelihood are all involved; so is the very structure of our society.

In the councils of government, we must guard against acquisition of unwarranted influence, whether sought or unsought, by the military-industrial complex. The potential for the disastrous rise of misplaced power exists and will persist.

—President Dwight Eisenhower

The military-industrial complex is an integral part of the nuclear arms race, feeding it at the social and economic levels and its growth is relentless. There are three fundamental sources of the arms race at the socioeconomic level: (1) domestic forces within each country that press for continued increases in military spending and new weapons programs; (2) global commercial expansion and the projection of power (especially by the superpowers), which rely upon a vast military machine; and (3) the nature of international reciprocity, which involves charges and counter charges, actions and reactions.

The fundamental argument of this chapter is that the entire institutional structure of the modern socioeconomic order is organized in a way that escalates the arms race indefinitely and moves human society toward a nuclear confrontation. Nowhere is the sociological character of the arms race more clearly demonstrated than in an analysis of the military-industrial complex. All of humanity is trapped in a nuclear cage.

It is not a conspiracy theory argument, although there are conspiracies in the sense that elites do meet and coordinate decisions regarding the arms race. Those decisions are not, however, about whether to have a war, or even whether to escalate or de-escalate the arms race as a whole. For the most part, they are very specialized decisions about small parts of the entire military structure; they consist of what C. Wright Mills ([1958] 1976) calls frenzied next steps. The overall questions about war and peace are seldom decided, rather, they are made by default as a consequence of the accumulation and interaction of thousands of small decisions that constitute the drift toward World War III. Mills (ibid.:40) observes that those who command the dominant institutions of the United States are

> within the drift and the thrust toward World War III.
> *Drift* means that the consequences of innumerable decisions coalesce and collide to form the blind and overwhelming events of historical fate—in the present case, of war.
> *Thrust* means, first, such fate insofar as it operates because of explicit default; and second, the explicit decisions that are making for war.

The ways in which those "innumerable decisions coalesce and collide" are examined here at several levels.

NATIONAL FORCES: MILITARY-INDUSTRIAL COMPLEXES

At the national level, the nuclear cage is maintained by a military-industrial complex, which exists in some form in virtually every country (see Feagin and Kurtz 1986). That complex constitutes a fundamental, central aspect of the American social and economic structure, and there is evidence that a similar situation exists in the Soviet Union, despite Soviet denials.

In both superpowers, there is a continuing effort on the part of civilians to control the military, but that effort has not been entirely successful since the Second World War. The U.S. political structure is clearly quite different from the military governments that dominate many of the world's countries. Yet, a combination of historical and economic circumstances have locked the United States into a sociopolitical system in which the relationships among big business, Congress, and the military make it virtually impossible to curb a spiraling arms race that benefits the power brokers.

The Structure of the Military Economy

The American military-industrial complex has its roots in the efforts to pull the American economy out of a depression in the 1930s with massive military spending, and in the events of World War II. During the 1940s, the United States established a permanent wartime economy (Mills [1958] 1976). Manufacturing facilities in the United States cost a total of $40 billion in 1939; within a mere fifteen years, an additional $26 billion worth of plants and equipment had been added to the infrastructure of the national economy, primarily through the mobilization of the war effort. That massive buildup caused a centralization of the economy because major government contracts were given to a few top corporations. In 1939, the top 250 corporations owned about 65 percent of all manufacturing facilities. During the war, they operated 79 percent of the new facilities built by government contracts.

The scope of the current military-industrial complex is staggering; it now involves 137,000 firms and divisions (Melman 1983:42). Since the end of World War II, more than half of all tax dollars have been spent on past, current, and future military operations, which together comprise the largest single activity of the U.S. government. The military enterprise is coordinated by a central office with a staff of about fifty thousand people—probably the world's largest industrial management staff (ibid.:82).

Boeing, Lockheed, and McDonnell Douglas together employed six thousand people to write proposals on the C-5A aircraft alone. The five major competitors on that program wrote proposals totalling 240,000 pages in length and weighing about 35 tons.

Like other bureaucracies, the military-industrial complex is organized so that it has a tendency toward expansion (see Chapter Four). It is unique, however, in several respects. First, unlike any other enterprise, it has *guaranteed profits*. Military contracts are written on a cost-plus basis; that is, a certain percentage of profit is guaranteed regardless of the costs of production. It is a corporate executive's dream. This practice was initiated in World War II, when the products for which military contracts were made were defined as "necessary regardless of the costs," since they involved national security.

Cost escalation has become a normal feature of military spending be-

Many individuals rely upon the military for their livelihood, such as these technicians placing cones on top of an MX Pathfinder missile's ring. Photo courtesy of U.S. Air Force/Deparment of Defense.

cause of the nature of the products involved and because of a continuation of wartime practices. Major weapons systems are particularly susceptible to cost overruns. In 1980, the Pentagon's Defense Science Board found that the prices of military goods were rising 50 percent faster than the general price index (ibid.:225). Such increases are formidable. In a single quarter of 1980 prices to be paid for forty-five major weapons systems *increased* by $45 billion.

Without precedents, it is difficult to estimate actual costs of complex weapons systems, and because of cost-plus contracts, there is no formal incentive for the bidding contractor to provide realistic estimates. In fact, if the estimate is too high, someone else might be awarded the contract. Furthermore, cost overruns increase a contractor's profit on signed cost-plus contracts.

Second, the military industry is essentially *recession-proof*. While much of the American economy was suffering from a recession at the beginning of the 1980s, the defense industry was booming. Stock prices for major military contractors soared during the period from the 1982 Dow Jones Industrial Index low to 2 March 1983 (see Table 6.1). Military contracting is subject to political, rather than economic, cycles.

Regional economies are often affected substantially by the growth of military spending, as members of Congress are well aware. When the drop of oil prices in 1986 resulted in widespread damage to the Austin, Texas, economy, one journalist (Weissmann 1986:41) observed,

> At a time when the comptroller of Texas has estimated a budget deficit of $1.3 billion statewide and a loss of 3,600 government jobs in Austin over the coming year, Pentagon-sponsored projects like the Lockheed strike system are more than a secret weapon; they may represent economic survival.

Third, the military industry commands the largest single block of capital resources in the U.S. economy (Melman 1983:xiii, 88ff.). Although military expenditures in recent years usually account for only five to six percent of the U.S. gross national product, they make up a much larger percentage of the capital resources available for the expansion of jobs and equipment, building industrial capacity, and so forth. In 1977, for example, the military spent $46 out of every $100 of new producers' fixed capital formation. Thus, it has an enormous impact on the way in which American management, technology, and productivity operate.

Fourth, military contracts procure goods that are not productive in the conventional sense. Although they "may be useful for political, military, and even aesthetic or religious purposes, . . . they are no part of what is ordinarily understood as the goods and services that the citizenry produces and consumes" (ibid.:82–83). Relatedly, military expenditures create far fewer jobs than the same amount of money spent in most other industries, because of waste and the highly skilled, highly paid personnel required

Table 6.1 Stock Price Changes for Military Contractors, 1982 Dow Jones Industrial low to 2 March 1983

Military Contractor	Stock Price Change (%)
Boeing	+145.8
General Dynamics	+125.3
Grumman	+135.7
Rockwell	+103.5

Source: "Defense Bucks" (1983).

(Figure 6.1). The military-industrial complex uses the services of an estimated 30 percent of the country's mathematicians, 25 percent of its physicists, and 47 percent of its aerospace engineers (Tempest 1983b:2).

Soviet commentator Fedoseyev (1985a:41) remarks,

> Not only does the unbridled arms race consume resources that could be used to resolve global problems, to heighten people's standard of living; it is also inescapably aggravating the crisis developments that originate from them. Military production is using up a huge amount of unrenewable energy and raw materials, and this most unproductively and irrationally.

Unlike other industries, the military can justify its spending by appeals to patriotism, making it extremely difficult to criticize. Those who dare to question the funding of a new weapons program, or the expansion of an existing one, leave themselves open to charges of being unpatriotic.

Finally, military contracting is an insiders' game and is consequently riddled with conflicts of interest. Less than 20 percent of defense procurement is obtained through formally advertised contracts. Instead, it consists primarily of individually negotiated contracts among insiders. It is impossible for most corporations to compete, because a relatively small number of corporations have a monopoly on building the major weapons systems (see Table 6.2). After all, how many companies could even attempt to be a major contractor on the Trident submarine? Such practices lead to

Figure 6.1 Jobs from military and other expenditures.

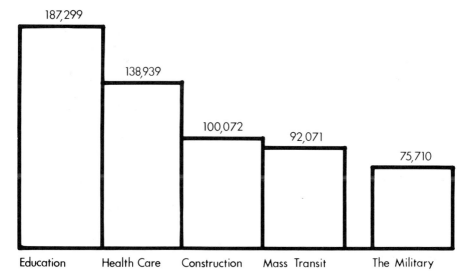

$1 BILLION SPENT — NUMBER OF JOBS CREATED

187,299 — Education
138,939 — Health Care
100,072 — Construction
92,071 — Mass Transit
75,710 — The Military

overpricing for defense products: One company charged the military $243 for an $11 circuit breaker, and the government was hit with a $639 tab for a tube that normally costs only $12. The most significant consequence of the insiders' game is the creation of a revolving door for circulating influence, money, and jobs among three major institutions—Congress, the Department of Defense (DoD), and the military contractors.

Table 6.2 Major Military Contractors

	Fiscal Year 1983 (Billions of U.S. $)	Fiscal Year 1980 (Billions of U.S $)	Fortune 500 No.	Weapons
1. General Dynamics	6.8	3.5 (1)	46	F-16, Trident subs, SLCM, DIVAD, M-1, M-60 tanks
2. McDonnell Douglas	6.1	3.2 (2)	42	F-15, F-18, KC-10, AV-8B aircraft
3. Rockwell Int.	4.5	0.9 (14)	43	B-1B, MX, Hellfire missile, nuclear weapon components
4. General Electric	4.5	2.2 (5)	10	Ship nuclear reactors, jet engines, ICBM reentry vehicles
5. Boeing Co.	4.4	2.4 (4)	27	C-135, B-52 upgrades, ALCM, AWACS, E-3A aircraft
6. Lockheed Corp.	4.0	2.0 (6)	50	C-5, P-3, C-130 aircraft, Trident missiles
7. United Technologies	3.8	3.1 (3)	18	Jet engines, UH-60, CH-53, SH-60 helicopters
8. Tenneco Inc.	3.7	1.5 (9)	19	Aircraft carriers, nuclear submarines
9. Hughes	3.2	1.8 (7)		AH-64 helicopter, Phoenix missile, electronics, radars
10. Ratheon Co.	2.7	1.7 (8)	59	Hawk, Sidewinder, Dragon, Sparrow missiles

Source: "The Top Ten Military Contractors," 1984, *The Defense Monitor* 13 (4):6. Reprinted with permission.

The Revolving Door

Military and industry people regularly get together to discuss common problems and create new weapons projects. After they leave the government, former Department of Defense employees who were responsible for key contract decisions are sometimes hired by military contractors to work on the same weapons system for which they had responsibility at the Pentagon. Such contract decisions are highly subjective and do not involve an open bidding process. These networks of personal contacts are extremely important, even when the individuals involved are trying to be objective and honest.

An in-depth study of eight major defense contractors by Gordon Adams (1982) highlights the interrelationship of the major institutional components of the military-industrial complex (see Figure 6.2). The eight companies (Boeing, General Dynamics, Grumman, Lockheed, McDonnell Douglas, Northrop, Rockwell International, and United Technologies) dominated the top-ten contractor list two-thirds of the time between 1970 and 1979, and received over $100 billion in DoD contracts (25 percent of all DoD awards). Each company received more than $1 billion per year in research and development contracts through the Department of Defense's Independent Research and Development (IR&D) and Development and Bids and Proposals (B&P) programs.

The Congress, of course, has the final word on military expenditures,

Figure 6.2   The iron triangle.

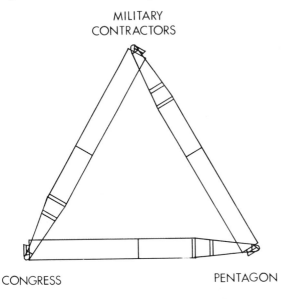

MILITARY
CONTRACTORS

CONGRESS   PENTAGON

and contracts are ultimately written with an eye on key congressional and senatorial districts. Components of the B-1B bomber are produced in forty-eight states, so members of Congress have a direct interest in the funding of the project. Senator John Tower, former chair of the Senate Armed Services Committee, complained: "Ironically, my colleagues who are the most vocal critics of higher defense spending are often also those who violently oppose reduced funding for defense programs located in their own states." When he challenged senators to suggest programs in their states that could be cut, only six responded, one of whom recommended an increase (Tempest 1983b:2).

Major military contractors maintain offices in Washington, D.C., to lobby members of Congress. Five of the companies in Adams's study[1] spent a total of $16.8 million between 1974 and 1975 to maintain Washington offices. Over $15.8 million of that total was charged to contracts; in other words, the government was charged for the cost of convincing the military and Congress that they needed what they were buying. Rockwell alone spent over $7 million on lobbying during the period studied (Adams 1982:136ff.).

A second avenue of influence on Congress is Political Action Committees (PACs). General Dynamics' PAC, for example, spent $510,000 from July 1977 to August 1980 in efforts to influence members of Congress. Each of the eight companies in Adams's study had a PAC that concentrated its contributions on key congressional committee members (see Table 6.3) and candidates from areas in which the company's plants were located. A campaign contribution of several thousand dollars is a trivial sum for a major military contractor, but it may be one of the largest donations a member of Congress receives.

In addition, military contractors use grass-roots mobilization to influence Congress. As one industry commentator put it,

> A few years ago we began to understand that while Government policies are executed in Washington, their impetus lies elsewhere, at the grass roots. Since then, we have involved more and more plant managers in letter and telegram writing, personal visits, and telephone calls on Governmental policies because their views are more important than those of the Washington lobbyist. (quoted in ibid.:134)

Washington offices of major contractors mobilize employees, shareholders, and local communities who benefit from their contracts in letter-writing campaigns, personal visits, and contributions to PACs.

Major military contractors develop intimate relationships with people in the Pentagon as well, since many decisions are made long before they reach the Congress. Contractors influence the military by hiring individuals who have worked in the military or Pentagon, by serving on advisory committees, and through the activities of trade associations.

Table 6.3 PAC Contributions to Members of Congress, July 1977
to August 1980

Member of Congress	PAC Contributions
Senate Armed Services Committee	
Sen. Strom Thurmond (R–SC)	$14,300
Sen. John Tower (R–TX)	13,175
Sen. John Warner (R–VA)	11,000
Sen. Sam Nunn (D–GA)	9,100
Sen. Barry Goldwater (R–AZ)	7,800
Senate Defense Appropriations Subcommittee	
Sen. Ernest Hollings (D–SC)	$13,000
Sen. Warren Magnuson (R–WA)	10,200
Sen. Jake Garn (R–UT)	5,500
Sen. Edward Brooke (R–MA)	5,300
Sen. Daniel Inouye (D–HI)	5,100
House Armed Services Committee	
Rep. Charles Wilson (D–CA)	$12,925
Rep. Jim Lloyd (D–CA)	11,650
Rep. Mendel Davis (D–SC)	10,100
Rep. Bob Wilson (R–CA)	9,700
Rep. Richard Ichord (D–MO)	9,925
House Defense Appropriations Subcommittee	
Rep. Joseph Addabbo (D–NY)	$10,800
Rep. Robert Giaimo (D–CT)	7,700
Rep. Jack Edwards (D–AL)	7,250
Rep. Bill Chappell (D–FL)	6,400
Rep. Bill Burlison (D–MO)	6,200

Source: Published by permission of Transaction, Inc., from *The Politics of Defense Contracting: The Iron Triangle*, by Gordon Adams, 1982, Copyright © 1981 by the Council on Economic Priorities, 84 Fifth Avenue, New York, N.Y. 10011.

The military-industrial complex is thus maintained through a vast network of interlocking reciprocal relationships, in which individuals and institutions profit and the arms race is expanded. The entire process is legitimized by an ideology of defense that permeates the cultures of both superpowers and lays the blame for the arms race squarely on the shoulders of the other power. An "elective affinity" (see Weber 1968) emerges between the growth of the military establishment, on the one hand, and the ideologies of militarism and "peace through strength" on the other.

In the face of this massive armaments program that commands a major proportion of the globe's resources, we are forced to ask the ancient question, Qui bono (Who benefits)? Some would argue that no one benefits from the nuclear arms race. Quite the contrary is true, however, as long as there is no nuclear war. In fact, there are two groups that benefit (at least in the short run) from the arms race and its accompanying ideologies: (1) the military sector of the domestic economy and (2) U.S.-based multinational corporations.

First and foremost, those who own and manage the defense industries benefit. In the United States, a small group of people in a specific sector of the economy reap great profits from the arms race and enjoy a privileged relationship with congressional decisionmakers. But what about in the Soviet Union? The official position is that there is no military-industrial complex in the Soviet Union.[2] Because, strictly speaking, there are no profiteers in the Soviet Union, there is not the same profit incentive that exists in the United States. As Soviet Embassy Information Officer Eugene Zykov puts it, "It makes no difference to the Soviet worker whether he is producing a tractor or a missile." The same factories, he claims, are engaged in military and civilian production.

There is, however, evidence that the Soviet military establishment has a privileged position in the Soviet economy; it receives funding priority and, according to Hedrick Smith (1976:312), "operates on a different system from the rest of the economy." Although the Soviets do not have large private military industries, their defense ministries and influential "design bureaus" fulfill a similar function (Tempest 1986:4). Trade consultant Samuel Pisar contends that the military sector is "the only sector of the Soviet economy which operates like a market economy, in the sense that the customers pull out of the economic mechanisms the kinds of weaponry that they want" (Smith 1976:312–13). According to a metalworker Smith interviewed, "export and military production pay better" than other sectors of the economy, and the "requirements are higher. More time is spent on the work and quality specifications are higher. Such work is usually given to highly qualified workers" (ibid.:313).

It is likely, furthermore, that the structure of Soviet bureaucracies involved in military production is similar in character to that of bureaucracies in the United States, with the same pressures for career advancement, personal interests, and territorial protection. Even if Soviet workers and bosses are not competing for monetary gain in the same sense as in the United States, the hidden economy of benefits and perks of various sorts help account for the fact that military production in the Soviet Union may capture twice the proportion of the GNP as it does in the United States.

In short, in both the United States and the Soviet Union, structural mechanisms have turned the military into the overwhelming sector of the economy. There are some variations between the two superpowers in their ideological justifications for militarizing their economies, but the results are similar.

The major rhetorical justification for defense expenditures in both countries is national security. What national security means varies, however, as reflected in the distinction between central and extended deterrence. Whereas central deterrence refers to protecting a nation's homeland, extended deterrence concerns the effort to prevent invasion of another theater. Despite enormous political and psychological difficulties with the notion of extended deterrence, it has been a key aspect of superpower politics in the nuclear age.

For example, if Europe is attacked by the Soviet Union, the United States is obligated under NATO treaties to consider such an invasion to be against the United States as well. As the two superpowers have extended their global influence since World War II, extended deterrence has entangled them in a vast network of economic and military activities.

The military establishment has unique access to sources of power and instruments of enforcement in the modern world, as John Kenneth Galbraith (1984) has suggested. This force has become a central feature of the modern socioeconomic order. "While we do not see it as a threat in the United States or generally in the older industrial countries, the near-monopoly that the military establishment retains of the use of force to obtain both internal discipline and external submission remains the major threat to democratic and civilian government throughout the world." It is to that global system that we must now turn in our search for the social and economic roots of the nuclear arms race.

THE GLOBAL PROJECTION OF POWER

The nuclear arms race is inextricably linked to the structure of the global economy. The growth of international trade and multinational corporations has resulted in what Peter Drucker (1969) calls the global shopping center, and like any shopping center, it needs a security patrol to maintain order. However, there is no administrative unit to ensure that security. The global system thus verges on anarchy, except for the raw power exerted primarily by the two superpowers through their vast network of military installations around the planet. In the final analysis, no one controls the global economy; it has a self-sustaining dynamic that is greater than the sum of its parts.

High wages in the United States and very cheap labor in the Third World have led to the flight of much American capital and production. Capital expenditures of foreign affiliates of U.S.-based multinationals have risen from $14.1 billion in 1970 to $45.5 billion in 1981 (see Table 6.4).

Beginning in the 1960s, a major proportion of the profit for the top U.S. corporations has been earned outside the country. A Department of

Table 6.4   Capital Expenditures of Foreign
Affiliates of U.S.-Based
Multinationals

Year	Capital Expenditures (Billions of U.S. $)
1970	14.1
1975	26.7
1980	42.4
1981	45.5

Source: U.S. Bureau of the Census (1982).

Commerce study (1970; cf. Barnet and Muller 1974:16) found that the top 298 U.S.-based multinationals earned 40 percent of their entire profits outside the United States. Furthermore, the rates of profit for overseas investment are much higher than for domestic investments. In 1972, for example, United Brands reported a 72.1 percent return on net assets, Parker Pen 51.2 percent, and Exxon 52.5 percent (ibid.:17). Whereas the rate of return on office equipment was 25.6 percent in overseas investments, it was only 9.2 percent in domestic enterprises. In the food industry, overseas profits were 16.7 percent and domestic profits 11.5 percent (ibid.:16–17).

American industries have thus expanded throughout the globe in an effort to exploit the mineral, agricultural, and labor resources of the Third World. A major consequence of that expansion has been the development of interventionary capabilities and of a nuclear umbrella that provides a threat to any nation or group perceived as hostile to U.S. interests.

The United States has a long history of intervening militarily, especially in Central and South America.[3] In recent years, perhaps in part because of the Vietnam fiasco, the United States has been somewhat more subtle in its military intervention. Using veiled threats and, in some cases, surrogate forces (as in El Salvador, Nicaragua, and Angola), it has been able to lessen somewhat the frequency of actual invasions witnessed earlier in this century. Nevertheless, the United States engaged in 215 "political uses" of military force between 1946 and 1975 without engaging in a continuing contest of violence (Blechman and Kaplan 1978:12) and continued to engage in combat on a regular basis. Recent revivals of the Monroe Doctrine by the Reagan administration have paralleled a major effort to increase the efficiency of secret commando units (see Gerth 1984) and interventionary forces, despite the fact that the United States has a substantial advantage over the USSR in intervention capabilities.[4]

The conventional military intervention of the superpowers is important to our examination of the nuclear arms race for two reasons. First, the escalation of nuclear forces is linked to the general militarization of the globe by the superpowers. The enormity of the military-industrial complex, fed by both nuclear and conventional forces, gives it widespread influence and stimulates further spending for nuclear and conventional forces. Second, because of the close coordination of nuclear and conventional forces as a deliberate aspect of U.S. policy (see, e.g., Weinberger 1983), it is virtually impossible to distinguish between the two in many ways. When the Marines splash ashore, they have tactical nuclear weapons at their disposal, and the larger nuclear umbrella stands behind them. Of that the adversary is well aware. Furthermore, there have been a number of times when the threatened use of nuclear weapons was applied to achieve political ends, the most recent being President Carter's response to the Iranian crisis in 1980. Blechman and Kaplan have identified nineteen separate incidents in which strategic nuclear forces played a key role in putting political pressure on America's adversaries (see Table 6.5).

In short, the global projection of power plays a key role as a source of the nuclear arms race by providing a justification for the buildup of mili-

Table 6.5 Incidents before 1975 in which Strategic Nuclear Forces Played a Key Role

Incident	Date
U.S. aircraft shot down by Yugoslavia	November 1946
Inauguration of president in Uruguay	February 1947
Security of Berlin	January 1948
Security of Berlin	April 1948
Security of Berlin	June 1948
Korean War: Security of Europe	July 1950
Security of Japan/South Korea	August 1953
Guatemala accepts Soviet bloc support	May 1954
China-Taiwan conflict: Tachen Islands	August 1954
Suez crisis	October 1956
Political crisis in Lebanon	July 1958
Political crisis in Jordan	July 1958
China-Taiwan conflict: Quemoy and Matsu	July 1958
Security of Berlin	May 1959
Security of Berlin	June 1961
Soviet emplacement of missiles in Cuba	October 1962
Withdrawal of U.S. missiles from Turkey	April 1963
Pueblo seized by North Korea	January 1968
Arab-Israeli War	October 1973

Source: Barry M. Blechman and Stephen S. Kaplan, 1978, *Force without War: U.S. Armed Forces as a Political Instrument*, Washington, D.C.: The Brookings Institute, p. 48. Reprinted with permission.

tary forces. As the economic interests of the superpowers (especially the United States) become global in scope, the power elites employ national military forces for police functions on the entire planet. National interests are expanded far beyond national borders and are legitimized by the social construction of evil and the manipulation of public opinion. The global projection of power benefits primarily a small but politically powerful group; at the same time it places the rest of the world at risk for short-term economic and political gains.

Such application of military power thus precipitates the drift and thrust toward World War III that Mills warned us about in 1958. The current escalation of the arms race on an unprecedented scale parallels the growth of the military-industrial complex during and following World War II, on the one hand, and the emergence of a global socioeconomic order dominated by the superpowers, on the other.

INTER-NATION RECIPROCITY

The nuclear cage is built on a foundation of reciprocal international inter-actions that transcend the economic motivations discussed in the previous sections. This is because economic factors are dialectically related to the drive for political global hegemony, spheres of influence, competition, and prestige. Although much of what motivates political and economic elites is economic, much of it is not. The notion of national security is somewhat arbitrarily constructed; in some ways it is instrumentally related to economic issues, in other ways it is of a largely symbolic character (e.g., the U.S. invasion of Grenada).

In thousands of offices around the globe individuals make minute decisions that propel the arms race. Such activities are largely economic and are rooted in occupational structures, but there are noneconomic elements as well. The latter sustain a major ideology of the modern world—nationalism. Nationalism has become a major means of organizing commitment and personal identity (Hirsch, Hodson, and Kurtz 1986).

The organization of the global political and military structure on the basis of competing nation states is what makes nuclear weapons so threatening. As Schell (1982:209) notes, the possession of nuclear weapons is not simply to prevent war and keep the peace, but "also to defend national interests and aspirations—indeed, to perpetuate the whole system of sovereign states. But now, instead of relying on war for this enforcement, as nations did in pre-nuclear times, they rely on the threat of extinction."

The logical contradiction in the nuclear threat, as Schell notes, is that the "actual execution of the threat would eradicate any national interest." Sometimes it appears as if "the nuclear powers put a higher value on national sovereignty than they do on human survival, and that, while they would naturally prefer to have both, they are ultimately prepared to bring an end to mankind in their attempt to protect their own countries" (ibid.:210). What appears on one level to be a series of rational acts (the protection of national security through the maintenance of a military organization) has absurd, irrational consequences.

Both the United States and the Soviet Union have been suffering a decline in hegemony in recent decades (see Chomsky 1982), resulting in a frequent escalation of belligerence in the international arena and the use of force against those who challenge their power (e.g., the Soviet invasion of Afghanistan and U.S. attempts to topple the Nicaraguan government). Historically, the consequence of such efforts would have been nationalistic expansion. Now the existence of nuclear weapons raises the stakes and puts not only targeted countries at risk, but the entire human race.

As a consequence of superpower aggression in many parts of the globe, other countries (with their own indigenous nationalisms) feel compelled to call upon one superpower or the other for nuclear protection, or to develop their own nuclear arsenals as a shortcut to self-determination. The nuclear cage thus becomes a complex, interconnected system that extends to the farthest reaches of the globe. The nationalistic structure of modern politics, with its reciprocating hostilities, strengthens and expands that cage to include every corner of the earth.

SUMMARY

Social and economic phenomena at several levels provide directional force for the drift and thrust toward World War III. First, in almost every country there exists a relationship among political, economic, and military forces that propels the arms race. The unprecedented growth in scale of the military-industrial complex emerged from the mobilization of national economies for the war effort during World War II. That militarization of the global economy left a legacy in most countries that centralized economic forces and created a unique mechanism for military production.

The military-industrial complex, although similar to any institutional structure, has some unique characteristics, all of which expand the arms race. In the United States, the defense industry (1) has guaranteed profits because of cost-plus contracts; (2) is free from economic cycles of recession; (3) commands the largest single block of capital resources in the economy; (4) exists for the creation of nonproductive goods; and (5) is legitimized by the ideology of patriotism, which makes serious criticism almost impossible. Further, the military industry is an insiders' game that takes place within a closed system—an iron triangle that links the Pentagon, military industries, and Congress by a revolving door of mutual reciprocity. The military-industrial complex is thus maintained through a vast network of interlocking relationships in which the individuals who would profit from the very expansion of the arms race are the very experts asked whether it should be expanded.

The arms race is perpetuated not only by forces within each country, but also by efforts (especially by the superpowers) to project military power for economic and political gain. The globalization of the economy, especially by U.S.-based multinational corporations, has led to the justification of a global military presence to protect national interests that lie far beyond the boundaries of any nation-states. The global social order is, at the same time, still organized around sovereign states that often operate on the basis of fervent nationalism. Such nationalism may appear rational or justified in the short run, from an official's point of view, but may have tragic long-term consequences.

The global projection of power inevitably provides further justification for the buildup of military forces. As the superpowers collide with other powers that threaten the profit-making activities of their corporations, or who undermine the perceived status of the encroaching nations and their citizens, the threat of armed conflict alone may further stimulate military preparations. Public opinion is manipulated by focusing on the threat presented by "opposing evil forces."

The question that haunts us is, How can we prevent such international conflicts from escalating into a nuclear holocaust? It is to that subject that we now turn our attention.

CHAPTER SEVEN

Alternative Strategies for National Security

Identifying the *sources* of the arms race is not easy, but even more difficult is knowing how to stop it. The two issues are obviously related, however, since any effort to diminish or reverse the arms race must attack its sources and change the conditions that fuel it. This chapter provides a broad overview of different approaches to the concept of national security and discusses the implications of reciprocity, bureaucracy, and ritual in looking for ways out of the nuclear cage.

PUBLIC DISCOURSE ON NUCLEAR WARFARE PREVENTION

Public discourse on any issue, including nuclear arms policy, evolves around a set of core images and symbols. As William Gamson (1984:3) points out, "Symbols are organized into packages of harmonious elements within a common organizing frame. These packages become part of a symbolic contest in which the weapons are metaphors, catch phrases, and other condensing symbols." Just as a wooden frame establishes boundaries around a painting hanging on a wall, a conceptual frame establishes the boundaries around a set of issues and defines how they are perceived and discussed. Information, theories, options, and ideas that lie outside that frame are generally ignored as irrelevant.

In any policy debate, comprehensive positions tend to coalesce and act as frames for the definition of a situation and the interpretation of the facts (see Goffman 1974; Bateson 1972; Glaser and Strauss 1964; Berger and Luckmann 1967). Ambiguity is never eliminated, but a relatively coherent posture is constructed and adhered to by people with shared interests. Groupthink and reciprocity reduce the ability of those involved in decisionmaking processes to "break frame" with the prevailing consensus of the groups with which they identify.

Positions on nuclear arms policy are no exception. Broad frames are constructed, out of which conclusions are drawn for specific policy decisions. A set of key metaphors, ritual responses, and symbolic meanings are packaged as a whole. We thus encounter ideas "not as individual items but as packages. One can think of the *set* of packages that are available for talking about the issue as its 'culture' " (Gamson 1984:2). Consequently, certain events and pieces of information are flagged as relevant, while attention is distracted from others.

Mainstream Positions in the U.S. Debate

In contemporary U.S. culture there are two mainstream packages of symbols, or frames, for answering the question, How shall we prevent a nuclear war? The first is the Peace through Strength position to which the Reagan administration adheres. We will call the second the Arms Control movement.[1] There are obviously other alternatives in American culture. A significant proportion of Americans subscribe to a disarmament frame, for example, but this has not been part of the mainstream political debate as a genuine policy option.

The Peace through Strength and Arms Control movement frames are central organizing packages, with both similarities and differences. To some extent, both involve technical fixes for security, although in rather different ways. Both focus on specific weapons systems rather than on broad political processes, even though each framework employs an underlying political theory in analyzing the problem.

We will discuss each frame in more detail in later chapters, but it is helpful to sketch out their main contours here. Each package contains a set of core metaphors (see Gamson 1984) and assumptions, according to which answers to such policy questions as the following are constructed: Can you trust the Russians? Should the United States build the MX? Should the Strategic Defense Initiative (SDI) be developed? Who is winning the arms race? Can a nuclear war be fought and won? Since the purpose of having a frame is to reduce ambiguity and complexity in order to facilitate concrete decisionmaking, there is often a tendency toward absolutism within the frames. The discussion that follows simplifies a complex debate in a manner similar to the simplification that occurs in real life.

Peace through strength. The Peace through Strength position is founded on time-tested military rituals that assume that the best way to preserve the peace is to prepare for war. As Richard Barnet (1984:162) puts it,

> These ideas are not mere rhetoric. They are deeply held beliefs of a generation of National Security Managers for whom the decisive learning experience was the Second World War. Staggered by the apocalyptic events of the war, the demonic Hitlerian vision of a world order, the death camps, the fire bombings, the saturation raids, and the nuclear attacks, this generation has believed with the first Secretary of Defense, James Forrestal, that "the cornerstone in any plan which undertakes to rid us of the curse of war must be the armed might of the United States."

The Peace through Strength frame has three fundamental assumptions. First, the United States must have a countervailing capability (see Chapter Eight) if it is to maintain the credibility of deterrence. That is, the nation must be able to reciprocate against any enemy aggression (primarily Soviet) at an appropriate level.

An implication of that assumption is that the United States must have the ability to wage a nuclear war in order to make deterrence credible. To do so requires a superior nuclear arsenal at every level and the ability to retaliate with weapons that can destroy the enemy's military capability. Thus the United States must modernize its weapon forces and deploy such weapons as could be used in "successfully" fighting a nuclear war, presumably through first strikes against military targets. The most recent addition to that position has been support for a ballistic missile defense to supplement offensive weapons (see Chapter Ten). Another implication of a countervailing strategy is the belief that a nuclear war can be limited and that it can be fought at several levels (each of which is intended to deter an adversary from escalating to a higher level of fighting).

A second major assumption of the Peace through Strength position is that the Soviets cannot be trusted. "The lesson of history, according to this argument, is that weak nations cannot 'buy' peace with treaties. 'Deals' with tyrants don't work" (Gamson 1984:11). The only way to keep the peace, according to this argument, is to deal with the Soviets from a position of strength.

A third, related assumption is that in the 1970s the Soviet Union engaged in a massive buildup of its nuclear arsenal, while the United States was "unilaterally disarming." As President Reagan stated in his speech before the United Nations on 17 June 1982,

> The decade of so-called détente witnessed the most massive Soviet build-up of military power in history. They increased their defense spending by 40% while American defense spending actually declined in the same real terms. . . . While we exercised unilateral restraint, they forged ahead and to-

U.S. weapons modernization programs in the 1980s include the Trident missile, shown here in a test flight on 31 August 1986. Photo courtesy of U.S. Air Force/ Department of Defense.

day possess nuclear and conventional forces far in excess of an adequate deterrent capability.

Furthermore, the president contends that the Soviets have not made concessions in negotiations because of the U.S. unilateral disarmament.[2] The current U.S. buildup, according to this view, is simply an effort to counter Soviet superiority and to regain the superiority lost in the 1970s.

Thus, according to this view, arms control agreements with the Soviets are problematic, if not futile. At this point in history, the argument goes, a major arms control agreement such as a nuclear freeze would lock the United States into a position of inferiority. The massive military buildup is felt to be a demonstration of American will in the face of a tough and ruthless adversary.

Arms control movement.   The significance of the Arms Control movement frame has increased in the 1980s because of the resurgence of the peace movement in the early years of the decade (see Chapter Fourteen). That movement was largely a backlash against the new Peace through Strength orthodoxy institutionalized as official U.S. policy under the Reagan administration. It is often identified in the public's mind with the Freeze proposal (see Forsberg 1982), which advocates a bilateral halt in the production, testing, and deployment of nuclear weapons. Although originally a minority position, the idea of the Freeze has captured the political imagination of much of the American public and was essentially adopted by the Democratic party establishment in the 1984 elections.[3]

The first major assumption of the Arms Control position is that even if deterrence works, it will not be aided by a further weapons buildup. Instead, the new generation of first-strike weapons being developed by the United States would seriously undermine security. According to this view, fifty thousand nuclear weapons in the superpower arsenals are already more than enough to ensure deterrence. At this stage, a military buildup simply precipitates further military buildup; the first step should be to stop the race. A key metaphor used by Arms Control proponents is that if one is speeding down a highway and wishes to go in the opposite direction, it is necessary first to stop, and then to reverse directions.

There are two slightly different arguments supporting such an assumption. The first is the "sufficiency" argument, which accepts the concept of deterrence but argues that beyond a certain level (long since passed), deterrence is not enhanced by additional weapons or modernization programs. The second argument is a more radical critique of deterrence, namely, that even if deterrence has been a factor in preventing nuclear war thus far, there is no assurance that it will work indefinitely. Ironically, this position has recently been used by President Reagan to justify SDI.

A second major assumption of the Arms Control position is that there is currently an approximate parity or essential equivalence in the super-powers' arsenals. Forsberg (ibid.:52) claims that "the time is propitious for a bilateral freeze. Today the U.S. and the U.S.S.R. are closer to parity in nuclear arms than they have been at any time since World War II. The U.S.S.R. has advantages in some elements of nuclear weaponry, the U.S. has advantages in others."

The Peace through Strength assumption that a freeze would lock the United States into a position of inferiority implies that now is not the time for arms control. The Arms Control parity assumption implies that we should take advantage of the moment by putting a stop to the upward spiral. Some even argue that if there was parity in the early 1980s, the Reagan buildup has shifted the balance in favor of the United States.

The third assumption of the Arms Control position is that arms control is the only long-range strategy that will work, although agreements must go far beyond previous accords. In effect, the Arms Control movement has accepted Mills' 1958 argument that *"the only realistic military view is the view that war, and not Russia, is now the enemy"* ([1958]1976:97; emphasis in the original).

The emphasis on war (or nuclear weapons) as a more important adversary than the Soviet Union strikes at the core of the Peace through Strength position and has provoked a predictable response. The image of the Soviets as evil incarnate, and the need to deal with them from a position of strength, is at the center of the Peace through Strength approach to nuclear policy. For Peace through Strength supporters, "freezeniks" are at best well-intentioned dupes of the Soviet Union.

Mainstream Positions in the Soviet Debate

> The Soviet Union has been the initiator of the struggle for peace and disarmament. Thanks to its efforts, about twenty international agreements have been concluded which to various extents curb the arms race in several areas.
>
> —Konstantin Likutov, *Soviet Foreign Policy*

As one might expect, the *public* face of the Soviet debate is not as tumultuous as in the United States, because of Soviet suppression of dissent. There are, nonetheless, policy differences within the Soviet Union as well. The primary division in Soviet opinion appears to be over the respective roles of the Soviet Union and the United States in perpetuating the arms race.

The official Soviet position.   The official Soviet position is close to the Arms Control movement position in the United States in many respects, and the Soviets have submitted a Freeze resolution to the United Nations that borrows much of Forsberg's wording (see Fedoseyev 1985b:395). The major difference between the official Soviet position and the U.S. Arms Control stance lies in the former's insistence that only the United States—

not both superpowers—is responsible for the escalating spiral of nuclear armaments.

There is a very strong official peace movement in the Soviet Union, organized primarily around the Soviet Peace Council (established in 1949; see Brown 1985:38). Peace councils around the country engage in a wide range of activities oriented toward the cessation of the arms race (but exclusively espousing criticisms of Western arms). To celebrate the United Nation's Special Session on Disarmament in 1982, about fifty million people participated in more than eighty thousand meetings, marches, and demonstrations during Disarmament Week in the Soviet Union (Kharkhardin 1985:275).

According to Vladimir Razmerov (of the USSR Academy of Sciences), whereas the official U.S. position is to oppose the peace movement, the Soviet government is in solidarity with it. He contends, however, that the antiwar movement in the West is sometimes misguided in protesting Soviet policy. Why, he asks,

> should the protest marches and demonstrations be against the Soviet Union which supports their demands?
> Clearly, the anti-war protest movements should be directed against those forces in the US and NATO who advocate an ever more dangerous escalation of the arms race and increase nuclear stockpiles instead of limiting them. (Brown 1985:52)

Thus, in addition to the three assumptions of the Arms Control movement in the United States, the official Soviet perspective on nuclear issues adds a fourth: Western countries, notably the United States, are the source of the arms race and present the only obstacles to arms control.

Finally, the official Soviet position includes a Peace through Strength component as well, advocated by the hard-liners in Moscow. Despite the fact that the USSR has adopted the peace movement's rhetoric virtually in toto for purposes of public discussion, it has also sustained a major nuclear buildup of its own. The memory of the Great Patriotic War is kept alive with hundreds of war monuments and elaborate rituals (see Chapter Eleven) that justify the expenditure of massive amounts of money to maintain a strong military machine.

The independent Soviet peace movement.   There is also an independent peace movement in the USSR, whose position is much more like that of the U.S. Freeze campaign. Although it is a tiny minority of the Soviet population, the independent peace movement in the USSR (and much of Eastern Europe) has carved out a position in the Soviet debate.

One part of that movement, the Group to Establish Trust Between the USSR and the USA (often called simply the Trust Group), was founded in June 1982, primarily by young scientists and artists. They issued an appeal lamenting that "the USSR and the USA have the means to kill in such proportions that it is possible to bring the history of mankind to an end" (Humanitas International 1985:4). In addition to the group in Moscow, which has been subjected to government harassment and jailings, other trust groups have been meeting in Odessa, Riga, Leningrad, and Novosibirsk (in Western Siberia). Other independent peace groups, such as Independent Initiative and the Group of Good Will have demonstrated publicly in Moscow and elsewhere in the USSR (ibid.).

What is interesting about the Soviet debate is the significance attached to one point of disagreement between the official and independent peace movements. Although the movements are in agreement on most assumptions, the key difference concerns the role of the Soviet government in perpetuating the arms race. This difference is the key to understanding Soviet policy and internal opposition to it. The complete lack of Soviet culpability is the *core* assumption of the official position.

Results of the U.S. and USSR Debates

The major consequence of the debates has been an extensive military buildup by both superpowers. Both sides speak loudly and frequently about peace and arms control, but their strategies for achieving them have produced an unprecedented militarization of international relations. The Peace through Strength argument has prevailed in many policy decisions made by both superpowers, resulting in an unprecedented U.S. escalation, new generations of destabilizing weapons, and the extension of the arms race into outer space.

The assumptions of deterrence and Peace through Strength are difficult to avoid in the present context of bloc politics, but they impose a high toll on the human population. First, there is the high psychological cost of living under the nuclear sword of Damocles. Second, it may be idealistic to assume that deterrence will continue to work indefinitely, as President Reagan has acknowledged. The gravest danger is the possibility that the search for an elusive technical fix is not preventing, but rather *postponing*, a nuclear holocaust. The task, therefore, is twofold: first, to find a way to break the action-reaction cycles, and second, to provide security for all of humanity. We now return to the conceptual framework developed in Chapter Four and its implications for developing alternative strategies for security.

RECIPROCITY, BUREAUCRACY, AND RITUAL

The social processes that precipitate the arms race also hold the promise for its reversal: Reciprocation, bureaucratization, and ritualization all contain potential exits from the nuclear cage.

Reciprocity

The nuclear arms race is perpetuated, in part, by a series of reciprocal actions, primarily by the superpowers (although increasingly complicated by nuclear proliferation). Reciprocal actions thus far in the arms race have been based on the doctrine of deterrence. Because of the assumption that a nuclear arsenal is necessary to deter aggression, the superpowers have responded to each new weapons development on the other side with what was perceived as an appropriate reciprocation. The deployment of a new weapons system on one side precipitates a new system on the other. The problems in defining appropriate reciprocation become quite clear when one looks at the uneven development of superpower arsenals and the continuous mutual perception of an imbalance in the exchange.

Profound hostilities between the superpowers persist. There are, however, also similarities in the way in which foreign policy is forged in both superpowers. First, each side responds to the other as a consequence of the way in which the arms race is structured. Hence, each superpower's nuclear policy is largely determined by the actions of the other side. Much of Washington's policy is admittedly not made in Washington, but is triggered in Moscow, and vice versa. This is one of the great ironies of the nuclear cage, which traps policymakers from adversary nations in a common process of diminishing sovereignty over their own resources and wills.

Second, on each side of the superpower conflict, nuclear issues are linked to a broad package of symbolically meaningful political, economic, and social issues. It is not simply the defense of national boundaries that is at stake, but also global interests. The superpowers, in short, act like superpowers, projecting military nuclear power across the globe and thus threatening the security of everyone on the planet.

The reciprocal process could, however, lead to de-escalation, as suggested by the concept of peace initiatives—nonmilitary steps taken outside of negotiations, designed to induce reciprocation by other states.

Peace initiatives. Peace initiatives are not necessarily based on trust but on (1) the nature of reciprocity and (2) shared interests. Most people would agree *in principle* that both superpowers should place limits on the nuclear arms race; the disagreement emerges over the means for doing so. There is some historical precedent for peace initiatives, such as Anwar Sadat's visit to Jerusalem. That action set in motion a peace-making process that (although not fulfilled) has produced major advances in the Middle East peace process. A more germane example is President Kennedy's unilateral cessation of American atmospheric nuclear testing, leading to the Limited Test Ban treaty (see Etzioni 1967).

The theoretical basis of peace initiatives was outlined by Charles Osgood, with his notion of graduated and reciprocated initiatives in tension reduction (GRIT). The GRIT strategy is an attempt to create a mirror image of the escalation that created the arms race. That escalation, according to Osgood (1984:338),

> is designed to push the villainous THEYs beyond their risk ceiling before the heroic WEs reach ours. This strategy has four salient features: first, the steps are unilaterally initiated (we did not negotiate with the North Vietnamese about increasing the tempo of our bombing or moving in closer to Hanoi; we just did it unilaterally). Second, each step propels the opponent into reciprocating if he can, with more aggressive steps of his own. . . . Third, such steps are necessarily graduated in nature. . . . But fourth, calculated escalation is obviously a *tension-increasing* process, the termination of which is a *military* resolution (victory, defeat, or in our time even mutual annihilation).

A peace initiative simply reverses the process, shifting from a calculated tension-induction to tension-reduction.

Most of the proposals currently on and off the table could be amenable to such initiatives, including a Comprehensive Test Ban, the Freeze, deep cuts, and a flight test ban. Peace initiatives do not substitute for bilateral negotiations, but are unilateral initiatives that attempt to set the stage for such negotiations. They save valuable time by setting agreements in motion before the excruciating negotiations over details have to be worked out, and they create a climate within which the mutual advantages of an agreement are more easily recognizable. Although often considered far out of the mainstream, significant endorsements of the concept have emerged.[4]

The most dramatic recent example of a peace initiative is the Soviet Union's unilateral moratorium on all nuclear testing, announced in July 1985. The original conditions of the moratorium were that it would be in effect until January 1986, or would continue indefinitely if the United States reciprocated with its own moratorium. When the United States failed to respond positively by the deadline, General Secretary Gorbachev extended the moratorium. Unfortunately, for a peace initiative to work, there must be an openness on both sides to the principle of the action, and in the case of this moratorium there was no such agreement on the U.S. side.[5] An example of a recent, successful peace initiative is the Soviet Union's unilateral moratorium on testing of its antisatellite (ASAT) system, which was followed by a U.S. Congress decision to cut off funds for the testing of its ASAT system.

The momentum of the arms race is so strong that it is very difficult to predict the outcome of a peace initiative. Each initiative thus involves some risk. Even one that fails, however, creates space and possibilities for a reciprocation. The other side, of course, must at least *appear* to respond positively. For example, the 1986 summit between Reagan and Gorbachev in Reykjavik, Iceland, allowed Reagan to seem to be responding to the Soviet test moratorium.

The idea of peace initiatives has found support in some unexpected quarters, including a group of American business leaders such as Harold Willens, a California industrialist (see Willens 1984). In the long run, however, it is necessary to change not only the social psychology of the arms race but its institutionalization as well, as discussed in the next section.

Bureaucracy

Institutionalization of nonmilitary establishments.   Institutions tend to do what they are organized to do, and the current military establishments in both superpowers are organized for warfighting or at least for deterrence through the threat of warfighting. As Mills argues ([1958]1976:82), "The immediate cause of World War III is the military preparation of it."

One thing is clear: Whereas the institutions organized for the purpose of fighting wars are gargantuan in scope, there has been very little institutionalization of nonmilitary means of resolving conflicts. That strategy has scarcely been tried.

The most obvious exception is the United Nations, which is weak and somewhat paralyzed by its own structure. That is not to say, however, that we should underestimate its role. One of the difficulties with historical arguments is that we have no parallel controls by which to make historical comparisons. The vast complex of factors involved is so varied that it is impossible to know what the postwar period would have been like without the UN.[6] Nevertheless, at this late date, political and legal institutions might still be established to resolve conflicts without the international violence that could lead to nuclear war. Admittedly, the idea seems rather far-fetched, but so did the American form of government a few hundred years ago. Limited steps have already been made with the creation of the United Nations, the World Court, and the International Monetary Fund.

At both national and international levels, arms control agencies could facilitate peacemaking. Such institutions are open to co-optation, but their creation in the latter half of this century constitutes a new development in human history. The current situation is not encouraging, however. The U.S. Arms Control and Disarmament Agency is headed by Kenneth Adelman, who has been quoted in the press as saying that "arms control is a sham." In the Soviet Union, the official peace committees have channeled the public's desire for disarmament into a mechanism for the denunciation of U.S. policy.

A more encouraging example of such an institution is the Standing Consultative Commission established by the United States and the USSR in December 1972 to deal with arms control compliance issues.[7] The commission considers questions concerning compliance with specific arms control agreements and works out procedures for implementing them. It discusses ambiguous situations and considers allegations of violations of treaties.

Since its creation, the commission has investigated charges of eight alleged Soviet violations and six alleged American violations. Each allegation has been resolved to *both* parties' satisfaction, at least prior to the Reagan administration, which has worked outside the framework of the commission. Since the procedure used by the commission relies on the good will of the parties involved, the erosion of détente has undermined the process.

A similar procedure was developed in 1980 during negotiations among the United States, the USSR, and the United Kingdom for providing on-site inspections as part of a comprehensive test ban treaty. Unfortunately, the United States walked out on the talks after the Soviets' invasion of Afghanistan. The negotiations were then scrapped by the Reagan administration.

There are obvious difficulties with the creation of such international organizations. Because the ultimate power of any nation-state's government is its monopoly on use of military violence, it is hard to imagine the nations of the world surrendering that monopoly to an international body.[8] But exactly this may emerge as a preferable alternative to the continued military resolution of conflicts.

Because of the close coordination of nuclear and conventional forces, international institutions in a nuclear world must mitigate both types of conflicts. Nuclear and conventional weapons are linked on both sides in an overall strategy, which the Soviets call the correlation of forces. In such a strategy, nuclear weapons are primarily seen as a backup force, to be called on when a conventional conflict cannot produce imperative victory.

Nuclear and conventional weapons are related, first, because of the massive increase in conventional armaments. The United States alone sold $97.6 billion of arms under the Foreign Military Sales program from 1971–80—approximately eight times the total amount for the preceding two decades (Klare 1984:2). World arms transfers rose from $3–4 billion per year in the early 1960s to $25–30 billion per year in the early 1980s (in constant dollars; ibid.:7). Second, the nuclear threshold has been blurred as nuclear and conventional arsenals have become increasingly similar. For example, the large cluster bomb units used by Israel against civilians in Lebanon are nearly as destructive as the new so-called mini-nukes (although they lack global ecological and health consequences). Small guided missiles with multiple warheads pose a similar danger, and some of the new cruise missiles can carry either conventional or nuclear warheads.

Rethinking the military institution. Another issue, bureaucratic in nature, concerns the military itself and efforts to check its growing power. Randall Forsberg calls for a narrowing of the role of the military to truly *national* defense; her plan does not contain short-term goals, but has a 50-to-100-year timetable. According to the plan, the international community should first delegitimize the most aggressive military functions— conventional unilateral superpower intervention, and nuclear superiority aimed at backing up such interventions. One hopeful sign that such limits on the military would be welcome is the international outrage now expressed at interventions (e.g., in Afghanistan and Grenada).

Next, Forsberg argues that we should stabilize and substantially reduce the very large, technically advanced military forces of the major industrialized countries and China; those forces should be maintained only for defense and mutual deterrence. Following that, she contends that we should create and strengthen nonmilitary mechanisms for conflict resolution and peacekeeping, while encouraging the relaxation of East-West and Sino-Soviet tensions. Ideally, such a process would include the democratization of political and economic structures in the Third World and the global spread of civil liberties.

A penultimate goal would be to phase out military alliances and forces other than short-range antiaircraft, antitank, and antiship forces suitable for national territorial self-defense. Finally, we should attempt to replace national military defenses with nonmilitary defenses and international mechanisms, perhaps including an international police force. While Forsberg's goals may appear utopian, the nuclear threat calls for a radical rethinking of the institutional bases of defense.

Civilian-based Defense and Nonviolent Action.

> Then they came up and laid hands on Jesus and seized him.
> And behold, one of those who were with Jesus stretched out
> his hand and drew his sword, and struck the slave of the
> high priest, and cut off his ear. Then Jesus said to him, "Put
> your sword back into its place; for all who take the sword
> will perish by the sword."
>
> —Matt. 26:50–52

One of the most comprehensive plans for institutionalizing alternative forms of defense has been elaborated by Gene Sharp, of the Program on Nonviolent Sanctions in Conflict and Defense, Center for International Affairs at Harvard (see Sharp 1973, 1985b). Since contemporary military technology has essentially abolished conventional means of geographical defense and since no nation can protect its citizens against nuclear attack, Sharp (1985b:16) proposes the creation of a new defense system that is based on the following assumptions:

1. Military power today often exists without real capacity to *defend* in struggle the people and society relying upon it. Often it only threatens mutual annihilation. More importantly . . . defense capacity can today be provided without military means.
2. Military occupation does *not* necessarily give the invader political control of the country, and the occupation can be destroyed *without* military resistance.

Although outside the boundaries of most contemporary definitions of defense, the idea of a civilian-based defense may not be as farfetched as it first appears. In order to rule a society effectively, a modest degree of cooperation is required. Civilian-based defense operates on the premise that civilians can deny cooperation on an organized basis, thus reducing the incentive for invasion and subverting efforts to rule a conquered society.

Historical precedents for more spontaneous noncooperation provide some hope for the possibility of a well-prepared, coordinated campaign set up in advance of any invasion or coup. Sharp and his colleagues have identified 198 specific methods of nonviolent action (see Appendix A), including nonviolent methods of protest and persuasion, noncooperation, and intervention.

Civilian-based defense, although perhaps impractical at this stage, may be a silver lining in the mushroom cloud. Without the threat of nuclear war, it is possible that such measures would never have been taken seriously. As it is, the nonviolent tradition of the early Christian Church and of Thoreau, Tolstoy, Gandhi, and Martin Luther King, Jr., has become the object of systematic investigation and serious consideration.

In Poland, the philosophy and tactics of Gandhi and King have had an influence on the growth of Solidarity and the Polish resistance. As Lech Walesa puts it,[9]

> Victory can be achieved by various means. It can be gained with tanks and missiles, but I think that one wins better with truth, honesty and logic—in running the economy, in everything. And just take our example, and note that we have not fired a single shot. And we do not know what other means would have to be employed here to win such a victory as ours, except without firing a single shot. I think that the 20th and 21st century should be modeled on a struggle such as the one we have demonstrated. This is a new weapon. Well, not a new one. Actually, an old one. But it is very effective, and tailored exactly to the needs of the 21st century.

Despite Solidarity's shortcomings, it has transformed Polish society over a short period of time. There are many new civil liberties (despite marshal law), a strong independent labor movement, and a massive underground press that is almost as extensive as the official press. Similarly, in the Philippine Revolution of 1986, millions of citizens engaged in civil disobedience and nonviolent actions to oust Marcos. Priests and nuns led large crowds to surround military headquarters, to prevent shooting of rebels by government troops, and so forth. Although still in its infancy, the idea of civilian-based, nonviolent defense has captured the attention of policymakers and scholars, especially in Sweden and Great Britain.

Nonviolent action, as stated by Sharp, "resembles war more than it does negotiation; it is a technique of struggle" that "involves the use of power, but in different ways than military violence" (Sharp 1985b:21). The key to a civilian-based defense is the widespread, systematic training of a major portion of the population *prior* to any invasion or coup. Although it involves risk and would require prior cultural changes, it may be an idea whose time has come.

Conflict resolution and crisis communication.   A more immediate and less far-reaching step, not requiring a major structural transformation, is the use of crisis management techniques to resolve conflicts short of war. Several gains have been made in this area in recent years (see Volpe 1985; Fisher and Ury 1981; Kriesberg 1982).

One proposal is the creation of a Crisis Communication Center staffed twenty-four hours a day with people from the United States and the Soviet Union, and perhaps other countries as well. Communication between the superpowers is at present remarkably crude. Even the "hot line" is a simple teletype machine.

The importance of person-to-person communication can be seen in the case of Paul Nitze's experience while negotiating for the Reagan administration in Geneva in 1983. Despite his reputation as a Soviet affairs hardliner, Nitze and his Soviet counterpart were reportedly able to draft a mutually agreeable treaty during their famous "walk in the woods" session. Although eventually vetoed by Washington and Moscow, the proposal suggests that agreement might be found if there were more interaction between adversaries.

Much has been learned in recent years about the processes of conflict resolution, including the application of techniques developed in labor disputes and elsewhere. The National Institute for Dispute Resolution, the Special Committee on Dispute Resolution of the American Bar Association, the National Institute of Justice, and the Society of Professionals in Dispute Resolution represent a few of the institutions cultivating such techniques. Social scientists have played a key role in these developments, including James Laue and the Conflict Clinic at the University of Missouri at St. Louis, Louis Kriesberg, as well as the scholars at the Harvard Negotiation Project.

The use of arbitration and mediation bodies was applied to international affairs in the Camp David process and in international trade agreements that could serve as models for others. The creation of international legal institutions such as those associated with the Law of the Sea treaty, the International Court of Justice, and human rights conventions could pave the way for the peaceful resolution of world conflicts.

International peacekeeping forces.   One alternative to traditional defense that continues to attract considerable attention is the introduction of international peacekeeping forces into areas of violent conflict (see Coser 1963; Clande 1963). The use of UN troops in Korea, Cyprus, and elsewhere has not been as successful as hoped, but must be evaluated in light of their difficult contexts.

Since a major cause of the arms race is the desire for national security, provision should be made for international security forces that would limit each nation's need to protect its own borders. Aaron Tovish, of the Parliamentarians for Global Action, suggests that international security forces should be trained to be just as reliable and automatic as internal police forces. A nation should, in a sense, be able to pick up the telephone and dial the 911 emergency number if it is being attacked, and expect someone to come to its assistance.[10]

Institutions to address the causes of war. The threat of war is directly related to the poverty, disease, and hunger that feed discontent and international strife, especially in the Third World. With a major proportion of the world's human population living on the verge of starvation, it is little wonder that thousands of people die in wars every year. The superpowers often exploit such situations for their own benefit rather than helping to alleviate the problems.

When asked by the *National Catholic Reporter* how much it would cost to solve the problems of hunger in Africa, relief workers in the field estimated that it would take from $2 billion to $8 billion—the price of one of several major weapons programs in the U.S. budget alone! Although some relief programs to aid international development already exist—many of them carried out by United Nations agencies (such as UNICEF)—they are a drop in the bucket compared to what could be done. Increases in such efforts might provide more actual security to the people of the world than pouring arms and munitions into the world's hot spots. It might be possible (although not the most desirable scenario) to institute competition between the superpowers in development programs, so that they would try to "outdo one another in doing good," thereby alleviating the dire poverty in which much of the world lives.

A nonaligned peace movement. A final institutional process that undermines the threat of nuclear war is the growth (especially in the early to mid-1980s) of a nonaligned, worldwide peace movement, which will be discussed in more detail later (see Chapter Fourteen). Czechoslovakian peace activist Zdena Tomin suggests that such a movement is like a group of tiny mice eating away at the walls that separate the superpower blocs. Although seemingly insignificant, they weaken the structure of those walls piece by piece, until finally the walls may surprise everyone by suddenly collapsing.

In the final analysis, because the world is organized around bureaucratic institutions—political, economic, and cultural—the prevention of nuclear war may require the creation of alternative international institutions that break down nationalistic barriers.

Ritual

Many of the institutional alternatives suggested require a simultaneous cultural reorientation away from the ritual elements of the arms race and toward habitual responses to security threats that do not include immediate recourse to violence. In the current situation, superpower elites and citizens alike stress the potential catastrophe that a strategic nuclear exchange would cause, and yet they continue to prepare for it (see Frank 1982). There is an institutionalized, habitual propensity to resort to violence that must be undermined in order for a stable peace to emerge (see Boulding 1978). However, despite the threat of nuclear annihilation, the "taboo lines" that establish boundaries for warfare have been moved increasingly toward mass destruction of civilians in modern warfare, a situation that was unthinkable in earlier centuries.[11]

The process of reality construction involves the imaging of alternatives, much of which occurs at a preconceptual or symbolic level. Therefore, the power of ritual behavior can either perpetuate existing reciprocal networks and institutions or be harnessed to help shift paradigms in matters of national policy.

An instructive example is the abolitionist movement of the nineteenth century, which took on a seemingly impossible task and won. That movement employed a series of rituals to provide a symbolic underpinning to its efforts. First, there was a ritual public denunciation of the institution of slavery, employing a rich set of symbolic images. Drawing upon Judeo-Christian images and symbols, the abolitionists developed songs, metaphors, and ritual activities oriented toward the immediate liberation of some slaves (using the underground railroad), and the eventual elimination of slavery altogether.

These ritual activities of the abolitionists helped create new, shared definitions of the situation, so that it became increasingly impossible to speak publicly in favor of slavery. Eventually a new consensus emerged within the population and within the dominant political structure. Opposition to slavery became attached to the interests of the Union and served as a rallying cry for the North during the Civil War.

The relatively fluid nature of culture (at least when compared to bureaucracies and social networks) makes it possible to change cultural definitions to undermine the legitimacy of existing institutions. Ritual activities can also reenforce and fortify alternative institutions, giving them legitimacy and authority to combat dominant institutions. Sometimes indirect actions, such as cultural, educational, and artistic exchanges, are more effective at breaking down transnational barriers than direct government-to-government interactions.

A characteristic of rituals that would provide alternatives to the nuclear arms race, then, is that they help redefine the problem that created and sustains the nuclear cage. The enemy that is ritually denounced might be the nuclear threat itself, rather than another group or nation. The peace movement has already utilized popular rituals borrowed from religious, labor, and civil rights movements: public demonstrations and marches, songs, speeches, letter writing, sit-ins, and so forth. In the fall of 1986, for example, United Campuses to Prevent Nuclear War held an international event called Give Peace a Dance, which occurred on campuses around the world and emphasized the solidarity of students and faculty across national boundaries. (There are plans to make it an annual event.)

Such rituals may occur on two levels: first, a series of stop-gap rituals directed at the denunciation of particular policies, weapons, or actions, and second, a series of rituals focused on a deeper level, identifying the underlying causes of the arms race—injustice, violence, and threats worldwide to security, dignity, and human rights. Public events might operate on both levels simultaneously. One aspect of such rituals would be the construction of new attitudes and strategies for encountering enemies, on both a cognitive and an affective level. For example, Gandhi's effort to differentiate between the act and the actor might be reenforced by public declarations, songs, and symbols that do not vilify individuals or types of people, but instead condemn certain actions, while outlining ways in which those who commit them might change.

Similarly, "new" strategies could be implemented, such as Jesus' suggestion that his followers overcome evil with good. Through rituals people can often practice what Sharp (1985b:22) calls political *jiu-jitsu*, which involves highlighting the sharp distinction between protesters and the violence of the system attempting to repress them, so that even the oppressors may recognize the repugnance of the repression.

Similarly, instead of attacking core symbols of the opposition head-on, it may be possible to redefine those symbols in a more positive light. Daniel Berrigan has suggested, for example, that rather than burning the American flag (as some protesters did in the 1960s), protesters should wash the flag as a simultaneous expression of respect and criticism. The ritual celebration of other symbols can be used as occasions for transforming the international system (for example, in cultural, scientific and economic exchanges) by attesting to the common interests of people across national boundaries.

The creation of new rituals and symbols may open new cracks in the nuclear cage. Because rituals are rooted in experience, it may be helpful to systematically investigate the kinds of activities and symbols that have helped underscore positive international relations and reduce violence in the past. The Live-Aid concert in the summer of 1985, for example, helped millions of people identify with the drought-stricken people of Africa. It reenforced an empathy for people of other lands and showed participants that it feels good to help others. Sometimes existing institutions and rituals can accomplish the desired purposes, as seen by the efforts within Christian churches in the United States and the Soviet Union to heighten congregants' awareness that as they worship, Christians on "the other side" are worshipping as well.

Finally, since rituals tend to reify the social structures and institutions in which they occur, the creation by a nonaligned peace movement of ritual occasions might fortify those institutions and give them new legitimacy. Although the structures of bloc politics and global systems of power are not going to change overnight, the ritual celebration of transnational structures might undermine the nationalism that legitimizes war-making. One consequence of the peace movement is that both Reagan and Gorbachev have gone to great lengths to co-opt its rhetoric in public pronouncements that emphasize their own commitment to peace and arms control.

SUMMARY

This chapter provided an overview of alternative strategies for national security, starting with the mainstream packages used in public discourse in both the United States and the Soviet Union. Because public discourse tends to evolve around a set of conflicting core images and symbols (each of which has its own internal consistency), it is helpful to examine the assumptions and consequences of each approach.

Two mainstream positions exist in the United States. The dominant symbolic package is the Peace through Strength approach to national security, which rests on three fundamental assumptions. First, a system of nuclear deterrence has kept the peace for forty years, but must be modernized in order to provide the capability to fight and win a limited nuclear war with first-strike weapons. Second, the Soviets cannot be trusted and therefore must be dealt with from a position of strength. Third, during a period of détente in the 1970s, the Soviets allegedly engaged in a massive military buildup, while the United States followed a line of unilateral disarmament, resulting in a Soviet arsenal superior to that of the United States. Peace through Strength advocates contend that the United States is now vulnerable to Soviet attack, and so any major arms control agreement like the Freeze would lock the United States into a position of nuclear inferiority.

The other major U.S. position is the Arms Control movement. Its advocates assume that even if deterrence works, any further buildup will seriously undermine security. The Arms Control approach also argues that there is currently an approximate parity between the two superpower arsenals, thus providing an opportunity for a major arms control agreement. Finally, Arms Control advocates argue that only international agreements will work as a long-range strategy for the security of the human species. Either everyone is secure, or nobody is.

Within the Soviet Union, the two major positions on nuclear weapons policy are those of the government and of the small independent peace movement. Soviet officials have adopted the rhetoric, and many of the assumptions, of the U.S. Arms Control position, with two major differences: the Soviets feel that (1) the United States is solely responsible for the nuclear arms race; and (2) they must deal with the United States from a position of strength, because of the untrustworthy, warlike nature of U.S. policymakers.

The independent Soviet peace movement has a position much like that of Arms Control advocates in the United States, arguing that the two superpowers must be forced to end the arms race. The Soviet government has highlighted the distinction between its own position and that of the independent peace movement by harrassing and jailing the movement's leaders.

As a consequence of the shared Peace through Strength elements of the elites in both superpowers, both countries have been engaged in an endless military buildup. In the second section of this chapter, we returned to the analytical concepts of the framework developed in Chapter Four: reciprocity, bureaucracy, and ritual. These social processes hold out the prospect of exits from the nuclear cage.

Reciprocal actions have precipitated an escalation of the arms race, but they could also facilitate its reversal. Peace initiatives capitalize on the nature of reciprocity in an effort to induce beneficial, rather than harmful, exchanges. They are nonmilitary steps taken outside of negotiations, which are designed to prod adversaries into taking steps to reduce tensions and reverse the arms race. Thus, one side may unilaterally act to initiate a comprehensive test ban (or some other measure) in an effort to break a stalemate in arms negotiations.

In examining the concept of bureaucracy, we discussed efforts to establish institutions that transcend the existing conflictual international arrangements. Some examples include the United Nations, arms control agencies, the Standing Consultative Commission, systems of civilian-based defense, institutions for conflict resolution and crisis communication, international peacekeeping forces, and institutions that address the root causes of war, such as poverty, disease, and injustice. The emergence of an international, nonaligned peace movement holds out the possibility of creating alternative institutions that can undermine the power of nation-states to define international relations in military terms.

Finally, the creation of rituals that transcend bloc politics was discussed as a means by which an alternative reality might be imagined, and in which people from around the world might participate. Although such rituals cannot exist without an infrastructural base, they can facilitate the creation of nonmilitary institutions and approaches to settling cross-national differences.

In the following chapters, we will examine in more detail the alternatives that various parties to the contemporary nuclear policy debate have proposed, beginning with a discussion of strategic policy and the concept of deterrence.

CHAPTER EIGHT

Deterrence Policies and Assumptions

"Vengeance may not be a pretty word, but it's what's expected of us."

"Right!" said Sverre. "We owe it to all those millions of dead people to make more millions of dead people. Be careful how you rewrite strategic doctrine, General, or you'll come out of this war without a single medal."

—James Morrow, *This Is the Way the World Ends*

THE LOGIC OF DETERRENCE

The most widespread response to the threat of nuclear annihilation has been to continue the ritual, bureaucracy, and reciprocation of a military buildup based on the logic of deterrence. In its simplest form, deterrence is a promise to do what one might be expected to do anyway—to reciprocate when one is harmed. An effective deterrence must convince the adversary that one can retaliate effectively enough to inflict unacceptable damage.

Deterrence is both simple and complex at the same time. On the one hand, it is the schoolyard dare: "Don't cross this line, or I'll knock your block off!" On the other hand, it is a complicated interaction that requires psyching out one's adversaries, convincing them that the threat is credible.

Deterrence operates on the same principle as all human interaction: It involves the social construction of definitions of a situation that are created by "taking the role of the other." Decisions about what creates an effective deterrence involve predicting an adversary's potential reactions. Intelligence-gathering activities provide some of the necessary information, but the process is never perfect; even when two close friends interact, one never knows fully what the other is thinking. It is even more difficult to anticipate the reactions of a government, especially when there is little person-to-person interaction and available information is deliberately deceptive. Normal processes of cue-giving and cue-receiving are driven underground.

Deterrence was complicated immeasurably by the development of nuclear weapons. In some ways, the threat of retaliation is clear enough with nuclear weapons: They are so immensely destructive that anyone who uses them against a similarly armed opponent obviously risks unbelievable retaliation. If, however, one admits openly that the use of nuclear weapons would be suicidal, the very notion of deterrence is called into question. (That may be why the Pentagon is so anxious to insist that the nuclear winter hypothesis will not affect nuclear policies.)

Consider, for example, the NATO policy that nuclear weapons be used in Western Europe if a Warsaw Pact invasion cannot be repelled by conventional weapons. NATO's thousands of tactical nuclear weapons make no sense if the Warsaw Pact allies are not convinced that the weapons would be *used*. Consequently, one inevitable outcome of the NATO policy is the contention that a nuclear war could be fought on a limited basis, without escalating to an all-out holocaust. If a nuclear power were to admit that no one could actually win a nuclear war, its threat to use nuclear weapons might become empty.

Nuclear strategists are not working with real-life situations based on hard data and experience; they are instead forced to speculate about what might happen in the event that a nuclear war occurred. In the absence of concrete information, people tend to operate in a ritual fashion, in this case along the lines of responses established within military and political traditions long before the development of nuclear weapons. We simply do not know with any certainty what the results of a nuclear war would be, and no sane person wishes to find out. Nuclear policymakers do not have the luxury of testing their ideas in the real world to see if their assumptions are correct. The situation is aptly described by a bumper sticker that reads, Nuclear war: See one, you've seen them all.

American Nuclear Policymakers: Victims of Groupthink?

Throughout the nuclear age, American nuclear policies have been shaped by a small group of strategists (see Porro 1982). The political leanings of the party in power have had little effect on those policies. Even the commander in chief, the president, and the cabinet have had minimal direct effect, although the president's actions can bring about changes.

Early American strategic policy relied upon what was called *massive retaliation.*[1] That doctrine, originally defined in the 1950s by Secretary of State John Foster Dulles, consisted of a plan to use overwhelming force when responding to a threat to American vital interests. In the nuclear age, however, that policy places the president in a very awkward situation: For what kind of threat will he or she be willing to risk a nuclear war? The United States cannot respond with massive retaliation (or threaten to do so) every time its interests are threatened. Consequently, during the early years of the Kennedy administration, American policy evolved toward a doctrine of *controlled response*, as outlined by Defense Secretary Robert McNamara.

The controlled response doctrine rests on a distinction between counterforce and countervalue attacks. As discussed in Chapter One, counterforce attacks are directed against a nation's military forces (weapons installations, bases, command centers, and so forth); countervalue policies refer to assaults directed toward the enemy's cities. Whereas massive retaliation required no such distinction, the controlled response doctrine contained two elements that relied on it. The first was the notion of damage limitation, a plan to attack the other side's weapons before they could be used. The damage to be limited, therefore, was not in the adversary's country, but in one's own. The second element was the idea of city withholding, based on the assumption that if Soviet cities were destroyed, there would be no reason for the Soviets *not* to retaliate.

Controlled response sounds attractive in the abstract, but it was abandoned during the Cuban missile crisis as unworkable. Concerned that the Soviets—in the heat of the crisis—would not understand the subtle innuendos involved in a threat of controlled response, the Kennedy administration sent a simple, harsh message to the Soviets, and a new strategic doctrine, *assured destruction*, emerged.

The popular term for assured destruction is Mutual Assured Destruction (M.A.D.), although the strategy is much more complicated than that term implies and strategists argue that assured destruction is not M.A.D. The strategy relies on an assured destruction capability, roughly defined as the ability to destroy two-thirds of the population and three-fourths of the industrial base of the adversary. It combines elements of massive retaliation and controlled response, incorporating a "ladder of escalation" strategy

---

Central (homeland) attack

↑

Theatre conflict

↑

Tactical nuclear conflict

↑

Conventional warfare

Figure 8.1   The ladder of escalation.

where attempts are made to stop the escalation of conflict at the lowest possible level, as suggested in Figure 8.1.

In theory, the strategy requires superior force at the top of the ladder; otherwise, the enemy could continue to escalate a conflict until it reached a level at which it was superior. If, for example, the Warsaw Pact invaded Western Europe, NATO allies would attempt to stop the invasion with conventional forces. If that failed, they could escalate the conflict with tactical nuclear weapons, such as the neutron bomb, nuclear land mines, short-range artillery rounds, and Lance missiles. If they were unsuccessful with those weapons, theater nuclear weapons (e.g., intermediate-range missiles and GLCMs) could be used. If all else failed, NATO could launch a central attack, that is, an attack on the Soviet Union. Such a strategy is often called flexible response because it includes options other than massive retaliation. It is very similar to the Kennedy-McNamara doctrine of controlled response, and is subject to some of the same uncertainties. How long would it take, once the "nuclear threshold" were crossed, to escalate from tactical to theater weapons? A week? Two hours? How long would it be before strategic weapons were employed? What would happen if communications were destroyed by an electromagnetic pulse?

As the Soviets began to reach parity with the American arsenal, the notion of assured destruction became increasingly problematic. Once the United States lost the margin of superiority it had enjoyed through the early 1960s, the doctrine became unusable because of the requirement for superior capabilities at the top of the ladder of escalation.

Since the late 1970s, the United States has moved toward what is termed a *countervailing strategy*, which incorporates aspects of the flexible response strategy of assured destruction. Countervailing attacks are those considered appropriate by the party reciprocating in response to a prior attack. It is a cost-imposing strategy, in that the objective is to inflict enough damage on an opponent to deter it from taking any aggressive action. The plan calls for the capability to impose whatever costs are deemed necessary for deterrence. As weapons delivery systems became increasingly accurate, nuclear strategists became convinced that the use of nuclear weapons did not have to be an all-or-nothing proposition.

Because countervailing strategies require (1) superiority at all levels along the ladder of escalation and (2) highly accurate, survivable weapons for counterforce attacks and retaliation, many nuclear strategists embrace the Peace through Strength option for preventing nuclear war.

PEACE THROUGH STRENGTH

As suggested in Chapter Seven, much of the recent public debate over strategic policies in the United States has focused on the proposals of two social movements: Arms Control and Peace through Strength. A Peace through Strength resolution has been endorsed by ten state governors, passed by thirteen state legislatures, and cosponsored by a majority of both houses of Congress. Despite widespread support for the Freeze in Congress, political elites in the United States (like those in the Soviet Union) find it difficult to support the rhetoric of the Freeze without also embracing the principle of Peace through Strength, however contradictory that may sometimes be. A recent film produced by the American Security Council Foundation, "Countdown for America," provides a graphic summary of the Peace through Strength position.[2] It presents four basic arguements: (1) the Soviet Union has gained military superiority; (2) since 1967, the Soviets have been engaged in a massive arms buildup, while the Americans were unilaterally disarming; (3) the Soviets cannot be trusted, they (like the Nazis in 1939) are determined to dominate the world, and negotiations with them are therefore impossible; and (4) the nuclear freeze campaign, while supported by many well-meaning people, is manipulated by Moscow and would lock the United States into a position of nuclear inferiority.

I have already argued (see Chapter One) that it is virtually impossible to evaluate who is ahead and who is behind in the arms race because of the different kinds of weapons systems employed by each side and that after a certain level of destructive force such comparisons are irrelevant. However, it is still important to examine the Peace through Strength argument, because it approximates official policy in the United States and is frequently espoused in the media by government officials.

According to Senator Tower, since the time of the Cuban missile crisis, "in a very unrelenting way, the Soviet Union has built its own strategic capability to the point that now it is superior to that of the United States of America" (American Security Council 1982:3). Peace through Strength advocates argue that since 1967 the United States has placed a freeze on building ICBMs and SLBMs, whereas the Soviets have continued to build their arsenal.

Peace through Strength advocates continue their argument by talking about civil defense. Whereas the Soviets have a civil defense program with shelters for military and civilian leaders and a large percentage of their industrial labor force, the United States "has a civil defense program in name alone." Consequently, "because we have no defense against nuclear missiles, if an all-out nuclear war were ever started by the Soviets, the United States could suffer up to 60% casualties; whereas Soviet casualties could be less than 10%"(ibid.:7).

If the assumptions of the Peace through Strength argument are accepted, the United States must modernize its nuclear forces. The image of the Soviet Union as the evil empire and the idea that the United States is engaged in a battle of right against wrong lend support to that position. As President Reagan stated in his speech before the United Nations on 17 June 1982, "The United States has fought four wars in my lifetime. In each, we struggled to defend freedom and democracy" (Reagan 1982).

Caspar Weinberger furthered the Peace through Strength argument, addressing the nuclear freeze issue:

> I think it's apparent why the Soviets are for a nuclear freeze. It would leave them in a position of permanent superiority, and that would be a very dangerous thing for America and her allies because it would mean that the credibility of our deterrent, our ability to prevent war, would be seriously weakened. (American Security Council 1982:2)

Consequently, the Soviets are actively supporting the freeze movement. As Major General Richard X. Larkin[3] put it, "The KGB, I believe, claims this is one of their most successful enterprises, that is, this World Peace Council orchestrating the nuclear freeze movement." According to Larkin, the World Peace Council is a communist front organization set up to manipulate the Freeze movement in the United States. Through it, there is

> a direct communications and guidance and direction link from the office of the chief of the Information Directorate in the Central Committee of the Soviet Union right down to city hall. . . . The guidance is there, the funding is there, the direction is there. . . . You can imagine the difficulty of organizing a mass rally as held in New York[4] . . . the advertising that has to go out, the mailing that has to go out, the reservations that have to be made. We would probably conservatively say that it would cost them $300 million to put on a year's activity in the United States. This is apart from their salaries and their travel expenses.

Despite the conclusion of the FBI in 1982 that the Freeze movement was *not* manipulated by the Soviets, the allegations persist, spurred on in part by a *Reader's Digest* article (Barron 1982), which President Reagan quoted publicly.

The major problem with the Peace through Strength argument is its selective use of information. Although the United States does not have as many weapons delivery systems as the Soviet Union, it actually has more warheads (see Chapter One). Other "deficiencies" in the American strategic arsenal are the consequence of deliberate policy decisions: The bomber program has been given low priority because of an emphasis on ICBMs and SLBMs; American weapons have smaller total megatonnages because of a concentration on smaller, more accurate weapons. In almost every category of weapon, the United States is more advanced technologically than the Soviet Union. Because of sophisticated guidance systems, American rockets are more accurate and reliable; because of solid fuel, they can be smaller and more manageable.

In some areas of the arms race the Soviet Union is superior; in other areas the United States is more advanced. By selectively focusing on one aspect of the arms race at the exclusion of others (and ignoring the larger question of whether such comparisons are even meaningful), one can always make the case that one side or the other is behind. Both superpowers do just that to justify a continued arms buildup.

U.S. claims of inferiority and of the need for new types of nuclear weapons are not necessarily deliberate deceptions, but are a consequence of a particular strategic doctrine, that of counterforce targetting. We will now turn our attention to an examination of the contemporary American strategic policy in an effort to question some of the assumptions on which it rests.

ASSESSING THE ASSUMPTIONS

Defining the Situation

President Reagan claims that the United States was "never the aggressor," but that "America's strength and, yes, her military power have been a force for peace, not conquest, for democracy, not despotism, for freedom, not tyranny" (Reagan 1982). General Secretary Gorbachev claims that "since the very beginning of the nuclear age the Soviet Union has consistently and vigorously fought for ending the accumulation of nuclear arsenals, for curbing military rivalry and for strengthening trust and peaceful cooperation between states" (Gorbachev 1985b:1).

On the one hand, Defense Secretary Weinberger (1983) tells us that U.S. strategic research and development must increase by 41 percent if the United States is to modernize its weapons forces to the extent needed to overcome a marked Soviet advantage. Admiral Hyman Rickover (1982), on the other hand, argues that one nuclear submarine would be sufficient to deter the Soviet threat and that we could sink the rest of the submarines.

The Federal Emergency Management Agency contends that more than 80 percent of the American population could be saved from a major nuclear attack if a crisis relocation plan were implemented (FEMA

1980h:5). Robert Jay Lifton, however, insists that "whatever tiny bands of survivors might exist will be at a stone-age level of struggle for the means of maintaining life" (1982:20).

How can such intelligent, presumably informed people provide such diametrically opposed answers to these important questions? There are some areas of consensus: There is virtual unanimity on (1) the fact that nuclear weapons are horribly destructive; and (2) the types and numbers of weapons possessed by the major nuclear powers. Whether one reads the report of the Joint Chiefs of Staff, those from the London-based Institute for Strategic Studies, or those from the Stockholm Peace Institute, one finds essentially the same figures. With such substantial agreement on the details, why is there so much disagreement on the overall picture and on how to get out of the nuclear cage?

It is a classic sociological question, because its answer is found in the social processes by which people make decisions and process information. Individuals develop an overall picture of an issue (a definition of the situation, or a frame) and then filter the details through that picture, selectively perceiving the information that supports their position and ignoring that which undermines it. Sociologist W. I. Thomas (1966) contends that "situations defined as real are real in their consequences." A fundamental sociological premise, therefore, is that different definitions are constructed by people in different positions in the social structure.

The question that must be asked is whether our current nuclear strategies, based upon our current definition of the situation, will prevent nuclear war. One's answer to that question will depend, to a large extent, upon his or her position in the policymaking business. My answer is an unfortunate no. I do not believe that we are moving in a direction that will help us avoid the holocaust. It is clear, however, that I am outside the group of people who make such decisions, and I encourage the reader to be conscious of that fact while reading this book.

A plan of action, and a definition of the situation that justifies it, is only as good as the assumptions on which it rests. The remainder of this chapter critiques the four major underlying assumptions of current U.S. nuclear policy, namely, that nuclear deterrence works in essentially the same manner as conventional deterrence, that actors in a nuclear conflict will behave in an essentially rational manner, that nuclear war can be limited, and that the protection of national interests is worth the risk of a potential nuclear exchange.

Nuclear and Conventional Deterrence

Almost as soon as the United States military acquired them, atomic weapons were integrated into American foreign policy. They were originally conceived of as an extension of conventional weapons, and early strategic nuclear theory was based on ideas of strategic bombing. National Security

Council Document No. 30 (NSC 30), resulting from NSC discussions in early 1948, stated this quite clearly: The national military establishment "must be ready to utilize promptly and effectively all appropriate means available, including atomic weapons, in the interest of national security and must plan accordingly" (Pringle and Arkin 1983:50). The primary strategic response to nuclear weapons was thus simply to include them in the military rituals of the prenuclear age.

In recent years, nuclear weapons policies have been woven into the Single Integrated Operating Plan (SIOP), which specifies how all U.S. military forces are to operate in a time of crisis. As Weinberger (1983) puts it, "all our nuclear forces are governed by a single coherent policy that governs the linkage among our conventional, non-strategic nuclear and strategic forces."

An early critic of that linkage between nuclear and conventional weapons, Bernard Brodie, argued that the introduction of nuclear weapons had to change the nature of military thinking. "Thus far," Brodie argued, "the chief purpose of our military establishment has been to win wars" (1946:76). However, because the costs of a nuclear confrontation would far exceed any potential benefits, he contended that Clausewitz's ([1832] 1968) classic notion of war as a means to achieve political objectives no longer made sense. "From now on," Brodie argued, "[the military's] chief purpose must be to prevent . . . [wars]. It can almost have no other useful purpose" (Brodie 1946:76; cf. Brodie 1959, 1966, 1978). He could not conceive of any political objective that could justify the loss of a hundred cities or millions of people. No one, according to Brodie, would win a nuclear war.

Herman Kahn (1960, 1962, 1965), on the other hand, rejected Brodie's assumptions. Nuclear wars, like any other, he claimed, could be won or lost. The debate between Brodie's position and Kahn's has continued throughout the nuclear age (see Porro 1982). Its implications for strategic policy and weapons programs are rather obvious. If one accepts Brodie's assumptions, a military with nuclear weapons must simply have a sufficient deterrence to retaliate if attacked. If one accepts Kahn's assumptions, however, sophisticated counterforce weapons make sense, and highly accurate, survivable weapons (such as the cruise and Pershing missiles and the Trident II/D-5) are necessary in order to carry out a protracted nuclear war. For Kahn, nuclear wars are won or lost on the same criteria as all other wars: weapons superiority, troop strength, the will to fight, and so forth.

President Eisenhower was apparently thinking along Brodie's lines when he told his naval aide, Captain Aurand, "We have got to set [target] limits. We've got to get this thing right down to deterrence." Pringle and Arkin (1983:119) suggest that Eisenhower and Kennedy both attempted to develop a minimum war plan, a finite deterrence (such as a fleet of relatively invulnerable submarines), but "the politicans allowed the military to bully them out of it." Some of the resistance was a consequence of the bureaucratic organization of the armed forces; whereas the Navy proposed such a minimal deterrence, the Air Force opposed it (ibid.:119–20).

The push toward the Kahn position makes sense from the point of view of those with responsibility for making decisions about nuclear weapons. The Kennedy-McNamara notion of controlled response (or flexible response) was an effort to provide the president with more options. The notions of counterforce targeting and limited damage are quite appealing to those making decisions about the actual use of the weapons. In the Nixon and Ford administrations, there were strong leanings toward the Kahn side of the argument and a return to counterforce and nuclear warfighting strategies.

In the Carter administration, the initial policy leanings were Brodie-like, but officials moved toward a countervailing strategy in order to obtain a sense of having a flexible response. Thomas Powers (1982) suggests that Carter began to shift his position as he became engrossed in the details of nuclear policy. A known detail-afficionado, Carter demonstrated more interest in the contingency plans for nuclear war than any president since Harry Truman (Pringle and Arkin 1983:39).

From Brodie's perspective, bean-counting (the precise calculation of who is ahead and behind) is obsolete. With the introduction of any new military technology bean-counting activities are problematic—military planners are faced with the task of comparing apples and oranges. Traditionally, however, methods of calculating equivalences could be tested on the battlefield. Over years of experience, planners could make informed estimates about the rough equivalences involved—for example, one soldier on horseback is worth X soldiers on foot. But how does one make such evaluations about nuclear weapons? What does *overkill* mean?

Even Weinberger began to qualify earlier claims that a nuclear war is winnable. "We, for our part," he wrote in his 1984 report to Congress, "are under no illusions about the dangers of a nuclear war between the major powers; we believe that neither side could win such a war" (Weinberger 1983:51). Rather, we will employ military force to restore the peace. The objective (rather than to *win*) would be "to restore the peace on favorable terms" (ibid:32). But what is the distinction between winning and restoring the peace on favorable terms?

The bind for military planners is a difficult one: If there are no winners, how does one plan? In the absence of concrete solutions to the problem, strategists are forced to rely upon ritualistic formulas, making calculations of simple aggregates and weapons capabilities. Like most rituals, they appear perfectly rational to participants although they may not make sense to an outside observer. They give the strategic planner a sense of rational control, which leads us to the second assumption of current U.S. nuclear policy, that the key actors in the arms race behave in a rational manner.

The Assumption of Rationality

The assumption of rationality behind current deterrence theories is questionable along four lines: (1) rationality is a slippery concept that is neither objective nor empirically verifiable; (2) it assumes that adversaries will perceive our intentions in the way we think they will, and that our assessment of their behavior is correct; (3) rationality requires nearly perfect information; and (4) it implies that doctrines and practices are the same thing.

German sociologist Max Weber ([1904–5] 1958), a noted authority on rationality, points out that rationality is always a perception derived from a particular point of view. Another dimension of rationality is that what appears rational from a short-term point of view for an individual may be irrational in the long run for a collectivity. As Weber points out, rationality at one level frequently has irrational consequences at another. Andre Gunder Frank makes that point by developing an analogy between the nuclear arms race and the Third World debt crisis, on the one hand, and the game of chicken,[5] on the other.

> What is rational for each of the players taken individually in the short run is irrational in the medium or longer run (which can turn out to be quite short) for all of the players put together. . . . But nobody is prepared to give in until the last moment, and at the last moment it may be too late, that is, the last moment may indeed be the last. (1985:70)

Charles Osgood (1962) observes that people *can* behave rationally, and often do; but people can also behave *ir*rationally, and often do. Furthermore, as emotional stress increases, nonrational mechanisms become more prevalent. In a state of international crisis that might lead to nuclear war, we can expect people to have strong tendencies toward nonrational behavior, to employ defense mechanisms such as projection and reaction formation, and to be more easily influenced by the distortions created by groupthink.

The fate of the earth thus rests on the quite shaky assumption that the adversary in a nuclear conflict will perceive our intentions in the way we *think* it will, and vice versa. That is, we assume similar definitions of the situation, but we are blind to mirror imageries and projections. We often apply a double standard, or shift standards altogether, when attributing rationality or irrationality to an opponent. Our actions are rational; the adversary's are irrational. There is a logical contradiction built into deterrence theory. Deterrence only works if both sides are rational, and yet we all sense that if both sides were, they would find a way to stop the arms race. We have a haunting suspicion that the arms race itself is irrational.

On the other hand, when it serves our purposes, we assume that our opponent is rational, when in fact the adversary may be acting irrationally. We may assume, as Osgood notes, that the primary motive behind an action is aggression when it is actually fear. Therefore we assume that an action that appears threatening is deliberately so.

Countervailing policies assume extreme rationality and make no sense without it. The basis of a counterforce attack, for example, is that the adversary will calculate the risks of further military action and stop its aggression. In other words, we decide that the adversary is rational or irrational depending upon which viewpoint confirms our definition of the situation.

For people to act in a rational fashion, they require nearly perfect information. This requirement is reflected in the Reagan administration's placing of the highest priority (see Weinberger 1983) on what is called C^3I (C-cubed-I), that is, command, control, communications, and intelligence. All C^3I aspects of military planning are honed to the finest details, including such specifics as a presidential airborne command post, which is supposedly designed in such a way as "to ensure continued operation during nuclear war."

Ample anecdotal evidence exists, however, to suggest that perfect information is not available to defense planners. Emma Rothschild (1983) notes, for example, that the 1984 Department of Defense report includes a map of the Middle East in which Albania has an extensive land border on southeast Italy; the northeast African country of Djibouti is misspelled in two different ways; and, more astonishing, Jordan is depicted as having a 100-kilometer Mediterranean coastline separating Israel and Lebanon.

Admiral Noel Gayler argues that warplanners are deceiving themselves when they plot elaborate scenarios:

> Real war is not like these complicated tit-for-tat imaginings. There is little knowledge of what is going on, and less communication. There is blood and terror and agony, and these theorists propose to deal with a war a thousand times more terrible than any we have ever seen, in some bloodless, analytic fashion. I say that's nonsense. (1984:396)

As John Dewey (1929) suggests, we must give up our futile "quest for certainty." We simply cannot obtain it. The question is not "How can we obtain certainty?" but "On what kind of uncertainty are we willing to risk our lives?" In that context, the oft-asked "Can you trust the Russians?" becomes rhetorical nonsense. Deterrence is, to some extent, based upon trust. We can never have full knowledge of their knowledge of our knowledge.

Finally, the assumption of rationality implies that deterrence doctrine and practice are the same thing, but that is a questionable assumption, as shown by U.S actions during the Cuban missile crisis. Although the notion of flexible response is attractive in the abstract, for example, it becomes unworkable in the real world. How does one communicate to one's adversary that the missile launch they detect on their screens will cause only *limited* damage, and that there is no intention to launch a full-scale attack?

Such thinking on the part of American strategic planners is based on a faulty understanding of human behavior. How would the United States respond to a message from the Kremlin that Soviet missiles were going to destroy Kelly Air Force base in San Antonio but that the attack was intended as a limited strike? It would be Remember the Alamo! all over again. Would the president suddenly throw his or her hands up in despair and capitulate to Soviet demands? That is not likely.

Countervailing strategies rely upon very complicated definitions of the situation and work only if the adversary does, in fact, respond as expected. The United States has a rather poor record on second-guessing its adversaries. During the Vietnam War, for example, members of the Johnson administration became convinced that the bombing of Hanoi would bring the Vietnamese to their knees. On the contrary, the destruction of their capital city strengthened their resolve to fight.[6]

Powers (1982) argues that new targeting theories are actually only attempts to frighten or injure an enemy with weapons grown more accurate and numerous. Theories thus often emerge after the fact to explain technological developments, a case of what William F. Ogburn called cultural lag (Powers 1982; Ogburn 1922).

The ritual effort to develop nuclear policies that provide a sense of control leads us to a third assumption of current theories of deterrence, that nuclear war can be limited.

Limiting Nuclear War

Current strategic thinking in the United States is generally dominated by the Kahn side of the nuclear policy debate. In assuming that nuclear wars can be won or lost, one must also believe that such conflicts can be limited in scope. Although that is a fundamental policy of our government (and has been since the Nixon presidency), it is quite debatable and involves high risks.

An assumption of the notion of limiting nuclear war is that one has the capability to stop escalation at the lowest possible level along a "spectrum of violence" (Weinberger 1983). Weinberger insists that only with accurate weapons such as the Pershing II and short-range nuclear weapons can we escalate the intensity of a conflict in a controlled fashion.

It is highly unlikely, however, that *anyone* would be in control in a nuclear war; conventional wars have always been difficult to control, and a nuclear war would be much more difficult. As Bernard Brodie wrote in 1959, "What we have done must convince us that Thucydides was right, that peace is better than war not only in being more agreeable but also in being very much more predictable."

The principle of reciprocity suggests, in fact, that there is a built-in escalation component that moves a conflict beyond the control of its participants. As Lifton (1982:15–16) asserts, "The psychological key is the assumption that a preplanned combination of bold, limited nuclear action and equally bold, more or less *unlimited* nuclear threat can enable us to *control* the situation and keep it *limited*. That assumption defies virtually all psychological experience."

Furthermore, the illusion of limit and control undermines the so-called threshold of use (and the distinction between conventional and nuclear weapons); it may increase the probability that nuclear weapons will actually be fired. Some have even drawn an analogy between the limited use of nuclear weapons in a counterforce attack and the imposition of economic sanctions.

Such assumptions should be questioned by nonexperts precisely *because* they are not strategic planners and are therefore not blinded by the kind of abstract, unreal decisions that strategic planners make. These sorts of theories are developed because a small group of policymakers convince each other that they are correct. Within the frame of their debate—if their assumptions are accepted—it is almost impossible to logically disagree with their theories. What is faulty, however, are the assumptions, such as the notion of limited nuclear war, on which such theories are based.

Limited-nuclear-war policies in the United States are justified largely by the argument that the Soviets have developed similar strategies (see Gray 1976, 1979; Pipes 1977). Pipes (1977) argues that because the Soviets have a warfighting strategy, the United States must develop one as well. Not to do so threatens the credibility of deterrence. Pipes discounts the statements by Soviet politicians from Khrushchev through Gorbachev that point out the futility of nuclear war, summed up in Khrushchev's often-quoted (but seldom-cited) declaration that the survivors would envy the dead.

Likutov (1985:39), in an officially approved Soviet publication, claims:

> The Soviet Union has repeatedly pointed out that all talk about a "limited nuclear war" is extremely dangerous and utterly divorced from reality. Can one seriously talk about any limited nuclear war whatsoever? For it must be clear to everyone that the aggressor's actions would inevitably and instantly invite a devastating retaliatory blow from the side that is attacked. Only utterly irresponsible persons can claim that nuclear war can be fought according to some kind of rules worked out in advance, whereby nuclear missiles will go off under a "gentleman's agreement," hitting only specific targets and leaving the population intact. There can be no such thing as a "limited" nuclear war. There is no guarantee that such a war, once started, would not develop into a global nuclear catastrophe.
>
> The USSR also totally rejects the concept of a "protracted" nuclear war and the possibility of winning such a war, for if the potential of destruction now available in the world should be put into action the human race would probably cease to exist.

Instead of accepting such public pronouncements, Pipes examines Soviet military documents and concludes that the USSR has adopted "a policy diametrically opposed to that adopted in the United States by the predominant community of civilian strategists: not deterrence but victory, not sufficiency in weapons but superiority, not retaliation but offensive action" (1977:31).

There are, however, contradictory positions on nuclear policy in *both* superpowers. One thing is clear: Military planners in both the Soviet Union and the United States do not plan to lose any kind of war, nor *can* they plan to do so. The development of winning scenarios and warfighting strategies is a primary task of any war planner's job.

Such plans have been around since long before the recent round of warfighting strategies. In a briefing in 1954 by the commander of the Strategic Air Command, for example, Navy officers were informed of plans to reduce the Soviet Union to a "smoking, radiating ruin in two hours." Ironically, the Pipes argument (and similar arguments by others, such as Colin Gray) has resulted in the shift of warfighting talk in the United States from the military to the political arena.

A related issue is that of survival. The assumption that with proper planning and preventive action a large proportion of the population would survive a nuclear conflict is one of the most questionable assumptions of all. It goes against the grain, of course, to suggest that nothing can be done in the event that deterrence should fail. Many people rebel against the suggestion that if the holocaust comes, we should just lie down and die. There is, in fact, a strong survivalist movement, in which people are building shelters in remote areas and stockpiling supplies.

The major problem with the assumption of survival is that increased confidence in the ability to fight and win a nuclear war and to survive may increase the tendency to view the use of nuclear weapons as a real foreign policy option. We may never know with any real certainty what would happen if a nuclear war were actually to occur unless it happened, and then most of us would not be around to discuss which theories were correct. The more we learn, however, the more illusory any hope for survival appears.

Still another element of the concept of limited nuclear war is the argument that certain kinds of nuclear weapons and policies are moral, which implies that others are immoral. We have already discussed the difference between offensive and defensive military actions in the context of reciprocity. Few people would raise moral objections about defensive actions, although there is a strong nonviolent tradition in most of the world's major religions which suggests that military action is never appropriate. Most nations attempt to foster the impression that all of their military activities are defensive in nature and that their enemies' actions are offensive and aggressive.

In arguing for the notion of limited nuclear war, some strategic planners have raised another moral issue: the idea that plans to strike cities, rather than military targets, are immoral. Thomas Powers (1982:86) points out that "it is a kind of unwritten rule among strategic planners that one does not target 'population per se.' " Even in the earlier period of the nuclear age, American war planners used circumlocutions to insist to themselves that they were not directing weapons at people. As McNamara attempted, in 1962, to move toward a flexible response, an SIOP was developed that included a "low-option attack" on Soviet nuclear forces alone. It still would have killed millions of Soviet citizens, of course. In shades of Orwellian nukespeak, urban-industrial targets were called war supporting industry and targets critical to recovery, in order to make their planned destruction sound less ghastly.

In his 1984 Report to Congress, Weinberger argued in favor of funding counterforce weapons by claiming that the "mass destruction of civilians . . . is neither moral nor prudent" (1983:55). Such a theory fails to point out, however, that the collateral damage from a counterforce exchange would wreak such ecological havoc that everyone would be at risk, and that the distinction between counterforce and countervalue attacks is a mere academic exercise.

One should not necessarily jump to the conclusion that the advocates of counterforce weapons are themselves immoral, even if (from a personal point of view) one considers counterforce strategies immoral. A fundamental sociological insight into the nature of morality is that morality is not simply related to individual decisions, because people with good intentions often make decisions that have immoral consequences. On the other hand, it would be naive in terms of the overall picture to argue that strategists and policymakers are always pure in their motives. We have been deliberately deceived too many times. But even if they had only good intentions, they might come up with the same results, because of the structural limitations of morality. There is a tendency in U.S. culture to overemphasize the psychological factors involved in the arms race—fear, greed, etc. Although all of those elements are involved here, the *structure* of the arms race itself provides sufficient cause for it to continue. Simply replacing a few individuals with others who are of high moral standing would probably not solve the problem, which stems from the bureaucratic organization of ritual reciprocity.

Nor is deterrence theory a matter of party politics; it is an establishment line with remarkable continuity over time and across party lines. The experience of Jimmy Carter is an informative one. Powers (1982a:83–84) argues that when Carter took office in January of 1977,

> he probably would have done away with nuclear weapons altogether given the choice. . . . He took office with a visceral dislike of the vast, indiscriminate power of nuclear weapons. In a briefing at Blair House shortly before his inauguration, he astonished the Joint Chiefs of Staff with a suggestion that we could make do with a retaliatory force of 200 nuclear weapons.

As an outsider, Carter was viewed with intense suspicion by the Pentagon, but following an extended debate and study, the Carter administration gradually came into line. According to Powers, "shifting to 'realistic' planning for limited war, so alarming to the general public, was not anything Carter or his advisers *chose* to do. They were pushed every step of the way by the weapons themselves" (ibid.:84). It was not simply the *weapons*, of course, but the arms race ritual with all of its actors, technological imperatives, and bureaucratic organization.

The Assumption of National Interests

What, in the final analysis, is worth the risk of nuclear war? One's answer to that question will be related to one's position on the assumptions already discussed in this chapter. If one believes that nuclear war and its consequences can be limited, one is more likely to believe that a nuclear response to threats to national interests are worth the costs. The arguments in favor of that position are well known: Better Dead than Red, better to risk nuclear war than to "succumb to communist bullies."

Deterrence policies have, in fact, served the national interests of both superpowers in that they have helped keep them from a nuclear exchange thus far. The value of deterrence cannot be discounted. On the other hand, the definitions of deterrence that have developed in recent decades, and the actions taken as a result of them, have increased the frequency of the very factors we have identified as the origins of the arms race: reciprocal belligerence, fear and mistrust, bureaucratic entrenchment and expansion of the military-industrial complex, and destructive ritual behavior. Deterrence defined as an ever-spiraling arms race has increased international tensions and conflicts, and has swollen the globe's warmaking machinery to gargantuan proportions.

A central issue we have identified is the existence of an evil enemy who justifies an arms buildup. As one Reagan administration official put it, "The threat of political coercion is infinitely more important than the threat of nuclear war."

The question is, then, what would constitute a sufficient threat to justify the risk of nuclear war? An attack on an area of vital interest? An invasion of a close ally? The use of conventional weapons or nuclear weapons? These are not idle questions, although they are too seldom taken seriously.

Any individual's answer to those questions would depend, of course, on the way in which he or she framed the issue and the assumptions with which the potential outcomes of a nuclear war would be evaluated. If one believes that a nuclear war could be fought like a conventional war, in a rational manner and on a limited basis, then the nuclear threshold might be rather low. If, however, one believes that a nuclear war could not be won, fought rationally, or contained, then *any* consideration of the use of nuclear weapons appears foolish.

The issues raised in this chapter call the rationality, if not the morality, of nuclear weapons use into question. We have, indeed, created a nuclear cage that has trapped us all. The nuclear weapons issue is not simply an issue of freedom, but of existence itself. The democracy for which we would sacrifice lives is not protected by those nuclear weapons, either. As Richard Falk (1982) argues, the very existence of nuclear weapons interferes with democratic governance in fundamental ways. It results in unsurpassed reification of social structures and turns democracy on its head. Falk contends that nuclear weapons thus endanger democratic structures by granting to a fallible, flawed human being or a small, hidden inner group of advisors an awesome capability:

> Traditionally, divine right prerogatives even if pathologically abused could only produce limited damage. . . . Increasingly, the leadership of the main nuclear powers possesses a capacity for destruction commensurate with what traditional religions attributed to the divine, a capacity to cause in the fullest sense a global or human apocalypse. (ibid.:58–59)

Similarly, Lifton argues that it is no accident that 1950s McCarthyism was associated with efforts to guard the unprecedented power and anxiety created by nuclear weaponry.

Although the concept of deterrence may have some validity in the short run, it cannot be seen as a permanent solution. This fact has been recognized by a wide spectrum of individuals, including President Reagan.[7] There is, in fact, considerable historical evidence to suggest that when deterrence means military buildup, the most likely result is eventual war (see Richardson 1960; Richardson et al. 1960; Wilkinson 1981). Indeed, Martin Luther King, Jr., could have been talking about the superpowers' contemporary strategic policies when he said that we must all learn to live together as brothers and sisters, or all die together as fools.

CHAPTER NINE

Civil Defense and Crisis Relocation

A reasonably effective crisis relocation program could result in total survival of over 80 percent of the population.

—Federal Emergency Management Agency,
Questions and Answers on Crisis Relocation Planning

He said, "If there are enough shovels to go around, everybody's going to make it." The shovels were for digging holes in the ground, which would be covered somehow or other with a couple of doors and with three feet of dirt thrown on top, thereby providing adequated fallout shelters for the millions who had been evacuated from America's cities to the countryside. "It's the dirt that does it," he said.

—Robert Scheer, interview with Pentagon official
T.K. Jones in *With Enough Shovels*

One natural response to the nuclear threat is to seek ways to protect oneself should deterrence fail. Few issues are as emotionally volatile as that of civil defense, because it raises questions about one's own survival and the fate of one's friends and family. For some, civil defense is an essential element of a nation's overall deterrent; for others, it is a reminder that deterrence may not last indefinitely. Taking steps to protect the U.S. population during and after a nuclear war is the responsibility of the Federal Emergency Management Agency (FEMA), created in 1979 (Murphey 1982) to coordinate responses to both natural and human-made disasters.

FEMA officials claim that more than 80 percent of the U.S. population would survive a major nuclear attack if residents of high-risk areas were evacuated, upon warning that attack was imminent, through a crisis relocation plan (Federal Emergency Management Agency 1980d:5).[1] Civil defense experts are trying to turn around a sense of fatalism that has developed in the nuclear age. As one British expert, Eric Alley,[2] puts it, although the experience of a nuclear war "would be terrible beyond imagination and description . . . there is much that can be done to make sure that it would not mean the end of life for our country" (1982:101). According to Alley, millions of survivors would have adequate resources to rebuild the country; the real danger facing the survivors of a holocaust is psychological. "Self-pity and a high sense of tragedy are going to build nothing at all. They must be thrown out, for the survivors have to become builders, and they will have the means, the health, and the strength to build again" (ibid.).

THE IDEA OF CIVIL DEFENSE

Civil defense is an old concept, but it has taken on new significance since the aerial bombing of Great Britain by Germany in World War I. It is a passive defense as opposed to an active defense, such as a ballistic missile defense system.

During World War II the U.S. government established an Office of Civilian Defense, whose function was to develop plans to protect the population in the event of a direct attack on the United States. The major U.S. civil defense program was developed under the Kennedy administration; the president called it an "insurance we trust will never be needed—but insurance which we could never forgive ourselves for foregoing in the event of catastrophe" (Kennedy 1961:9–10). A community shelter program was initiated, and civil defense expenditures jumped from $138 million in 1961 to $580 million in 1962 (see Murphey 1982:202; Kerr 1983:116ff). Although the shelter program was proclaimed with fanfare, it set off a stormy debate and was essentially abandoned by 1964. As Kerr (1983:193) put it, the program was "rendered largely irrelevant by the doctrine of mutual assured destruction." Many critics of civil defense feel that such an effort to protect the population could be perceived by the nation's adversaries as a provocative act designed to undermine the deterrent policy.

A 1977 study by the U.S. Defense Department examined a number of civil defense options and evaluated their potential effectiveness. As shown in Table 9.1,[3] the study concluded that in the event of a heavy, mid-1980s attack on U.S. military and urban-industrial targets, about 20 percent of

Table 9.1 Projected Effectiveness of Civil Defense Programs

Program	Percent of Survivors	Cost/Survivor/10 Years ($)
No civil defense	20	0
Fallout shelters	54	10
Blast shelters	79	74
Evacuation	89	31

Source: Federal Emergency Management Agency (1980h).

the U.S. population would survive if there were no civil defense program at all. A blast shelter program for high-risk areas, at an estimated cost of over $60 billion, was deemed too expensive.[4] The preferred scenario, later called the Crisis Relocation Plan, is evacuation. According to the study, crisis relocation would save approximately 89 percent of the U.S. population at an average annual cost of about $230 million in fiscal years 1980 through 1984 (in 1979 dollars). The Reagan administration revived civil defense in earnest, with an emphasis on crisis relocation.

CRISIS RELOCATION PLANNING

Crisis relocation planning (CRP) is based on three assumptions: (1) there would be some advanced warning of the nuclear attack; (2) the primary targets would be military and industrial installations (rather than cities); and (3) by relocating the population from high-risk areas before an attack, people would have to contend only with radioactive fallout, and not with the direct effects of the explosion, and could therefore survive. Responding to a nuclear attack would be similar to reacting to any natural disaster.

The first assumption holds that any attack would probably be preceded by a period of heightened international tensions and posturing on both sides, perhaps even a conventional military conflict. U.S. intelligence forces would be able to detect Soviet preparations for attack because of troop movements, increased military preparations, and radio traffic (all of which are monitored by U.S. agencies).

The second and third assumptions suggest that people evacuated from high-risk areas can escape the most devastating effects of a nuclear war. One FEMA pamphlet (1980h:2) states that "because a distance of as little as ten miles will remove people from the blast and heat effects of a nuclear explosion, FEMA feels it is prudent to develop plans to relocate high risk area populations." However, as Leaning and Keyes (1984:6) contend, "At the heart of the argument supporting CRP for nuclear war lies the belief that the disaster resulting from a nuclear attack is fundamentally similar to other kinds of natural and manmade disasters."

The FEMA publication *In Time of Emergency: A Citizen's Handbook on Emergency Management* explains that

> people can protect themselves against fallout radiation, and have a good chance of surviving it, by staying inside a fallout shelter. In most cases, the fallout radiation level outside the shelter would decrease rapidly enough to permit people to leave the shelter within a few days. . . .
> Information from trained radiological monitors, using special instruments to detect and measure the intensity of fallout radiation, would be used to advise people when it is safe to leave shelter. (FEMA 1980d:7)

Another FEMA publication[5] suggests that it may not be too late to protect yourself even in the "unlikely" event that "your first warning of an enemy attack might be the flash of a nuclear explosion in the sky." "If there should be a nuclear flash, . . . take cover *instantly* in the best place you can find," the pamphlet instructs.

> You should take cover in any kind of a building, a storm cellar or fruit cellar, a subway station, or tunnel—or even in a ditch or culvert alongside the road, a highway underpass, a storm sewer, a cave or outcropping or rock, a pile of heavy materials, a trench or other excavation. Even getting under a parked automobile, bus or train, or a heavy piece of furniture, would protect you to some extent. If no cover is available, simply lie down on the ground and curl up. (FEMA 1980d:14–15)

An entire chapter of *In Time of Emergency* is devoted to fallout shelters—how to identify existing shelters and how to build one in your home. Options include permanent basement shelters, outside shelters, and even a "preplanned snack bar shelter" (a snack bar built of bricks or concrete blocks that can be converted into a fallout shelter by lowering a false ceiling into place).

About four hundred high-risk areas have been identified in the United States, encompassing about 35 percent of the population but less than 15 percent of the nation's total land mass. Each high-risk area has been assigned a designated host area, in which the government has identified potential shelters in schools, colleges, armories, and other nonresidential buildings. If officials became convinced that a nuclear attack was imminent, the president could declare a state of emergency. Extensive plans are already in place for how the evacuation would take place, where people would go in the designated host areas, what provisions would be made for enhancing fallout protection, and so forth. Copies of the plans would be distributed in local newspapers in the event of a crisis. They would include instructions on evacuation routes, what to do before leaving home,[6] and what to take when relocating to a safer area. Employees of "critical governmental and industrial organizations" located in high-risk areas would be designated as key workers and would commute from their designated reception areas to work twelve-hour shifts in the high-risk areas.

Upon arrival in a host area, evacuees would proceed to an assigned reception area (by following signs with the number of the last digit on their auto license plate), where they would register with the authorities. Those assigned to public buildings would be instructed to

> elect a leader and form working groups to help local officials and volunteers with such tasks as cooking and feeding services, providing water supply, cleaning up trash and garbage, maintaining order, assuring quiet during sleeping hours, organizing recreation and religious activities, arranging medical care for the sick and assisting the handicapped. (ibid.:55)

The next task would be to construct fallout shelters. As stated in *In Time of Emergency,*

> Upgrading existing structures by piling earth outside them can be done by adding an average of one cubic yard of earth for each 10 square feet of shelter space to be developed (more for some buildings, less for others). Moving a cubic yard of earth is not easy—it's about 80 to 100 buckets full—but can be done if everyone works for their survival. (ibid.:56)

A chapter on shelter living discusses what supplies and equipment are needed for life in a shelter, including food, water, sanitation supplies, and medicines. A subsequent chapter examines emergency care of the sick and injured, providing basic first aid information, since medical care may not be available. In addition to instructions about how to treat people who have stopped breathing, have received burns, or are in shock, there is a section on radiation sickness. Because there is no cure for radiation sickness, the treatment is symptomatic: aspirin for headaches, salt-and-soda solution or kaolin and pectin for diarrhea, and so forth.

The bottom line of civil defense plans is that with a proper plan, adequate knowledge of weapons effects and first aid, and the will to survive, a major proportion of the population will survive. Such a proposition is an essential component of the system of deterrence itself.

CIVIL DEFENSE AS A COMPONENT OF DETERRENCE

> An effective civil defense program is an important element of our total defense effort.
>
> —President Lyndon Johnson, quoted in Office of Civil Defense, *Civil Defense, U.S.A.: A Programmed Orientation to Civil Defense*

For many who work on crisis relocation and other civil defense plans, the only purpose of the plans is to save lives if a nuclear war occurs. Civil defense is, however, a central component of overall deterrence policy. Civil defense programs play a key role in the psychology of deterrence and constitute a logical extension of nuclear warfighting strategies (see Mavor 1982; "Civil Offense" 1978). As Jennifer Leaning (1982:94) put it, "The validity of the concept [of waging nuclear war] is based on the notion of survivability. . . . Without civil defense, the U.S. military cannot use its weapons. Civil defense closes the loop in U.S. offensive strategy." The deterrent role of civil defense has been a key argument of its proponents from the time of the Kennedy administration[7] to the Peace through Strength perspective of the Reagan administration. When President Reagan outlined his civil defense proposal in March 1982, he claimed that "civil defense as an element of the strategic balance, should assist in maintaining perceptions that this balance is favorable to the United States."[8] It makes less sense within a mutual assured destruction doctrine, which relies upon the vulnerability of the populations of both sides.

Advocates of nuclear warfighting doctrines, including President Reagan, point to the Soviet civil defense program as yet another indication of the Soviets' rejection of M.A.D. The president claims that the Soviets have practiced evacuations of their cities: "We learned that in one summer alone, they took over 20 million young people out of the cities into the country to give them training in just living off the countryside" (quoted in Scheer 1982:106). The CIA claims, however, that there is no evidence that the Soviets ever carried out practice evacuations (ibid.). Nonetheless, the Soviet civil defense program has been cited by many proponents of an American program as evidence that the Soviets have a warfighting strategy (see Goure 1983).

A 1982 Reagan administration proposal for a $4.3 billion, seven-year civil defense program encountered many of the same objections raised about civil defense in the 1960s. A *New York Times* editorial (3 April 1982) argued that "the mischief in this kind of planning goes beyond the waste of money" and linked it to the "idea that it is feasible to fight a general nuclear war and to 'survive.' That idea is not merely irresponsible; it is mad." Scheer (1982) discovered that the person responsible for the civil defense commitment, whom the *New York Times* called "mad" and said "should be fired," was Ronald Reagan himself. According to two Reagan appointees in the Office of Management and Budget interviewed by Scheer, the president intervened personally in the development of the proposal, overruling his own Office of Management and Budget and even Air Force General David C. Jones, then-chairman of the Joint Chiefs of Staff (ibid.:108). Reagan had been persuaded of the importance of the program by presidential counselor Edwin Meese III, an old friend of FEMA director Louis Guiffrida.

The civil defense program is important to Reagan because it is an integral component of a nuclear warfighting strategy. The Soviet Union's development of a civil defense program is somewhat puzzling, however; civil defense would seem to be in direct contradiction with consistent statements by Soviet leaders through the years echoing Khrushchev's sentiment that the survivors would envy the dead.

THE SOVIET CIVIL DEFENSE PROGRAM

In a popular joke that reportedly circulates in the Soviet Union, one citizen asks another, "What does the government expect us to do in the event of a nuclear war?" The response is, "Put a sheet over your head and walk slowly toward the nearest graveyard." "Why slowly?" the inquirer asks. "So as not to provoke a panic." The Soviet program's title, Grazhdanskaya Oborona ("civil defense"), has been dubbed "grob" (taken from the first two letters of each part of the program's name). Grob is also the Russian word for coffin (ibid.:182).

Despite the apparent hesitancy by many Soviet citizens to take the idea of civil defense seriously, the program has a substantial budget.[9] British Soviet expert Chris Donnelly argues that the Soviet civil defense effort is "a useful tool of policy," and that the Soviets have a nuclear warfighting strategy. However, he feels that the effectiveness of their program should not be exaggerated. "We believe," Donnelly writes, "that the Soviet CD effort is considerable, but still far from adequate to give sufficient protection to the country for strategic nuclear war to be considered as a viable option" (1982:254). Fred Kaplan (1978) insists that although the Soviet civil defense program looks good on paper, it is weak and full of discrepancies.

The Soviet program grows out of a historic commitment to defense against repeated invasions, especially those that occurred during World War II. Leonid Brezhnev called for an upgrading of the Soviet civil defense system in 1966, which has since been integrated into the overall Soviet civil defense system (Donnelly 1982:260). According to Donnelly's (1982:262) study of Soviet civil defense publications, protection of the Soviet population in times of war is to be achieved by a number of measures, including early warning, dispersal and evacuation, shelters, food and water stockpiles, medical services, and rescue operations in areas of destruction.

At the core of Soviet civil defense efforts are (1) an evacuation plan to move people out of the cities and into the countryside, and (2) blast shelters for key leadership and essential segments of the workforce. Although the Soviets have a more extensive blast shelter program than the United States has, it accommodates only a small fraction of the total Soviet population. John M. Weinstein (visiting research professor at the U.S. Army War College's Strategic Studies Institute) notes that

> Soviet evacuation plans call for 17 million urban residents to walk 30 miles (1.5 mph for 20 hours) and then build expedient protection. How the very

young, the very old, and the sick are to make such formidable progress (while carrying two weeks' worth of food, water, and supplies) is not clear. . . . A heavy concentration of urban citizens results in certain obstacles to successful evacuation. . . . Citizens from [Moscow and Leningrad] would face major problems evacuating to rural reception centers or areas suitable for the construction of expedient shelters. Finally, how evacuees in expedient shelters would survive the higher levels of radioactive fallout that would result if the U.S. retaliatory strike included ground bursts is unclear and is seldom addressed by those who assert the effectiveness of Soviet civil defense. (Weinstein 1982:2)

Despite the many problems with the Soviet civil defense scheme, it is taken very seriously by many in the Reagan administration, including Thomas K. Jones, deputy under secretary of defense for research and engineering, Strategic and Theatre Nuclear Forces. When interviewed by Scheer (1982:22), Jones produced pictures from Soviet manuals showing Soviet shelters "that were little more than holes in the ground covered with some thatching." "This little primitive-looking thing in this picture," Jones explained,

> is a Soviet-designed shelter. . . . In essence, you dig a hole, take lumber, small saplings or something like that, and build this thing and cover it with dirt . . . that cuts the lethal area of that megaton weapon down to about two square miles. . . . [The] Russians have twenty to thirty designs. The idea is you pick a design to match the material you have on hand. (ibid.:22–23)

Jones believes that the United States should emulate the Soviet model: "Turns out," he postulates, "with the Russian approach, if there are enough shovels to go around, everybody's going to make it" (ibid.:23).

It is hard to reconcile the Soviets' program with their claims that a nuclear war is not survivable (see Leebaert 1981). As noted in Chapter Eight, there are contradictory policies in both superpowers on the survivability of a nuclear war: The politicians usually say it is impossible to survive a nuclear war, whereas military planners must operate on the assumption that survival is possible. This contradiction in Soviet and American policies can probably best be understood as a reflection of two factors: (1) the ambivalence of most people toward civil defense and (2) internal debates within both superpower governments. Even those who think that a nuclear war is unwinnable and unsurvivable have trouble accepting the thought of just giving up and dying if a nuclear war should occur—it seems to go against our instincts of self-preservation.

CRITICISMS OF CIVIL DEFENSE

Few government programs have provoked as much controversy as civil defense, which highlights public fears about a nuclear holocaust. A number of themes have persisted over the decades in criticisms of civil defense.

First, many critics argue that civil defense diverts attention from the real issue—the need for nuclear disarmament—and provides a false sense of security. California Department of Health Services Director Beverlee A. Myers claims that it would be unethical even to participate in the creation of plans that create the "illusion that the public health community can offer any assurance of health protection" in the event of a nuclear war. She argues that "to plan for a hoax is a disservice [to the people of her state]" (quoted in Scheer 1982:107).

FEMA's crisis relocation plans have provoked much satire and nervous laughter. One demonstrator at the June 12, 1982, rally in New York City carried an umbrella labeled Fallout Shelter, and someone has created a poster that looks much like the fallout shelter signs, except that it reads "Shellout Falter." There is even a *nuclear war manual for dogs* (Kurtz and Gilliam 1983).

A second criticism is that a strong civil defense program can be perceived as provocative by a nation's adversaries. Advocates often hold a double standard, saying that our nation's program is purely humanitarian and designed to save lives, while theirs is an act of aggression. As Weinstein (1982:9) puts it,

> If our preparations to save Americans are defensive and non-threatening, why aren't the preparations of the Soviets viewed the same way? Is it not likely that the Soviets will view American civil defense plans in the same manner that we view theirs: as a threatening capability that betrays sinister intentions to pursue a warfighting scenario? In other words, the distinction between offense and defense is neither unambiguous nor mutually recognizable. Serious attempts by the Soviets or the Americans to pursue ambitious civil defense programs may contribute to fear and uncertainty about the adversary's intentions, thereby placing a hair trigger upon the arsenals of each and perhaps contributing to the very circumstances each seeks to avoid.

Erich Fromm and Michael Maccoby (1962:89) suggest that "the more credible we make our resolve to strike first, the more the Russians will expect us to attack during a crisis, and hence the more they will be likely to launch a preemptive strike." Further, we must look at the potential consequences of actually implementing a crisis relocation plan. One of the warning signs that the Soviets are preparing an attack would be the evacuation of their cities. It is unlikely that such an event, as any defensive measure, could be perceived as anything but threatening to the other side.

When civil defense is perceived as an element of deterrence, it can also be interpreted as providing a shift in the balance of power. The introduction of a serious civil defense system in one country might be met with an increase in the level of offensive armaments on the other side. Admiral Noel Gayler (1983) argues, however, that the effort to use civil defense plans to tip the strategic balance are based on false assumptions. He contends that civil defense is harmful because it "generates a mind-set toward nuclear war."

A third theme expounded by the critics of civil defense (and perhaps the most serious criticism) is that civil defense proponents do not understand the extent of the damage that could result from a major nuclear exchange. Although many civil defense planners are highly intelligent, a survey conducted in the early 1960s (Rose 1963) found that the more educated individuals were, the less likely they were to say they would build a fallout shelter in the event of a nuclear attack. The major flaw in the assumptions of civil defense plans is their reliance upon specific effects of individual nuclear explosions and not on the widespread environmental effects of nuclear war. Proponents respond that their critics overestimate the effects of a nuclear war and use scare tactics to mislead the public. If a nuclear exchange would result in global climatic catastrophe, however, even the most elaborate system of civilian protection would be worthless. Any survivors of a nuclear war, on any part of the planet, might emerge from their shelters into a long, dark, radioactive nuclear winter only to face slow starvation in a hostile climate.

Even before the nuclear winter theory was advanced, Leaning (1982) provided a thorough critique of civil defense assumptions in her testimony before a congressional subcommittee. According to Leaning, if the Soviets were to attack, they would probably attempt to destroy major military installations and industrial plants. Approximately two-thirds of the U.S. population (about 145 million people) would be directly affected by the blast effects of weapons hitting those targets (ibid.:96). Beyond the staggering logistical problems involved in moving such a large number of people in a three-to-five-day period, such a migration would create tremendous public health problems.

A study of bombing victims in Northern Ireland conducted from 1963 to 1977 found that there was an increase in criminal and homicidal behavior among the victims. Evacuation plans for New York City call for about 7.5 million people to relocate during a five-day period. New York City experiences an average of 21.6 murders, 44.5 violent rapes, 520.5 aggravated assaults, and 2,733.6 burglaries during a five-day period. It is a city of well over a million handguns, according to police department estimates. As Leaning puts it, "The usual forces for law and order will be so occupied helping the population cope with an extraordinary situation that they will have less time and attention to spend on monitoring and controlling more deviant behavior" (ibid.:98). Moreover, people not normally prone to violent behavior may react more violently under the stress of the situation, as witnessed during the 1974 shortages at gasoline pumps around the country.

Once people are located in shelters, the problems have just begun. Each shelter will have to be stocked with food and water for a thirty-day period, and waste material will have to be stored in the shelter, resulting in an increased risk of odor pollution and disease. Air ventilation will present serious problems. Since radioactivity can pass through standard commercial air systems, the shelter may actually receive radioactivity. Difficulties in maintaining reasonable temperatures in the shelter would compound the ongoing medical needs of the sheltered population. One FEMA plan calls for body bags for each shelter for storage of the bodies of those who die during the thirty-day period.

Psychological stress in the shelter would be severe, with people of different ethnicities and classes forced to live together in cramped quarters. The likelihood of conflicts over food, water, space, and other scarce resources would be great. "Even very stable people will find their equilibrium stressed by the tremendous social disruption, disorientation about future security, anger and grief at the turmoil and destruction, guilt about personal behavior" (ibid.:99; cf. Abrams 1981). Under such conditions, Soviet plans for holes covered with dirt seem a cruel joke.

Finally, Leaning (1982:101) suggests that those who survive "will not recognize their world when they emerge from the shelters. . . . Fires and blast effects may have destroyed or damaged much of the rural environment. Radioactive contamination of the land and water will present an incessant, uncertain hazard."

Meeting the most basic human needs will be a major undertaking, with shortages of shelter, food, and water, primitive sanitary conditions, a thriving insect population, and millions of decomposing corpses (both human and animal). Diseases that are now controlled (e.g., cholera and typhus) would run rampant. Recent analyses of Hiroshima data suggest that current estimates of the health impact of radiation effects should be at least doubled (ibid.:103; cf. Marshall 1981).

Almost 80 percent of the food production in the United States would be destroyed in a nuclear attack, since most food is produced in high-risk areas. With the normal means of food distribution certain to be destroyed during the war, the scarcity of food would be a catastrophic problem. Within six months, all stored grain would have been eaten, and the ability to produce new food supplies would be minimal, in part because the major components of American food production (such as fertilizer, pesticides, heavy machinery, and irrigation) would be nonexistent. Thus, Leaning concludes that the post-attack world would be characterized by persistent famine.

Severe alterations in the ecosystem were anticipated even before the nuclear winter studies, by which previous estimates of ecological damage pale in comparison. It might take at least thirty years for the ozone layer to regenerate (National Research Council 1975, 1985), during which time "humans and animals would sustain third-degree burns on exposed surfaces after one hour outdoors" (Leaning 1982:106). "The post-attack terrain may well be burnt barren of vegetation, stripped of animal life, infested by insects, and blistered by the unfiltered ultraviolet rays of the sun" (ibid.:107).

In the midst of such a hostile environment, it is likely that large numbers of people would simply lose the psychological will to live. Dazed by the vicissitudes of daily survival, weak from illness and disease, overtaken by grief from the loss of family, loved ones, homes, jobs, and so forth, it is likely that a major proportion of the surviving population would simply be unable to cope.

What Leaning presents, however, is virtually a best-case scenario that assumes that crisis relocation will work as planned and ignores the effects of a nuclear winter (not yet discovered at the time of her testimony). What is more likely, recent studies suggest, is that each of these problems would be compounded dramatically by the destruction of the ecosphere and the inability of life to survive under the harsh environmental conditions. Given such disastrous scenarios, it is unlikely that even the most successful crisis relocation program would be of much help. It is doubtful that most alive in the post-attack world would be grateful.

SUMMARY

The highly controversial issue of civil defense was discussed in this chapter primarily in terms of U.S. and Soviet efforts to develop measures to protect a proportion of their populations in the event of a nuclear war. The Federal Emergency Management Agency (FEMA), which has responsibility for civil defense in the United States, claims that more than 80 percent of the U.S. population could be saved in a nuclear war if high-risk areas were evacuated. Most civil defense planners emphasize the importance of overcoming a tendency toward fatalism and developing a will to survive after a nuclear attack.

The idea of civil defense is an ancient one, although it has taken on a new importance in the twentieth century as civilians have become targets of warfare. In the United States, a community shelter program was initiated during the Kennedy administration but was quietly abandoned. It was replaced in the 1970s by crisis relocation planning (CRP) after a defense department study estimated that CRP could save 89 percent of the population at a relatively low cost.

CRP is based on three assumptions: that there would be advance warning of an attack; that the primary targets would be military and industrial; and that relocating people from about four hundred high-risk areas would eliminate the need to protect them from blast and heat effects—with protection from fallout, they would survive.

Although many who work on civil defense plans see the purpose of the plans being only to save lives in the event of a nuclear war, policy-makers see the civil defense program as a central component of an overall deterrence policy and, in recent years especially, of a nuclear warfighting strategy. The idea of fighting and prevailing in a nuclear war is based on the notion of survivability.

There is some debate about the implications of Soviet civil defense plans. Since a strong civil defense makes little sense except in the context of a warfighting strategy, some Peace through Strength advocates point to the Soviet program as an indicator of the Soviets' rejection of M.A.D. The Soviet program contradicts consistent statements by Soviet leaders through the years denying the possibility of fighting and winning a nuclear war.

Soviet civil defense plans also call for crisis relocation, but the plans primarily call for urban residents to walk out of the cities and construct their own makeshift shelters. There is some provision, as well, for blast shelters for key leadership. There is considerable debate as to the overall effectiveness of the Soviets' program.

A number of criticisms have been leveled at civil defense planning. First, some argue that it diverts attention from the real issue—the need for arms control—and provides a false sense of security. Second, critics argue that a strong civil defense program might be perceived as aggressive by a nation's adversaries. It may also be perceived as providing a shift in the balance of power, thus provoking an increase in the level of offensive armaments on the other side or an impetus to strike first. Third, critics contend that civil defense advocates do not understand the extent of the damage that would be caused by a major nuclear exchange. The major flaw in civil defense plans is their neglect of widespread environmental effects, most notably nuclear winter. No matter how efficiently the most thorough crisis relocation plans might be carried out, survivors would probably emerge from their shelters into a long, dark, radioactive nuclear winter, only to face slow starvation in a hostile climate. Problems created by shortages of shelter, food, and water, primitive sanitary conditions, a thriving insect population, and millions of decomposing corpses would be compounded by prolonged low-level exposure to radioactivity, freezing temperatures, and a decimated social structure. The most likely result is Khrushchev's prediction that the survivors would envy the dead.

CHAPTER TEN

"Star Wars": The Strategic Defense Initiative

> Up until now we have increasingly based our strategy of deterrence upon the threat of retaliation. But what if free people could live secure in the knowledge that their security did not rest upon the threat of instant U.S. retaliation to deter a Soviet attack; that we could intercept and destroy strategic ballistic missiles before they reached our soil or that of our allies?
>
> "National Security Address to the Nation,"
> —President Ronald Reagan,
> 23 March 1983

In the search for the elusive solution to the nuclear threat, President Reagan proposed (in March 1983) a program to render nuclear weapons impotent and obsolete. The president's proposal, the Strategic Defense Initiative (immediately dubbed Star Wars, much to the president's dismay), calls for a five-year, multi-billion dollar research, development, and testing program. Its long-term goal is to develop a ballistic missile defense system to protect the United States against attack by intercontinental ballistic missiles. Its short-term impact has been to provoke a storm of controversy.

The Strategic Defense Initiative (SDI) is more than a purely technical issue. It is a social and political issue, as well. It provides an instructive example of the social construction of reality and the confluence of reciprocal, bureaucratic, and ritualistic elements of the nuclear arms race. The social processes involved in the construction of knowledge are revealed in the rhetoric of the debate between the proponents and critics of SDI. The issue is one of framing and perspective, rather than of facts. Therefore, it is essential that we look at the assumptions behind the rhetoric.

THE CASE FOR SDI

A number of justifications for the SDI program have been put forth by its proponents. From their perspective, SDI is (1) a pragmatic political decision by the president, (2) a critique of deterrence theory, (3) the alleged failure of arms control, (4) a series of technological breakthroughs, and (5) the Soviet threat to U.S. land-based missiles.

Packaging a Program

According to Colonel Allan Myer, a member of the White House staff who helped write the president's SDI speech, the initial motivation for President Reagan's proposal was a pragmatic one. In some candid remarks at a 1984 conference at Texas A&M University,[1] Myer explained that the president's speech was originally designed to gain support in Congress for his military budget. The SDI section of the speech was added to increase public and media interest and to make a stronger case for the budget. Much of the research for the program was already underway; the address simply brought together a number of projects under the same rubric.

The SDI vision proclaimed by the president was thus primarily an effort to package a set of existing projects and present them in a more palatable manner for public consumption. The key selling point was that the new technologies would provide a *defensive* approach to the nuclear threat, as opposed to the "no defense" policy of Mutual Assured Destruction. SDI is consistent with the Peace through Strength orientation of the Reagan administration and its critique of assured destruction. At the same time, it uses a defensive military rhetoric and strategy. It combines two ideas that are sometimes in tension: (1) a hard-line approach that is (2) justified by its defensive nature. It is acceptable to be tough when merely engaged in a reciprocal response to an aggressive adversary.

The SDI strategy had actually been outlined earlier in a paper entitled "High Frontier: A New Option in Space," which was prepared by a major conservative think tank with close ties to the Reagan administration.[2] The paper presents a carefully outlined proposal for a project to sell ballistic missile defense (BMD) to the American public. The author states that a primary objective of the BMD sales pitch is

> to force a drastic reorientation of US arms control debate in such a way as to make it politically risky for BMD opponents to invoke alleged "arms control arguments" against a . . . BMD system. In fact, the project should unambiguously seek to recapture the term "arms control" and all of the idealistic images and language attached to this term.

The author argues that "BMD proponents should begin to stress nuclear disarmament as a new end-point, perhaps using such descriptors as 'arms control through BMD = nuclear disarmament.' " In discussing specific strategies, the author argues that the proposal is

> a radical approach that seeks to disarm BMD opponents either by stealing their language and cause (arms control), or putting them into a tough political corner through their explicit or *de facto* advocacy of classical anti-population war-crimes. Ideally, both tactical routes should seek to involve as many big names as possible.

The author points out that care should be taken in choosing who is to promote the program publicly. The group or person chosen would have to turn around the perception that "BMD is primarily a 'right-wing' cause because assent to a pro-BMD position generally means subscribing to a whole array of other 'conservative' pro-defense arguments or programs."[3] One option discussed in some detail is seeking the public support of someone like Henry Kissinger, who would appeal to liberals and centrists.

Most importantly, according to the author, the selling of SDI should consist of a "heavy overlay of theology, ethics, [and] 'high road' " rhetoric. According to the author, "Very little attention has ever been put into techniques for converting, or otherwise neutralizing, peace groups or arms controllers to a pro-BMD stance." The author suggests that a "quick co-opting of 'arms control' arguments is very important to the long-term survival of BMD," and that the program "will be driven by ethical urgency, rather than by technology availability." According to the proposal, "It is important to try to capture—and capitalize on—existing 'urgent' movements, of which the freeze is the most prominent example."

I have no information about the role of this proposal in the Reagan administration's strategies for promoting SDI, but two things suggest that it may have been influential: (1) the ongoing close consultative relationship between the think tank and the administration, and (2) the fact that the package put forth by the president and others in the administration capitalizes on exactly the arguments outlined in the think tank's plan.

Will Deterrence Work Forever?

Many proponents of SDI claim that it provides an alternative to U.S. policies that depend upon the threat of retaliation as the only defense against nuclear attack. Their claims are related to a second justification for SDI—the inherent flaws in current definitions of the doctrine of deterrence.

Ironically, in considering SDI the president asked some of the same questions of deterrence as his critics, especially, Can it work perfectly and forever? His conclusion was that it probably cannot. Leslie Gelb (1985b:1) writes that "Mr. Reagan's vision has done nothing less than to assault the core of nuclear philosophy, namely deterrence based on the threat of retaliation. He and his senior aides are saying that the 40 years of nuclear peace built on that threat cannot last and [that threat] is, in any event, immoral."

The moral argument figures strongly in the case for SDI presented by strategic planners uneasy about targeting Soviet cities. Weinberger (1983:55), for example, makes the argument in his 1984 Annual Report to Congress that there is a vast difference between cities and military targets:

> Some believe that we must threaten explicitly, even solely, the mass destruction of civilians on the adversary side, thus inviting a corresponding destruction of civilian populations on our side, and that such a posture will achieve stability in deterrence. This is incorrect. Such a threat is neither moral nor prudent. The Reagan Administration's policy is that under no circumstances may such weapons be used deliberately for the purpose of destroying populations.
>
> For this reason, we disagree with those who hold that deterrence should be based on nuclear weapons designed to destroy cities rather than military targets. Deliberately designing weapons aimed at populations is neither necessary nor sufficient for deterrence.

The defense secretary concludes that a weapons modernization program is necessary in order to develop accurate weapons that can hit military targets rather than cities. That logic sustains the conservative critique that assured destruction holds innocent civilians hostage. Lewis E. Lehrman (1985)[1] contends that a strategic defense would "enable us to abide by a just-war doctrine . . . which rightfully requires us to discriminate between innocent civilian and military targets."

According to former Air Force Secretary Hans Mark,[5] the president was quite disturbed by the U.S. Catholic Bishops' (National Conference of Catholic Bishops [NCCB] 1983) critique of the concept of deterrence and found aspects of their argument quite convincing. Mark claims that the bishops' critique was a major motivating factor in the president's decision to go ahead with the SDI proposal, which some of his advisors had been encouraging him to support for some time. As the president stated in his 23 March 1983 speech, "It is better to save lives than to avenge them."[6] George Ball (1985:38) concedes that the moral argument is an appealing one. "It is heartwarming to think that our weapons would no longer be used to kill people but only to shoot down weapons of the adversary. . . . It all seemed too good to be true—and, of course, it was."

In addition to the moral critique of deterrence, there is a practical one. Among the briefings the president received when he entered the Oval Office, according to Myer, none was more powerful than the one that described the American intelligence community's understanding of the Soviets' plan for a nuclear attack. Myer (1984) describes the president's response to the briefing this way:

> The president asked a question—I heard it with my own ears: "This M.A.D. concept has worked for about three decades. It's worked perfectly. And it *must* work perfectly, because if it doesn't work perfectly, it fails utterly. How long can we, the human race, expect deterrence to work perfectly? How long can we bank on perfection? . . . Unless you have perfection forever, you have catastrophe."

That sense of helplessness in the face of such a grave threat is one of the most difficult features of the nuclear cage; it creates cognitive dissonance, especially for the leaders who are given the authority and responsibility to protect the country and its citizens. Earlier questions about what to do if deterrence fails led to nuclear warfighting doctrines. The SDI is an attempt to respond to the same gnawing doubts.

The Failure of Arms Control

A third reason for the administration's support of SDI is that the president looked at the history of arms control and concluded that it has not controlled arms (ibid.). Furthermore, the president believes that arms control agreements cannot be verified and cannot be trusted because of Soviet violations (see Chapter Eleven). The president has never shown any confidence in the arms control process, largely because of his deep mistrust of the Soviets, and he has opposed every major arms control agreement between the superpowers. Furthermore, the record is quite clear: The arms control process has not solved the nuclear dilemma.

From the perspective of many proponents of SDI, a major reason for the failure of the arms control process is a series of alleged violations made by the Soviets. One violation they point to is the construction of a phased-array radar in the interior of the Soviet Union (in south-central Siberia). This type of radar, although permissible on a nation's periphery as part of an early warning system, is forbidden by the ABM treaty to be located in the interior of the United States or the USSR (see Jastrow 1984:24).

The conclusion of SDI proponents is that arms control is not the way out of the nuclear cage. As the president's speechwriter put it (Myer 1984), "In 50 years, we can expect to have half the number [of nuclear weapons] we now have, or one-third—even in the best case. If you agree up to that point, do you just throw up your hands and say, 'Hell, that's the best I can do?' Or do you sniff around for another alternative?" From the president's point of view, the Strategic Defense Initiative was the way out of the seemingly insolvable nuclear dilemma—and the experts told him it would work.

The Technologists' Proposal

Support for SDI has also been motivated by the conviction of several scientists, primarily working in weapons laboratories, that such a system is technically possible in the long run, provided sufficient resources are dedicated to research on the topic. Such a technological solution is especially appealing in a cultural milieu that places great faith in technology. The key to these technologies is the miniaturized computer (see Jastrow 1984:28ff.). The central characteristic of any ballistic missile defense is accuracy—one must be able to hit a rapidly moving target thousands of miles away. That task has been made possible only recently by the development of "smart missiles," which are programmed by miniature computers that can adjust the course of the missile to direct it toward its target. Some of the technology required for SDI is already in use in the new generation of counterforce weapons being deployed by the United States. Some proponents (see Brzezinski et al. 1985:29) contend that a two-layer defense could be deployed by the early 1990s and would be 90 percent effective.

The Soviet Threat

A final reason for the administration's decision to pursue SDI is the growth of the Soviet ICBM arsenals in the 1960s and 1970s, and the consequent vulnerability of American ICBMs and bombers. Jastrow (1984:25ff.) argues that two of the three legs of the U.S. strategic triad are now vulnerable to attack from the Soviet Union. Increased numbers and improved accuracy of Soviet ICBMs have resulted in a concern among many security analysts that a window of vulnerability has developed that would leave U.S. land-based missiles open to a Soviet attack. Despite the problems with that notion,[7] it is clear that the Soviet weapons program has decreased the number of U.S. warheads that would be available for a retaliatory strike.

Calculations of who is ahead and who is behind in the nuclear arms race have little to do with the actual outcome of a nuclear war, in which there would be no winners. What is "significant" are the comparative calculations that can be made about the nuclear capabilities of the two countries. From that perspective, there has been a shift from a clear preponderance of American superiority to a situation of relative parity. A U.S. space-based defense would provide a way to neutralize a portion of the Soviet arsenal. It would make little difference in the outcome of a nuclear conflict, but it would make a difference in the ongoing, ritualistic calculations carried out at the Pentagon—calculations that have an effect on the policymaking process. This principle can be seen in Payne's (1983:6) argument about another element of BMD, the hardening of targets against blast effects:

> In a sense, it does not ultimately matter whether HPD [hardened-point targets such as ICBM silos] can "really work" or not. What is critical is that BMD

can inject a sufficient degree of *uncertainty* into the Soviets' evaluation of their capability to strike U.S. retaliatory forces successfully so that they would never risk striking at U.S. strategic forces. . . . In other words, a U.S. BMD system for HPD need not perform flawlessly in order to achieve its primary purpose of enhancing deterrence stability.

Thus, according to Payne and others, the real purpose of SDI is not to replace deterrence with a new concept of defense, but to fortify the same old notions of deterrence with yet another layer of uncertainty. The rhetoric of SDI thus vacillates between visionary discussions about making nuclear weapons impotent and obsolete and the more pragmatic arguments that SDI would be a way of enhancing deterrence.

The sociological insight most important here is that *politicians*—especially President Reagan and Defense Secretary Weinberger—tend to make the more ideological, sweeping attacks on the notion of deterrence. Most scientists and military officials (who are more familiar with the technical characteristics of SDI), on the other hand, are more modest in their claims and argue from the basis that SDI would be a supplement to other aspects of an overall deterrent.

Convinced that SDI was potentially viable, President Reagan called for a $26 billion budget over a five-year period to investigate the feasibility of its deployment.

SDI: HOW IT IS SUPPOSED TO WORK

The Strategic Defense Initiative, as outlined by the president and his advisors, is a concept that involves the coordination and conceptual linking of a number of ongoing R&D projects. With the creation of the Strategic Defense Initiative Office (SDIO), more than ninety line items already in the Pentagon budget were unified into approximately five areas under the direction of Lt. General Abrahamson.[8] The proposed system is focused on a defense against ballistic missiles—short-range and especially ICBMs (it is not directed against cruise missiles or bombers, and is of only questionable value in defending against submarine-launched missiles). The system has three layers, each of which would engage weapons to disable the missiles in a different phase of their flight: the boost, midcourse, and reentry phases (see Figure 10.1). The weapons to be used to intercept missiles are sometimes divided into three categories on the basis of their speed: lasers (which travel at the speed of light), particle beams (which travel at almost the speed of light), and the slower, computer-guided (smart) projectiles (see Broad 1985c:19).

The first phase of ballistic missile flight, the boost phase, is the most crucial for missile defense, but this phase lasts only forty to three hundred seconds (Bowman 1986:20). Consequently, to disable missiles in their boost phase, they must be detected, a decision must be made to activate the de-

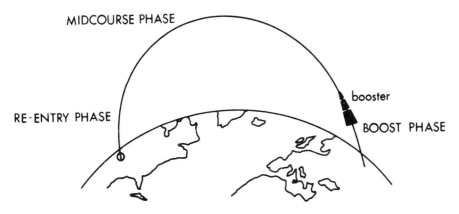

Figure 10.1   Phases of a ballistic missile defense.

fenses, and they must be tracked and hit, all within the span of a very few minutes. The boost phase is critical to defense, however, because there are fewer targets to attack at that point—the multiple warheads and decoys have not yet separated from each missile (see Bethe et al. 1984). Furthermore, the booster rocket is easier to track than the reentry vehicles because of its strong infrared signal, and it is a "softer" target, that is, easier to hit (UCS 1984:1). Defense against missiles in the boost phase would be based primarily on directed-energy technologies, such as particle beams and lasers (Daniel 1984).[9]

During the midcourse phase, directed-energy weapons or smart projectiles could be used, although the difficulties in disabling a missile in this stage are almost insurmountable. As the UCS (1984:2) report on space-based defenses puts it, "In the midcourse, the defense could be confronted with hundreds of thousands of objects, all of which would have to be tracked and intercepted, since discrimination between warheads and decoys would be impossible in the vacuum of space."

The third layer of the defensive strategy is a point defense, which involves attacking ICBMs during their reentry phase, as they return to the earth's atmosphere and speed toward their targets.

The engineering problems associated with the development of SDI weapons are mind-boggling but are also an intriguing challenge to the engineers working on the projects. Pentagon officials boast that the SDI program dwarfs research for both the Manhattan Project and the Apollo moon program (Broad 1985:19).

Laser Weapons

The technology behind laser weapons is based on the ancient knowledge that focused light can burn things. Archimedes reportedly used mirrors to concentrate sunlight and burn the fleet that was attacking Syracuse during the Peloponnesian War (Tsipis 1983:201ff.). Several types of laser weapons are currently in development. The chemical laser uses hydrogen (or deuterium) and fluorine to create the energy for the lasing light. Rockwell's Rocketdyne division in Los Angeles has developed a chemical laser called Sigma Tau, although it is still in an experimental stage (see Biddle 1985b:6). Another type of laser is the X-ray laser being developed by the Lawrence Livermore Laboratories. Despite the nonnuclear rhetoric of SDI, the X-ray laser channels nuclear explosions into laser rods that emit lethal bursts of radiation (Broad 1983:17).

Laser systems could be based in space on orbiting battle stations, on the ground, or on missiles that would be "popped up," or launched, when an attack is detected (see Figure 10.2). Orbiting battle stations could be at a low altitude of several hundred miles or in geosynchronous orbit at 22,500 miles. Such stations (in addition to being extremely expensive) would be very vulnerable to attack. A station in higher orbit (and therefore less susceptible to attack) would require a sighting telescope 100 to 150 meters in diameter—twenty or thirty times the size of the world's largest telescope (UCS 1984:2).

Presidential science advisor George Keyworth has supported the development of the ground-based laser, which would require a mirror stationed in space to reflect the laser back onto the target. The pop-up system is favored by physicist Edward Teller, who is associated with the Livermore

Figure 10.2 Ground-based laser system.

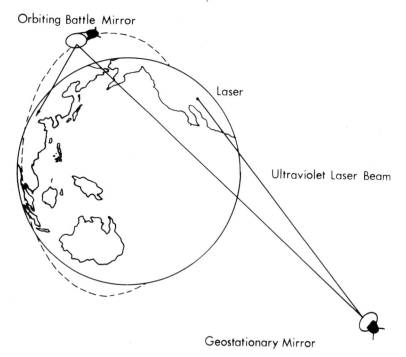

Orbiting Battle Mirror

Laser

Ultraviolet Laser Beam

Geostationary Mirror

Laboratories. Because of the earth's curvature and the short period of time in which ·missiles can be attacked in the boost phase, the weapon would probably have to be based on a new fleet of submarines stationed close to the Soviet Union (ibid.).

Particle-beam Weapons

Particle-beam weapons are similar to lasers, but instead of emitting light (photons), they direct high-energy particles toward a target. They have one advantage over lasers—one cannot shield against particle beams. But they have their own problems: They are very bulky; it is difficult to aim them; it is hard to tell if they have hit the target (they do not leave much of a "signature"); and the beam has to be held on the target for several seconds (for example, the beam would have to be held for one to ten seconds on a fast-moving 10-meter target 3,000 miles away). If a particle-beam weapon shoots electrons, it does so at almost the speed of light. When the electrons hit the target they unravel the lattice of atoms and molecules in the target, which then appears to melt (Tsipis 1983:185–6).

Space-based particle-beam weapons would have to be placed on large satellites in low orbit around the earth. Tsipis (ibid.:189) argues that a defense based on such weapons would require as many as one hundred satellites.

"Smart" Missiles or "Kill Vehicles"

The prime candidates for a space-based defense against missiles in the midcourse phase are homing kill vehicles, or smart weapons, which are de signed to seek out their targets by use of miniaturized computers on boa rd that make adjustments in their flight paths. The basic technological pri nciple was demonstrated in 1985, when an Army missile successfully inter cepted an unarmed warhead in a flight test. Such weapons would have to be launched at tremendous speeds, probably with what is called an electr omagnetic railgun, which uses electromagnetic fields in a vacuum to acce lerate the projectiles. Several models of the railgun have been built at the Center for Electromechanics at the University of Texas at Austin. Worker s at the lab have nicknamed the weapon the Gedi Gun. (It could not be named the Jedi Gun because of the copyright on that name.)

The SDI System

In addition to the weapons themselves, there are a number of other aspects to a space-based defense, each of which has problems that have to be solved.[10] Daniel (1984) has suggested, for example, that there would be four major segments to the SDI system: a surveillance segment, a spacecraft segment, a launch and servicing segment, and a C^3 (command, control, and communications) segment. The surveillance portion of the system requires a catalog of everything visible in space—stars, satellites, and so forth—and must have the capability to recognize anything that is new, so that it can relay the information to a human or a computer. The C^3 segment would make decisions about the nature of the novel object in space and relay the decision to activate or not activate the system. Because of the short time span involved, all of the decisions and subsequent follow-through have to be made in a matter of minutes. The launch and servicing segment would have to get the systems into space and then provide ongoing maintenance. Because the space shuttle could not accommodate payloads as large as those required by some aspects of the strategic defense system, a new rocket (like the Saturn V) is being considered. The spacecraft segment would comprise not only the weapons and the battle stations but also escort vehicles designed to protect the weapons.

Although the idea of a defense against nuclear weapons is obviously very appealing, it is also remarkably complicated, and a number of problems with SDI have been noted by its critics.

SDI AND ITS CRITICS

Five major arguments have been leveled against the SDI: (1) it is technologically impossible; (2) it is cost-prohibitive; (3) every aspect of the program is subject to many countermeasures; (4) SDI would exacerbate the political problems it is supposed to address, especially since it would undermine the arms control process; and (5) contrary to its formal name, the Strategic Defense Initiative is not strictly defensive, but has offensive capabilities as well.

The Technology Critique

Almost no scientists—within or outside the defense establishment—are willing to claim that it is technically possible to create a leak-proof defensive system. That is not to say that many specific technical difficulties cannot be overcome. Phenomenal advances in the technology required to build such a system have been a major motivating force behind the SDI proposal.

The most confusing issue is whether the system is to be a total defense or a more limited supplement to existing deterrent forces. Clearly the president promises a complete defense against nuclear weapons, and a shift from offensive to defensive weapons. His public statements on the topic have been designed to take the higher ground, with an emphasis on defensive technologies. That is a major aspect of the popular appeal of SDI, because of the role of defensive actions in negative reciprocity (as discussed in Chapter Four). "The only weapon we have is MAD—Mutual Assured Destruction," the president said in an interview reported in the *New York Times* on 12 February 1985 (Weinraub 1985:1). "Why don't we have MAS instead—Mutual Assured Security?"

In an effort to clarify the administration's position on the issue, the president's science advisor, George Keyworth, suggested in December 1984 that Reagan's idea of a total defense remained an ultimate goal but that it had been set aside for the present (Gwertzman 1984b). Even Secretary Weinberger, who had been adamant about the total defense concept, conceded under questioning that there would be a transitional phase of a more limited nature.

Weinberger advocates a complete defense, however, as he suggested during an interview on "Meet the Press" on 27 March 1983 (*Bulletin of the Atomic Scientists* 1983:5):

QUESTION: What would [a space-based ABM system] do for cruise missiles, which hug the ground and presumably could come through that system?
WEINBERGER: Well, the defensive systems the President is talking about are not designed to be partial. We want to get a system which will develop a defense that is—
QUESTION: Total? Against all incoming missiles of any kind?
WEINBERGER: Yes, and I don't see any reason why that can't be done.

In contrast, SDI proponents such as Payne (1983) envision SDI as a supplement to offensive weapons; Jastrow (1984) perceives SDI as a way of reducing the Soviet threat to American ICBMs. Major General Donald L. Lamberson, head of the Defense Department's directed-energy weapons program, testified before a Senate Armed Services subcommittee that "a constellation of space laser platforms might . . . possess the capability to negate, say, 50 percent of a large-scale ICBM attack on U.S. strategic forces by engaging several hundred missiles in boost phase as the first layer of a ballistic missile defense" (*Bulletin of the Atomic Scientists* 1983:6). A 50 percent success rate in disabling ICBMs is far from a leak-proof defense, even if an additional percentage of missiles were destroyed in subsequent layers. With almost five thousand warheads on their ICBMs, the Soviets could mount a devastating attack even in the unlikely event that the defense system was 99 percent effective and only 1 percent of the warheads made it through the shield. If the worst-case scenarios of the nuclear winter studies are correct, only 1 percent of the superpowers' current arsenals might trigger a nuclear winter.[11]

A detailed technical analysis of the proposals, conducted by the Union of Concern Scientists (1984:4), concluded that "there is no realistic hope of achieving the president's goal of an impermeable defense against nuclear attack." SDI proponent Daniel O. Graham[12] argues that "the president doesn't have time to wait for a technological consensus to form inside the regular government. It takes the U.S. 12 to 18 years to produce a major weapons system" (*Bulletin of the Atomic Scientists* 1983:6).

Among the expert critics of SDI is a group of highly influential engineers, physicists, and political scientists at Harvard, MIT, Cornell, Stanford, IBM, and the Brookings Institution (see Wilford 1983:1, 8). These critics include informal Pentagon advisors and weapons experts, such as Richard L. Garwin, a nuclear physicist at IBM, and Robert Bowman, a retired lieutenant colonel who once headed the Air Force's advanced space programs development. According to Bowman (quoted in ibid.:8) all the SDI technologies

> have staggering technical problems. All are likely to cost on the order of a trillion dollars. All violate one or more existing treaties. All are extremely vulnerable. All are subject to a variety of countermeasures. All could be made impotent by alternative offensive missiles and therefore would be likely to reignite the numerical arms race in offensive weapons. All would, if they worked, be more effective as part of a first strike than against one.

The real Achilles heel of SDI may be the complicated computer software that would have to be designed to control a defensive system. The extent of the problem in developing such software was clearly revealed by David Parnas, a respected computer scientist who, in 1985, resigned from the Panel on Computing in Support of Battle Management convened by the SDIO. Although he had not objected to previous defense-sponsored research, he believes that the SDI effort is unwise and submitted with his resignation a series of essays outlining his objections. According to Parnas, the requirements of the system are simply unreachable, and the project should be discontinued. He claims that "because of the extreme demands on the system and our inability to test it, we will never be able to believe, with any confidence, that we have succeeded. Nuclear weapons will remain a threat" (Parnas 1985:1329).

Excessive Costs of the SDI

A second criticism is the cost of a space-based defense. The expenditures required to develop and deploy the entire system might total a trillion dollars—the most expensive project ever undertaken by any government in human history. The Union of Concerned Scientists' study (1984) estimated that it would cost $70 billion just to place chemical lasers in orbit, and $60 billion for the kill vehicles, based upon current shuttle flight costs. Tsipis (1983:196) estimates that it would take 1.8 million shuttle trips—or, with ten shuttles making three trips a year, 60,000 years—to provide space-based particle-beam weapons with the explosives needed to destroy 1,500 ICBMs.

Paul H. Nitze, the Reagan administration's senior arms control adviser, claims that if the system is not cost-effective, it will not be deployed

(Gwertzman 1985b:1, 6). However, proponents of SDI counter that no price is too large to eliminate the threat of nuclear annihilation and that the American people would be willing to make a sacrifice for that kind of security. Fred C. Ikle, the under secretary of defense for policy, contradicted some of Nitze's stringent criteria for deploying SDI (see Wicker 1985:27), and Lt. General Abrahamson has replaced the earlier notion of marginal cost-effectiveness with cost goals, which completely obfuscate Nitze's concern.

Former Defense Secretary James R. Schlesinger, testifying before the House Armed Services Committee's panel on defense policy, claimed that a defensive system that intercepted 50 percent of Soviet missiles would be "much more expensive than an arms control agreement that would reduce their missiles by 50 percent" (Mohr 1985a:3).

Countermeasures

A third argument leveled at SDI is that it is susceptible to simple countermeasures. According to Broad (1982:1372–4), "the exotic weapons and other military satellites could be easily destroyed by a single nuclear blast in outer space." That blast, he contends, would

> instantly set up an electric pulse of up to a million volts per meter in hundreds of satellites and battle stations, disabling them and replacing the bold vision of a *Star Wars* conflict with the dreary reality of a nuclear graveyard. A 2-megaton blast just outside the earth's atmosphere would set up a pulse in objects as far away as geosynchronous orbit, some 36,000 kilometers above the earth. The effects of a larger bomb would reach even further.

Critics of SDI argue that even if the system were to be perfected (which they say is impossible), countermeasures would render it useless. To those who argue that it was once thought impossible to fly people to the moon, the moon did not take evasive action or fire at approaching spacecraft.

The UCS study (1984) suggests that there are many countermeasures that might be taken against each aspect of a space-based defense. The most obvious countermeasure is a buildup of offensive weapons designed to overwhelm the system, or to circumvent it (as with cruise missiles). Schlesinger argued before Congress that the deployment of a space defense against ballistic missiles would probably result in the Soviets placing a large number of submarines armed with cruise missiles just off the U.S. coast. According to Schlesinger, "There is no way we can hope to head off intrusion into U.S. airspace" by cruise missiles (Mohr 1985a:3).

Other countermeasures would be directed at the system itself, such as shortening the boost phase of ICBMs by fitting them with more powerful engines. The UCS study suggests that reaction time might be reduced to as little as one minute. Other measures might include hardening, shielding, or rotating the booster rockets to protect them from the effects of beam weapons (1984:3).

Several of the segments of a space-based system would also be vulnerable to attack. Space mines or other weapons could be used to attack the weapons deployed in space.[13] Components of the system based on the ground could be attacked by submarine-launched missiles at short range (to prevent adequate response time for the United States to detect and destroy them) or by cruise missiles. The explosion of a large nuclear warhead might blind a system with an electromagnetic pulse, although efforts are being made to develop shields to protect the system from EMP.

Garwin and Gottfried (1985) argue that the Soviets already have a weapon—their Galosh missile (deployed since the 1960s)—that could eliminate the U.S. space trucks. They suggest a scenario in which the Soviets launch a salvo of Galosh missiles that would punch a hole in the "shield," through which ICBMs would then be launched. "The Galosh demonstrates," they argue, "that a relatively crude nuclear weapon can negate a sophisticated defense" (ibid.:A19).

Political Problems with SDI

A fourth criticism of SDI is that it would make the political problems associated with the nuclear arms race more difficult, rather than lessening them. The controversy about the SDI research program has already cooled relationships between the superpowers and damaged the arms control process.

SDI has been perceived as threatening and aggressive by the Soviet leadership. Yuri Andropov, speaking four days after President Reagan's "Star Wars" speech in March 1983, contended, "Should this conception be translated into reality, it would in fact open the floodgates to a runaway race of all types, both offensive and defensive" (Mohr 1985b:8). Because the program is designed to defend the United States against ICBMs, it is likely that the Soviets will respond by stepping up their development of cruise missiles, depressed-trajectory missiles, and SLBMs.[14] A U.S. space-based defense, therefore, might provoke the Soviets not only to join a new arms race in space but also to escalate the current offensive race. In addition to weapons designed to circumvent or overwhelm the defense system, SDI will no doubt provoke the rapid development of antisatellite weapons and an entire arsenal created to defend space battle stations (Daniel 1984).

No matter how loudly the United States objects, the Soviets are likely to see a defense system as a supplement to a first-strike strategy. As we have already seen, some strategic planners in the United States are already justifying SDI as an adjunct to the overall deterrent force rather than as a replacement for it (see, e.g., Jastrow 1984). It is a short inferential step from perceiving SDI as an element of deterrence to seeing it as a supplement to a first strike. Such fears are fueled by NATO's first-use policy.

Perhaps the most significant immediate political cost of SDI is its impact on arms control. Harvard Law School treaty expert Anram Chayes contends that "the stated goal of the [SDI]—to provide [an ABM] defense of the country—is presently illegal" under the terms of the 1972 Anti-Ballistic Missile treaty (Raloff 1985:39). Similar charges are made by a group called the National· Campaign to Save the ABM Treaty (Mohr 1985c).[15] The U.S. Defense Department, however, has interpreted the ABM treaty more broadly, arguing that many SDI technologies can be tested in space and on land because they are in gray areas of the treaty and are not explicitly forbidden. Furthermore, the Pentagon asserts that the United States reserves " 'the right' to disregard provisions of the treaty in reprisal for purported Soviet violations, raising the possibility that experiments would proceed even if they did not comply with the treaty" (Keller 1985b:1).

The pursuit of a space-based defense places the United States on a collision course with explicit prohibitions in one of the most effective treaties of the nuclear age. Article V of the ABM treaty explicitly forbids the superpowers from efforts to "develop, test or deploy ABM systems or components which are sea-based, air-based, space-based, or mobile land-based."

The impact of SDI on the arms control process is wide ranging. Thus far most alleged superpower violations of agreements have concerned loopholes and ambiguities. However, the testing and deployment of a space-based defense would be a clear and unambiguous violation. It would no doubt unravel the tattered fabric of détente and plunge the superpowers into a frigid cold war. SDI calls U.S. credibility at the negotiating table into question, yet negotiation is critical because of the new generation of weapons currently being deployed—the counterforce weapons, which might increase the chances of an accidental war, and cruise missiles, which are small and difficult to detect.

SDI has already become a major stumbling block for the Soviets in current negotiations in Geneva. Just as it plays a key role in current U.S. policy, the prevention of its deployment has become a key factor in Soviet nuclear policy. As Konstantin Likutov (1985:44) puts it, "We . . . regard the prevention of the militarization of outer space as one of the urgent problems facing mankind, on whose solution the future of our planet depends."

Some proponents of SDI have suggested that the ABM treaty should be scrapped or modified to allow the deployment of a space-based defense, because of "the possibility that strategic, technical, and political developments during the past decade have rendered the ABM Treaty potentially anachronistic and dangerous" (Payne 1983:1). They argue that although the ABM treaty might have made some sense at the time it was signed, when a defensive system did not seem technologically feasible or cost-effective, the situation has changed because of technical developments.

White House officials have waffled in responding to charges that SDI will violate the ABM treaty. They argue that since SDI is merely a research program, Soviet concerns are premature (Gwertzman 1984a:A1). On the other hand, administration official Paul Nitze (who was involved in the ABM negotiations) called the treaty a "living accord" that can be amended to permit SDI (Biddle 1985a). Delicate negotiations would, however, be required in altering an antiballistic missile treaty into one that permits an antiballistic missile system.

Johansen (1985) points out that SDI poses a current as well as a future threat to the ABM treaty. A passage leaked to the press from the secret 1984–88 Defense Guidance statement shows the U.S. commitment to initiate "the prototype development of space-based weapons systems . . . so that we will be prepared to deploy fully developed and operationally ready systems" (ibid.:201; cf. Kennedy 1984:19). A January 1984 National Security Decision Directive signed by President Reagan requires major tests of that system before 1990, which would unquestionably violate the ABM treaty.

Some experts have concluded that U.S. experiments to "flight test demonstrations of high altitude optical homing and nonnuclear kill" also appear inconsistent with treaty limits.[16] Further, the testing of ASAT weapons launched from F-15 fighters raises questions about a gray area in the ABM treaty, because ASAT technologies can be adapted for ABM systems (Johansen 1985). Similar questions are raised by tests of Patriot and Hawk missiles to determine if they can be used as antitactical missiles.[17] Gerard C. Smith, former director of the Arms Control and Disarmament Agency and chief negotiator at the time the ABM treaty was signed, claims that "we are already in an anticipatory breach of contract" (ibid.).

It is clear, then, that SDI poses grave threats to the ABM treaty and in doing so poisons the climate for the entire arms control process. Whereas the U.S. administration is making SDI a central focus of its strategic policy (see Gwertzman 1985a), the Soviets have made its cancellation a major priority. There seems to be some hope in the United States that the Soviets will come around to the American point of view. As Leslie Gelb pointed out (1985a:1), the superpowers had switched roles in the debate over missile defenses by the time they met in Geneva at the beginning of 1985. "Less than 20 years ago," Gelb wrote, "American officials began the process of convincing skeptical Soviet leaders that defenses against missile attacks would undermine mutual deterrence. [Now] Secretary of State George P. Shultz is set to preach the virtues of missile defenses, and the Soviet Foreign Minister, Andrei A. Gromyko, is expected to condemn them." Gromyko explained that the difference between the American and Soviet position on arms negotiations

> consists in the fact that the U.S.A. wished to leave space aside and concern itself only with those types of armaments on which talks were already held.
> The Soviet Union categorically objected to such a viewpoint. There is an arms race in outer space and it is increasingly getting a filling in the form of corresponding arms. This would not only bring to naught but also surpass what has been done on the earth. ("Excerpts from Interview" 1985:4)

The political problems of SDI became most evident at the summit in Reykjavik, Iceland, in October 1986. SDI may have been the only stumbling block preventing Reagan and Gorbachev from reaching a major arms reduction agreement.

The Offensive Side of Strategic Defense

A fifth criticism of the Strategic Defense Initiative is that it is not truly defensive. The technological capabilities that make SDI a potentiality—the capability to hit targets from great distances with high accuracy—are those involved in the latest generation of counterforce missiles like the MX, the Trident II/D-5, and the Pershing II (see Jastrow 1984:29; Aldridge 1983a).

According to a number of weapons experts (both critics and supporters of SDI), SDI could serve several offensive functions (Boffey 1985b:10). First, it could be used as a defensive supplement to an offensive attack, thus limiting the enemy's retaliatory capability. Second, it could be used to destroy space satellites, which are much more vulnerable than the fast-moving ballistic missiles SDI would be designed to disable. Third, it could even be used against ground targets in an attack. Defense analyst Robert Bowman (1986:114) contends that "Star Wars has become a program to develop offensive weapons disguised as a defense."

Laser expert John D. G. Rather (an SDI supporter) claims that such targets as airplanes, oil tankers, power plants, and grain fields could be attacked by space-based weapons, igniting instantaneous fires and causing damage that could "take an industrialized country back to an 18th-century level in 30 minutes" (ibid.). Henry W. Kendall, chair of the Union of Concerned Scientists, conjectures that lasers might even be used for selective assassination; they might, for example, be directed against the top Kremlin officials observing the annual May Day parade in Moscow (ibid.).

According to an article by Richard Halloran (1985:6) there is some evidence (although it has been both confirmed and disputed by administration officials) that "the Defense Department is devising a nuclear war plan and command structure that would integrate offensive nuclear forces with the projected antimissile shield." Halloran contends that as part of a warfighting strategy to make deterrence credible, SDI "is intended to coordinate the potential use of [Pershing and cruise missiles] . . . plus others still being developed with the shield of weapons on land and in space that is being fashioned with the aim of destroying long-range missiles and their warheads before they strike the United States" (ibid.). However, Under Secretary of Defense for Policy Fred C. Ikle, one of the sources cited in the article, disputed Halloran's contention that new war plans would integrate offensive forces with the projected antimissile shield (Molotsky 1985). The controversy was provoked by concern raised in Canada, where a similar story was carried by the Canadian Broadcasting Corporation; Ikle's comment was issued as a clarifying statement.

Whether or not the offensive uses of SDI are a technical possibility, there is considerable evidence that the Soviet Union *perceives* them to be. According to one Soviet pamphlet ("Star Wars" 1985:31–32), "the true purpose of the 'strategic defense initiative' is to obtain an opportunity for launching a nuclear attack with impunity, and for continuously harrassing the Soviet Union and other countries by means of nuclear blackmail." If the offensive capabilities of the system are genuine, and it is most likely that some of them are, then the Star Wars nickname may be more accurate than the formal name of the project.

TOWARD A SOCIOLOGY OF "STAR WARS"

Evaluation of the proposed Strategic Defense Initiative depends more on one's basic assumptions and interpretations than on the actual facts of the case. SDI is primarily a political and sociological issue rather than a purely technical one, despite the widespread tendency to view it as the latter. The social construction of the case for SDI has emerged from a complex network of reciprocal interactions and institutionalized interests. Clearly the debate needs to be widened beyond its current focus on the technical merits and demerits of such a system.

The desire to discover a technical fix for what is at base a political problem is a tendency deeply rooted in American culture and is a central element of the arms race ritual. Thus, it is not surprising that SDI has struck a popular chord with much of the American public. The ritual nuclear arms buildup has failed to provide a sense of security—the American public continues to feel vulnerable because of the massive Soviet nuclear arsenal.

U.S. officials have thus turned to the ritual experts for a solution to the problem, and they have been offered the hope of a technological solution, which diverts attention from the real problems at hand: (1) the use of violence as a means for settling international disputes, and (2) the sad state of U.S.-Soviet relations. Furthermore, the SDI "package" incorporates elements of both sides of the mainstream debate on nuclear policy in the United States—Peace through Strength versus the Freeze. Although the peace movement has rejected the SDI proposal, claiming that it is merely an escalation of the arms race, some of the movement's supporters in the general public are attracted to the SDI vision of making nuclear weapons impotent and obsolete.

Whereas government officials feel that they have only limited control over the political processes that perpetuate the arms race, technological rituals give them an illusion of control based upon the alleged objectivity of science. The pursuit of a technical solution is reinforced by institutionalized processes of both positive and negative reciprocity. Positive reciprocity (the return of good for good) sustains the relationships among the various elements of the iron triangle: the military contractors (and weapons labs), the administration (including the Pentagon), and the Congress. SDI has provided an opportunity for each element of the iron triangle to profit from their reciprocal relations: The scientists and engineers have offered the president a technical possibility that could give him a sense of control as well as political capital. The administration offered Congress a share of that capital in exchange for a multi-billion-dollar research program, which was in turn given to the military contractors and weapons labs to work on the project.

Furthermore, the "defensive" theme of SDI proponents was an appropriate symbol with which to uphold the norms of negative reciprocity. The blame for the arms race is shifted squarely on the shoulders of the adversary—it is only because the Soviets have engaged in a massive arms buildup, thereby threatening our security, that the United States is ostensibly building weapons in the first place. SDI is merely an attempt to reciprocate, not by returning harm for harm (or so the argument goes), but by putting up a protective shield against potential harm. Thus, the motivation for a continuation of weapons research, development, and deployment is justified on high moral grounds.

One of the most interesting elements of the pro-SDI rhetoric is the debate between those who proclaim it as pure defense and those who envision it as a supplement to existing deterrent forces, that is, as an element of a warfighting strategy designed to make deterrence credible. Robert McNamara (1987) refers to these two positions as SDI 1 and SDI 2. As usual, one's position on this issue is closely related to his or her role in the debate. Public salespersons for the program (like Reagan and Weinberger) tend to subscribe to SDI 1; those designing the technology or integrating it into strategic doctrine tend to subscribe to SDI 2. Public discussion of SDI by its supporters has shifted somewhat from SDI 1 to SDI 2, although the idea of making nuclear weapons obsolete keeps creeping into administration pronouncements. The dilemma for public proponents of the program is that nuclear warfighting rhetoric has not played well with the American public or with European allies who are concerned about being the immediate victims of a nuclear conflict between the superpowers. The best sales pitch for SDI is that it is purely defensive. Nonetheless, the R&D people truly believe in the system and insist that it will work, although their understanding of it is limited.

A certain myopia is created by the process of bureaucratic specialization. Scientists in the weapons laboratories and military industries work in narrow, technical fields in which they have been able to create dazzling technologies. Yet, it is one thing to shoot down one ICBM in a test and quite another to erect an elaborate system of detection and defenses that can destroy thousands of missiles in a few minutes. The experts upon whom we rely to offer advice about the feasibility of a particular technology are (1) the specialists who work on a small portion of a problem without seeing the entire picture; and (2) the very people who would gain from the funding of such a program and would lose if it were not approved.

Thus, no matter how objective a scientist or engineer might try to be in assessing the viability of a particular technology, it is always in his or her best interest to have faith in it. Further, the scientists and engineers working on military projects are often our "best and brightest," because those projects are often the most intellectually intriguing and well funded. Those scientists and engineers are highly motivated individuals who invest a great deal of themselves in their work and are attached to their ideas and projects. As Wayne Biddle (1985b:6) put it, "The business of the engineers is to make things work, so they carry a ubiquitous optimism in the face of admittedly horrendous technical problems."

It is no accident that the strongest arguments for SDI are made by those who have advocated the deployment of counterforce weapons and have taken a Peace through Strength posture in the arms race debate.[18] The notion of a defensive system apparently accomplishes two things for them: First, it promises a technological edge in the bean-counting game by negating a certain percentage of Soviet missiles and thus restoring a measure of U.S. superiority in the comparative calculations. Second, it addresses nagging doubts about the whole structure of deterrence and its indefinite viability. The idea of creating a solution to that problem is so appealing that it has captured the imagination of people such as the president who do not believe that deterrence by threat of annihilation can work perfectly and forever.

These two goals of SDI are contradictory, but contradictions are nothing new in the construction of the nuclear cage. The confusion and ambiguity surrounding the public presentation of the program are probably not so much a matter of deliberate deception (although deception is a part of the presentation) as a consequence of sociological ambivalence (see Merton and Barber 1976). A number of people—politicians, planners, scientists, and engineers—are placed in situations in which conflicting demands are imposed upon them. The vision of a defense against nuclear weapons is so powerful, not to mention extremely profitable, to those making the decisions that they convince themselves that opposition to strategic defense is simply narrow-minded or uninformed. They are therefore able to screen out any evidence that contradicts their perceptions that the SDI program is the most desirable way to enhance security.

The Strategic Defense Initiative is thus a subtle *coup-de-plume* that packages the continued militarization of the planet and extends militarization into outer space. Although it is presented as a defensive system that will render missiles impotent, it is a technological leap in the direction already traveled. Because it is impossible to create a complete defense against nuclear weapons, the SDI program should prove to be most useful as a supplement to nuclear warfighting strategies. Unlike the concept of fighting prolonged or limited nuclear wars with counterforce weapons, which has provoked global opposition, SDI presents nuclear warfighting with a positive face, because it holds out the false hope that no matter how horrible a nuclear exchange might be, we may be able to survive it.

CHAPTER ELEVEN

Superpower Relations

We have a different regard for human life than those monsters [the Soviets] do.

— Ronald Reagan, quoted in Robert Scheer,
With Enough Shovels: Reagan, Bush and Nuclear War

"What about the Russians?"

"What about the Americans?"

These two questions are often intended to be the last word in arguments about the arms race. They are the bottom-line justifications for every new military program in the United States and the Soviet Union, respectively. The logic implied by the questions is: "Of course, we would rather not do such-and-such, but the Russians [Americans] are, so we have to do it as well." In short, the major issue of the nuclear arms race, at least at this point in history, concerns the hostile relationship between the superpowers.

MIRROR, MIRROR ON THE WALL

Perhaps the most striking feature of superpower relations in the nuclear age is that despite obvious differences between the two countries, enemy images within each bear such a remarkable resemblance. Both superpowers have a tendency to act like superpowers, justifying their own behavior and condemning that of the other.

Images of evil are important for a number of reasons. First, they frame the nature of global politics and define "our" role in it as positive and the adversary's role as negative. Second, they are used to legitimize the expenditure of massive amounts of money on weapons programs for defense against a malicious, evil enemy. Third, they facilitate boundary maintenance, sharpening both internal and external boundaries in each nation. Finally, they provide occasions for ritual denunciations of alleged transgressions, which reaffirm prevailing world views.

The social construction of evil is only one aspect of superpower relations, however. It should not blind us to the rich texture of conflict and cooperation, of hate and respect, of hostility and mutual regard. The superpowers are bound together in a relationship that Raymond Aron (1973) aptly labels "friendly enemies." They are forever engaged in reciprocal exchanges and have a powerful impact on one another. Their interaction is fraught with nuance and ambiguities that are difficult to unravel.

Furthermore, each superpower's evil image of the other—like all stereotypes and caricatures—contains an element of truth. Indeed, each superpower has engaged in aggressive behavior in the global arena and has contributed extensively to the militarization of life in the twentieth century. Despite their different domestic political structures, their foreign policies exhibit many similarities, some of which may be inherent in the role of superpower. The clearest fact of all is that each nation *does* threaten the health and security of the other.

In this chapter, we analyze each nation's image of the threat posed by the other and then note some of the ways in which those pictures are both false and true.

THE SOVIET THREAT

The Evil Empire

The image invoked most frequently in the United States by those highlighting the threat posed by the Soviet Union is that of Hitler's Germany just before World War II. Norman Podhoretz (1980:27) contends that

> the Soviet Union is a revolutionary state, exactly as Hitler's Germany was, in the sense that it wishes to create a new international order in which it would be the dominant power and whose character would be determined by its national wishes and its ideological dictates. In such an order, there would be no more room for any of the freedoms we now enjoy. . . . In short, the reason Soviet imperialism is a threat to us is not merely that the Soviet Union is a superpower bent on aggrandizing itself, but that it is a Communist state armed to the teeth, and dedicated to the destruction of the free institutions which are our heritage and our glory. In resisting the advance of Soviet

power . . . we are fighting for freedom and against Communism, for democracy and against totalitarianism.

This theme of similarities between the Soviet Union and Hitler's Germany appears frequently in postwar political rhetoric (see Adler and Paterson 1970) and has three major implications. First, it implies that the Soviet Union is an expansionist power. Advocates contend that contemporary Soviet expansionism emerged from the combination of a long-standing Russian tradition with a communist ideology. Colin Gray (1977:35), one of the major exponents of the Soviet threat interpretation, insists that "territorial expansion was 'the Russian way,' just as it has been 'the Soviet way' " (cf. Pipes 1976). Furthermore, he contends that "the Soviet commitment to world dominion is nonnegotiable" (Gray 1977:38). Another influential scholar, Richard Pipes, perceives a Soviet grand strategy that "takes for granted the inevitability of unremitting global social conflicts until ultimate victory" (1984:60).

Such beliefs were expressed primarily by the far right during the détente of the 1970s but became a guiding principle of U.S. foreign policy in the 1980s. President Reagan contends that relentless Soviet expansion continues without the restraint of morality that guides U.S. behavior. "As good Marxist-Leninists," the president observes,

> the Soviet leaders have openly and publicly declared that the only morality they recognize is that which will further their cause, which is world revolution. . . . Morality is entirely subordinate to the interests of class war. And everything is moral that is necessary for the annihilation of the old, exploiting social order and for uniting the proletariat. (Reagan 1984:113–14)

Gray insists that because the Soviet Union has ambition without boundaries, the United States and its allies must either "sustain a very robust local denial capability," or "invest in a significant margin of strategic nuclear superiority" (Gray 1977:53).

A second implication is related to the first: The United States must develop a nuclear warfighting capability, which, in turn, requires a superior nuclear arsenal (see Chapter Eight). The effort to obtain (or retain) military superiority requires a continuous modernization of weapons and delivery systems, all of which would be unnecessary except for the Soviet threat.

Finally, this vision of the Soviets as ruthlessly bent on world domination implies that treaties made with them are not worth the paper on which they are printed. A major faction in the United States believes that the Soviets have been violating the SALT agreements deliberately and are untrustworthy, and the only viable response is therefore one of strength and military superiority. The major lesson to be learned from this perspective of the Soviet Union, its proponents argue, is that one must avoid the appeasement accorded Adolf Hitler before World War II. America and its allies must stand strong in the face of a dangerous enemy.

There is, of course, some truth in the evil empire image of the Soviet Union. In the period since World War II, the Soviet government has been engaged in a massive arms buildup and an intensive nuclear weapons program, developing a rough parity with the United States despite the fact that it has only half of the U.S. gross national product to support such a program. During that period the USSR has used direct military intervention on three occasions—in Hungary, Czechoslovakia, and Afghanistan—and has used proxy troops and covert actions to undermine the governments of other countries. It has bullied people in nations under its indirect control in the so-called Eastern bloc, forcing the governments of such countries as Poland and East Germany to follow its bidding in many areas, including both domestic and foreign policies.

Human Rights Abuses

Much of the public outcry in the United States against the Soviets concerns their domestic policies, in addition to foreign interventionism. Mainstream America often perceives Soviet foreign policy as a symptom of the general depravity of the Soviet Union. Princeton Soviet specialist Stephen F. Cohen (1985:5–6) summarizes the orthodox view of U.S. sovietology as follows:

> In October 1917, the Bolsheviks (Communists), a small, unrepresentative, and already or embryonically totalitarian party, usurped power and thus betrayed the Russian Revolution. From that moment on, as in 1917, Soviet history was determined by the totalitarian political dynamics of the Communist Party, as personified by its original leader, Lenin—monopolistic politics, ruthless tactics, ideological orthodoxy, programmatic dogmatism, disciplined leadership, and centralized bureaucratic organization. Having quickly monopolized the new Soviet government and created a rudimentary totalitarian party-state, the Communists won the Russian civil war of 1918–21 by discipline, organization, and ruthlessness. Exhausted and faced with the need to settle the Lenin succession, the party then retreated tactically in the 1920s from its totalitarian designs on society by temporarily adopting less authoritarian policies known as the New Economic Policy (NEP). But in 1928–29, its internal house having been put in order by Stalin, the party, driven by ideological zealotry, resumed the totalitarian assault on society. The process culminated logically and inevitably in the 1920s, the years of imposed collectivization and forced industrialization, as the party totalitarianized society through mass terror and expanded structures of bureaucratic control. A total party-state emerged; autonomous social institutions and processes, indeed the boundary between state and society, were destroyed. Full-blown totalitarianism had to abate somewhat during the war with Germany in 1941–45. But it then reemerged—a monolithic, ideological, terroristic party-state, headed by Stalin, ruling omnipotently over a passive, frozen society of atomized new citizens.

There is little question that the Soviet government has frequently treated its citizens in a repressive fashion. The most vivid images of Soviet human-rights violations come from statements of Soviet dissidents, such as Andrei Sakharov and Anatoly Scharansky, from the writings of Alexander

Solzhenitsyn, and from stories about the Stalinist era, which even *Izvestiia* has referred to as a "dreadful and bloody wound."[1] Those who emphasize the evil nature of the Soviet Union remind us vividly of the horrors of the Stalinist period, in which "millions of men, women, and children were arbitrarily arrested, tortured, executed, brutally deported, or imprisoned in the murderous prisons and forced-labor camps of the Gulag Archipelago" (ibid.:95). In terms of sheer numbers of victims—totaling in the millions— Stalin's holocaust may have been more devastating than Hitler's.[2] The continued mistreatment of political prisoners and the horror stories told by emigres who were subjected to atrocities are seen as evidence for a continuity between the contemporary Soviet Union and Stalinist Russia. Although mass executions have been discontinued, abuses of human rights persist.

If the Soviet government is ruthless and untrustworthy and stops at nothing in deceiving its own people, how can it be trusted in relations with its adversaries? One of the ironies of the human-rights argument about the Soviet Union is that the period of the worst human-rights abuses by Stalin was the same time period in which the U.S. relationship with the Soviets was closest (the countries were allies against Hitler). The United States is quick to overlook the domestic "shortcomings" of its allies when to do so furthers U.S. interests (just as the Soviets will support anticommunist governments if it serves their interests).

At the same time as sovietologists in the U.S. academic community began in the 1960s and 1970s to raise serious concerns about the orthodox image of the Soviets, concern about the Soviets enjoyed a resurgence among policymakers within the Reagan administration. It is important to examine perceptions of the Soviet threat in historical perspective.

Constructing the Soviet Threat

> After the Czech coup in 1948, it wasn't a matter of whether they [the Soviets] were going to attack [the United States], it was just when. Would it come in 1950 or 1951? Or would they wait until 1955?
>
> For years the military would come in with these inflated estimates of Soviet military capabilities and intentions. They were *all* aimed at the budget. The Air Force would argue [the Soviets have] got the capability of building such-and-such a number of bombers, so they're *going* to build them, so three or four years from now they *will* have 800 bombers.
>
> —DeForrest van Slyck, an early member of the CIA's Board of National Estimates, quoted by Thomas Powers, *Thinking about the Next War*

As with virtually every process sustaining the nuclear cage, disagreements within the United States over the true nature of the Soviet Union and its intentions emerge from the differing frames through which information is interpreted. Responsible scholars and sincere individuals come to sharply differing conclusions. Although some version of the Soviet threat picture painted in this chapter has usually been a guiding image of American foreign policy since World War II, there is a strong counterframe in the United States that emphasizes the significance of the Soviet Union's fears about its security.

As a result of being invaded twice by the West in this century and suffering twenty million casualties in World War II alone, the Soviet Union has developed an obsession with security that is difficult for Americans to understand. From this point of view, the primary objective of U.S. actions toward the Soviets might be to reassure them that their security is not threatened by the United States.

George F. Kennan, who as a scholar and diplomat has observed the Soviet Union for four decades, expressed in the 1980s a view of that country and its leadership that is quite different from the threat model he expounded immediately following World War II. Rather than an aggressive regime intent on destroying the West, Kennan sees "a group of troubled men . . . whose choices and possibilities are severely constrained" by a number of factors. They are prisoners of their personal and national past, an antiquated ideology, a rigid system of power, and

> certain ingrained peculiarities of the Russian statesmanship of earlier ages—the congenital sense of insecurity, the lack of inner self-confidence, the distrust of the foreigner and the foreigner's world, the passion for secrecy, the neurotic fear of penetration by other powers into areas close to their borders, and a persistent tendency, resulting from all these other factors, to overdo the creation of military strength. (1982:153)

For Kennan, the Soviet Union's efforts to expand its influence bring neither surprise nor alarm. "Most great powers have similar desires. And the methods adopted by the Soviet Union are not very different from those adopted by some of the others" (ibid.). Instead of an evil empire pursuing new territories, Kennan sees a nation distinguished not so much by success as by a lack of it.

These competing images of the Soviets in much of the U.S. foreign policy debate in the 1980s correspond to the alternative strategies for national security outlined in Chapter Seven. The Peace through Strength alternative is a logical implication of the Soviet threat model, and the Arms Control movement position is based on an image of the Soviets that emphasizes their ultimate concern for security and an interpretation of their actions as more defensive than aggressive.

The latter view of the Soviet Union waxes and wanes in popularity but has usually been a minority position. At any given moment the behavior of U.S. policymakers contains some mixture of these seemingly incompatible positions. There are also areas of agreement in these opposing views, such as the Soviet Union's concern about invasion, its feelings of isolation and conflict with the hostile powers that encircle it (including communist countries), its inevitable conflict with Western capitalist countries because of ideology, and its tendency to rely greatly upon military power (see Ground Zero 1982:192–93).

Beyond a narrow range of consensus, however, the two frames have radically diverging implications for U.S. policy. The ascendancy of the threat frame during the 1950s, and again in the 1980s, can be attributed to a number of factors, not the least of which is the effort by an organization called the Committee on the Present Danger.

The Committee on the Present Danger

> It is not an easy matter to sell to the general public a domestic program based on impoverishing a large part of the population for the benefit of the wealthy, destroying the environment, eliminating health and safety standards, and subsidizing the production of high-technology waste. There is a classic means for achieving this end: heightening international tensions and creating a war scare.
>
> —Noam Chomsky, *Towards a New Cold War*

The most effective ideological mechanism for mobilizing the American population since Nazism has been the communist or Soviet threat, which is invoked time and again. Jerry Sanders (1983:2) states that the basis of post–World War II American foreign policy has oscillated between managerialism and a position of containment militarism. The most recent shift— from managerialism to militarism in the late 1970s and early 1980s—is largely a response to a "well-organized and well-financed 'Soviet threat' campaign led by the Committee on the Present Danger [CPD]."

There have been two CPDs in the American political scene, the first at the beginning of the cold war, at the time of the secret policy review carried out in 1950 under the direction of Paul Nitze, which emphasized the danger of a growing worldwide communist threat. Nitze, along with Eugene Rostow, later founded the second CPD, formed in the late 1970s.

The current committee played a key role in the U.S. Senate's failure to ratify the SALT II agreement and the Carter administration's shift to a hard-line position. It promoted the presidential candidacy of Ronald Reagan (a member of the committee's board of directors), who claimed that the SALT II treaty was fatally flawed because the United States had given in to tough Soviet negotiators in the drafting of the treaty (see Rostow 1979). A CPD publication explains why the Soviet Union is not a reliable treaty partner:

> The Soviet military buildup of all its armed forces over the past quarter century is, in part, reminiscent of Nazi Germany's rearmament in the 1930s. The Soviet buildup affects all branches of the military: the army, the air force and the navy. In addition, Soviet nuclear offensive and defensive forces are de-

signed to enable the USSR to fight, survive and win an all-out nuclear war should it occur. (quoted in Scheer 1982:37–38)

The extent of anti-Soviet sentiment in the United States is reflected in the controversy created by an ABC news show's decision to allow a Soviet spokesperson (Vladmir Posner) to respond to a speech by President Reagan on 27 February 1986. President Reagan reportedly remarked, "I don't know why the hell the media is so willing to lend support to the Soviets" (Neuman 1986:1). *Washington Post* Executive Editor Benjamin Bradlee claimed that ABC's action was inappropriate. "You don't go to a Nazi for an opinion on a domestic dispute in Israel," he insisted. "There are two sides in a democratic society. Communism is not a third side" (Boyer 1986:10).

When Ronald Reagan took office in 1981, so did the Committee on the Present Danger. Its impact on current U.S. policies is remarkable. In addition to the person in the Oval Office, members of the Committee's board of directors have taken the following key foreign policy posts during Reagan's administration.[3]

1. U.S. Ambassador to the United Nations: Jeane Kirkpatrick
2. National Security Council staff: Geoffrey Kemp and Richard Pipes
3. Key Pentagon posts: Amoretta Hoeber, Fred Charles Ikle, Richard Perle, R. G. Stilwell, and Navy Secretary John Lehman
4. State Department: Secretary of State George Shultz, as well as James Buckley and W. Allen Wallis
5. President's Foreign Intelligence Advisory Board: W. Glenn Campbell, John B. Connally, John S. Foster, Jr., Clare Boothe Luce, Peter O'Donnell, Jr., Paul Seabury, Seymour Weiss, and Edward Bennett Williams
6. Arms Control and Disarmament Agency: Directors Eugene Rostow and, later, Kenneth Adelman
7. General Advisory Committee on Arms Control and Disarmament: William Graham, Colin Gray, Francis Hoeber, Charles Burton Marshall, John Roche, Donald Rumsfeld, Laurence Silberman, and E. R. Zumwalt, Jr.
8. Chief Negotiator for Theater Nuclear Forces: Paul Nitze

The president had a strong visceral antagonism toward the Soviets that began long before his election; he had been warned of the Red menace by his longtime actor friend and former California senator, George Murphy, who had heard from J. Edgar Hoover that "Franklin D. Roosevelt's New Deal was masking a plot to socialize America" (Scheer 1982:42). Reagan claims to have battled communists in Hollywood in the 1950s when he served as president of the Screen Actors Guild.

The basic themes raised by the committee were also those raised by candidates Reagan and Bush, namely,

that the Soviets were in the process of attaining superiority in nuclear and conventional weapons; that they were bent on world conquest; that the

United States, misled by the spirit of détente, had disarmed during the seventies while the Soviets went barrelling ahead in the arms race; that nuclear deterrence and the assumption of Mutual Assured Destruction were no longer adequate; and that the Soviets were in fact preparing to fight and win a nuclear war. (ibid.:48)

When the Soviets are framed in such terms, efforts to negotiate agreements with them are nonsensical. Soviet overtures are perceived as sheer propaganda, and the only U.S. option is the Peace through Strength approach. Although the administration's rhetorical denunciations of the Soviets were muted during Reagan's reelection campaign, committee members retained their control of key foreign policy posts, and adherents to the Soviet threat model (for example, Paul Nitze and John Tower) were sent to Geneva to represent the United States in negotiations.

The United States does not have a monopoly on threat construction, however; there is a similar process in the Soviet Union. Most Americans will have trouble recognizing their country in the Soviet image of an evil United States, just as Soviet citizens are shocked by the U.S. image of the USSR.

THE U.S. THREAT

> The dominant note of exterminating Russians to the last man runs through all of the [CIA] staff planning since Harry Truman's time, and has, if anything, gained still greater resonance today.
>
> —Nikolai Yakovlev, *CIA Target—The USSR*

From the Soviet point of view, the United States constitutes a unique threat to its security and its status as a superpower. Such fears are rooted in the long history of hostilities to which the Russian and later Soviet nations have been subjected. What appears to some Americans to be an unwarranted paranoia on the part of the Soviets is a long-standing security problem best symbolized by the Second World War.

In that bloody war (the Great Patriotic War) the Soviets lost twenty million people; virtually every survivor was personally affected. The grief from that war and the memory of its heroes are kept alive by both government and people in the USSR. Every village has its memorials to fallen citizens, who are honored on numerous ritual occasions—even weddings often include a trip to lay flowers at the memorial. As Gottlieb (1982:26) puts it,

> History has taught the inhabitants of the Soviet Union that they live in a hostile world. Over the centuries their land has been invaded by Mongols, Turks, Swedes, Poles, Frenchmen and Germans. In 1918 Great Britain, France, Japan and the United States sent troops to the Soviet state in an effort to sup-

press the Bolshevik Revolution in its infancy. Many American textbooks gloss over this. Yet it is one of the factors, within the living memory of older citizens, that make the Soviets fearful of encirclement. . . . For the Soviets it is not a reassuring picture.

For many Soviets, the U.S. government provides the most vivid symbol of the general threat to Soviet security. Such fears are compounded by the U.S. alliance with two historic enemies of the Soviets: Germany and China. A quick look at a map of U.S. military bases around the world demonstrates the reality on which Soviet fears of encirclement are based. The Soviets are covered on every flank by the United States and its allies, except for buffer zones in Eastern Europe, Afghanistan, and recently Iran. Most Americans are not conscious of the insecurity that creates for a war-weary people. They do not realize, for example, that Beirut is closer to the Soviet Union than Grenada is to the United States.

Soviet versions of the American threat focus on three themes: (1) the direct threat to the Soviet Union posed by the United States and its allies, with their many military bases, history of aggressive behavior, and repeated attempts to undermine Soviet security; (2) the nuclear arms buildup (for which the United States is responsible); and (3) U.S. imperialism in the Third World.

The Threat from Hostile Capitalist Neighbors

Capitalism and socialism will have to work out a common stand on the practical issues of peaceful coexistence.

The world now faces the danger of total destruction. There is no alternative other than peaceful coexistence. We have to work out concrete, practical measures. The main task of the policy of peaceful coexistence is to promote cooperation between the two social systems in every way and lower the level of confrontation.

—Vladimir Razmerov, quoted in
Wilton John Brown, *Do Russian People Stand for War?*

To some Soviet commentators, U.S. rhetoric about the Soviet threat is a deception that masks true American intentions. A. Y. Yefremov (1979:144) contends, for example, that "all talk of the 'Soviet menace' was intended to camouflage the fact that the military-industrial complex pursued as before the objective of securing for the United States the possibility to achieve world supremacy." According to these commentators, whereas the socialist countries are pursuing a policy toward peace and disarmament, the United States and its allies are preparing for war. Gorbachev (1985c:33) has stated that "the declared 'crusade' against communism . . . implies far-reaching hegemonistic ambitions." This tendency toward militaristic behavior, so the argument goes, has its roots in the nature of capitalism and the intolerant political tradition of the United States. According to Yakovlev (1984:10),

Irrespective of the tone and tenor of the official rhetoric, the ruling American political tradition is intolerance. It dates to the days when the Pilgrim Fathers, who hadn't got on with the Old World, crossed the ocean to set up a state fitting their views. That was when the we-they outlook took shape. And any careful observer will see that the U.S. statesmen who speak for political pluralism are really intolerant of it, for they worship the form of government in the United States as the only possible and in every way superior form. For reasons rooted in this American political tradition, the permanent conflict between the U.S.A. and the rest of the world is in fact inevitable.

Just as some in the United States see parallels between the Soviet Union and Nazi Germany, some Soviets see similarities between the United States and the Nazis. Gorbachev (1985c:104) complains (with an allusion to the United States) that "the ill-intentional myth of a 'Soviet military threat,' exploited so noisily by Nazism, is still in circulation." The cold war was "launched by militaristic circles in the West" in order to deprive the Soviet Union and its allies of "the fruits of their victory" in World War II (ibid.:107).

Nowhere is the American threat seen more clearly than in U.S. plans to use atomic weapons against the Soviet Union in the postwar period. Yakovlev (1984:29) observes that the Joint War Planning Board adopted a plan on 14 December 1945 that called for the bombing of twenty Soviet cities with the entire atomic stockpile of 196 bombs. Pyotr Fedoseyev (1985a:43) reports that

> in 1949, President Truman endorsed Dropshot, a plan for total nuclear war against the Soviet Union that was to be started in 1957. Dropshot was declassified in 1978 and is now widely known. It was aborted by the rapid development of Soviet nuclear weapons, which came as a surprise for the US strategists. Yet plans of a similar kind have been nursed by US reactionary elements all down the years.[4]

According to Yakovlev (1984), these plans were supplemented with psychological warfare against the Soviets. In addition to spreading "subversive and incendiary" ideas about the Soviet Union in Western Europe, the CIA, Yakovlev contends, tried to cultivate discontent among the Soviet peoples. At the same time that the United States was "getting ready to shower the Soviet Union with atomic bombs," the CIA (especially through Radio Liberty and Radio Free Europe) was using "flattery to lull [the Soviet people] into a false sense of security" (ibid.:123–24).

In more recent years, Yakovlev (ibid.:245) argues, the United States has presented "old merchandize in a new wrapping," with the Reagan administration's "crusade against the Soviet Union and socialism." This anti-Soviet revival is, furthermore, shrouded in religious rhetoric: "It has invoked ethical and other norms of Christianity. On its ideological banner is inscribed the name of God" (ibid.).

Soviets contend that in the 1970s the CIA and others began a campaign to spread false propaganda about the level of Soviet defense spending. These reports, Yefremov (1979:252) claims, inaccurately compute Soviet spending in American prices.

> Such cost and prices, however, defy comparison because the Soviet and US systems of price formation are widely discrepant. The Soviet Union is not plagued by inflation. Many other factors, such as the military payroll differentials, etc., should also be taken into account. Hence the CIA method of computation yields nothing like an accurate result.

The reason for "circulating the myth about the Soviet Union's intention to tip the balance of strategic forces in its favour," Yefremov (ibid.) contends, is to "hold back the process of drafting a new strategic arms limitation agreement."

Finally, recent developments in U.S. and NATO policy are seen as provocative and threatening. The "US imperialists and their allies" are creating

> plans of preventive, "limited," protracted, and total nuclear wars, of "star wars," and the like. Recently, this activity was crowned by the insane idea that the imperialist coalition can win a nuclear-missile war. The US military establishment and President Reagan's Administration turn a deaf ear to the obvious facts, to all incontestable scientific proof that a worldwide nuclear-missile conflict would most likely wipe out civilisation and life on earth. (Fedoseyev 1985a:44)

This allegation raises a second important theme of the American threat model—that the United States is responsible for the nuclear arms race.

U.S. Responsibility for the Nuclear Arms Race

> Any serious and factual analysis in the military field shows that it was the US that started the dangerous escalation of the arms race. The real threat is not the "Soviet military threat." History shows that from the invention of the atomic bomb to this day US policy has been based on the continuous build-up of nuclear weapons. The Soviet Union has never wanted to take part in the arms race. It was forced to do so for its own security and that of its allies.
>
> —Lt. General Mikhail Milstein, quoted in
> Wilton John Brown, *Do Russian People Stand for War?*

From a Soviet perspective, there is no question about who is responsible for the nuclear arms race: The United States initiated and perpetuated it. According to Likutov, "the United States has always taken the lead in the arms race while the Soviet Union has only reacted in the interests of its security, to dangers created by the United States" (1985:41). As he sees it,

> The United States has invariably been the initiator of the development and deployment of new types of weapons, while the Soviet Union has only been

taking measures in response to the US challenge. But that is not the whole point.

Hasn't the USSR put forward one initiative after another aimed at removing the war danger and really limiting and ending the arms race? Hasn't the USSR declared its readiness to limit, reduce and prohibit any type of weapons?

On the all-important question of today, that of stopping the arms race and reducing armaments, the Soviet Union has a clear conscience before all peace-loving people. It is not Moscow's fault that the West has for years failed to respond to the numerous constructive Soviet proposals aimed at curbing the arms race and reducing armaments.

Soviet understandings of the mechanisms of the arms race are traced to Lenin, who warned that imperialist militarism would result in the expansion of the military apparatus, creating military monsters (Ponomarev 1985:15). For the Soviets, the source of the arms race is the pressure of the U.S. military-industrial complex (Brown 1985:40–41). On the one hand, "militarism is a tool of the aggressive policy of monopoly capital," and on the other hand, it is "one of the most important sources of superprofits" (Ponomarev 1985:15). As such, it is seen as an inherent consequence of the capitalist system. According to Soviet leaders, the Soviet Union has no military-industrial complex, the United States has led in the development of new nuclear weapons, and the Soviet Union bears no responsibility for the continued escalation of the arms race. On the contrary, according to Ponomarev (ibid.:24), it is "the aggressive policy followed by the United States and NATO [that] compels the Soviet Union and the other countries of the socialist community to take measures to safeguard their security."

Soviets contend that whereas U.S. nuclear weapons are provocative and dangerous, the effect of Soviet weapons on the world has been positive. "There is no doubt," Lev Feoktistov (1985:77) writes, "that the Soviet Union's possessing nuclear arms has always had a sobering effect on the US imperialist circles and thus has stabilised the international situation." According to a recent Warsaw Pact declaration, evidence for this difference between the weapons policies of the two countries can be found in recent U.S. doctrines, such as first strike.

> The new US arms build-up programs are inseparable from the escalation of the strategic concepts and doctrines, such as the "first disarming nuclear strike," "limited nuclear war," "protracted nuclear conflict," and others. All these aggressive doctrines which jeopardise peace are based on the assumption that it is possible to win a nuclear war through the first use of nuclear weapons.
>
> The states represented at the meeting stress emphatically that it is folly to hope to unleash and win a nuclear war. There can be no winners in a nuclear war once it breaks out. (Zhivkov et al. 1985:318)

The Soviets raise a similar objection about SDI. As Konstantin Chernenko wrote in a letter to U.S. scientists, "The Soviet Union reaffirms that it is ready to do its utmost to prevent the sinister plans to take the arms race into outer space from becoming a reality." He contends that the Soviets "are vehemently against the development of large-scale anti-missile defence systems which can only be regarded as systems designed to carry out nuclear aggression with impunity" (Chernenko 1985b:360).

The major alleged difference, then, between U.S. and Soviet policies is that the former seeks superiority and continually escalates the arms race, whereas the latter, as Gorbachev puts it, does "not strive for unilateral advantages, for military superiority over the United States, over NATO countries; we want a termination, not a continuation of the arms race" (Likutov 1985:42). In keeping with this policy, the Soviets have made numerous proposals of steps to reduce the nuclear threat, including no first use, steps for nuclear disarmament and nuclear free zones, and a freeze resolution adopted by the UN General Assembly. Vladimir Razmerov observes that the Soviets have "submitted more than 100 positive proposals to the United Nations" (Brown 1985:61).

Finally, the American threat interpretation of U.S. foreign policy argues that the United States engages in imperialistic activities and exploits the Third World. Soviet military strength, from this perspective, is a necessary deterrent to U.S. imperialism.

U.S. Imperialism and Third World Exploitation

The driving force behind the nuclear arms race, from the Soviet perspective, is the capitalist system and its internal dynamics. As Gorbachev (1985c:23–24) puts it,

> The striving for maximum profits, for the perpetuation of a society of oppression and exploitation, for world domination is the real basis of imperialism. . . .
> The capitalist system is in the throes of a deep crisis which has engulfed the economy and politics and the material and spiritual life of bourgeois society.

Whereas the "war party" (as Lenin called it) has triumphed in the United States as a consequence of that crisis, Gorbachev contends that "there are no forces in the Soviet Union and the fraternal socialist countries that need war" (ibid.:24). One indicator of the "critical economic convulsions" currently afflicting the capitalist world, according to Fedoseyev (1985a:38), is the militarization of the capitalist economies. It is a result of counter-crisis measures and an effort to dampen the effect of the contradictions within the capitalist system (cf. Martynov 1985:207); it "spells salvation for capitalist companies that have run aground."

Thus, "imperialism is forcing the whole world, all the peoples and states to spend many billions of dollars for military purposes" (Fedoseyev 1985a:40). Today, according to Fedoseyev, "truly fantastic sums are being spent senselessly and unproductively, while many hundreds of millions of people are still dragging out a poverty-ridden, miserable existence." This waste affects not only capitalist countries, but the socialist countries as well, so that

> the people of the Soviet Union have an incontestable stake in stopping the arms race. They know that this would not only reduce the war threat but also enable them to tackle their economic tasks more effectively. . . . The chief obstacle . . . is the militarist policy of the extreme reactionary forces of modern-day imperialism." (ibid.:42)

The American threat model implies that the Soviets must continue to reciprocate to U.S. escalations of the arms race in order to protect the security of the Soviet Union and its socialist allies, but it also must act as a brake on imperialist activities in the Third World and elsewhere. The model provides an external reason for failures of the economy. Because "Washington has raised terrorism to the level of state policy" (Likutov 1985:13), the United States threatens the peace and security of the entire world.

Constructing the American Threat

Because policy debates among the ruling Soviet elites are not matters of public record, it is difficult to sketch the outlines of those debates. As in the United States, there are conflicting currents of opinion, often held simultaneously by the same people but emphasized by different factions at various times.

Soviet foreign policy contains a tension between views of the United States and its allies as evil, on the one hand, and of the need to cultivate peaceful coexistence, on the other. Consequently, the 1977 Constitution of the USSR outlines two basic principles of Soviet foreign policy:

> *the principle of peaceful coexistence with states with different social systems*, and *the principle of proletarian, socialist internationalism in relations with other socialist countries and with the peoples and states fighting for social emancipation and national liberation, against imperialism and colonialism.* (quoted in ibid.:9; emphasis in the original)

Contemporary Soviet statements attempt to reconcile the tension by returning to Lenin's analysis of the problems of war and peace. There are two elements of his argument. First, the war about which Lenin was writing in 1917 was an imperialist war: "Lenin and his associates proceeded from the fact that in the minds of working people a desire for emancipation from exploitation and a desire for peace were fused together" (ibid.:7). Vadim Zagladin (1985:135) argues that fighting wars . . . to preserve or expand the positions of monopoly capital . . . was an indissoluble feature of imperialism."

Second, because the transformation from capitalism to socialism would not be simultaneous in all countries, peaceful coexistence is essential in the transitional period. According to Zagladin (ibid.:133), "ever since the time of Marx and Engels, Communists have held that the working class . . . [is] deeply interested in securing a peaceful passage from capitalism to socialism by means of primarily political instruments."

There have been shifts in emphasis between the two themes in Soviet history, one of the most significant being the result of Khrushchev's détente policies (see Zimmerman 1969:213). The détente policies were "considerably at variance with conventional Bolshevik notions about the main enemy" (ibid.). The primary difference between the two positions is whether one admits to some independence of various sectors of the ruling U.S. elite and whether one recognizes an important pro-disarmament segment within the American business community (ibid.). Within the détente frame, the United States was seen as less monolithic in its decisionmaking structure.

Special attention has been paid to the American antiwar movement, for which the Soviet government has shown much support. The task of the peace movement, according to Razmerov (in Brown 1985:52) should be to criticize

> those forces in the US and NATO who advocate an ever more dangerous escalation of the arms race and increase nuclear stockpiles instead of limiting them.
>
> I am sure that more and more demonstrators will see the Soviet Union's peaceful intentions and realise where the real threat comes from.

There is no need, from Razmerov's perspective, for peace forces within the United States and elsewhere to criticize the USSR, because Soviet weapons exist only as a deterrent to others. "Were the Soviet Union to have no such great military power," he insists, "there might appear some irresponsible persons in Western extremist circles who would be ready to resort to nuclear war regardless of the consequences for the future of the human race" (ibid.).

FACTS, FACTIONS, AND FICTIONS

This thumbnail sketch of threat models in the two superpowers only begins to reflect the complexity of the respective positions, but it provides a starting point for our analysis of superpower relations. Although there are competing currents in each country, the dominant picture in each is that the other is an evil power that is a threat to the security and well-being of the globe. These images (and the social and economic structures they legitimate) must be redefined in the process of dismantling the nuclear cage. The obstacles are formidable, but perhaps not insurmountable. In this section, we examine some of the steps that might be taken in that process.

The Politics of Threat Assessment

In March 1985, an exasperated Jimmy Carter defended his presidency against criticisms by Ronald Reagan, insisting that Reagan habitually misstated the record of U.S. weapons modernization. The strategic weapons modernization for which Reagan was taking credit, Carter argued, was initiated long before Reagan took office. He also disputed Reagan's perception of Soviet behavior and pointed out that there were persistent differences between CIA threat assessments and those developed at the Pentagon. He attributed those differences to the complicated nature of developing such reports and to the impact of political goals. "I think the Commander in Chief generally gets what he wants," Carter insisted, "and if the goal is to rapidly escalate the American defense budgets, then those are the kind of estimates he will get" (Mohr 1986:18).

Both Soviet and American threat frames establish boundaries for the interpretation of information about the enemy. Although objectivity in these matters is an admirable goal, it is an impossibility. As Oxford professor Michael E. Howard observes, "one of the oldest 'lessons of history' is that the armaments of an adversary always seem 'brutal' and threatening, adjectives that appear tendentious and absurd when applied to our own" (Scheer 1982:50).

It seems clear that whatever one's perspective on U.S. and Soviet behavior, there are many parallels between the two. True believers in the threat paradigms would never concur, of course, with that assessment. The balance sheet on foreign military interventions (leaving aside domestic considerations for the moment) may be somewhat startling to those living in the United States who are accustomed to the Soviet threat frame (see Daniels and Mogey 1981:12; Barnet 1979) (see Table 11.1).

Of the sixty nationalist revolutions that swept the globe after World War II, only two—in Vietnam and China—were actually communist-led di-

Table 11.1 Balance Sheet of Military Interventions

U.S. Interventions		USSR Interventions	
Iran	1953	Hungary	1956
Guatemala	1954	Czechoslovakia	1968
Lebanon	1956	Afghanistan	1979
Vietnam	1960		
The Congo	1960		
Laos	1960		
Dominican Rep.	1965		
Cambodia	1970		
Grenada	1983		

rectly, and none were led by the Soviets, although the Soviets aided others, often because the rebels found the Soviet Union to be their only source of aid.

The Soviets have more than half a million troops in Eastern Europe, as well as military bases and thousands of troops in Yemen, Ethiopia, Cuba, and elsewhere. Still, according to the Joint Chiefs of Staff (1978:19), the United States is the only nation capable of projecting and sustaining its power, globally by military force. The Rand Corporation reports that the "gross Soviet capabilities to project power abroad do not remotely equal the United States' and could not sustain an occupation or invasion beyond its own immediate border state areas" (Klare 1979:676).

The United States is the only nation with hundreds of thousands of troops stationed on over two hundred bases and military installations around the world. It gives military aid, training, and advisors to sixty-one countries. Whereas the Soviet threat is not to be taken lightly, it must be seen in the light of U.S. activity as well (see Daniels and Mogey 1981).

But, does not the United States support freedom? Despite many good intentions, the U.S. military aligns itself with those who provide stability for American business interests, frequently military dictators. One Brookings Institution report identified 215 times between 1945 and 1975 in which the United States used military force to gain political or economic ends short of actual invasion or battle (Blechman and Kaplan 1978). In short, U.S. activity in global politics does not quite fit the peace-loving image most Americans have of their country.

There is considerable ambivalence in the behavior of both sides. There is also a misleading tendency, within both threat frames, to perceive the other side as monolithic in its decisionmaking structure. Contrary to the American threat paradigm, U.S. decisions are not made by a simple monolithic capitalist elite that dictates exactly what the government shall do in every instance. However, there is, of course, some truth in the Soviet contention that wealthy interests have an inordinate voice in policymaking that contradicts U.S. rhetoric. Nor is the Soviet Union a monolith, as the Soviet threat paradigm would suggest, although there is a centralized decisionmaking apparatus that discourages the sort of public wrangling over policy issues so common in the United States. Elite power structures in both countries manipulate and, to a large extent, control the decisionmaking process.

The issues of freedom and constraint in the political East and West are complex and hotly debated. As Jeffrey Goldfarb (1982:26) points out, "Any sociological analysis of freedom necessitates an analysis of social control. The notion of freedom without any sort of systematic constraint, of a totally free society or individual, does not make any sociological sense." Furthermore, one of the great ironies of the differences between the socialist and capitalist countries is that their differing definitions of freedom are then used to legitimate mechanisms of social control in their respective governments (ibid.).

Within the academic communities of the United States and the USSR, the threat frames have shaped research and discourse about superpower relations. Even in the more open U.S. universities, the academic study of the Soviet Union has been greatly influenced by the cold war. Princeton sovietologist Stephen Cohen (1985:8) contends that "American Sovietology was created as a large academic profession during the worst years of the cold war."

The academic study of the Soviet Union in the United States became highly politicized by the 1950s; Daniel Bell observed that sovietological theories of the time were "designed to shape the behavior of the free world in its opposition to Communism" (quoted in ibid.:11). Sovietologists were drafted to serve in the cold war, and those who resisted became victims of McCarthyist politics. Major figures in the field were branded "a member of the Communist conspiracy" by Senator McCarthy, and the associate director of the Harvard Russian Research Center was forced to resign. As Cohen (1985:18) writes,

> The field took shape . . . in a poisonous atmosphere of witch-hunt in the educational profession that included HUAC's investigation into "Communist Methods of Infiltration" in 1953, the firing of at least six hundred professors and teachers across the country, [and] disloyalty allegations against many more.

The legacy of that period contributed to what Cohen considers a crisis in Soviet studies in the 1960s and 1970s. Although there may be problems with the revisionist scholarship that has emerged in recent years, it is important to critically examine the images of the Soviet Union that have developed in U.S. academia.

If it is difficult to obtain any objectivity in the relatively open universities of the United States, the problems in doing so in Soviet universities seem virtually insurmountable. In short, any studies of the United States or the Soviet Union—in either superpower—must be explored in terms of the interests implied in their conclusions. Although far from being a perfec t solution, one step in that direction is to explore efforts by other part ies to frame the superpower conflicts from other perspectiveᶜ

Other Frames: Europe and the Nonaligned Movement

> Every day we remain alive is a day of grace as if mankind as a whole were a prisoner in the death cell awaiting the uncertain moment of execution. And like every innocent defendant, we refuse to believe that the execution will ever take place.
> We find ourselves in this situation because the nuclear weapon states have applied traditional doctrines of war in a

world where new weapons have made them obsolete. What is the point of nuclear "superiority" or "balance" when each side already has enough weapons to devastate the earth dozens of times over? If the old doctrines are applied in the future, the holocaust will be inescapable sooner or later. But nuclear war can be prevented if our voices are joined in a universal demand in defence of our right to live.

—"Delhi Declaration" by six heads of state:
Raul Alfonsin (Argentina),
Rajiv Gandhi (India),
Miguel de la Madrid (Mexico),
Julius Nyerere (Tanzania),
Olof Palme (Sweden),
and Andreas Papandreou (Greece),
28 January 1985

Outside the privileged and exclusive superpower club, many view the behavior of its members with increasing alarm. The heads of state comprising the Five Continents Peace Initiative quoted above speak on behalf of a growing number of people from nonnuclear nations who have become increasingly critical of U.S. and Soviet policies.[5] Concerns expressed by Europeans in the early 1980s have spread throughout the world, especially since the publication of the nuclear winter studies, which imply that the rest of the world is at risk along with the superpowers.

One of the most promising perspectives is the idea of détente from below, which encourages the growth of an independent peace movement that bypasses the bipolar division of the world. As Czech peace activists Jan Kavan and Zdena Tomin (1983:9) suggest, "Each side must learn to sort the wheat from the chaff and there is no better way than through direct contact." Although these non-superpower voices are not without biases and political agendas of their own, they can serve as a check on the restricting frames developed within the United States and the USSR.

Solving the Puzzle

Economist Kenneth Boulding points to two elements of conflict management that are essential components of the move to abolish warfare. The first is what he calls mature conflict behavior, "the ability to manage conflict without overt violence and even without undue tension or emotions of hatred" (Boulding 1982:235). The second element is intervention by third parties, which have the benefit of bringing alternative frames or perspectives to a conflict. They can provide mediating and teaching roles that enable conflicting parties to understand the limitations of their own definitions of the situation. According to Boulding (ibid.:236–37),

the abolition of war then requires a twofold learning process, one whereby the values and behavior states themselves change toward long-sightedness, toward accurate reality testing of power systems, and toward a value system which lays stress on the welfare of all mankind. The other is a learning pro-

Citizen diplomacy involves interpersonal interaction among U.S. and Soviet citizens. Here Jenifer Turpin (second from left) meets Soviet students on the beach while attending a conference in the USSR as a representative of United Campuses to Prevent Nuclear War (UCAM).

cess whereby we develop the institutions of third-party intervention on a world scale.

A number of concrete steps can be taken within the spirit of Boulding's prescriptions—all of which imply that we should identify the possibility of nuclear annihilation as the major threat to security faced by the superpowers. It is a bilateral threat, rather than a unilateral one, and our efforts need to focus on how to reduce the fears it produces.

First, we need to deconstruct the images of evil that have been built up over time between the superpowers. That is not to say that conflicts can be eliminated, but that the threat assessment should be more sober. There is a certain inevitability to the conflict. Nonetheless, the form that rivalry has taken during the forty years of the nuclear age need not persist. Denunciations of evil in which both sides engage are self-fulfilling prophecies that provoke the very animosity that has been predicted.

A simple reduction of the level of negative rhetoric is not possible, however, without institutional measures that reenforce the common interests of the superpowers: a reduction in (1) the threat of nuclear war, (2) the vast expenditures on armaments, and (3) the proliferation of nuclear weapons to other countries. This step could encompass specific proposals suggested in recent years, such as the development of confidence-building measures and the establishment of a crisis communication center.

A third step would be the institutionalization of ongoing personal contact and the cultivation of mutual interests. This would include an increase in economic and cultural exchanges, large-scale travel and personal contacts between the two nations, and regular face-to-face meetings among political leaders. Occasions for balanced, beneficial reciprocal exchanges and rituals of friendship could help to reduce tensions and redefine the nature of the relationship.

Fourth, bold visionary arms control agreements must be concluded, with adequate verification measures and a framework for settling ambiguities. Comprehensive treaties that are more verifiable than the partial agreements already concluded would increase the possibilities for building trust and would enhance security for both sides.

Finally, the superpowers must demilitarize their global competition. It would be naive to think that these two great systems would suddenly give up their efforts to maximize their political and economic interests in the world. However, rivalries between the superpowers could be institutionalized in a more nonthreatening way from which they would continue to profit. Such measures must take into account the genuine desire for independence and self-determination of other peoples, so that an era of neo-détente is not simply an occasion for increasing U.S. and Soviet domination of the rest of the world.

Although all of these measures may appear to be mere wishful thinking, we must remind ourselves of the alternative to solving the problem of superpower conflict: the potential extinction of the human race.

SUMMARY

The major issue of the nuclear arms race is the hostile relationship between the superpowers. Although there is debate and ambivalence surrounding the policies of both the United States and the Soviet Union, forces in each country engage in the social construction of evil to frame global politics in a way that puts their own policies in a positive light and lays the blame for the arms race on the other superpower. Images of evil thus legitimate massive military spending, sharpen social boundaries, and provide occasions for ritual denunciations that reaffirm prevailing world views.

In the United States, the Soviet threat model compares the Soviet Union to Nazi Germany just prior to the Second World War. Several implications follow from that perspective: Because the Soviets are an expansionist power bent on world domination, the United States is forced to develop a nuclear warfighting capability as a deterrent to Soviet aggression. The Soviets are not to be trusted in light of foreign adventurism and human-rights abuses in their own country, so efforts to reach arms control agreements with them are impractical and dangerous.

Although the Soviet threat model has been the dominant view in the United States, reenforced by the Committee on the Present Danger and the current U.S. administration, an alternative perspective sees the Soviets as a defensive nation obsessed with security and fearful of invasion (because of a long history of attacks by Western and other forces).

In the Soviet Union, an American threat model views the United States as a unique threat to Soviet security and its status as a superpower. Soviet versions of the American threat focus on three themes: (1) the direct threat to the Soviet Union posed by the United States and its allies, with their many military bases, history of aggressive behavior, and repeated attempts to undermine Soviet security; (2) the nuclear arms buildup (for which the United States is responsible); and (3) U.S. imperialism in the Third World. From the Soviet point of view, U.S. rhetoric about the Soviet threat masks true American intentions to engage in imperialist expansion and militaristic behavior—the nuclear arms race is a logical consequence of the capitalist system. Because the USSR allegedly has no military-industrial complex like that of the Western countries, and because the United States initiated the nuclear arms race and continues to escalate it, the Soviet military buildup is simply a defensive response intended to counter American efforts to undermine Soviet security and exploit the Third World.

During the period of détente, a revised version of the American threat emerged in ruling circles of the Soviet Union that emphasizes the need for peaceful coexistence between the superpowers. This perception of U.S. behavior sees the political decisionmaking process in the United States as less monolithic than does the American threat model and emphasizes that the threat of a nuclear holocaust is more dangerous than the threat of U.S. aggression.

Any effort to evaluate the two threat models, or frames, is difficult because of the complexity of the issues involved and the interests served in both superpowers by the social construction of evil. Nonetheless, a balance sheet of aggressive actions and military interventions shows that both superpowers have engaged in belligerent behavior in the global arena, and each threatens the other's security.

It is helpful to examine third-party perspectives of the United States and the Soviet Union, especially the perspectives of nonaligned and nonnuclear countries, which increasingly protest the threat to everyone's security posed by the superpower arms race. Peace activists in many countries are encouraging a détente from below that bypasses the bipolar division of the world and emphasizes personal contacts and shared interests among people of all nations on the planet.

Concrete steps for reducing the fears on both sides produced by the arms race include a reduction in the level of negative rhetoric, the creation of institutional measures that reenforce the common interests of the superpowers, and the institutionalization of ongoing personal contacts, cultural and economic exchanges, and so forth.

Finally, a solution to the superpower conflict requires visionary, verifiable, and comprehensive arms control agreements that actually reverse the upward spiral of the arms race and reduce superpower tensions by increasing security on both sides.

CHAPTER TWELVE

Arms Control
and Disarmament

> If you figure you can't have arms control unless the Rus-
> sians are nice guys, then it seems to me that you're being
> totally illogical. If the Russians could be trusted to be nice
> guys, you wouldn't need strategic arms control. And you
> wouldn't need strategic arms.
>
> —SALT II Negotiator Paul Warnke, quoted in
> Robert Scheer, *With Enough Shovels: Reagan, Bush and Nuclear War*

Arms control negotiations have provided some of our greatest hopes and
worst disappointments in the nuclear age. An evaluation of our progress in
that crucial area depends on one's predispositions. An optimist would point
to the complex (and to some extent workable) structure that provides a
procedure for negotiations. This period of human history, the optimist
feels, will not only be viewed historically (provided humanity survives it) as
one of intense militarization, but also as the beginning of an arms control
and disarmament process that made war truly obsolete. The pessimist,
however, would point out the dramatic increase in nuclear armaments
since negotiations began. Although a series of treaties was greeted with
great fanfare, the pessimist would say, it was accompanied by a relentless
military buildup.

One of the major problems in evaluating progress in this area is that we do not know what the world would be like at this point in history *without* arms agreements. Would it be pretty much the same, since negotiations have conceded only the most expendable aspects of the weapons race? Or would it be radically different? Without the Limited Test Ban treaty and the Nuclear Non-Proliferation treaty, for example, would we now live in a world clouded with radioactive fallout, in which dozens of countries had nuclear weapons?

Despite sincere and profound yearnings for arms control, negotiations have often been exercises in international impression management rather than substantive progress. While pursuing myopic national interests in practice, the major powers vie for a peace-loving image.

In this chapter, we examine some of the major treaties negotiated thus far, as well as proposals that are now under discussion in official and unofficial circles.

PROGRESS IN ARMS CONTROL?

The history of arms control since World War II is a familiar pattern of offers and rejections, counter-offers and rebuffs, as well as some agreements. It is, as Alva Myrdal (1982) puts it, a story of lost opportunities. A summary of the major treaties is included in Appendix B and should be consulted while reading this chapter.

© 1985, Washington Post Writers Group, reprinted with permission.

One of the first arms control proposals was the Acheson-Lilienthal Report prepared by Truman's Under Secretary of State Dean Acheson and David Lilienthal. The report proposed turning over U.S. nuclear technology to an international atomic development authority, which would maintain a monopoly over the research, development, and use of atomic energy. U.S. opposition emerged, however, to relinquishing its nuclear monopoly. Instead of the Acheson-Lilienthal Report, a significantly altered proposal, the Baruch Plan, was presented to the United Nations.

Unlike the Acheson-Lilienthal Report, the Baruch Plan included a set of sanctions and eliminated the Soviet veto in the UN Security Council. Furthermore, the Baruch Plan gave the (U.S.-dominated) UN control over the Soviet Union's military and economic practices. The Soviets rejected it. Their counterproposal to destroy all atomic weapons within three months, followed by penalties for violation, was rejected by the sole nuclear power of the time, the United States.

These proposals reveal a pattern that has characterized many arms control proposals: They are offered in a way that fosters the impression that the initiator is peace-loving, but they contain provisions clearly unacceptable to the other side. In that way, elites try to demonstrate that they have taken peace initiatives but the adversary has failed to reciprocate.

Agreements that have been made in the nuclear age address the following issues: (1) preventing the proliferation of nuclear weapons to nonnuclear states; (2) limiting nuclear tests; (3) enhancing intersuperpower communication; and (4) limiting weapons and delivery systems.

Limiting Proliferation

It was fourteen years after Hiroshima that the first arms control agreement was reached: the 1959 Antarctic treaty prohibiting nonpeaceful uses of the continent. It was the first successful effort to limit the spread of nuclear weapons to nonnuclear areas. Similar agreements have been reached prohibiting nuclear weapons in outer space (the 1967 Outer Space treaty), on the ocean floor (the 1971 Sea-bed treaty), and in Latin America (the 1967 Treaty of Tlatelolco). Although each treaty has significant provisions, each is also riddled with problems. Alva Myrdal (ibid.:99) points out, for example, that the Sea-bed treaty involves "the well-known game of distracting attention from the major problem of the arms race of the seas which concerns, of course, mobile rather than fixed weapon capabilities." In general, such treaties focus on areas (such as Antarctica) in which agreement could be reached without sacrifice.

The most important effort thus far to curb proliferation is the 1968 Treaty on Non-Proliferation of Nuclear Weapons (NPT). The treaty obliges each nuclear-weapon state signing the agreement not to transfer nuclear weapons or control over them to any recipient directly or indirectly. The nonnuclear signatories agreed not to receive nuclear weapons in exchange for information from the nuclear powers about the peaceful uses of nuclear energy. Finally, according to Article VI of the treaty,

> each of the Parties to the Treaty undertakes to pursue negotiations in good faith on effective measures relating to the cessation of the nuclear arms race at an early date and to nuclear disarmament, and on a treaty on general and complete disarmament under strict and effective international control.

The NPT is thus designed to prevent both horizontal nuclear proliferation (i.e., proliferation to nonnuclear powers) and vertical proliferation (the growth of nuclear arsenals within existing nuclear states).

From one point of view, this treaty has been successful: It has minimized proliferation despite the refusal of several key states to sign or ratify it. The major problem is the nuclear powers' gross violation of Article VI, which obliges them to end the arms race. The article is written in such general terms, lacking deadlines and sanctions, that the nuclear powers have responded to protests that they are not working to end the arms race by simply asserting that they are trying to do so.

Limiting Tests

A second significant area of concern in arms control has been nuclear weapons testing. To date, the most important agreement addressing this concern is the 1963 Limited Test Ban treaty (LTBT), which drove nuclear testing underground. It was signed by 111 nations, including all NATO and Warsaw Pact states except France, and most major powers except China. Several nonaligned countries (such as India) have refused to sign, claiming that the treaty discriminates against nonnuclear powers. Following a Chinese nuclear explosion in 1964, the Indian ambassador to the United Nations, Birendra Narayan Chakravarty, told the Disarmament Commission that

> it is no use telling countries, some of which may be even more advanced in nuclear technology than China, that they should enter into a treaty which would stipulate only that they must not acquire or produce these weapons. . . . Unless the nuclear powers . . . undertake from now on not to produce any nuclear weapons or vehicles for weapons delivery and, in addition, agree to reduce their existing stockpile of nuclear weapons, there is no way of doing away with proliferation. (Epstein 1975:57)

Many Indians think that (despite the government's current nonnuclear policies) if Pakistan gets the bomb (which seems likely) India will revive their nuclear weapons program as well.[1]

This successful treaty, now more than twenty years old, was initiated by Kennedy and Khrushchev in the wake of the Cuban missile crisis. Concern about testing had become a major public issue following the Bravo tests of a multimegaton bomb by the United States in the Bikini Atoll, which produced massive fallout that endangered hundreds of Marshall Islanders and fell on some Japanese fishermen in the area. The final step toward the treaty was a unilateral moratorium announced by Kennedy, with a challenge to the Soviets to reciprocate.

Two subsequent agreements in the 1970s closed two loopholes in the treaty,[2] one of which contained detailed procedures for on-site inspections of nuclear test sites, which Soviet Foreign Minister Gromyko indicated the Soviets would be willing to consider. Both new treaties were signed, but neither was ratified by the United States.

The LTBT is, in the final analysis, more of a public health measure than a disarmament treaty (Myrdal 1982:95). It unfortunately demonstrates the character of many treaties; it provides a sense of accomplishment for the elites of the signing states but is more notable for what it does not control than for what it does.

Superpower Communications

The importance of increasing superpower communications has long been recognized, but there has been only one major agreement on that topic: the Memorandum of Understanding between the United States and the USSR Regarding the Establishment of a Direct Communication Link, signed in 1963. The "hotline" agreement provided for a telegraph-teleprinter link between the two countries. It was the result of Kennedy administration concern about its inability to communicate directly with the Soviets during the Cuban missile crisis. (Modernization agreements were reached in 1971 and 1984, providing for additional circuits and satellite links.)

Widespread misconception of the hot line and how it works has been spread by such popular films as *Dr. Strangelove* and *Fail Safe*. Although it makes a better dramatic scene to show the American president talking to the Soviet premier on the telephone, the real hot line does not provide voice or visual contact. Messages from Moscow to Washington are typed and transmitted in Russian; those from Washington to Moscow are in English.

Limiting Weapons and Delivery Systems

The Strategic Arms Limitation Talks (SALT) were initially the source of some optimism that nuclear arms would finally be limited. When Richard Nixon visited Leonid Brezhnev in Moscow in May 1972, two arms limitation agreements were signed: the Anti-Ballistic Missile (ABM) treaty[3] and an interim agreement. The ABM agreement initially limited the deployment of ABM systems to two each in the United States and the Soviet Union: one to protect ICBMs and another to protect the nation's capital. The United States had no ABM system at the time (although it was beginning construction of two sites); the Soviets had one ABM system functioning near Moscow. At another Nixon-Brezhnev summit in 1974, the number of installations on each side was reduced to one. The Soviet Union left its system around Moscow operational, and the United States maintained a system around ICBM bases in North Dakota, although the system was eventually dismantled because it was believed to be ineffective.

The ABM agreement was facilitated by the climate of détente, the high cost of building ABM systems, and the questionable effectiveness of a missile defense. The Soviets claim that there was a fourth reason for the agreement: The United States had achieved "considerable military-strategic superiority" (Yefremov 1979:158) and was thus willing to enter into a treaty with the USSR.

The 1972 Interim Agreement provided for a freeze (for a period of five years) of the aggregate number of ICBM launchers and ballistic missile launchers on submarines. It gave the Soviets an advantage in the number of launch vehicles, but left the United States with a substantial technological advantage. Although the agreement has expired, both sides have continued to adhere to it. The major loophole in this agreement (and there are always loopholes) is that it does nothing to limit the adaptation of single warhead missiles to MIRVs. First the United States and then the USSR simply added more warheads to each launcher.

The SALT II agreement, signed by both countries in 1979 but not ratified by the United States, sets limits on particular types of weapons systems and the number of MIRVs. It restricts the testing and deployment of new types of ICBMs, bans the SS-16, and sets ceilings on the launch-weight and throw-weight of strategic ballistic missiles.

As a presidential candidate, Ronald Reagan attacked the SALT II treaty, saying that it gave the Soviets an unfair advantage. As president, he maintained a two-fold attitude toward the treaty until 1986: (1) It is fatally flawed, but (2) the United States will abide by its provisions. The anti-SALT faction within the administration won at least a temporary victory in May 1986, when the president announced that the United States would no longer be bound by the treaty.

Controversy around the agreement has thrived in the United States. In 1984 two conservative Republican senators, John P. East (North Carolina) and Steven D. Symms (Idaho), complained that continued compliance with the unratified treaty "could easily be interpreted as appeasement of the Soviet Union." They argued that the administration's behavior was unconstitutional and illegal because the Senate, which is given the responsibility of ratifying treaties, refused to ratify SALT II (Mohr 1984). The two senators also threatened to vote against the deployment of the MX if the president did not stop abiding by the treaty's provisions (Gwertzman 1984a). The president's decision not to observe the limits of the treaty provoked worldwide protests and efforts in the U.S. Congress to prevent funding of programs that would exceed the SALT boundaries.

Perhaps the most important aspect of the SALT agreements is that over a period of seven years they established a set of procedures for further negotiations that would have imposed far-reaching limits on the arms race. Since the election of the Reagan administration, however, the SALT process has been jettisoned by the United States.

Russett and Blair (1978:118) suggest that "a common view of SALT is that it is more a symbol of détente and a means of keeping détente alive than a means of controlling the arms race. Accordingly, the results of SALT are often cosmetic, glossing over substantive disagreements on the most vital issues." Within the Peace through Strength context of Reagan administration foreign policy, attitudes toward détente have been ambivalent at best, so that there has been no desire to pursue the SALT process. Consequently, the major achievement of the SALT accords—the creation of a mechanism for truly significant agreements—appears for nought, unless a future administration returns to them.

MAJOR PROPOSALS

Since the collapse of the SALT process, a number of arms control proposals (both official and unofficial) have emerged from several quarters. A resurgence of the peace movement in the 1980s, first in Europe and then in the United States and elsewhere, has put pressure on the superpowers to negotiate further agreements, thus far without success.

Bilateral Nuclear Freeze

The general principle of the bilateral nuclear freeze proposal, already discussed in some detail in Chapter Seven, was first discussed in 1964 and was recently revived by Randall Forsberg and others. Forsberg's proposal calls for a "mutual freeze on the testing, production, and deployment of nuclear weapons and of missiles and new aircraft designed primarily to deliver nuclear weapons" (1980:52). The proposal has received much popular attention in the United States and was adopted as official policy by the Soviet Union, but it has encountered stiff resistance from the Reagan administration.

START: Strategic Arms Reduction Talks

The arms control climate changed considerably with the 1980 election of Ronald Reagan. Influenced by the Committee on the Present Danger, the administration has evaluated the arms control process from a Peace through Strength position, assuming that arms control will not work with untrustworthy Soviet adversaries. The solution to the problem of U.S. security, therefore, does not lie in the failed arms control regime (according to this argument), but in a return to a crude preponderance: Build another seventeen thousand strategic warheads, beef up all aspects of the strategic triad, and develop accurate new weapons.

Under strong pressure (both domestic and from European allies), the president in 1982 proposed a new round of talks in Geneva. The administration's attitudes toward arms control are reflected in the people appointed to represent the United States in those negotiations, such as Peace through Strength founder Paul Nitze and retired Senator John Tower, long-time chair of the Senate Armed Services Committee who helped lead the fight against SALT II in the Senate. Kenneth Adelman, who was appointed director of the U.S. Arms Control and Disarmament Agency, reportedly said that arms control is a sham.

In the Geneva talks, the Reagan administration made a two-phased START proposal (shown in Table 12.1), which it claimed would result in deep-cuts in the superpowers' strategic arsenals. Although one expects negotiating positions to have elements each side is prepared to give away in the bargaining process, the START proposals could scarcely have been taken seriously by the Soviets. The first part of phase one would have had about the same impact on both sides, but a further reduction to 2,500 warheads would have resulted in the Soviets giving up 2,500 warheads and the Americans being permitted to add 900. The reason for the inequity is the focus on land-based missiles: The Soviets have approximately three-fourths of their warheads on land-based missiles, whereas the United States has only about one-fourth of its arsenal there.

The second phase of START focuses again on ICBMs, resulting in each side reducing its ICBM arsenals to 850 missiles. The United States would give up only 204 ICBMs, whereas the USSR would have to dismantle 550. Similarly, the reduction in total throw-weight would affect the Soviet arsenal more than that of the United States, since Soviet missiles are larger and heavier (and consequently less accurate) than U.S. missiles.

Much of the arms control community in the United States was quite disturbed by the START proposals. Former Secretary of State Edmund Muskie contended that START "may be a secret agenda for sidetracking *disarmament* while the United States gets on with *rearmament*—in a hopeless quest for superiority in these things" (quoted in Scheer 1982:7). When the

Table 12.1 The Start Proposal

Phase I	Phase II
1. Reduce number of weapons on ICBMs and SLBMs by ⅓, from 7,500 to 5,000	1. Reduce number of ICBMs to 850
2. No more than 2,500 warheads on ICBMs	2. Reduce *throw weight* to equal level

Source: U.S. Department of State (1982)

United States began to deploy cruise and Pershing missiles in Europe at the end of 1983, the Soviets suspended the Geneva talks.

The Build-down Proposal

Another Reagan administration proposal, the so-called Build-down proposal, calls for (1) a reduction in the number of SALT-accountable warheads from about 8,500 to 5,000 on each side, and (2) a reduction of the "potential destructive capability" of delivery vehicles, a decrease from 15,000 to 8,500 standard weapon stations. According to the build-down plan, each new missile deployed would result in the retirement of two existing missiles. The theory behind the proposal is that the greatest threat to security is MIRV technology and that multi-warhead missiles should be replaced with new cruise and Pershing missiles and eventually with the single-warhead Midgetman. As with the START proposals, build-down is focused on multiple-warhead land-based missiles, that is, the heart of the Soviet arsenal.

Although the proposal sounds good on the surface, it involves trading old weapons for new ones, and it does not control any arms—it would not overtly ban the development or deployment of any type of weapon (Paine 1983). It reflects a U.S. determination to build a new generation of counterforce weapons. The result would be Soviet reciprocation.

European Force Reduction Talks (INF)

The INF negotiations were another casualty of the Soviet walkout from the Geneva talks following NATO deployment of U.S. cruise and Pershing II missiles. In those negotiations, the Reagan administration proposed a so-called zero option—the United States would not deploy its cruise and Pershing II missiles if the Soviets removed their SS-20s stationed in Eastern Europe. The primary stumbling block of the INF negotiations was the status of French and British missiles, which should carry 1200 warheads by 1990. The USSR claimed that they had to be counted because they posed a threat to Soviet security; the United States claimed that they were irrelevant in bilateral talks.

Comprehensive Test Ban

One of the oldest proposals for slowing the arms race is a comprehensive test ban (CTB). That was the original goal of the negotiations that led to the 1963 Limited Test Ban, and the goal was revived in 1977 by the USSR, the United States, and Great Britain. Major agreements were reached by the negotiators in Geneva in 1980, but the United States walked out of those talks. The most significant area of agreement was the provision for limited on-site inspections for verification of compliance (see Goldblat 1982). Prior to the CTB negotiations, the Soviets had regarded on-site inspections as unnecessary because of satellite monitoring capabilities, and therefore a technique used by western diplomats "to thwart the conclusion of any disarmament agreements" (Yefremov 1979:140). More recently, the Soviets have agreed to a broad range of on-site inspections.

The major advantages of a *comprehensive* test ban are that it would eliminate ambiguity and would be easily verifiable.[4] A major push by several peace movement organizations for the United States and the Soviet Union to end testing on 6 August 1985, the fortieth anniversary of the bombing of Hiroshima, was unsuccessful. The Soviet Union, however, announced a unilateral moratorium on all nuclear testing in July 1985, to last until January 1986 or as long as the United States also observed the moratorium. Following the January deadline, the Soviets extended the moratorium, even though the U.S. administration had dismissed the moratorium as mere propaganda and refused to reciprocate. The Soviets refrained from testing any nuclear weapons for a total of eighteen months.

No-First-Use Proposal

Another proposal that has gained support in many quarters is a "no first use" of nuclear weapons policy. Such a position is official Soviet policy but has been rejected by the NATO allies, which reserve the option to initiate the use of nuclear weapons to turn back a conventional Soviet attack. A no-first-use proposal by McGeorge Bundy, George Kennan, Robert McNamara, and Gerard Smith (1984) received considerable attention but has not been taken seriously by the U.S. government.

Whereas the Reagan administration considers such a policy unthinkable, it is important to the Soviets, who claim that the reason the United States refuses to adopt such a policy is that the Pentagon is really preparing to deliver a first nuclear strike.

The New Abolitionist Movement and Nonviolent Civilian Defense

For some, such proposals as a bilateral freeze, a CTB, and no-first-use are insufficient to provide a long-term means of escape from the nuclear cage. Although they support some of those proposals as immediate stop-gap measures, they claim that it is essential to go much farther. Many advocate more sweeping demands, such as the complete abolition of nuclear weapons.

The New Abolitionist movement is primarily a religious movement inspired by the nineteenth-century movement to abolish slavery. Advocates draw parallels between false claims against the earlier abolitionists that it was idealistic to think that slavery could be abolished and the current response to their call for the abolition of nuclear weapons. Some abolitionists advocate the civilian-based defense proposals discussed in Chapter Seven. They contend that the entire concept of security needs to be redefined and that in the long run it is important to establish new, nonviolent means of security.

Ironically, the abolitionist rhetoric has been co-opted by both Reagan and Gorbachev. At their summit in Reykjavik, they discussed the possibility of completely eliminating all strategic nuclear weapons, and perhaps *all* nuclear weapons. In the stormy debate following the summit, U.S. officials at first denied that Reagan had agreed to eliminating anything but ballistic missiles. The confusion was probably a result of their attempts to "clarify" what had happened at the summit—they could not believe that the president had actually done what the Soviets were saying he had done. Similarly, the Joint Chiefs of Staff essentially admitted that they were caught unawares by the Soviet proposals because they had never even considered the option of scrapping all strategic nuclear weapons. Nine months prior to the summit, however, Gorbachev had proposed just that—apparently he was not taken seriously at the Pentagon.

Gorbachev's proposal had three stages. In the first, the superpowers would "reduce by half the nuclear weapons that can reach each other's territory."[5] It would include the total elimination of medium-range missiles (ballistic and cruise missiles) in Europe and would ban the development of space-based weapons. England and France would not build up their nuclear arsenals, and the United States (and presumably the USSR) would not supply other countries with weapons.

In the second stage, which would start no later than 1990, all nuclear powers "would pledge to freeze all their nuclear arms and not to have them on the territories of other countries." The United States and USSR would continue their reductions, eliminating medium-range and tactical weapons, stopping nuclear tests, and banning all nonnuclear weapons based on new techniques like particle beams.

Finally, in the third stage, beginning no later than 1995, all remaining nuclear weapons would be eliminated, so that "by the end of 1999 there will be no nuclear weapons on earth." The Soviet proposal includes the suggestion that "verification of the destruction or limitation of arms should be carried out both by national technical means and through on-site inspections." The proposal states, further, that "the USSR is ready to reach agreement on any other additional verification measures."

In short, although it has not been taken as a serious proposal by the United States, the Soviet proposal offers a program for complete nuclear disarmament by 1999. If Gorbachev is bluffing, Reagan could call his bluff by taking him up on the offer.

ARMS CONTROL: SOME CONCLUSIONS

President Reagan's conclusion that the arms control regime has failed to control arms is unfortunately accurate. Even the most successful agreements have rationalized an escalation, rather than facilitated any retrenchment, in the arms race. On the other hand, it is impossible to evaluate what might have happened had there not been any agreements, and past failure does not necessarily imply the impossibility of future success.

A series of obstacles lie in the path of arms control, however, including the nature of international politics, worst-case scenarios, problems of equivalency, issues of enforcement and verification, and vested interests that lobby for escalation.[6] These are discussed in the following sections.

The Nature of International Politics

The global political order is structured around a system of nation-states, each seeking to further its own interests, and a system of bloc politics controlled primarily by the United States and the Soviet Union, each vying to manipulate less powerful states to support its own bloc.

As long as national elites continue to define security within the bounds of a nationalistic ideology rather than recognizing the common, global nature of security in the nuclear age, there will be strong resistance to major arms control agreements. That does not mean, of course, that such agreements are impossible to achieve even within a nationalistic context, because one might legitimately define arms control as in the national interest. However, the major impact of nationalism is to undermine disarmament attempts in a radical manner. International politics are characterized by deceit, fraud, destruction, lying, and violence rather than by the pursuit of peace, and the leaders of all countries tend to be profoundly distrustful of other states—including their allies.

Any head of state who reaches agreement with other states suffers accusations within his or her nation of being soft on the enemy. Any successful treaty requires two sets of negotiations—one external (with other nation-states) and one domestic. Khrushchev, for example, was accused by the Stalinists of being "soft on capitalism" for signing the Limited Test Ban treaty. Kennedy was able to avoid that type of criticism, to some extent, because of his belligerence toward the Soviet Union during the Cuban missile crisis. It is no accident that Richard Nixon concluded the largest number of agreements in the nuclear age. He had made his political career in the 1950s as part of Senator McCarthy's anticommunist campaign. Thus, ironically, the head of state most likely to be *able* to conclude an agreement is often the one least likely to attempt to do so.

Worst-Case Scenarios and Problems of Equivalency

The dynamics of planning, which involve the construction of worst-case scenarios, constitute another obstacle to negotiations. There is always a fear on the part of policymakers and planners that some stoppage of research and development might result in a secret, quantitative leap by the other side, thus fueling the climate of mistrust and fear that helps feed worst-case scenarios in the first place.

Worst-case scenarios are often precipitated by the problem of equivalency. As Myrdal (1982) suggests, the Soviet Union and the United States are locked in a race "out of step" with one another. It is difficult to compare different types of weapons systems, strategies, and so forth; it takes years to negotiate an intricate treaty and to decide how to equate offensive and defensive weapons (or even to define which is which).

The SALT II agreements, for example, were mutually agreed upon as equitable when signed by the superpowers. Before the treaty was ratified by the U.S. Senate, however, two major events changed the U.S. political climate and undermined the consensus on the treaty: The Soviet invasion of Afghanistan fueled anti-Soviet fears, and the election of Ronald Reagan put an opponent of arms control in the White House. Although the terms of the agreement did not substantially change, the perceptions and definitions of those matters did.

Enforcement and Verification

One of the most significant stumbling blocks to arms control is enforcement and verification.[7] Two basic ways to verify arms control agreements are by national technical means and by cooperative international technical means. The former are carried out unilaterally by one country to verify for itself how well another nation is keeping an agreement. Satellites, specialized radars, and other devices are used. To monitor test firings, a nation can use cameras, infrared detectors, radars tracking ICBMs in flight, and radios receiving the adversary's telemetry signals.

Former Defense Secretary Brown claimed that national technical means enable us to monitor all key aspects of Soviet strategic programs. According to Brown,

> There is a double bind which serves to deter Soviet cheating. To go undetected, any Soviet cheating would have to be on so small a scale that it would not be militarily significant. Cheating on such a level would hardly be worth the political risks involved. On the other hand, any cheating serious enough to affect the military balance would be detectable in sufficient time to take whatever action the situation required. (Committee on Foreign Relations 1979:221)

The current administration, however, has less confidence in such means and has made the verification issue a major rationale for not concluding further agreements.

Although national technical means of verification will probably not prevent all cheating, they probably can prevent any *significant* cheating that would result in a change in the strategic balance of power. It takes about eight to fifteen years to develop a new weapons system from the gleam in a designer's eye to the deployment of the system; it is impossible to develop a weapons system in secret. The extent of the U.S. capability to determine the state of Soviet weapons was hinted at the SALT I talks; U.S. negotiators actually told Soviet negotiators how many weapons the Soviet Union had.

Cooperative international technical means of verification include such measures as seismic monitoring stations, which can detect nuclear explosions with considerable confidence. Information from the stations can be exchanged through the World Meteorological Organization, so that all signatories (e.g., to a comprehensive test ban) could obtain information about such explosions. In the event of a comprehensive ban on nuclear weapons tests or flight tests, a combination of national and cooperative international technical means would provide a wide measure of confidence in verification procedures.

Another cooperative means is the creation of international commissions as forums for resolving issues of compliance. The model for such institutions is the Standing Consultative Commission (SCC) created to monitor compliance with the SALT agreements. The SCC was established on 21 December 1972 (see Article XIII of the ABM treaty) and meets twice a year. Each superpower has a commissioner, a deputy commissioner, an executive secretary, and various advisors on the commission.

In response to a film entitled *The SALT Syndrome*, produced by the American Security Council,[8] an interagency group composed of representatives of the Department of Defense, Joint Chiefs of Staff, State Department, CIA, Arms Control and Disarmament Agency, and the National Security Council issued a statement claiming that the

> specific charge that the Soviets cheated on SALT I is inaccurate. We raised a number of issues with the Soviets in SALT I—as they did with us—but in every case the activity in question either ceased or subsequent information clarified the situation and allayed our concern. SALT II will actually help us monitor Soviet strategic forces by establishing rules for verification. (Center for Defense Information 1982:1)

Ambassador Robert Buchheim, until recently the U.S. commissioner in the SCC, has stated that "The SCC has never yet had to deal with a case of real or apparent clear and substantial non-compliance with an existing agreement" (ibid.).

A summary of SCC actions prepared by the Center for Defense Information (ibid.) shows a general pattern in Soviet responses to charges taken before the SCC by the United States. First, the Soviets have claimed that they were not doing what the Americans claimed they were doing. They then contend that even if they were doing it, it would not be a violation of a treaty. Finally, the suspect activity has ceased. For example:

> During 1973 and 1974, U.S. observation of Soviet testing led to conclusions that an air defense radar was being used in an anti-missile role in possible violation of the ABM Treaty. It raised the issue with the USSR in the SCC.
>
> The Soviets insisted that no air defense radar had been tested in an ABM role. They also maintained that the activities in question (range safety and in-

strumentation) were not limited by the ABM Treaty. A short time later the radar activity of concern during Soviet missile tests had ceased. (ibid.:2)

The United States has raised eight possible Soviet violations with the SCC, and the Soviets have raised questions about six possible U.S. violations. Each of the issues was resolved to the satisfaction of both parties.

To summarize, a number of observations might be made about the arms control process. First, the most progress has been made in areas of no immediate consequence, such as the creation of a nuclear-free Antarctica. A second area of progress has been with questionable or extremely expensive options, such as the ABM system, although controversy surrounding that issue has been revived by recent discussions about SDI.

Third, the most discouraging conclusion is that arms control talks thus far have legitimated the arms race and allowed for its escalation. Nonetheless, a framework for negotiations has been established that *could* lead to more meaningful agreements. That development is historically unprecedented and a hopeful sign, and both public and elite opinion generally affirm arms control, at least in principle.

Finally, it must be noted that time is running out. For agreements to be achieved, the superpower elites must be *forced* to negotiate. A new generation of weapons is creating a verification nightmare, with small missiles that are virtually undetectable and the expansion of the arms race into outer space. Without a renewed will and dramatic changes in our negotiating approach, the era of arms control may soon pass us by.

CHAPTER THIRTEEN

The Church and the Bomb

> Jerry, I sometimes believe we're heading very fast for Armageddon.
>
> —Ronald Reagan to Jerry Falwell,
> quoted in the *Boston Globe*, 2 May 1982

"Where you stand depends on where you sit." That aphorism has been a major theme of this book and can be seen nowhere more clearly than in an examination of the role of the Christian church in the debate over the nuclear arms race. The church has a special position in that debate, in large part because of its transnational character: It is the only major institution that bridges the people of the two major nuclear powers. It rivals the most powerful multinational corporations in its scope and influence on a global basis, and it has no rivals in terms of its historical roots. The church's ideology simultaneously provides the most radical opposition to and legitimation for the arms race.

By its emphasis on the familial ties of all humanity, the church provides institutionalized rituals that undercut the nationalistic basis of the arms race. It thus offers a vantage point from which the arms race can be viewed that differs substantially from that of most institutions with high visibility in modern society.

How an individual perceives the rationality of a position on any issue always depends on that individual's point of view. As already argued, differing frames for examining security issues are constructed from different positions within the decisionmaking structure of a society. Nuclear policy positions like a countervailing strategy appeal to those who make decisions about the deployment and use of nuclear weapons. Further, beliefs about how best to acquire security are highly correlated with one's relationship to the actual decisionmaking process. Those who sit in the seats of power cannot understand why people with whom they agree about the importance of preventing nuclear war cannot recognize the necessity of deploying warfighting weapons that provide a flexible response in the event that deterrence fails. Similarly, many outside that circle of policymakers have trouble understanding why those within it are blind to the inevitability of a holocaust if the arms race is not stopped. Religious leadership defines the arms race from an outsider's point of view.

One of the most interesting aspects of this debate is the fact that the Christian church is at the core of the peace movement, at least in the United States. The church's position has puzzled many people, for at least two reasons. First, there is a wide diversity of opinions regarding war within the church; the Roman Catholic Church membership, for example, runs the gamut from Defense Secretary Weinberger and Alexander Haig to Archbishop Hunthausen in Seattle, who calls the Trident submarine base in his diocese the Auschwitz of Puget Sound. Second, Christian groups throughout history have traditionally legitimated warmaking, from chaplains in uniform to blessings on the battlefield. Yet condemnations of the nuclear arms race have become strict orthodoxy in most Christian denominations. As one *Christian Science Monitor* reporter put it, when the Pope and Billy Graham agree on something, religious people must sit up and take notice.

RELIGIOUS CRITIQUES OF THE NUCLEAR ARMS RACE

> In the words of our Holy Father, we need a "moral about-face." The whole world must summon the moral courage and technical means to say "no" to nuclear conflict; "no" to weapons of mass destruction; "no" to an arms race which robs the poor and the vulnerable; and "no" to the moral danger of a nuclear age which places before humankind indefensible choices of constant terror or surrender. Peacemaking is not an optional commitment. It is a requirement of our faith. We are called to be peacemaker, not by some movement of the moment, but by our Lord Jesus.
>
> —National Conference of Catholic Bishops,
> *The Challenge of Peace: God's Promise and Our Response*

Christian institutions, and individuals within the church, are providing leadership in a burgeoning global movement against the nuclear arms race.

Opposition to nuclear weapons has spread within the church from grass-roots organizations, such as Pax Christi and the Inter-faith Task Force, to the very top of the ecclesiastical hierarchy. There continues to be considerable controversy, especially among the laity, but there is a remarkable consensus developing at the top and in many sectors of the grass roots that the nuclear arms race is a sin and opposition to it is a Christian duty.

Why has there been such a dramatic shift from the mainstream Christian legitimation of war (as in World War II) to the widespread opposition the churches are now posing? It is a rather complicated matter, but two major changes have occurred that have affected the church's position.

The first is the change in the nature of war brought on by nuclear weapons, which has undercut the traditional Christian basis for legitimating war—the just-war theory. A second concerns the evolving relationship between the Christian church and the power structure of Western society. The traditional alliance between the church and the ruling powers of society since the fourth century A.D. has been unraveling since the eighteenth-century Enlightenment. That alliance consisted of the legitimation of the state by the church in exchange for a special status for the church in society. It reached its apex in medieval Europe, when the ruling aristocratic and ecclesiastical elites were virtually one and the same. The breakdown of the medieval alliance has resulted not in a simple consensus of opposition to the Western power elite but in a divided church characterized by splits within and between religious organizations, as well as shifting alliances from issue to issue, country to country, and over time. Within the ruling bodies of mainline Christian denominations in the United States a consensus has emerged around a relatively abstract opposition *in principle* to the arms race.[1] There is, however, some disagreement over specific policies and means for affecting them.

Pockets of opposition to that leadership consensus do exist, especially on the Christian right, yet a substantial proportion of the population equate a nuclear holocaust with Armageddon. A number of themes and responses have emerged within the church, ranging from the traditional legitimation role that supports the nuclear arms race as an element of deterrence to the call for a radical rejection of nuclear weapons by members of the new abolitionist movements.

CRITICAL THEMES WITHIN THE CHURCH

Three Traditions on War:
Pacifism, Just War, and the Crusade

Within the Christian tradition, there are three major strands, held in tension over the centuries, that address the problems of war and peace: (1) the pacificism and nonviolence of the early church,[2] (2) the just-war teachings (see Hollenbach 1983; Johnson 1981), and (3) the crusade, in which fighting is a sacred cause (see Bainton 1960; Hinson 1982:52; Johnson 1981; and Walters 1973).

Pacifism. There is considerable evidence that the early church was pacifistic. Among the reasons for repudiating participation in warfare was the fact that it required Christians to engage in such pagan exercises as the worship of the emperor (see Bainton 1960). The primary reasons, however, were the example of Jesus' life and teachings, and the Christian principle of agape (love that was to be directed toward all humanity), as suggested by a number of the Church Fathers.

Tertullian, for example, asked: "Whom have we to hate? If injured, forbidden to retaliate, . . . who can suffer injury at our hands" (*Apology*). Tertullian held that love and killing were incompatible with one another and that the injunction to love one's enemies was the final test of one's relationship to God. He did not even allow for self-defense, but counted it "better to be slain than to slay." Similarly, Origen argued (in *Against Celsius*, III.7) that Jesus "did not consider it compatible with his inspired legislation to allow the taking of human life in any form at all." Saint Cyprian of Carthage, in the third century, praised the Christians of his day by noting,

> They do not even fight against those who are attacking since it is not granted to the innocent to kill even the aggressor, but promptly to deliver up their souls and blood that, since so much malice and cruelty are rampant in the world, they may more quickly withdraw from the malicious and the cruel.[3]

The early church allowed converts already in the army to remain in the military but under the strict condition that they were not to kill or they would be excommunicated. As suggested in the Canons of Hippolytus, a "soldier of civil authority must be taught not to kill men and to refuse to do so if he is commanded." Thus, Saint Martin of Tours lay down his arms after his conversion, claiming, "Hitherto I have served you as a soldier. Allow me now to become a soldier of God. . . . I am a soldier of Christ. It is not lawful for me to fight."[4]

That position was criticized by some non-Christians, who claimed that the church was merely playing into the hands of the state's enemies, and ultimately the church's enemies. One famous early critic, Celsius,[5] complained,

> If everyone were to do the same as you, there would be nothing to prevent [the emperor] from being abandoned, alone and deserted, while earthly things would come into the power of the most lawless and savage barbarians and nothing more would be heard among men either of your worship or of the true wisdom.

Hinson (1982:52) suggests, however, that Celsius apparently had a limited acquaintance with Christianity, because one segment of the church had already been drawn into service under Marcus Aurelius.

Johnson (1981:xxvi) is probably correct when he observes that it is dangerous to draw a clean line between the pacifist and just-war traditions in Christianity. "Like the concept of the just war," he argues, "that of pacifism is not absolute. Rather, there are many forms, theoretical and historical, of both."

The clear turning point for the church on issues of war and peace was the conversion of the Emperor Constantine to Christianity in 312, which resulted in the forcible Christianization of the Roman Empire. Before a decisive battle, Constantine reportedly had a vision in which he saw the sign of a cross in the heavens and the words "In This Sign Conquer." He had the sign painted on his troops' shields, won the battle, and became convinced that the Christian God was a great god of war.

The pacifism of the early church was not well suited to Constantine's plans, and eventually Christian doctrines were modified under the new conditions in which Christianity was the official religion of the empire. The result was the development of the just-war theory, a dominant Christian position since the time of Saint Augustine.

Just-War theory.   At the core of many Christian critiques of the nuclear arms race is an analysis of the contemporary implications of the just-war tradition (see National Conference of Catholic Bishops [NCCB] 1983:26ff.; United Methodist Bishops 1986). According to the Catholic bishops, the just-war doctrine "begins with the presumption which binds all Christians: we should do no harm to our neighbors; how we treat our enemy is the key test of whether we love our neighbor; and the possibility of taking even one human life is a prospect we should consider in fear and trembling" (NCCB: 1983:26). In short, the original purpose of just-war teaching was an effort to prevent war: The decision to go to war should require "extraordinarily strong reasons for overriding a presumption *in favor of peace and against war*" (ibid.:27).

When attempting to determine if such conditions exist, two types of criteria must be applied: those relating to the decision to fight—*Jus ad Bellum* criteria—as well as standards for the conduct of war once the decision to fight has been made—*Jus in Bello* criteria (cf. Johnson 1973a, 1973b; Hollenbach 1983).

The former (*Jus ad Bellum*) rely primarily upon the issue of *proportionality*; i.e., Is the good to be gained from the battle proportionate to the cost to be incurred? According to the U.S. Catholic Bishops (NCCB 1983), a decision to go to war is possible only when the following conditions are met: (1) just cause, (2) competent authority, (3) comparative justice, (4) right intention, (5) last resort, (6) probability of success, and (7) proportionality.

In order for a war to have *just cause*, there must be a "real and certain danger," such as the need to protect innocent lives and to secure basic human rights. However, "as both Pope Pius XII and Pope John XXIII made clear, if war of retribution was ever justifiable, the risks of modern war negate such a claim today (ibid.:28).

The second criterion, *competent authority*, refers to a belief that the decision to go to war must be for the common good, rather than for private gain. Generally, therefore, declarations of war must be made by public officials, although there are extreme cases in which revolution may be considered legitimate.

The third criterion, *comparative justice*, requires that the decision to go to war be made in light of the presumption against war and the limits of any just cause. In particular: "Do the rights and values involved justify killing? For whatever the means used, war, by definition, involves violence, destruction, suffering, and death" (ibid.:29). Relatedly, the path of war must be taken only with *right intention*, which means that there must be a just cause and that during the conflict one continues to pursue peace and reconciliation, "including avoiding unnecessarily destructive acts or imposing unreasonable conditions [e.g., unconditional surrender]" (ibid.). The insistence by the United States that Japan surrender unconditionally to bring World War II to an end, for example, would not meet the traditional criterion of right intention.

The fifth standard by which the decision to go to war must be evaluated is that of *last resort*: All other alternatives must have failed. Today, even if all of the previous criteria were rigorously met (which is difficult to imagine), the major powers would have difficulty demonstrating that all other means of resolving a conflict had been tried, considering the current disproportionate expenditure of resources on military means for resolving conflicts. The current global geopolitical system is organized not so much to prevent wars as to make them an inevitability in the event that a nation feels itself wronged.

It is impossible to envision any way in which a nuclear war could meet the final two criteria of the just-war tradition: the *probability of success*, and *proportionality*. Except in the most limited of nuclear conflicts, how could any party waging the war be successful in preserving the values for which the war was allegedly waged? The purpose of this criterion is "to prevent irrational resort to force or hopeless resistance when the outcome of either will be clearly disproportionate or futile."[6] Finally, the "damage to be inflicted and the costs incurred by war must be proportionate to the good expected by taking up arms" (ibid.:31). As with the probability of success, proportionality in a nuclear war is possible only in a strictly limited nuclear war. One must ask, therefore, in the most optimistic scenarios, what objectives would legitimate the destruction of a nation's heartland, or several major cities? Nuclear winter theories suggest, of course, that it is unlikely that a catastrophe of enormous proportions could be prevented even in a limited nuclear exchange.

Even after the decision is made to go to war, the conduct of war itself must be subject to two principles: *proportionality* and *discrimination*. As the U.S. bishops put it, "Response to aggression must not exceed the nature of the aggression. To destroy civilization as we know it by waging a 'total war' as today it *could* be waged would be a monstrously disproportionate response to aggression on the part of any nation" (ibid.:33).

The principle of discrimination prohibits action against innocent civilians (see Ramsey 1961, 1968; Johnson 1981:350). One must discriminate between retaliation against aggressive parties and actions taken against noncombatants. As the Vatican Council stated, "Any act of war aimed indiscriminately at the destruction of entire cites or of extensive areas along with their population is a crime against God and man himself. It merits unequivocal and unhesitating condemnation" (Vatican Council II:1982).

The implications of the church's stance are profound. It prohibits much of the conduct of World War II, notably the bombing of population centers. Although originally considered ghastly and immoral, the bombing of cities gradually became acceptable to much of the citizenry on both sides of the war, a process that Kenneth Boulding calls moving the taboo line. What had been taboo becomes defined as permissible.

On the basis of these principles, and the qualitatively different nature of modern warfare, the possibility of waging a nuclear war is impossible within the just-war criteria. For these reasons, the Second Vatican Council reaffirmed "the condemnation of total war already pronounced by recent popes" (NCCB 1983:33).

As with most principles, however, there are loopholes in just-war theory, especially in the principle of discrimination, which prohibits directly intended attacks on noncombatants. Does the fact that there are sixty potential military targets in Moscow mean that Moscow is a military target and that the deaths of millions of civilian inhabitants as "collateral damage" would be "unintended" (see ibid.:57; Walzer 1977:276–77)? Although admitting that the issues are not easily resolved, the bishops contend that "entire classes of human beings such as schoolchildren, hospital patients, the elderly, the ill, the average industrial worker . . . may never be directly attacked (NCCB 1983:34).

The Catholic bishops conclude that the nature of modern war requires, in the words of the Vatican Council, "a completely fresh reappraisal of war," with attention to both the just-war teaching and nonviolence. These two elements of the Christian tradition "diverge on some specific conclusions, but they share a common presumption against the use of force as a means of settling disputes" (ibid.:37).

The crusade tradition. The United Methodist Bishops (1986:35) observe that "the fusion of political and religious authority in the Middle Ages fostered a third Christian tradition in matters of war and peace: crusades against infidels." Although this tradition is, in some ways, an embellishment of the just-war tradition, the crusade is offensive rather than defensive (and is carried out under "God's orders").

There are two major currents of the crusade tradition in the contemporary church. First, there is the anticommunist crusade waged by many on the Christian right, which views the Soviet Union as the anti-Christ, a godless nation that must be resisted by a virtuous America. Second, there is the "Armageddon perspective" of an imminent nuclear holocaust. F. H. Knelman, in his book, *Reagan, God, and the Bomb* (1985:178), argues that

> in its most frightening aspect, the Reagan administration couples its warfighting policy with a fundamentalist, religious world view. The end of the world is engrained in the minds of the reborn. Armageddon is not a mere tenuous prophecy, but an absolute prediction. For key members of the administration, Armageddon is the basis of policy.

For fundamentalist clergy like Moral Majority leader Jerry Falwell, such parallels are a justification for a Peace through Strength position.

For others, like the popular evangelist David Wilkerson (1985:1), the coming nuclear holocaust is a sign of God's judgment, which will be visited upon both the United States and the Soviet Union:

> America is going to be destroyed by fire! Sudden destruction is coming and few will escape. Unexpectedly, and in one hour, a hydrogen holocaust will engulf America—and this nation will be no more.
> It is because America has sinned against the greatest light. Other nations are just as sinful, but none are as flooded with the gospel light as ours. God is going to judge America for its violence, its crimes, its backslidings, its murdering of millions of babies, its flaunting of homosexuality and sadomasochism, its corruption, its drunkenness and drug abuse, its form of godliness without power, its lukewarmness toward Christ, its rampant divorce and adultery, its lewd pornography, its child molestations, its cheatings, its robbings, its dirty movies, and its occult practices.

Although Wilkerson is certainly not mainstream, he does have millions of followers, thanks in part to support by such television evangelists as Jimmie Swaggart. It should be noted, however, that not all evangelicals take such a position. One national organization, Evangelicals for Social Action, issued a statement in 1983 entitled "An Evangelical Commitment to Nuclear Disarmament," inviting Christians to promote a verifiable bilateral freeze, to reexamine their jobs and investments "to assure that they are consistent with our peacemaking efforts," and to "encourage leaders of all nuclear nations to 'renounce unequivocally and publicly the first use of nuclear weapons' " ("Evangelicals" 1983).

The Armageddon theory is comforting to many Christians, as Mojtabai (1986) observes in her book, *Blessed Assurance*, because it assures them that Jesus will save them from personal harm by taking them to heaven. The concept of the Rapture, according to Amarillo minister Charles G. Jones, includes the idea that "Jesus shall descend with a shout and the trump of God, and the dead in Christ shall rise first, and we which are alive and remain shall be caught up together in the clouds to meet the Lord in the air. And so shall we ever be with the Lord" (quoted in Mojtabai 1986:159).

Although the Crusade tradition has been rejected by most mainline Christian leaders, it is a strand of Christianity that runs deep throughout the church and should not be discounted.

Evaluating the Traditions

The Catholic bishops reach some sobering conclusions. First, "under no circumstances may nuclear weapons or other instruments of mass slaughter be used for the purpose of destroying population centers or other predominantly civilian targets" (NCCB 1983:46), even in retaliatory strikes. Second (in contradiction to NATO policy), the bishops "do not perceive any situation in which the deliberate initiation of nuclear warfare, on however restricted a scale, can be morally justified" (ibid.:47). Finally, despite the complexity of the issue, the bishops are "highly skeptical" about the notion of a limited nuclear war: "The first imperative is to prevent any use of nuclear weapons and our hope [is] that leaders will resist the notion that nuclear conflict can be limited, contained, or won in any traditional sense" (ibid.:50).

Although unequivocal in their rejection of the *use* of nuclear weapons, the Catholic bishops are less sure about the issue of maintaining a deterrent force. They cite Pope John Paul II's statement that the concept of deterrence may be morally acceptable "certainly not as an end in itself but as a step on the way toward a progressive disarmament" (ibid.:55). Because military facilities and production centers are dispersed throughout population centers, however, the moral issue of proportionality emerges. Reagan administration officials consulted by the bishops

> agreed that once any substantial numbers of weapons were used, the civilian casualty levels would quickly become truly catastrophic, and that even with attacks limited to "military" targets, the number of deaths in a substantial exchange would be almost indistinguishable from what might occur if civilian centers had been deliberately and directly struck. (ibid.:57)

The bishops thus qualify their endorsement of a deterrent force to reject (1) the idea of planning repeated nuclear strikes or "prevailing" in nuclear war, and (2) the quest for nuclear superiority. Furthermore, certain specific proposals must be rejected, including first-strike weapons, strategic planning that "seeks a nuclear war-fighting capability" beyond the most limited function of deterrence, and proposals that blur the difference between nuclear and conventional weapons.

In conclusion, the bishops support a policy of sufficiency. They recommend the following as steps toward disarmament:

Religious critiques of the arms race are often directed against new counterforce weapons, such as the ground-launched cruise missiles fired from this transporter-erector launcher. Courtesy of the U.S. Air Force/Department of Defense.

(1) Support for immediate, bilateral, verifiable agreements to halt the testing, production, and deployment of new nuclear weapons systems.[7]

(2) Support for negotiated bilateral deep cuts in the arsenals of both superpowers, particularly those weapons systems which have destabilizing characteristics; U.S. proposals like those for START . . . and INF . . . negotiations in Geneva are said to be designed to achieve deep cuts; our hope is that they will be pursued in a manner which will realize these goals.

(3) Support for early and successful conclusion of negotiations of a comprehensive test ban treaty.

(4) Removal by all parties of short-range nuclear weapons. . . .

(5) Removal by all parties of nuclear weapons from areas where they are likely to be overrun in the early stages of war, thus forcing rapid and uncontrollable decisions on their use.

(6) Strengthening of command and control over nuclear weapons to prevent unauthorized use. (ibid.:60)

Some critics contend that the bishops did not go far enough (see Farrell 1982), but the bishops' statement was a historic departure for the heretofore hesitant and conservative U.S. Catholic Church. Some of the bishops, such as New York's Terence Cardinal Cooke, warned their colleagues that the issue could divide both church and nation (Ostling 1982:68).

With criticism reminiscent of Celsius's critique of the early church, Representative Henry J. Hyde (Republican of Illinois) claimed that the bishops' letter would make it impossible to fire a nuclear weapon, possibly leaving the nation defenseless (Halloran 1984). National Security Adviser William Clark, a Catholic layman who publicly criticized the bishops, expressed similar concerns, contending that the Soviets had mounted a massive arms buildup to which the United States must respond.

The United Methodist Bishops (1986) go even further than their Catholic counterparts in condemning the nuclear arms race. "For forty years," the Methodist bishops argue, "the moral function of deterrence doctrine has been to justify the threatened use of nuclear weapons and an unending arms race." As a consequence,

> deterrence has too long been reverenced as the unquestioned idol of national security. It has become an ideology of conformity too frequently invoked to disparage dissent and to dismiss any alternative foreign policy proposals. In its most idolatrous forms, it has blinded its proponents to the many-sided requirements of genuine security. There can be no unilateral security in the nuclear age. Security has become indivisible. Our vulnerability is mutual. Our security must be mutual. (ibid.:46–47)

This perspective is explicitly drafted from a position that claims to be within the "kingdom of God," another theme in religious critiques of the nuclear arms race.

The Kingdom of God

Within traditional Christianity, the kingdom of God is a fundamental idea with roots in Judaism. It has both spiritual and political implications, and is believed to have been inaugurated with Jesus, although there is always a tension between the already established nature of that kingdom and the fact that it is not yet a fulfilled reality. As the Catholic bishops put it, "Christians are called to live the tension between the reign of God and its concrete realization in history. The tension is often described in terms of 'already but not yet': i.e., we already live in the grace of the kingdom, but it is not yet the completed kingdom" (NCCB 1983:18–19).

Living within the kingdom of God means living in covenant with God and with other humans. Thus, for the Christian, the ultimate symbol of the meaning of Jesus' love is the cross: "Victim of the forces of violence, abandoned by most of his closest followers, Jesus gave his life in a cruel death. . . . In all of his suffering, as in all of his life and ministry, Jesus refused to defend himself with force or with violence" (ibid.:15–16).

Christians are thus to live *as if* they were already within the kingdom of God. The test of one's relationship with God is one's relationship with others, including one's enemy, just as one of Jesus' last words on the cross was to forgive his executioners (see Ford 1984).

The Methodist bishops emphasize the ancient Hebrew concept of *shalom*. As they put it,

> At the very heart of the Old Testament is the testimony to *shalom*, that marvelous Hebrew word which means peace. But the peace which is *shalom* is not negative or one-dimensional. It is much more than the absence of war. *Shalom* is positive peace: harmony, wholeness, health, and wellbeing in all human relationships. It is the natural state of humanity as birthed by God. It is harmony between humanity and all of God's good Creation. All of creation is interrelated. Every creature, every element, every force of nature participates in the whole of creation. If any person is denied *shalom*, all are thereby diminished. (United Methodist Bishops 1986:24)

It is within that context that the Methodist bishops condemn the "idolatry" of nuclear deterrence as un-Christian.

The Arms Race as a Misappropriation of Resources

A final theme that emerges frequently in religious critiques of the nuclear arms race is that the expenditure of vast amounts of money on arms, in the midst of poverty and hunger, is an offense to God. The United Methodist Bishops (ibid.:72) observe that

> current military spending, close to $1 trillion annually or more than $2.5 billion everyday, is thirty times as great as the world's total of official development assistance from all governments. The military expenditures of the two superpowers alone exceed the total value of world trade in agricultural prod-

ucts. The cost of just one nuclear aircraft carrier exceeded the gross national product of fifty-three countries in 1983.

The link between peace and justice is a resounding theme in Christian critiques of the arms race, as reflected in the National Council of Churches' annual Peace with Justice week (in October), in which many churches across the country participate. In many religious circles, the Swords into Plowshares slogan from Isaiah represents a demand for the conversion from military to social spending. From that point of view, massive defense expenditures are an injustice perpetrated against the poor.

AN ETHICAL SPECTRUM ON NUCLEAR ARMS

The United Methodist Bishops (1986:39ff.) identify a sevenfold ethical spectrum on the nuclear arms race that ranges from first-strike policies to traditional pacifism (see Figure 13.1). Many Christians in the United States express sincere and legitimate concern about the Soviet threat to American security, just as many Christians in the Soviet Union are concerned about the American threat to Soviet security. The traditional position of the church in the United States (despite a strong minority undercurrent of pacifism) has been to legitimate national military establishments and the need to fight wars, stockpile weapons, and maintain a strong defense. The official atheism of the Soviet Union, and the persecution of Christians in the USSR and elsewhere, provide motivation for that position today, so that the issue is often posed in terms of Christianity versus "godless communism."

Many Christians thus support four of the positions along the ethical spectrum: first-strike policies, counterforce superiority, first-use deterrence (which retains the option of nuclear retaliation to a conventional attack), and no-first-use deterrence, which allows for the possession and possible use of nuclear weapons but rejects the use of nuclear weapons to defend against a conventional attack.

The U.S. Catholic bishops took what might be called a Yes/No Deterrence position—"They say Yes to having [nuclear weapons] but No to using them" (ibid.:41). Critics have dubbed the position bluff deterrence, or even clergy deterrence, because of its ambiguity and its proponents' opposition to retaliation (ibid.:42).

Other Christians take a nuclear pacifist approach, in which they support conventional military forces (and the possibility for armed defense or revolution) but reject all use of nuclear weapons. Finally, others insist that the only option for a Christian is a repudiation of all warfare, in the context of the traditional pacifism that has long been supported by a significant segment of the church.

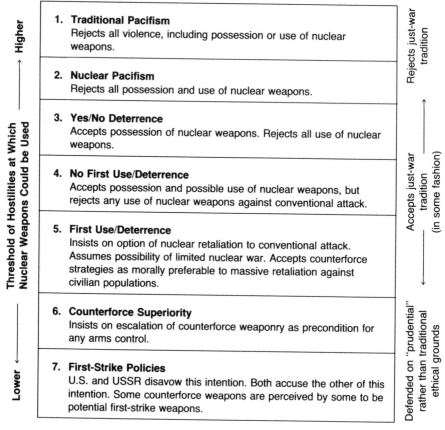

Figure 13.1   An ethical spectrum on nuclear arms. *Source*: Gary L. Ball-Kilbourne and Jack A. Keller, Jr., 1986, *In Defense of Creation: The Nuclear Crisis and a Just Peace, Guide for Study and Action*, Nashville, Tenn.: Graded Press, p. 17. Used with permission. Copyright © 1986 by Graded Press.

A SPECTRUM OF STRATEGIES

Public Protest: Bilateral Disarmament

Religious people are at the core of the Bilateral Freeze movement in the United States and elsewhere. The 12 June 1982 rally in New York City, which drew a larger number of people than to any other protest march in the history of the country, was cosponsored by a wide variety of religious groups, from the American Friends Service Committee to the National Federation of Temple Youth. Support for bilateral disarmament may be the most widespread position among mainstream Christians in the United States who are actively engaged in opposing the nuclear arms race. Contrary to what many contend (see Barron 1982), the major force behind this protest is not the KGB, but the Christian church.

Public Protest: Unilateral Disarmament

Some Christians believe that disarmament is so urgent that they have moved toward an advocacy of unilateral disarmament, often in the form of peace initiatives, to break the nuclear stalemate. Archbishop Raymond Hunthausen, for example, argues:

> I believe that one obvious meaning of the cross is unilateral disarmament. Jesus' acceptance of the cross rather than the sword raised in his defense is the Gospel's statement of unilateral disarmament. . . . I am struck by how much more terrified we Americans are by talk of disarmament than by the march to nuclear war. We whose nuclear arms terrify millions around the globe are terrified by the thought of being without them. (Hunthausen 1982:6–7)

The Netherlands Reformed church has also reached the conclusion that because multilateral agreements have failed, it is necessary to undertake unambiguous unilateral action. In a resolution, church leaders stated that "as we related these considerations to our own responsibility in our own society, we conclude that denuclearization of the Netherlands will be such an unambiguous step" (Donaghy 1981:21).

The most radical undercurrents of the peace movement thus often paradoxically arise out of what is one of society's most conservative institutions.

Nonviolence, Civil Disobedience, and Noncooperation

Within the church, there are major pockets of radical resistance to the arms race. In evaluating the stance of the church toward war, German theologian Helmut Gollwitzer (1982:47–48) concludes that there is only one answer to the question of what the church should do about war. According to Gollwitzer, "the church ought probably to have refused to participate in war much sooner; at any rate, this is its very last chance to do so." Christians who engage in various forms of civil disobedience (or "direct action") claim to be operating in the tradition of Jesus, Gandhi, and Martin Luther King, Jr. Such action involves the deliberate violation of civil laws in alleged obedience to a higher authority. Those who undertake civil disobedience believe that they are already living in the kingdom of God (which is characterized by justice and peace) and that their actions are a witness to their faith. Although we shall discuss this approach in more detail in Chapter Fourteen, it is helpful to sketch some of the forms of nonviolent protest that have emerged in the churches.

Civil disobedience takes different forms in different countries. In East Germany, for example, many people have broken the law simply by wearing a symbol on their clothing with the words "Schwerter zu Pflug-schwaren" (Swords into Plowshares), which represents the biblical image of the promise of peace made through the prophet Isaiah. They have been harassed by the German police, who sometimes strip the symbol from protesters' clothing.

Sit-ins and demonstrations at military installations, weapons factories, and embassies provide other forms of nonviolent civil disobedience. At the time of the 12 June rally in New York, for example, demonstrators staged sit-ins at the diplomatic missions of the five major nuclear powers: the Soviet Union, the United States, China, Great Britain, and France.

Others have entered factories where nuclear weapons are made to call attention to those weapons as symbols of death. Protesters often pour vials of their own blood onto warheads and other weapons to dramatize the reality of the weapons. Similarly, tax resistance heightens the argument that tax dollars should not be spent lavishly on the arms race. Archbishop Hunthausen, along with many others, refuses to pay 50 percent of his federal income taxes as a catalyst of nonviolent action based on faith.

Ritual Alternatives to the Arms Race

Finally, many Christians have called for rituals that affirm the kinship of all humanity and provide concrete actions for people to undertake in the pursuit of peace. The Catholic bishops have recommended that Christians engage in prayer, fasting, and penance in their quest for peace. The function of prayer is to open people up to God's power, or, in sociological terms, to allow people to gain a new perspective on the arms race by transcending personal and national loyalties.

For Henri Nouwen (1979), prayer is an act of "letting go of all things," an "act by which we divest ourselves of all false belongings and become free to belong to God and God alone." The connection between prayer and the arms race is thus a beginning, at a personal level, of renouncing those things that lead to war. "In the final analysis," asks Nouwen (ibid.),

> isn't the nuclear arms race built upon the conviction that we have to defend—at all cost—what we have, what we do, and what we think? Isn't the possibility of destroying the earth, its civilizations, and its peoples a result of the conviction that we have to stay in control—at all cost—of our own destiny?

Similarly, the Catholic bishops argue that the act of penance is an important part of the Christian's opposition to the arms race, a conversion that includes turning from violence. Consequently, the bishops proclaimed:

> As a tangible sign of our need and desire to do penance we, for the cause of peace, commit ourselves to fast and abstinence on each Friday of the year. We call upon our people voluntarily to do penance on Friday by eating less food

and by abstaining from meat. This return to a traditional practice of penance, once well observed in the U.S. Church, should be accompanied by works of charity and service toward our neighbors. Every Friday should be a day significantly devoted to prayer, penance, and almsgiving for peace. (NCCB 1983:91)

SUMMARY

The Christian church has traditionally provided both justification for and critiques of the waging of war. In recent years, however, most mainstream religious leaders (who stand outside policy circles) have consistently condemned the nuclear arms race and have developed extensive moral critiques of nuclear weapons.

Church participation in the disarmament movement is related to two major changes that have affected religious opinion on issues of war and peace: (1) the change in the nature of modern warfare—especially with the development of nuclear weapons, which has undercut just-war theories; and (2) the breakdown of the traditional alliance between the Christian church and Western power elites.

A number of themes have emerged from religious deliberations on the arms race. First, the church has reevaluated traditional Christian teachings in light of the nature of modern war. Two of those traditions—pacifism and just-war theory—raise serious ethical questions about the use of nuclear weapons and in some cases deterrence itself. Whereas the early church was largely pacifistic, just-war theories emerged after the Christianization of the Roman Empire by Constantine in the fourth century. A third tradition, the crusade, is used by some fundamentalists to justify the nuclear arms race and to provide assurance that they will escape personal harm.

On the basis of two key principles of just-war theory, proportionality and discrimination, it is impossible to justify the use of nuclear weapons. The good to be obtained from a war must be greater than the cost incurred, and noncombatants must be immune from attack. A nuclear war would fail to meet either criterion.

The U.S. Catholic bishops condemn the nuclear arms race and the development of a new generation of weapons, and they propose a number of steps to move toward disarmament, including a bilateral nuclear weapons freeze. They do, however, allow for a deterrent nuclear force as morally acceptable on a temporary basis, "as a step toward a progressive disarmament." The United Methodist bishops, on the other hand, condemn deterrence as an "idol of national security" that blinds its proponents to the "many-sided requirements of genuine security" and is used to justify a spiraling arms race.

A second theme that has emerged from the church's deliberations on the arms race is the Christian concept of the kingdom of God, which requires church members to love one's enemies and give ultimate loyalty to God, even if that means coming into conflict with one's national obligations. A third theme is that the expenditure of vast amounts of money on weapons is unjustified in light of widespread human needs.

Within the church, there is a spectrum of ethical positions on the nuclear arms race, from support of a first-strike policy to nuclear and traditional pacifism. There is also a spectrum of strategies against the arms race, from public protest favoring bilateral or unilateral disarmament, to nonviolence and civil disobedience, to the development of ritual alternatives.

Although the church has expressed a diversity of opinions concerning what should be done about the nuclear dilemma, there is a remarkable consensus among mainline Christian leaders in condemnation of nuclear weapons and the arms race. Furthermore, the church and its leadership have, to a large extent, energized and shaped the movements of protest against the nuclear cage that have emerged in recent decades.

CHAPTER FOURTEEN

The Nuclear Disarmament Movement

Robert D. Benford

> I like to believe that people in the long run are going to do
> more to promote peace than are governments. Indeed, I
> think that people want peace so much that one of these days
> governments had better get out of their way and let them
> have it.
>
> —President Dwight D. Eisenhower

By the early 1980s, millions of people throughout the world were rattling
the nuclear cage. Why, after living in relative complacency under the
shadow of the bomb for over three and one-half decades, were people suddenly so aroused? What accounts for the emergence of what may be the
first genuinely global social movement? Why were literally thousands of organizations established in opposition to the nuclear arms race? Which strategies and tactics have tended to be successful? And, finally, what are the
peace movement's future challenges? Though we will not attempt to offer
comprehensive answers to these questions, each will be briefly addressed as
we outline the nuclear disarmament movement, one of but a few rays of
hope in avoiding a cold, dark, radioactive future.

The author would like to thank John Bandy, Lester R. Kurtz, Sam Marullo, and
John MacDougall for their insightful comments on earlier drafts of this
chapter.

"Come on, Brian—let's don't get involved!"

© Punch/Rothco

A fundamental assumption shared by peace activists throughout the world is that people, who were able to construct a nuclear cage, should be equally capable of tearing it down. There are, however, those who have no interest in dismantling nuclear weapons and those who believe that such a task is impossible. Such skeptics assert that we must learn to live with nuclear weapons (Carnesale et al. 1983a). Hence, a major objective of movements to rid the world of these destructive instruments has been convincing people that nuclear disarmament is not only desirable but achievable.

Even among those who believe that we should and can eliminate nuclear weapons, there are profound disagreements over how this can be accomplished. Should attention be concentrated on one bar of the cage at a time, as reflected by peace groups that focus on a single weapon, such as the MX? Or should efforts be devoted simultaneously to several of the cage's bars, as illustrated by the Nuclear Weapons Freeze Campaign? Or is it better to exert energies toward shaking the very foundations of the cage, as exemplified by traditional pacifist groups like the American Friends Service Committee (AFSC)?

Given the variety of explanations as to why the nuclear cage came into existence, it is not surprising that a number of seemingly incongruous approaches toward its demolition have emerged. This, then, is a basic characteristic of today's peace movement: It is incredibly *diverse*. It is at once radical and moderate, structured and amorphous, organized and chaotic, religious and secular, routinized and spontaneous, simple and complex. Its members include blacks and whites, old and young, union members and corporate executives, Republicans and Democrats, antiabortion people and pro-choice advocates, atheists and archbishops (Barash and Lipton 1982:14).

Despite its diversity and apparent internal contradictions, the peace movement is bound together by a set of interrelated assumptions. First, its members believe in the sanctity of life. Second, they accept the claim that nuclear parity exists between the two superpowers. They further assume that, given the trend in the arms race, the likelihood of a nuclear war is increasing. A fourth assumption is that a nuclear war is not winnable and that a nuclear war of any size would have devastating, if not irreparable, effects on civilization and the ecosphere. Finally, peace activists agree that if an unprecedented disaster is to be prevented, individuals must act collectively to oppose it.

EARLY PEACE ACTIVISM

Peace activism and pacifism are not products of the nuclear age. American resistance to war occurred at least as early as 1637, when the peaceable Algonquin Indians refused to pay taxes to the Dutch to improve a fort in what is now Manhattan (Hedemann 1982). Every war in which the United States engaged—from the Revolutionary War to those being waged today in Central America—has been accompanied by the conscientious opposition of pacifists.

Organized peace activity emerged on the U.S. scene at the beginning of the nineteenth century. It was at first "a largely religious phenomenon," the roots of which extended from biblical times, gaining expression through the historic peace churches: the Society of Friends (Quakers), the Brethren, and the Mennonites (Chatfield 1973:x). To engage in fighting and killing, according to these peace pioneers, was a crime against God and violated the teachings of Christ.

By the mid-1800s pacifism had spread from the religious spheres to the secular. Rather than opposing war on purely religious grounds, secular pacifists tend to take a more intellectual approach. War is seen as an irrational means of resolving conflicts (Boulding 1984). Throughout the remainder of the century and into the 1900s, secular pacifists sought alternatives to military intervention and violent conflict.

But it was World War I that became the catalyst for the emergence of the modern peace movement in the United States. A wave of disillusionment swept across this country with that conflict, due in part to a steady flow of grisly books, many of which were authored by the combatants themselves, depicting "a gory and senseless slaughter" (Wittner 1984:1–2). Americans felt betrayed.

Peace activism, secular and religious, expanded. By the mid-1930s the clergy, women, and college students had joined forces in a powerful triad for the cause of peace. The rise of fascism in Europe, however, led to the beginning of the collapse of expanding pacifism, and Pearl Harbor nearly dealt a death blow to the organized peace movement. Public opinion shifted against pacifist views, and many pacifists fell silent. But despite the loss of millions of peace supporters with war's arrival, a substantial nucleus of Americans retained their pacifist ideals.

THE EBB AND FLOW OF NUCLEAR PACIFISM

Traditional pacifists played a central role in each of the three waves of antinuclearism that have swept the globe: the scientists' movement of the 1940s, the test-ban movement of the late 1950s and early 1960s, and the antinuclear movement of the 1980s. They were not, however, the first to oppose construction of the nuclear cage. Indeed, antinuclear activities began even before the first atomic bomb was produced.

Scientists' Movement

Ironically, the initial movement against the bomb emanated from the group who designed and eventually produced the first three nuclear weapons—the Manhattan Project scientists. Concerned about the "tremendous social and political implications of atomic warfare," top scientists at the project's Chicago Metallurgical Laboratory (referred to as the Met Lab) began meeting in 1943 to discuss their common anxieties (Novick 1946:400). These unauthorized meetings were quickly brought to a halt by Army security deputies (Smith 1965:15–16), but informal discussions did not cease. In the spring of 1945, word had reached the Met Lab scientists that Secretary of War Stimson would soon be appointing a committee on long-range planning regarding atomic weapons policy and postwar control. Fearful that the conclusions reached by the Interim Committee would primarily reflect military thinking, the Met Lab scientists organized their own committees to study the issues. One of these groups, the Committee on the Social and Political Implications, authored the Franck Report, in which the group concluded that the United States should not use the bomb to end the war with Japan (ibid.:32, 41–44).

Efforts to prevent nuclear warfare. Insightful and prophetic, the Franck Report identified key nuclear issues that continue to be debated today.[1] The document indicated that other nations would soon develop atomic weapons, that these weapons had reversed the relationship between offensive and defensive military capacities such that the former would forever be superior to the latter, that nations must be willing to sacrifice a certain degree of sovereignty in order to control nuclear armaments, and, finally, that it was necessary to institute international controls because "neither [the United States] or any other nation can stake its whole existence on trust in other nations' signatures [on paper agreements]" (ibid.:570). The report concluded that by using the atomic bomb the United States "would sacrifice public support throughout the world, precipitate the race for armaments, and prejudice the possibility of reaching an interim agreement on the future control of such weapons" (ibid.:571). The scientists proposed that instead of dropping the bomb on Japan, a demonstration of the weapon's destructive power be held on a remote uninhabited island.

On 12 July 1945, less than a month before the Hiroshima bombing, a straw poll taken at Chicago's Met Lab indicated that only 15 percent of the scientists favored "full military use" of the new weapon in the absence of some kind of demonstration (ibid.:57–58). Leo Szilard, one of the "fathers" of the A-Bomb, collected signatures from Manhattan Project scientists indicating opposition to dropping the bomb without a demonstration or a warning. But the scientists' petitions and the results of the Met Lab straw poll failed to reach President Truman in time.

Scientists unified for international control.   After World War II, the Manhattan Project scientists were fairly unified in their resolve that science should serve the cause of peace. There were, of course, dissenters who believed that scientists had no place in the political arena, yet most of the Project scientists were troubled by the possibility of a nuclear arms race and concerned that, as a consequence of the arms race, scientific freedoms would be undermined (ibid.:91). Szilard summed up the sentiments of many scientists: "In 1945, when we ceased worrying about what the Germans might do to us, we began to worry about what the government of the United States might do to other countries" (Wittner 1984:143). Placing atomic energy under the jurisdiction of an international body, they reasoned, would alleviate such concerns. The scientists formed separate organizations at each of the Project's sites, groups that eventually coalesced as the Federation of American Scientists (FAS).

The efforts of the FAS culminated in the Acheson-Lilienthal Report, which Smith (1965:490) suggests represented the apogee of hope for the scientists' vision of international control and cooperation in the common development of atomic energy for peaceful purposes. These hopes were soon shattered. The Acheson-Lilienthal Report was replaced by the Baruch Plan, a watered-down and more punitive proposal that was rejected by the Soviet Union when it was presented at the UN (see Chapter Twelve). The underlying fallacy in the scientists' thinking was their collective belief that they could successfully apply scientific methods to politics, i.e., isolate a problem and find its solution (ibid.:458–59, 530; Gilpin 1962).

Cold War dilemmas and the loss of unity.   By the end of 1946, the scientists' movement had lost momentum. The scientists faced a dilemma:

Realizing that the chances of reaching an agreement on international control of atomic energy and hence preventing a nuclear arms race were dwindling, they were unable to admit the likelihood of failure without diminishing what chances of success remained (Smith 1965:502). Membership in the scientists' movement declined as many scientists chose to leave behind the uncertainties of politics to return to the certitude of their research.

The year 1948 ushered in another dilemma, which eventually split what was left of the scientists' movement. It emanated from the schizophrenic nature of U.S. nuclear policy: On the one hand, political leaders espouse the goal of disarmament, but on the other hand, they have consistently increased the nation's dependency on nuclear weapons. In wrestling with this dilemma, the scientists aligned themselves into three distinct groups: (1) those who continued to support nuclear disarmament; (2) those who advocated international control but favored a U.S. nuclear arsenal to contain Soviet aggression; and (3) those who argued that the United States should not waste its time pursuing international agreements with its untrustworthy opponent, but rather should contain the Soviet Union at all costs, including pursuing an intensive program to develop the hydrogen bomb (Gilpin 1962). Though scientists were by no means through in the political arena, the unanimity they had briefly enjoyed in the postwar period disappeared, never to return again.

Despite the loss of many members from the scientists' movement, a few scientists carried the antinuclear torch through the ensuing three decades. In July 1955, Bertrand Russell, Albert Einstein, and nine other eminent scientists issued an appeal for an agreement renoucing nuclear weapons "as part of a general reduction of armaments" (Nathan and Norden 1981:635). While the nuclear powers ignored the Russell-Einstein appeal, the scientific community did not. Instead, scientists organized the first Pugwash Conference on Science and World Affairs in 1957. It heralded the start of a series of meetings in which scientists from around the globe have continued to work for comprehensive nuclear disarmament for nearly thirty years (Feld 1982:3). Pugwash is, in essence, a global scientists' movement that attempts to utilize the internationalism of science as a force for peace (Gilpin 1962). Perhaps the most significant aspect of the Pugwash movement is the participation of American *and* Soviet scientists. Pugwash scientists played a key role in the achievement of every nuclear arms control agreement.

Despite its lasting contributions to the disarmament movement—most notably, the FAS, the *Bulletin of the Atomic Scientists*, and Pugwash—the scientists' movement was a short-lived and primarily elitist struggle. As De-Benedetti (1980:149) suggests, the scientists

> failed in their highest ambitions at the moment of ripest opportunity. They who had derived untold powers of destruction from the physical universe could not move human politics beyond the reach of catastrophe. They could

affect governments, but not move them. They could acquaint citizens with the danger of nuclear war, but never drive home its full meaning.

Given the beating the scientists sustained in the political arena, the emergence of the cold war, and the rise of McCarthyism, it is not at all surprising that the lion's share of activity in the disarmament movement took place during a two-year span from 1945 to 1947 (Smith 1965). Ten years would pass before the next wave of protests against the bomb crested.

Test-Ban Movement

Although pacifists were outraged that the United States had dropped the bomb on Japan, their moral indignation was not shared by the majority of Americans. A poll taken between the bombings of Hiroshima and Nagasaki revealed that only 10 percent of U.S. citizens were opposed to the use of atomic bombs on Japanese cities, compared to 85 percent who approved. Ethnocentrism, vengeance, and beliefs that the nuclear attack would bring an early end to the war contributed to this massive support. This latter "humanitarian" justification was soon called into question, however, by a series of government reports that suggested that the bombings were unnecessary and did not substantially contribute to Japan's unconditional surrender (Wittner 1984:128–30).

If such postwar studies failed to generate anxiety, John Hersey's *Hiroshima* certainly did. His account of the effects of the Hiroshima bombing upon the lives of six people, first serialized in the *New Yorker* and read over a major radio network, became an instant best-seller. Hersey's work personalized the experience of atomic warfare such that survival became a mobilizing force. Readers put themselves in the shoes of the victims. Fear thus emerged as the postwar peace movement's greatest asset.

Traditional pacifists were ambivalent about this new wave of concern. "On the one hand, it smacked of a certain selfishness, and seemed to raise a banner of coarse pragmatism in place of a pacifist humanitarianism" (ibid.:132). On the other hand, however, veteran pacifists welcomed this new constituency, although they sarcastically referred to the newcomers as nuclear pacifists.

Cold War chills.   Just when peace activism was beginning to flourish once again, the cold war froze the movement. Scientists were not the only ones whose peace efforts were cooled; even some of the most radical pacifists, including Norman Thomas and Dwight McDonald, renounced their faith in pacifism (ibid.:183). The Fellowship of Reconciliation (FOR), the War Resisters League (WRL), and other pacifist groups suffered significant declines in membership (ibid.:212). "If you're for peace, you must be a communist" seemed to be the prevailing sentiment of the era. The outbreak of war in Korea and the rise of McCarthyism were final confirmations for many peace activists that their ship had struck an iceberg and was sinking.

Fallout fears.   In the mid-1950s, fear, once again, provided the impetus for a revival of the peace movement. The dangers associated with nuclear weapons became real and immediate when in March 1954 twenty-three Japanese sailors were contaminated by radioactive fallout from an American hydrogen bomb test near the Bikini Atoll (Toyoda 1984). Objections to the testing poured in from every corner of the globe, including India, Western Europe, and particularly Japan. In Japan, the incident prompted intense public revulsion and massive demonstrations (Knightley 1982:12), instigating what proved to be the largest antinuclear movement in the world (Suzuki 1984:29).

Fear of contamination was not nearly as prevalent in the United States, although a few American scientists and activists began investigating the hazards of nuclear testing (Wittner 1984:240). Then, in 1955, radioactive rain fell on Chicago, and a thousand-mile-long radioactive cloud from a Nevada test reached New York. By 1957, scientific and public concern over radiation had reached epidemic proportions. Gallup polls revealed that American sentiment had shifted from opposing a negotiated test ban in late 1956 to favoring it by the following April (Divine 1978:139). Scientists facilitated this dramatic transformation of popular opinion by publicly challenging government claims that people's fears were unwarranted (ibid.:137). On 24 April 1957, Albert Schweitzer broadcast an appeal, heard in fifty countries, to halt all nuclear testing (Wittner 1984:241). Less than two months later, Linus Pauling presented President Eisenhower with a petition, signed by nearly three thousand American and eight thousand foreign scientists, calling for a ban on nuclear tests (Pauling 1958).

As if this were not enough to arouse the public's anxieties, Nevil Shute's novel *On the Beach*, which chronicles the death of the human race from fallout in the aftermath of a nuclear war, was published that summer and became an immediate best-seller. Americans reacted to the book by pondering on more than just the dangers of nuclear tests; they worried about the threat of nuclear war, as well (Divine 1978:162). In fact, "nuclear fear" became a shaping cultural force throughout the remainder of the decade and into the early 1960s (Boyer 1984:823).

SANE

Traditional pacifists and world federalists added their voices to the collective cry for a test ban. Several veteran peace activists persuaded Clarence Picket from AFSC and Norman Cousins of the *Saturday Review* to serve as co-chairpersons of a new organization, the National Committee for a Sane Nuclear Policy (SANE), which soon provided the antinuclear movement with an organizational vehicle for mobilizing the alarmed public into action. SANE initially was intended to be nothing more than a temporary educational tool, but reactions to its first newspaper advertisement were so overwhelming that it became a permanent fixture on the antinuclear movement's stage (Wittner 1984:244). By the summer of 1958 SANE had emerged as a major force with 130 chapters and approximately 25,000 members.

SANE was at first a single-issue organization that, for the most part, employed traditional tactics: lobbying on Capitol Hill, running newspaper advertisements promoting a nuclear test ban, and educating the public (Divine 1978). In short, SANE's aim was to use the existing institutional mechanisms to stop nuclear testing, in much the same way that the Nuclear Weapons Freeze Campaign of the 1980s has approached halting the nuclear arms race.

Nonviolent direct action.   A quite different approach to bringing about change rose to prominence during this period: nonviolent direct action. Nonviolent direct action is a method of actively opposing the institutions and agents that resist change. Although its recorded origins extend from biblical days, it was refined in the twentieth century by Mohandas Gandhi as he led the struggle for India's independence. For Gandhi, nonviolent direct action was a tool of his spiritual philosophy, *satyagraha*, which translated literally means "truth firmness." Part of this truth is the inseparability of means and ends. In other words, a peaceful society cannot be built by employing violence.

Gandhi believed that violence is indicative of cowardice, that the sword is a weapon of the weak. The weapons of *satyagraha*, by contrast, are pickets, fasts, boycotts, ostracism, noncooperation, and civil disobedience. From this perspective, if one believes that a law, policy, or practice is unjust, one is morally bound to oppose it. It is, in short, an *active* pacifism.

By the time the second wave of nuclear pacifism had emerged in the form of opposition to nuclear testing, the civil rights movement was already applying Gandhi's nonviolent direct action tactics. Since numerous pacifists were active in both movements, it was only natural that tactics which proved useful to one movement would be adopted by the other. While the *liberal* pacifists and internationalists were in the process of getting SANE off the ground, *radical* pacifists formed the Committee on Nonviolent Action (CNVA),[2] which sought to "undertake direct action toward unilateral and immediate disarmament" (DeBenedetti 1980:160–61). Unlike their counterparts at SANE, CNVA leaders were unwilling to limit themselves to the traditional avenues for bringing about change. Instead, they "gently invaded" U.S. missile installations and atomic test sites, refused to pay taxes, and organized international walks for peace and disarmament.

Pressures from within and without. Tensions developed between the radical pacifists and those who advocated a more moderate approach to dealing with the nuclear threat (DeBenedetti 1983). These intramural differences were not, however, limited to the question of appropriate tactics; the scope of the movement's goals was also contested. Radical pacifists advocated unilateral disarmament. SANE, by contrast, decided to focus initially on ending bomb tests rather than deal with the broader and more complex issue of disarmament (Divine 1978; Wittner 1984). When SANE did decide, in the summer of 1958, to expand its goals to encompass disarmament, it explicitly avoided the term "unilateral."

Ironically, it was SANE, rather than it's more radical counterpart, that came under attack from conservatives. Given SANE's effectiveness in arousing public opposition to the nuclear cage, it was not surprising that pro-nuclear forces attempted to discredit SANE. What was surprising, though, was that SANE leaders facilitated the conservative attack. SANE Executive Committee President Cousins caved in to pressure from Senator Dodd, who, in May 1960, accused the organization of being influenced by and sympathetic to communists. When the senator urged SANE to purge itself of any communists, Cousins cooperated in a secret investigation. By the time the witch hunt had run its course, a rally organizer had been fired, three board members resigned, and half the Greater New York SANE chapters were expelled from the organization for refusing to cooperate. Although SANE survived as "the largest and most influential peace group" of the era, the intended damage had been done (Wittner 1984:259–60). It was not the first such attack the peace movement had suffered; nor would it be the last.

New constituents and new tactics. Despite external attacks and internal divisions, antinuclearism was developing into a major political force by the end of the 1950s. It had become increasingly diverse with the addition of several constituencies, including those of women, students, and intellectuals (DeBenedetti 1980:165–66). Momentum continued into the early 1960s. Washington-area feminists organized several women's peace action groups and Washington, D.C., housewives into the national organization, Women Strike for Peace (WSP). In November 1961, WSP organized disarmament rallies in sixty cities, and women took to the streets in unprecedented numbers to call attention to the fact that as a result of atmospheric testing, milk was contaminated with radioactive strontium-90. Approximately fifty thousand women attended rallies, sent telegrams, and went on strike for a day, refusing to work in their kitchens and offices (MacDougall 1984:13).

Nuclear pacifism began to take hold on college campuses, as well. In 1959 Chicago-area pacifists and socialists formed the Student Peace Union (SPU), which became the "first major student peace organization of the

American sixties" (DeBenedetti 1980:166). SPU was committed to working "independently of existing power blocs" via "new and creative means" in its efforts toward disarmament and a "free and peaceful society" (ibid.; Wittner 1984:267). By 1960, it boasted five thousand members and twelve thousand subscribers to its bulletin.

Professionals also began clamoring for changes in nuclear policy. One of the guild-type antinuclear organizations established during this period was Physicians for Social Responsibility (PSR). Inaugurated in 1961 by a group of physicians "who were troubled by the health implications of nuclear weapons testing in the atmosphere and the lack of data on the medical consequences of nuclear war," PSR "played a major role in developing public understanding of the devastating capabilities of thermonuclear weapons," thereby contributing to the achievement of the Limited Test Ban treaty of 1963.[3] Although PSR's initial thrust into the antinuclear arena was short-lived, it reemerged in 1979 to become the prototype for scores of other professional groups that helped create the third wave of antinuclear activism.

While the movement grew more diverse, so did its tactics. On 3 May 1960, approximately two thousand peace advocates refused to participate in New York City's annual civil defense drill. As the sirens were about to sound, protesters assembled in City Hall Park and ignored orders to take shelter. Meanwhile, students at several area colleges and high schools resisted the drill, and two professors at Queens College refused to dismiss their classes (Wittner 1984:265–66).

Drama, innovation, and perseverance characterized the antinuclear campaigns of the early 1960s. "Why don't you go tell it to the Russians," the movement's opponents frequently asked. In 1961, that is precisely what the antinuclear activists did. Led by CNVA, a group of American activists were joined by participants from eight other countries on a San Francisco to Moscow peace walk. Once in Moscow, they "spoke almost nightly to public meetings, demonstrated against a Soviet radar base, conducted a two-hour vigil in . . . Red Square, and distributed 80,000 antiwar leaflets" (ibid.:277).

The Decline of Nuclear Pacifism

Despite infighting and occasional storms brought on by opponents, the future of the antinuclear movement looked sunny in the early 1960s. Movements against the bomb had emerged in Japan, Great Britain, and the United States. Each were diverse and resolved to tear down the nuclear cage. Antinuclear sentiment and activities had reached an unprecedented level. Then, as quickly as the wave had come in, it receded, not to return again for nearly two decades. What accounted for the movement's sudden dissipation?

Several explanations have been offered to account for nuclear pacifism's decline from 1963 through the 1970s, including: (1) a perception of diminished control, (2) a perception of diminished threat, (3) the loss of immediacy of the threat of the weapons themselves, and (4) the diversion of activists' energies toward stopping the Vietnam War.[4] While some factors may have contributed more to the decline of antinuclear activism than others, it is likely that the confluence of all of these overwhelmed the movement.

The perception of diminished control.   Paradoxically, the Cuban missile crisis, the world's closest brush with global nuclear war, was followed by the beginning of the demise of the nuclear disarmament movement in both Great Britain (Driver 1964:141–48) and the United States (DeBenedetti 1980:168–69). Although the October 1962 crisis could be viewed as having presented activists with another opportunity to capitalize on existing fears and anxieties about the prospects of a holocaust (and peace groups tried, albeit unsuccessfully, to do just that), the crisis could also be interpreted as proof of how ineffective and powerless the peace movement really was (Taylor and Pritchard 1980:12; DeBenedetti 1980:169).

Not only did peace activists begin to question their effectiveness, but ordinary citizens also felt more powerless in the face of strategic developments. *Sputnik* led to mechanization of the nuclear arms race and to greater reliance on ICBMs. One consequence of these changes was a depersonalization of the bomb (Lowther 1973:80). Given the interrelated facts that the Soviets could launch a missile strike against U.S. cities and that the United States had shifted to an assured destruction policy, it is not surprising that Americans began to feel more vulnerable. Such fears were temporarily assuaged by Kennedy's bomb shelter program. Just as Americans today would like to believe that "Star Wars" technology will one day provide a foolproof shield against the nuclear menace, citizens in the early 1960s hoped that bomb shelters would secure their protection. However, when the administration shifted away from a policy of city-avoidance, the case for a shelter program was substantially weakened (Freedman 1982:251), and the shelter craze faded.

The perception of diminished threat.   It is also possible the apathy of this era was not due to perceptions of diminished control, but rather to the fact that people felt *less* threatened (Wittner 1984:279–80; Boyer 1984:826–27). The world had, after all, survived the Cuban missile crisis. When push came to shove, Khrushchev backed down. Superpower tensions seemed to be easing; Kennedy established the Arms Control and Disarmament Agency in late 1961, and a Washington-to-Moscow hot line was installed eighteen months later. Moreover, ratification of the 1963 Limited Test Ban treaty signaled the thawing of the cold war. However, the treaty not only fell short of the movement's goal of a comprehensive ban on testing, it also eliminated a crucial mobilizing tool—the immediate threat of radioactive contamination from weapons tests.

Loss of immediacy.   Another plausible explanation for the decline in antinuclear activities in this period is that nuclear weapons and their effects became less visible and hence less immediate. As the horrors of Hiroshima and Nagasaki faded into the past, the dramatic above-ground tests ceased, civil defense drills were deemphasized, and nuclear weapons no longer seemed so real (Wittner 1984:280). Reenforcing this loss of immediacy was the fact that nuclear weapons "literally went underground after 1963" (Boyer 1984:830). Furthermore, the acronyms and slang of "nukespeak" desensitized people to the doomsday potential of nuclear weapons (Hilgartner et al. 1983). Finally, entrepreneurs of popular culture—writers, reporters, and television and film producers—no longer sustained the images of a holocaust (Boyer 1984:830–31).

The Vietnam war.   According to another theory, the nuclear disarmament mo vement was one of the first casualties of the escalation of the Vietnam War. Undoubtedly, the concreteness of the Vietnam War contributed to the shift from antinuclear pacifism to antiwar activism. Young American males were being drafted by the hundreds of thousands. Tens of thousands of Americans and Indochinese were being wounded or killed. And it was on the six o'clock news every evening for all to see. Interest in the potential menace of the bomb simply could not be sustained in the face of Vietnam's actuality (ibid.:836).

Traditional pacifist groups such as WRL, nuclear pacifist organizations like SANE, and other groups on the Left—most notably Students for a Democratic Society (SDS)—turned their efforts to opposing the war. When President Johnson announced his plan for escalating the war and ordered aerial bombings, antiwar protests intensified, thereby pushing nuclear disarmament to the movement's back burner.

But if Vietnam diverted activists' resources and efforts from the nuclear threat, it also created another peace movement layer upon which future generations would stand in their quest for a way out of the nuclear cage. The war radicalized many citizens who otherwise may have never raised their voices in dissent. The sweeping participation in and proliferation of antiwar groups exposed people to a wide range of group structures, tactics, and ideals. Thousands were trained in the politics of protest. Organizational forms such as the Mobe (Mobilization Committees to End the War in Vietnam) and SDS were experiments in group process that would be reincarnated in the radical environmental and nuclear disarmament movements of the 1980s (Benford 1984:63). But most important from the activists' perspective, the peace movement helped end the war (Wittner 1984:292; Kissinger 1979:261, 297).

REVIVAL OF NUCLEAR PACIFISM

A few pacifists carried the nuclear disarmament torch during the Vietnam War, but the flame had dwindled to a dim flicker. As the war came to a close, most peace activists did not return immediately to confronting the nuclear threat. Some joined in the pursuit of other causes, such as women's rights, farm worker mobilization, and the environment. Others, exhausted from the decade-long struggle against the war, took a break from political activities.

This lack of organized opposition to nuclear weapons during the era from 1963 through 1978 gave the appearance that Americans had indeed learned to live with the bomb. Détente and the ratification of a host of nuclear treaties seemed to provide evidence that something was being done in the way of decreasing the likelihood of Armageddon.

Beginning in the late 1970s, however, a series of disturbing events rudely awakened at least some Americans and most Europeans from their complacent slumber. By 1982 millions of people worldwide were clamoring for an end to the nuclear madness.

Precipitating Factors

The question of "Why now?" often haunts scholars of social movements. The answer is seldom simple or singular. The confluence of several events apparently contributed to the dramatic reescalation of nuclear disarmament activity, first in Europe and shortly thereafter in the United States.

Revival of nuclear disarmament activity in Europe.   Most peace groups in Northern Europe were established or revived in 1979 and 1980 (Mowlan 1983:28), primarily as a result of the December 1979 U.S./NATO decision to deploy 108 Pershing IIs and 464 ground-launched cruise missiles in West Germany, Great Britain, Belgium, Italy, and the Netherlands (Jones 1982). Following the Italian government's 1981 announcement of its decision to site 112 cruise missiles near Comiso (Sicily), the antinuclear movement in Southern Europe also began to gain momentum. In Eastern Europe, particularly in East Germany, an independent peace movement has been established, in spite of state attempts to suppress it (Hochschild 1982; Pooley 1983).

The demise of SALT II signaled the end of an era of détente and thus the potential for a renewal of the East-West cold war. For many Europeans, the NATO decision to deploy U.S. missiles on their soil confirmed that concern. In July 1980, the Carter administration issued Presidential Directive (PD) 59, which institutionalized the idea of flexible response. PD 59 "aimed to improve deterrence by improving the capacity for a prolonged nuclear war" (Freedman 1982:393). The implication, particularly in light of the planned creation of 572 additional European-based nuclear targets, was that if a nuclear war began, the two superpowers would attempt to keep it confined to Europe. Public comments by the newly installed Reagan administration regarding the efficacy of fighting and winning a protracted nuclear war exacerbated such concerns. These elements, combined with increasing world tensions—in Iran, Afghanistan, El Salvador, Poland, and Nicaragua—contributed to Europeans' fears.

Fear alone, however, seldom provides the basis upon which to build and sustain a social movement. To mobilize hundreds of thousands to the streets requires, among other things, organization (Tilly 1978). The existence of traditional peace groups such as WRL, Pax Christi, and the British Campaign for Nuclear Disarmament (CND), as well as newcomers like the Dutch Inter-Church Peace Council (IKV), were crucial to mass mobilization. Political parties and trade unions also played important roles. Finally, the fact that the antinuclear movement had been active and relatively successful throughout most of Western Europe in the 1970s (Nelkin and Pollak 1981) contributed organizationally and psychologically to the growth of the European peace movement.

In the fall of 1981, Europeans took to the streets in record numbers to protest the missile deployment plans. On 5 September, a women's peace encampment began at Greenham Common (a cruise missile deployment site in England). A little over a month later, 300,000 turned out in Bonn. Over 750,000 marched two weeks hence in London, Brussels, Oslo, Helsinski, Paris, and Madrid. Even skeptics took notice on 21 November when more than 350,000 people protested in Amsterdam. Meanwhile back in the United States the movement's revival was scarcely under way.

Revival of nuclear disarmament activity in the United States.   European disarmament leaders appealed privately and publicly to American activists for assistance in their struggle to prevent the NATO missile deployment. International media coverage of the massive demonstrations in Europe further enhanced awareness of the threat. Both led to actions in the United States. The growth of a U.S. movement, in turn, helped to sustain and encourage the European movement (Mowlan 1983:31).

As European peace activists prodded their American counterparts into action, President Reagan inadvertently became an even greater mobilizer for nuclear disarmament. Although his strategic policies were, at least initially, nothing more than a continuation of President Carter's program, Reagan's rhetoric was considerably more bellicose than his predecessor's. The casual manner in which he publicly talked about "fighting and winning" "protracted" or "limited" nuclear wars frightened not only Europeans but Americans as well. The weapons were made real again and took on a new immediacy. Slumbering pacifists and thousands of previously indifferent citizens were thus awakened.

Meanwhile, a series of events were unfolding that proved crucial to the revival of the U.S. nuclear disarmament movement. In 1980, Randall Forsberg, founder of the Institute for Defense and Disarmament Studies, wrote a paper entitled "Call to Halt the Nuclear Arms Race," in which she noted the trend toward a greater probability of nuclear war and outlined a proposal stating that "rather than permit this dangerous future to evolve, the United States and the Soviet Union should adopt an immediate, mutual freeze on all further testing, production and deployment of nuclear weapons and of missiles and new aircraft designed primarily to deliver nuclear weapons" (Forsberg 1980:1). Forsberg had come to believe that the key to disarmament lay in the identification of intermediate steps for which a variety of groups could rally support (Leavitt 1983a:12). The freeze proposal seemed to fit the bill. "In order to achieve disarmament, you have to stop first" soon became a familiar freeze slogan.

The simple but comprehensive idea spread rapidly (Niedergang 1982). Vermont and Massachusetts passed nuclear freeze resolutions in 1980, earning the freeze the label of a grass-roots movement. A petition drive to place a freeze initiative on a California ballot resulted in the collection of over a half million signatures (Kalven 1982). Meanwhile, Senator Edward Kennedy and other politicians became interested in the Freeze proposal, thereby enhancing the movement's media exposure and credibility. The freeze provided the movement with what many felt was *the* missing ingredient: a concrete solution to the nuclear predicament.

Antinuclear Proliferation

By the end of 1981, the peace movement's revival was clearly under way. This time, unlike during the Vietnam War peace movement, campuses were not the center of the movement's strength (Gordon 1982). Instead, support came from professionals, churches and their congregations, scientists, and the general public. Nonetheless, some signs of interest among college students surfaced toward the end of 1981. On Veterans Day in 1981, approximately 100,000 students on over 150 campuses attended teach-ins on the threat of nuclear war "reminiscent of college forums during the Vietnam era" (Walker 1982:10).

From the streets to the voting booth. The following summer the rapidly growing disarmament movement demonstrated its capacity to mobilize supporters. On 12 June 1982, 750,000 people marched past the United Nations building, where the UN's Second Special Session on Nuclear Disarmament was being held, and converged on Central Park for the largest protest rally in U.S. history. Two days later, police arrested approximately 1,700 demonstrators who staged sit-ins at the UN missions of the five major nuclear powers. Before 1982 ended, over 4,000 Americans were arrested engaging in various acts of civil disobedience directed against the nuclear arms race.

The U.S. disarmament movement had succeeded in garnering massive popular appeal. Public opinion polls consistently indicated that an overwhelming majority of Americans (as high as 78 percent) favored a bilateral, verifiable nuclear weapons freeze agreement between the two superpowers.[5] Hundreds of cities and counties and a dozen states passed resolutions endorsing the freeze. The Nuclear Weapons Freeze Campaign as well as other disarmament groups organized intensive lobbying campaigns on Capitol Hill. These concerted efforts finally paid off in the spring of 1983, when the House passed a freeze resolution. Though the freeze legislation had been slightly watered-down by an amendment that called for its repeal if it was not followed by negotiated arms reductions by both superpowers, most freeze activists interpreted the House vote as a major victory (Leavitt 1983b:5).

The victory celebration was cut short, however, when the House voted a few weeks later to continue support for development of the MX weapons program. The fact that a number of representatives cast contradictory votes by supporting the freeze and the MX led some peace movement leaders to question traditional channels as a means of confronting the nuclear cage. For example, two leaders of the People's Test Ban wrote in *Nuclear Times* that "the freeze label has allowed many politicians to appear pro-disarmament without sticking their necks out by opposing the very weapons systems that will make a meaningful freeze impossible" (Solomon and Sanchez 1983:16). Despite intramovement concerns that the freeze was being co-opted by politicians and despite the subsequent failure of the freeze in the Senate, the Freeze Campaign, as well as other groups such as SANE, United Campuses to Prevent Nuclear War (UCAM), and Women's Action for Nuclear Disarmament (WAND), set their sights on the 1984 elections.

President Reagan's landslide reelection victory may have signaled the decline of the disarmament movement's influence in the U.S. political arena. Political action committees (PACs) organized by various peace groups were able to mobilize thousands of volunteers for the Freeze Voter 84 campaign, and the peace PACs collectively raised more than six million dollars, but the results were disappointing (Taylor 1985). A few pro-freeze House incumbents did credit the peace PACs for having made the difference in their narrow reelection bids, yet only one movement-backed challenger managed to win a House seat. Randy Kehler, national coordinator of the Freeze Campaign at the time, pointed out that the important message of the movement's failure at the ballot boxes was that "the American people are in favor of a freeze but they don't feel the freeze is an urgent necessity. To them it's not more important than short-term economics or personalities" (Corn 1984:12).

More time must pass before we can adequately determine whether the 1984 elections marked the beginning of a decline in this third and largest wave of nuclear disarmament activity. Regardless, the first half of the decade witnessed an unprecedented growth in the movement.

Reemergence of antinuclear culture.   In the 1980s, popular cultural elements resurfaced that were at once a cause and a consequence of the growth of antinuclear sentiments and activities. Jonathan Schell's *The Fate of the Earth* (1982), initially serialized in the *New Yorker*, became an instant best-seller. Arguing that the planet would become a "Republic of Insects and Grass" in the aftermath of a nuclear war, Schell pleaded for greater public awareness of the nuclear threat and suggested that a tragic nuclear fate could be avoided by doing away with archaic national sovereignty structures.

A plethora of nontechnical books, such as Ground Zero's *Nuclear War: What's in It for You?* (1982), facilitated the layperson's understanding of nuclear weapons and issues. Courses dealing with nuclear topics became popular on dozens of college campuses and further sensitized and educated the public (Cevoli 1983). Nuclear education even began to gain a foothold in some junior and senior high schools (Loeb 1983; Rizzo 1983b).

Nuclear fiction also enjoyed renewed popularity. One of several hypothetical accounts of life following a nuclear war, ABC's "The Day After," was watched by millions of television viewers in November 1983.

Organizational boom.   Not only had millions of Americans joined the ranks of traditional and nuclear pacifism by the mid-1980s, but the number of peace groups also increased dramatically. By 1984, some three thousand independent nuclear disarmament groups and another one thousand local chapters of national peace groups were rattling the nuclear cage. The organizational boom was both a cause and a consequence of the growth of disarmament sentiments. But even if a greater number of organizations provided citizens with a variety of participation choices, one must speculate whether the peace movement had not engaged in its own peculiar brand of overkill. Why were there so many different groups dealing with presumably the same issue?

THE STRUCTURE OF THE DISARMAMENT MOVEMENT

A naive observer of the peace movement is likely to be confused by the multitude of groups it comprises. The variety of specific objectives, strategies and tactics, and messages can seem baffling. Perhaps the very nature of the peace movement's challenge—finding a way out of the nuclear cage—breeds ambiguity and the appearance of schizophrenia. While there may be a grain of truth in such assessments, we suggest that the internal diversity of the disarmament movement is a result of social processes common to social movements in general. In this section we examine three sources of structural diversity: (1) common social bonds, (2) division of labor, and (3) multiple definitions of the situation.

Common Social Bonds

People tend to be recruited to movements through their social networks. That is, they join because a friend, relative, neighbor, or co-worker already belongs (Snow et al. 1980). In today's disarmament movement, shared professional, religious, or demographic characteristics frequently attract peace advocates to particular groups.

Professional ties.   We observed how scientists, doctors, and students formed their own peace groups during the first two waves of nuclear pacifism. Two such groups, the Federation of American Scientists and Physicians for Social Responsibility, managed to survive the era of nuclear apathy (1963–78) that plagued the disarmament movement. Established by the Manhattan Project scientists, FAS was the world's first nuclear disarmament organization. But it was the physicians group, PSR, that became the blueprint for scores of other professional groups (Rizzo 1983a).

PSR languished throughout the 1970s until Helen Caldicott, a charismatic Australian pediatrician, brought new life to the organization in 1979. PSR initially focused its efforts on warning the public of the horrifying medical effects of nuclear war. Doctors utilized slides, films, and graphic statistical data, in what were termed "bombing runs," to substantiate their fundamental message that there is no medical response to nuclear war. By 1983, PSR leaders decided that they were obligated to go beyond sounding the nuclear alarm. Thus, in 1983, they added "prescriptions for the prevention of nuclear war" to their public forums (ibid.:11).

In 1980, Bernard Lown, one of the founders of PSR, and other American doctors met with Soviet physicians in Geneva and formed the International Physicians for the Prevention of Nuclear War (IPPNW). Five years later the international umbrella organization won the Nobel Peace Prize for the collaboration of American and Soviet doctors in "spreading authoritative information" regarding the "catastrophic consequences of atomic warfare" (Miller 1986:11). By the end of 1985, IPPNW had spread to forty-one countries and boasted a membership of over 135,000 physicians.

PSR became the prototype for a spectrum of other peace groups organized around a common profession, and groups of lawyers, educators, business executives, architects, social workers, and artists, among others, were formed. Like PSR, most of these groups focus on education—informing members of their own particular professions as well as the general public about the dangers of an unabated nuclear arms race. Each professional group brings to the movement its specialized expertise and resources, which are drawn upon by the entire movement.

Perhaps the most significant contribution the professional groups have made to the disarmament cause is the doors they have opened. Audiences previously unwilling to listen to the hard-core peace activists listen when their doctors, lawyers, teachers, and business associates speak of an impending nuclear disaster. Professionals, by virtue of the prestige they enjoy, are seen as credible and rational. In short, the proliferation of peace groups with common professional bonds dovetails nicely with the Freeze Campaign's strategy of eliciting support from the middle class.

Religious ties. We noted earlier how the historic peace churches were the first to spread the ideals of pacifism in the United States. More recently, as we outlined in Chapter Thirteen, the church has become a powerful force in the international quest for disarmament. Not only have its documents, such as the Bishops' Pastoral Letter, had substantial impact, but congregations have also proven to be fertile recruitment channels. Millions of people around the world have joined the peace movement because of their religious beliefs and affiliations. Church-based peace groups have been established at every conceivable geographical level—city, state, national, and international—and across nearly every denomination.

In the United States, most Christian denominations have formed their own peace groups, calling on members to take seriously the teaching of Jesus to "love your enemies." This has led a growing number of Christians to consider nonviolent resistance to nuclear weapons (Rice and Collum 1985:10). For example, the Agape Community, a network of Christians and peace activists, has initiated actions against the Nuclear Train, which carries nuclear warheads from the Pantex weapons assembly plant near Amarillo, Texas, to depots and deployment sites. Vigils and protests have been organized along the train's route, and some protesters have been arrested for blocking its tracks. Members of other religious groups have been arrested for participating in peace "witnesses" at the Nevada nuclear test site.

Nonviolent direct action by one Christian group has caused controversy not only outside the disarmament movement but within it as well. In June 1981 the Plowshares Eight, which included a Catholic sister and two priests, broke into a Pennsylvania weapons plant and destroyed nuclear missile components with hammers. Subsequent Plowshares actions have resulted in prison sentences of up to eighteen years.

Demographic ties. In addition to religious and professional ties, segments of the disarmament movement have been structured along demographic lines. Some groups, such as the Children's Campaign for Nuclear

Disarmament, have been established on the basis of age. That group organized a campaign in 1981 which resulted in the delivery of over eight thousand pro-disarmament letters to the White House from children around the United States (Rizzo 1983b:29). Groups made up primarily of the elderly, such as ACORN and the Gray Panthers, while not explicitly peace groups, have increasingly raised the antinuclear banner.

Though women played an important role in the peace movement as early as 1915, it was not until the 1980s that women became a major force within the disarmament movement. Their new strength was in part a consequence of the women's movement. Women began to link feminism with peace activism. Many women saw the nuclear arms race and the more general militarism pervading the world as rooted in patriarchical structures and male-dominated societies.

Numerous women's peace groups, such as Women's Action for Nuclear Disarmament, Peace Links, and Women's Pentagon Action, have been formed in the wake of the third wave of nuclear pacifism. Dramatic testimony to the commitment of many women to the cause of nuclear disarmament is provided by the women's peace camp at Greenham Common, England. What began in 1981 as a march by a few Welch women to the site of England's cruise missile base became a permanent peace encampment that has been sustained for over six years. Initially, the women hoped to prevent cruise missiles from entering the base, but after the arrival of the missile transports on 14 November 1983, the women vowed to carry on their nonviolent community (Snitow 1985:42). Despite inclement weather, primitive living conditions, constant evictions, and frequent arrests, the Greenham Common camp has endured, a symbol of women's perseverance and commitment to nuclear disarmament and a nonviolent life-style.

Division of Labor

While much of the antinuclear movement's structural diversity can be attributed to the formation of a variety of groups based on some common social bond, other factors, such as the emergence of a *division of labor*, have played equally important roles.

Most disarmament groups have developed areas of task specialization. Scientists, doctors, lawyers, educators, business executives, and artists, for example, each bring their unique expertise, talents, and resources to the movement. However, even within any of these groups, more than one subgroup has emerged, each of which differentiates itself from the others by means of developing a unique set of tactics or by appealing to a particular audience. Lawyers, for instance, have formed such groups as Lawyers Committee on Nuclear Policy (LCNP) and Lawyers Alliance for Nuclear Arms Control (LANAC). LCNP has begun to challenge the legality of nuclear weapons (Meyrowitz 1983). By contrast, LANAC has organized mock negotiations to gain a better understanding of the dynamics of arms control processes (Rizzo 1983a).

Similarly, educators have formed three major groups: Educators for Social Responsibility (ESR), United Campuses to Prevent Nuclear War (UCAM), and Student/Teacher Organization to Prevent Nuclear War (STOP). ESR's members are teachers at the pre-college level who focus on "helping teachers and parents respond to children's fears of nuclear war through education" (Burbank 1982:6). UCAM's members, by comparison, are college professors and students who concentrate on promoting nuclear education on college campuses (Cevoli 1983). Finally, STOP, which is made up of high school students and teachers, is more action-oriented, as indicated by its organized opposition to local crisis relocation plans (Rizzo 1983b).

Multiple Definitions of the Situation

The diversity of the nuclear disarmament movement is most apparent when attention is directed toward its wide array of goals, strategies, and tactics. One way of understanding the source of the different ways in which peace activists and their organizations deal with the nuclear threat is to analyze the various definitions of the situation held by the movement's participants. As noted in Chapter Seven, individuals try to fit occurrences into a framework that organizes their definition of what is going on (Goffman 1974).

Peace activists apply a number of different frames—technological, economic, political, and moral—to the nuclear arms race (Snow et al. 1986; Snow and Benford, forthcoming). Those who view the arms race as a consequence of technological developments tend to join two different types of groups: groups that are anti-technological (e.g., those that advocate getting back to nature or rejecting all technological developments), and groups that seek technological solutions to the arms race, such as opposing the invention and production of additional weapons systems.

Other activists apply an economic frame to the nuclear predicament. Some holding this perspective view the arms race as a consequence of the undue influence of the defense industry on political processes. Some work on economic conversion campaigns in an attempt to turn nuclear weapons production facilities into factories that would produce consumer products. Others apply a wider economic frame, locating solutions in changing their society's way of distributing wealth.

Still others adopt a political frame. Some of these activists form groups that advocate world government. Others pursue a more traditional path of trying to persuade their country's leaders to either renounce nuclear weapons or negotiate a reduction in arms.

Finally, many peace activists employ moral or spiritual frames to the situation. Frequently, members adhering to this perspective believe not only that nuclear weapons are unethical but that every person is morally obligated to oppose them. Civil disobedience is a common tactical weapon. In short, divergent beliefs about why and how the nuclear cage came to be built result in different responses to the perceived threat.

Divergent goals. The issue of the scope of the change needed to reduce or eliminate the nuclear threat has led to intense debate within the antinuclear movement. Numerous disarmament groups such as the Freeze Campaign, SANE, and most occupational groups have taken a *single-issue* approach. This wing of the movement has committed most of its resources to stopping hardware, i.e., to opposing the deployment of additional and more destructive nuclear weapons (Solo 1985:10).

By contrast, Mobilization for Survival, the War Resisters League, and the American Friends Service Committee, among others, advocate a *multi-issue* approach to peace. These groups tend to link a variety of goals, including stopping military intervention, social and economic injustice, and the nuclear arms race. From their viewpoint, the nuclear threat is but one symptom of more deeply rooted maladies. Structural changes—from the ways in which humans treat one another to the ways in which economic and political institutions are organized—are seen as necessary.

A parallel debate pits the *total disarmament* advocates against those seeking *arms control* agreements. The former tend to view arms control agreements as "devices for further arming the superpowers" (Raskin 1982:105). Arms control advocates counter that, realistically, the only way the threat of nuclear war will be reduced is if the nuclear powers negotiate treaties that would contain the arms race before it gets further out of hand. Once this is achieved, they argue, it might be possible to gradually negotiate all of the nuclear weapons away. If not, at least the danger will have been reduced or limited.

Peace activists are also divided on the question of whether their respective countries should pursue *unilateral* or *multilateral* disarmament goals. Unilateralists argue that their nation should begin dismantling its nuclear stockpile regardless of what other countries decide or agree to do. In contrast, multilateralists adhere to the belief that limitations or reductions of nuclear forces should be contingent upon one or more of the other nuclear powers simultaneously making equal or comparable cuts in their arsenals. This debate has been more prevalent within the European peace community than in the United States. Some of the most influential European peace movement organizations, such as Britain's CND and the Dutch IKV, have taken purely unilateralist stances (Young 1983). Though some U.S. activists and groups have advocated that the United States take unilateral steps toward arms control and reductions of nuclear forces, few have advocated that the United States eliminate its entire nuclear stockpile regardless of whether the Soviets reciprocate.

Strategic and tactical diversity.   A host of seemingly incongruous strategies and tactics have also emerged in the antinuclear movement. One recurring tension throughout the history of the movement has been between advocates of institutional means of initiating change and those who believe that drastic new measures are needed for dealing with the nuclear threat. Groups such as the Freeze Campaign, SANE, and most professionals have fallen into the former category. They have opposed civil disobedience and have instead preferred grass-roots organizing along two interrelated paths: educating and eliciting support from the masses, especially the middle class, and pressuring politicians to support nuclear arms control measures. In pursuit of this strategy, movement traditionalists employ petition drives, letter-writing campaigns, referenda, and other legal tactics. The underlying assumption is that the existing institutions can be used to achieve their goals. To go outside these channels, they argue, would drive away their mainstream supporters and "powerful sympathizers" (Rizzo 1985a:9).

Proponents of civil disobedience, on the other hand, do not believe or have lost faith in the efficacy of restricting their tactical repertoire to legal channels. Instead, they prefer nonviolent direct action: blockading military installations, nuclear train tracks, defense industry buildings, and Trident submarine harbors; breaking into missile silos and pouring blood (sometimes their own!) on nuclear weapons; and refusing to pay taxes, which subsidize weapons.

Some of the peace movement's most rancorous conflicts have concerned the use of such tactics. For instance, the national coalition that organized the massive 12 June 1982 rally in New York splintered at one point over the issue. Because several of the groups involved in planning the march and rally were unwilling to be associated with sit-ins at the UN missions (Cagan 1982:9), a separate coalition was established to organize civil disobedience (Miller 1982).

Not all of the peace movement strategies have generated such fervent internal upheavals. One legalistic approach, the nuclear-free initiative, enjoys support across a diverse spectrum of disarmament groups. The strategy originated in Japan in 1958 and, to date, over 2,700 communities in seventeen countries have declared their jurisdictions to be Nuclear Free Zones. A Nuclear Free Zone (NFZ) is an area that prohibits the research, testing, production, transportation, storage, and deployment of nuclear weapons. At last count, 105 NFZs had been established in the United States. Campaigns to declare the states of Massachusetts and Oregon off limits to nuclear weapons are also under way. Over half of the populations of Australia, New Zealand, Ireland, Great Britain, and Spain live in NFZs (Donnay 1985:3; Mapes 1985/86:7).

One of the NFZ movement's strongholds has been the Pacific region. In 1984, New Zealand banned all nuclear-powered and nuclear-armed ships from its ports (Leadbeater 1985:3). Small islands including Palau, Polynesia, and the Marshall Islands have also struggled to shed the nuclear yoke (Zarsky 1982; Myers 1983). The strength of the Nuclear Free Pacific movement is not at all surprising given the fact that the inhabitants of many of the region's islands have been guinea pigs for U.S. and French nuclear tests (Keju 1982; Aldridge 1983b).

Many disarmament activists have concluded that the cold war must be thawed before a meaningful nuclear weapons freeze can be achieved (Solo 1985:10). Thus, rather than continue to wait for the superpower leaders to engage in a more constructive dialogue, numerous peace groups have undertaken a strategy of citizen diplomacy. These groups encourage face-to-face interaction and cultural exchanges between citizens from Eastern bloc countries and the West. The underlying assumption is that such people-to-people programs provide an avenue for improving relations between nations, particularly the superpowers, in part by encouraging mutual understanding and thereby eradicating negative stereotypical images fostered by the cold war.

At least one citizen diplomacy organization, Group for Establishing Trust Between the USSR and USA, has been founded by Soviet peace activists. Unfortunately, because this small group of Soviet peace activists has attempted to operate independently of the official Soviet peace movement, its members have been subjected to harassment and persecution by the Soviet government.

In the West, an assortment of religious, professional, and traditional peace groups have initiated citizen diplomacy campaigns. Although groups such as the AFSC, Citizen Exchange Corps, and People to People International have employed citizen diplomacy tactics for a number of years, the strategy was not widely practiced until the 1980s. The various tactics devised by these groups share a common characteristic: They all involve an exchange between Soviet and American citizens, including visiting one anothers' homes, swapping students' essays and art, exchanging letters, establishing U.S./Soviet "sister cities," and communicating via satellite hookups between the two countries. These people-to-people and "twinning" programs may eventually undermine justifications for the nuclear arms race and war (Winther 1985); however, it remains to be seen whether "détente from below" will be successful in the absence of a similar commitment from Soviet and U.S. leaders (Shore 1984:11).

SUMMARY AND FUTURE CHALLENGES

Perhaps no task has ever been more monumental than that of escaping from or tearing down the nuclear cage. With its origins in earlier layers of religious and secular pacifism, the nuclear disarmament movement has confronted the nuclear threat in three waves: the scientists' movement of the late 1940s, the test-ban movement of the late 1950s and early 1960s, and the antinuclear movement of the 1980s. Each wave borrowed strategies and tactics from its predecessor and each developed a variety of new approaches.

As we indicated throughout this chapter, the contemporary disarmament movement is extremely diverse. Much of its diversity is a result of the variety of social bonds upon which different organizations are founded, the emergence of a division of labor within the movement, and the divergent frames, or definitions of the situation, that peace activists have derived in their attempts to understand why the nuclear cage came to be constructed. The latter has resulted in a seemingly incongruous set of specific goals, strategies, and tactics, which at times has created tensions between wings of the movement.

These tensions reflect the fact that we are all caught in a dilemma. On the one hand, we need to respond immediately to the threat of nuclear war. This sense of urgency is reflected in the variety of frenzied steps and stop-gap measures advocated by disarmament groups, from various radical acts of civil disobedience to the more moderate Freeze proposal. On the other hand, in order to develop permanent solutions to the threat, we need to make fundamental and sweeping changes in the way our planet is organized and structured. Pacifists recognized this necessity even before the dawning of the nuclear age. Peace activists and groups that advocate converting individuals to nonviolent life-styles, establishing world government, or achieving détente from below all reflect a commitment to long-term social change. Obviously, such global social change will take a long time to bring about.

Given this dilemma, the nuclear disarmament movement's diversity may well be its greatest asset rather than its fatal flaw. Both sides of the dilemma must be confronted simultaneously. Those who call attention to the urgency of the situation are justified in doing so, for the more one learns about our predicament, the more one realizes how precariously we dangle by a thread over the nuclear abyss. Groups dealing with this problem call attention to the necessity of taking immediate steps to reduce the likelihood of a nuclear war. Indeed, in the absence of the activism of these groups, it is questionable whether arms control and disarmament negotiations would have been on the national agendas of the United States and the Soviet Union. Perhaps this wing of the movement will buy time for those preferring to deal with the disease rather than its symptoms.

Segments of the movement advocating deeper social change are equally correct in their approach. After all, even if the nuclear cage were completely dismantled, we would still have a variety of means of destroying one another at our disposal. This wing consequently seeks more permanent solutions. Its proponents remind us that we must explore new ways of resolving conflicts and establish new structures and processes that take advantage of those qualities shared by all humans to bring us closer to a vision of a peaceful and just world order. Without these visionary peace activists who seek a global transformation, we might be doomed to repeat our mistakes. Yet this segment has been criticized by many inside and outside the movement for being too idealistic. Perhaps this is a fair criticism, but to throw one's hands up in the air and believe that humans are innately warlike becomes a self-fulfilling prophesy.

In short, what were referred to as seemingly incongruous goals, strategies, and tactics may not be so incongruous after all. On the contrary, the divergent approaches to dealing with the nuclear threat complement one another.

A major challenge facing the nuclear disarmament movement, then, is to foster and sustain participation in both segments. This is no easy task. Of the first forty-one years of the nuclear age, approximately twenty-five saw little in the way of organized efforts to confront the nuclear cage. The first wave of antinuclearism was swept away by cold war currents and the winds of war. The second wave endured longer but also receded due to the confluence of a variety of factors, not the least of which was another war. And there are signs on the horizon that the most recent wave of nuclear pacifism may soon suffer the fate of its predecessors. As the sanctuary movement[6] gathers momentum and veteran activists turn their attention to the immediate threat of another colonialist war in Central America, fewer of the broader peace movement's resources are available for antinuclear work. This anti-interventionist focus is not entirely misplaced. If a nuclear war does occur it is likely that it would emerge out of a Third World conflict in which the superpowers align themselves on opposite sides. Moreover, those actively opposing U.S. intervention in Nicaragua are struggling on the side of peace and justice. Yet, if we reflect back on the movement's history during the Vietnam era, we see the potential for the Central American movement to subsume most of the antinuclear movement.

Another challenge associated with sustaining participation in the disarmament movement is burn-out. The meaning and causes of the phenomenon are multiple. But, basically, many veteran peace activists have become fatigued after several years of disarmament work and disillusioned by the fact that their efforts have yet to bear much fruit. Many "are struggling with the realization that not a single weapons system has been stopped" (Cevoli 1986:20). Widespread burn-out among peace workers is not surprising when feelings of impotence are combined with a sense of urgency. Many activists "tend to feel if they take a vacation there'll be a nuclear war" (ibid.).

It is no coincidence that the topic of burn-out has become popular in movement circles at precisely the time that the movement has moved into a transitional stage. The movement's poor showing in the 1984 elections and its failure to stop new nuclear hardware such as the MX, Trident, cruise, and Pershing II missiles led to a period of reassessment. Two conclusions emerged from the movement's self-evaluation: (1) peace activists must adopt a long-term perspective and (2) less ambitious short-term objectives should be developed—objectives that can be readily achieved and thus serve to empower participants (ibid.:21–22).

The media present another challenge to the future of the antinuclear movement. The honeymoon between the media and the movement is clearly over (Rizzo 1985b). As the third wave of antinuclearism came crashing onto the scene in the early 1980s, the media helped stir the waters of debate. Within two years, media interest dwindled, and by 1984 there was "a virtual blackout in national news coverage of the freeze" (Hertsgaard 1985:44). In part, this is a reflection of the fact that the movement was no longer "hot copy." Its demonstrations and freeze referenda had become commonplace and routine. The movement thus faces another dilemma. Because what is typically defined as newsworthy by the media are stories that are unique to the everyday experience of the audience, the movement must constantly develop new tactics to capture the media's attention. Yet engaging in activities that are unusual enough to garner media attention may be too far beyond the realm of the average citizen's everyday experience and may consequently alienate potential movement supporters and sympathizers.

Another obstacle associated with the challenge of sustaining participation in the antinuclear movement is rooted in the nature of the nuclear threat. How long can individuals dwell on the prospects and gruesome details of a nuclear holocaust without "numbing out"? It may, in fact, be psychologically healthier to ignore or deny the threat. But such ignorance may not turn out to be healthy for the future of the human race. In response to this problem, groups like PSR decided that they needed to articulate some *hope* (in the way of prescriptions for avoiding nuclear war) along with their "bombing runs."

A further challenge confronting the future of the nuclear disarmament movement is the development of alternatives to the nuclear arms race, or visions of a new world order, a topic we will take up in more detail in Chapter Fifteen. The Strategic Defense Initiative has forced peace activists to intensify their search for ways out of the nuclear cage. It represents an ingenious attempt on the part of the military-industrial establishment to co-opt the peace movement. The idea of an impenetrable shield that would protect us from the threat of nuclear war resonates well among a significant portion of the public. The peace movement is in the difficult position of not being able to endorse SDI because it is viewed as another escalation in the arms race (one that extends the dangerous contest to the heavens), but neither can it use one of the most powerful arguments against SDI—that it undermines deterrence—because that would in essence be defending a policy the disarmament proponents have historically attacked on moral grounds (Rothschild and Peck 1985:26). Thus the movement's response to SDI to date has been to oppose it on moral and technical grounds without suggesting any clear-cut alternatives.

In conclusion, if the present wave of antinuclearism is to avoid the fate of the preceding waves, it will have to meet a number of challenges head-on. The movement must continue to foster activism that deals with both the urgency of the situation and its structural roots. Moreover, peace activists must respond to the various obstacles that stand in the way of sustaining participation in the movement, from burn-out to feelings of powerlessness and psychic numbing. Finally, the peace movement must meet the challenge of developing and implementing visions of a new world order.

CHAPTER FIFTEEN

Visions of a New World Order

The Zen Buddhists have one of the most puzzling statements in the world's religions: "If you meet the Buddha on the road, kill him." Given the radical reverence for all life in Buddhism, the saying seems nonsensical. We suspect that is part of the purpose of the saying—in other words, it (like many Zen sayings) breaks the frames in which we operate. The Zen masters realize that even their own teachings can blind believers if they comfortably accept what words say about truths for which words are inadequate.

The nuclear cage traps humanity in a dilemma that may result in annihilation, and the military framework has limited our ability to pursue alternatives in the organization of global politics (see Falk 1985). If we are to free ourselves from the nuclear cage, we must see beyond the boundaries of our current options. We must stretch our minds and "break frame."

BREAKING FRAME

As Goffman (1974) points out, individuals spend a great deal of time maintaining the primary frameworks of their culture. In everyday life, we are, for the most part, careful to stay within the bounds of appropriate behavior, taking care not to offend those around us by clashing with the norms and values of our society. In short, not only do we generally stay within the framework, we actively maintain and reenforce it.

Even in the simplest matters, such as natural bodily functions, we strive to maintain the boundaries, and when we do not do so, we have ritual responses to correct the misbehavior. One example in everyday life is what we call muffings,

> namely, occasions when the body, or some other object assumed to be under assured guidance, unexpectedly breaks free, deviates from course, or otherwise slips from control . . . with consequent disruption of orderly life. Thus, "flubs," "goofs," and—when the guidance of meaning in talk should have occurred—"gaffes." (ibid.:31)

This tendency toward self- and social control is reenforced by the social processes surrounding the phenomena of reciprocity, bureaucracy, and ritual.

We expect those with whom we interact to reciprocate when we observe cultural boundaries. On a broader level, social institutions reenforce those expectations by providing approval for those who maintain frames and negative sanctions for those who do not. Career patterns, the subtle pressures of groupthink, and hierarchical systems all sustain behavior that is within agreed-upon frames, and change or expel deviants.

Ritual responses are constructed to address the behavior of those who transgress boundaries, in an effort to restore the order that has been eroded by frame-breaking. There is a momentum of human behavior that (although never totally consistent) pushes people in preconditioned directions. In the case of the nuclear arms race, it is a drift and thrust toward World War Three (Mills [1958] 1976).

Frameworks can be broken, however. If major questions about their legitimacy arise, the frameworks are sometimes difficult to keep in place, despite the efforts of many to do so. "Frame breakers," who call ordinary definitions of reality into question, are the great heroes and villains of history: the prophets and statesmen; the Einsteins and Newtons; the Genghis Khans and Hitlers; Moses, Jesus, Muhammad, and the Buddha. Most major religious figures have subverted existing frames in a radical way. Moses led a band of slaves out of Egypt toward a new homeland, convincing them that they did not have to live under a tyrant pharaoh. Krishna persuaded Arjuna that it was his duty as a warrior to fight family members in a battle despite kinship norms prohibiting such action. Jesus commanded his disciples to love their enemies and to do good to those who persecuted them.

Enemy Frames and the Boundaries of Violence

Frames that define who is friend and who is foe seem unchangeable but are arbitrary and can shift rapidly. Whereas Soviet nuclear weapons are considered menacing by most Americans, those of the British and French—

and now the Chinese—are not. Although the Soviets and Americans were allies during World War II, they are now bitter enemies, whereas the Japanese and Germans are now close allies.

There have always been boundaries of violence, but they have moved over time. People tend to see the boundaries of the moment as somehow given and inevitable; that is inherent in the nature of frames. We must determine how to reverse the damage caused in this century by the shifting of the taboo line of violence (Boulding 1982). Usually, taboo lines of violence follow in-group and out-group boundaries. "Thou shalt not kill" normally refers to killing within the tribe. The same societies that punish in-group killing often require the slaughter of outsiders. In the modern world, the tribal circle has expanded, in one sense, so that it encircles the entire globe. We have seen our planet as a bright blue globe hanging in space; from that perspective, we are all in the family. At the same time, we have been plagued by an epidemic of nationalism. Animosities have been amplified by weapons of enormous destruction that feed the insecurities—and hence the hostilities—of people around the globe. We live at a historic crossroads in history. It is a time of great hope and fear.

Global consciousness has aided the proliferation of international nongovernmental organizations in recent years (see Boulding 1985). People are weaving cross-national networks that undercut existing nationalistic frames and help to create détente from below. International cooperation that would not have seemed possible a hundred or even fifty years ago is now occurring in this global village. It is essential to our survival. Jonathan Schell (1982:231) does not overstate the case when he writes:

> Two paths lie before us. One leads to death, the other to life. If we choose the first path—if we numbly refuse to acknowledge the nearness of extinction, all the while increasing our preparations to bring it about—then we in effect become the allies of death, and in everything we do our attachment to life will weaken: our vision, blinded to the abyss that has opened at our feet, will dim and grow confused; our will, discouraged by the thought of trying to build on such a precarious foundation anything that is meant to last, will slacken; and we will sink into stupefaction, as though we were gradually weaning ourselves from life in preparation for the end. On the other hand, if we reject our doom, and bend our efforts toward survival—if we arouse ourselves to the peril and act to forestall it, making ourselves the allies of life—then the anesthetic fog will lift: our vision, no longer straining not to see the obvious, will sharpen; our will, finding secure ground to build on, will be restored; and we will take full and clear possession of life again. One day—and it is hard to believe that it will not be soon—we will make our choice.

This reframing process must take place not simply at the level of politics (although it must happen there) but also in the spheres of art, religion, and creative imagination. We must translate visions and dreams into concrete political action.

BEYOND THE FRENZIED NEXT STEPS

The president went to bed late after a long day of lobbying legislators, receiving dignitaries, and consulting with his aides. Weeks of escalating peace movement demonstrations had put the new defense budget in a precarious situation, and he faced substantial opposition in Congress on his defense budget. Twenty-eight congresspersons had been arrested at a demonstration at the Pentagon the day before.

Now he was taking his case to the American people. Tomorrow night he would address the nation on prime-time television. The speech was going to be a masterpiece.

An American agent in Moscow had discovered a new secret missile project and had managed to take pictures of the weapon! With computer enhancement it looked truly threatening and would show very well on camera.

The NSC staff calculated some projections on the potential impact of a crash production schedule and produced a chart that would be superimposed on the picture of the new weapon. If that speech did not rally the American people behind his budget, he did not know what would.

He couldn't get that picture of the communist missile out of his mind. Then, to make matters worse, an old friend from college called that evening after dinner. He hadn't seen Marcy in years.

She had gotten mixed up with a fringe peace group and had taken advantage of their friendship to call him about the budget. He agreed to talk with Marcy, but he wouldn't have had he known what she wanted. She had been one of his favorite people in college. They had dated a while before she dumped him for a football player. Then, as now, she had not seen things his way.

He kept seeing her face superimposed on top of that missile, like the chart that had been prepared for his speech. They were both haunting him. Perhaps he was just nervous about the speech and the thousands of demonstrators amassed on the Mall.

He was scarcely asleep when he was suddenly jolted by the sound of an intruder. After blinking his eyes to clear his vision, he lurched for the phone and called security. No answer.

He switched on a light. Looming above him was a large Oriental woman shrouded in a black robe. Her hair had fallen out and her face was covered with purple spots; part of it was burned away. He shrunk back in horror.

"What the . . . Who are you?" he demanded.

"I," she replied calmly, "am the Ghost of Hiroshima Past. Come. I want to show you something."

The president grabbed his wife's arm, but she slept on undisturbed. The ghost was insistent. Helplessly, he was drawn to follow her.

Suddenly the president found himself at Ground Zero, Hiroshima. It was the sixth of August, 1945. On the desolate spot where they stood, people had become nothing. There was no sound. One moment people had been walking down the street, talking. The next moment they were gone. One hundred thousand people were killed instantaneously. Another one hundred thousand faced a slow, painful death.

The president turned away, but gradually he was compelled to survey the scene. As far as he could see, there was rubble. Half a wall remained here and there. A cockroach scurried under a pile of twisted metal and concrete. And a dreadful silence rang in the president's ears.

They walked out from the center. There were more signs of the life that had been. An old man's body, burned beyond recognition, was clutching a young child. Shadows of human figures were burned against walls and on bridges. It was a moment frozen in time.

They came upon a moving mass of charred, broken humanity. Old and young together moved silently. Some huddled together in quiet desperation. The president had known tragedy, but nothing this hideous, nothing so moving. Hesitantly, he approached one of the silent walkers. "Can I get you something? A cup of water?" There was no response.

The Ghost of Hiroshima Past took him aside and whispered, "Do not think that man will survive. More than half of the doctors and nurses are already dead. Tens of thousands of people are dead or wounded. Most of the others will die."

It was more than the president could take. He had heard and read about Hiroshima and had even watched a few minutes of one of those grisly specials on television last August. It had looked wretched, but not this bad.

"Get me out of here!" he screamed. Suddenly he was back in his bed. He shook his head trying to erase the horrible image.

"Perhaps I was just dreaming." But somehow it all seemed so real.

No sooner had he fallen asleep than he again heard the sounds of another intruder. He sat up with a start and stared at a ghostly figure. It was not the same apparition. His immediate reaction was relief, but fear and anger quickly returned. "Who are you?"

He tried to visualize what John Wayne would do in this sort of situation. But he could not recall any time John Wayne had confronted a ghost. He peered into a face partially hidden by shadows and waited for it to speak.

"I am the Ghost of Hiroshima Present," came the clear voice.

The president turned over and buried his face in his pillow. He found himself lying on the hard ground, his mouth filled with dirt. Mortar fire and jets screamed overhead.

The Ghost of Hiroshima Present took his hand and lifted him up. "They cannot hurt you; but look . . ."

The president watched with horror as napalm dropped from the planes overhead. Villagers came screaming from small huts. Small children, bloated with malnutrition, ran from huts which burst into flames before his eyes. He remembered a similar scene from a PBS special he had come across one night while switching channels. It may have been Vietnam or Afghanistan; he was not sure. "Perhaps they are communist guerrillas," he thought. "Or freedom fighters." He strained to identify the planes overhead to find out which side was which.

It was as if the Ghost of Hiroshima Present was reading his mind. "These are the innocent victims of someone else's war," she said.

There was no reprieve. She took him throughout the globe, forcing him to look at village after village, city slums, rough shacks of tin and cardboard. They saw abject poverty, misery, oppression, wherever they went.

People were dying on the streets, or crouched in the sun of the parched desert. They had no shelter, or food, or clothing.

"I'll call Jim at the Ford Foundation tomorrow," he thought. "They should be doing something about this."

Poverty was not all that she showed him. There were also factories churning out guns, tanks, planes, nuclear warheads, and missiles. In one neighborhood, where there were small black and brown children playing in the streets beside tiny shacks, there was an enormous defense plant.

They walked by the guards apparently unnoticed. Inside, she showed him a vast production line where missiles were being made. "Today," the Ghost of Hiroshima Present said, barely audible above the din of the plant, "fifteen thousand children will die of hunger and related causes.

"The nations' governments will spend two billion dollars on arms. Every second, somewhere in the world another child dies or is injured for life from the diseases of poverty. In that same second, a million dollars goes to the military."

"But what can I do?" he asked, exasperated. "It's not my fault! What about the Russians?"

The Ghost of Hiroshima Present stared at him.

"You may be the most powerful man in the world. If not you, then who?"

"I can take no more!"

He found himself back in bed. But the long night hours were not yet over. The president had one more visitor. The most dreadful of all.

The Ghost of Hiroshima Future.

This figure had no face; only shadows behind a long dark robe. It reminded him of Death in *The Seventh Seal*. He had never been able to stay awake through the whole film, but he remembered the figure.

At first he thought that the third ghost had taken him back to Hiroshima. The same rubble, the same silence. But there were no people anywhere. There were no dogs whining through the streets, no birds singing. Cockroaches, yes; there were a few scurrying about their business as if nothing had happened.

Then he saw fragments that looked familiar, lying in a crater. He took a closer look.

"Yes," she whispered. "It is the Capitol. We have not left Washington."

Her voice pierced the deadly silence. "You are seeing the end. There is no more human life on earth. This is the true enemy, the real evil that you face."

The ghost vanished as quickly as it had appeared.

The president jumped out of bed; not stopping to dress, he rushed to the Oval Office. With tears streaming down his face, he grabbed his speech from the top of his desk and tore it in two.

He sat down and began to write a new speech.

When his staff arrived a few hours later, they found the president asleep in a chair, with his handwritten speech on his lap.

"I have a new speech, and I want the speechwriters here by 10 A.M., please.

"Also, get me General Turgeson on the phone, would you? Tell him it's urgent. And cancel all of my appointments for the day."

"But, sir, today you are supposed to . . ."

"I know. This is more important. You'll see."

The rest of the day, most of the White House staff was trying to figure out what was going on in the Oval Office. It was obvious that *something* was happening, but whenever one of the few people admitted came bustling out, they just smiled and refused to answer the probing questions.

"You would not believe me if I told you," was the most thorough answer anyone was able to extract from the enigmatic staffers.

"Watch the speech tonight."

The Press Corps caught wind of the rumors and pressed for an explanation.

"What's going on?" they asked the press secretary.

"I assure you, even I don't know. All I know is that you had better *all* be there tonight. You have never seen anything like this before. It will be the news story of the century, I assure you."

Most thought that he was exaggerating, but within minutes, the phones were ringing as reporters called their offices around the world to give them the news.

"Get ready for a late-breaking story," Helen told her boss at UPI. "I don't know what it is, but it's something big.

"All we know is that the president has thrown away his speech. We're not going to get an advance copy of this one.

"What they did tell us is that there will be only one advance copy—it's being sent on the hot line to Moscow. Whatever is going on around here, it doesn't look good."

There was a flurry of speculation on all the networks on the evening news. By 8 P.M. (Washington time), everyone in the world who had a television set was sitting in front of it.

The cameras moved in on the president, sitting behind his desk in the Oval Office. There was a smile on his face.

"My fellow Americans," he began. It seemed conventional enough so far.

"When the founders of our great nation declared their independence, they took a risk that has benefited every succeeding generation.

"When Thomas Jefferson penned those famous words about the inalienable rights of all humanity to life, liberty, and the pursuit of happiness, he knew that he was living in extraordinary times.

"Such times call for statesmen to step forth and take risks that are unthinkable under ordinary circumstances. Our history is full of great men and women who have had the courage to do so. It is what has made this country the noble experiment that we treasure.

"From the pilgrims who set sail from the Old World to the pioneers who conquered the perils of the frontier, ours has been a history of courage and of faith. Faith in ourselves, in each other, and in a power beyond ourselves that inspires us to transcend the present and forge a new future.

"Never before in the history of humankind have we faced the peril and the promise that we now face. President Kennedy eloquently warned us of the nuclear sword of Damocles that hung over our heads. It hangs there still, and the thread that holds it grows ever more weak.

"Despite the valiant efforts of my predecessors to free us from that final peril, we continue to live in desperation. It is as if we were trapped in a cage of our own building. A nuclear cage.

"For, after all, we have created this monster that now threatens to annihilate life on earth, and it is in our power to undo that which we have done.

"To meet this challenge will not be easy, but we must. The American people have shown great courage in the past, and we will show the way again to a new future. The true American dream is the dream of all peoples of the world. It is not simply a car and a house, or any material possessions, but a planet filled with peace, and with liberty and justice for all.

"It is not, finally, military might that makes this country great, although we are all indebted to those who serve to keep our country safe. It is the fortitude of every citizen of this land, and our ability to dream. Not only to dream, but to act on our visions. To work by the sweat of our brow to build a better world for our children and grandchildren.

"We have faced many tests in the past, but never one as dangerous—or as full of possibilities—as the one we now encounter. The very existence of human life on earth is threatened. We must say no to the possibility of nuclear annihilation, and we must say it now. We must take our stand before the world community, and put an end to the madness that has possessed us.

"We must declare our independence from tyranny, as our ancestors did in 1776. We must proclaim a new Emancipation Proclamation, as President Lincoln did the following century. In the twentieth century we need emancipation from the scourge of war.

"We can wait no longer. The time has come for us to act. Nuclear weapons must never be used again! Therefore, I now wish to issue a new Declaration of Independence, a new Emancipation Proclamation: All humans are created equal and are endowed by their Creator with an inalienable right to be free from the threat of nuclear war.

"But words are not enough to end our reliance on a balance of terror. Therefore, as commander in chief, I am calling an immediate moratorium on all research, production, testing, and deployment of nuclear weapons. That moratorium will include a comprehensive test ban, a flight test ban, and a complete cessation of new nuclear weapons programs. The groundwork for these steps has been prepared by many patriotic visionaries who have been working tirelessly for peace.

"I have placed a call to Moscow and hope to speak to the Soviet general secretary at the conclusion of this speech. I do hope that you are watching, Mr. General Secretary; we have much to talk about. I will propose that we put aside all other duties for the moment and meet in person as soon as possible for detailed discussions about our mutual hopes and dreams. I am prepared to fly to Moscow immediately, if he is willing to receive me. I hereby publicly challenge our Soviet friends to reciprocate each of the initiatives I am announcing here tonight.

"You patriotic Americans who work in our defense industries do not have to worry about job security. We appreciate the fine work that you have done, and we will provide every avenue necessary for the conversion of existing military research and production facilities into peaceful activities. The fine minds and skilled hands of our scientists and defense workers will be channeled into projects that improve our quality of life.

"At the conclusion of my speech, we will begin dismantling one-half of all American nuclear weapons. Observers from all nations, and especially the Soviet Union, are invited to watch the process. I met this afternoon with my cabinet and the Joint Chiefs of Staff, who have agreed graciously to follow my orders in this serious undertaking. Arrangements are now being made for an unprecedented invitation for international guests to see for themselves as we begin to dismantle the nuclear cage and restore dignity and security to the planet.

"If, within a two-month period, the Soviets begin to reciprocate our actions by dismantling their own arsenals, plans will be announced for another massive reduction in our weapons. In the meantime, a deterrent force will be provided by our superb, but excessive, arsenals.

"The above measures will, of course, make it possible to have an immediate decrease in overall defense spending. I call upon the distinguished members of Congress to approve these bold measures and to work with me in developing a plan for the wise expenditure of those funds.

"I propose that we begin with the following: First, we can initiate a large tax cut to stimulate the American economy and create new jobs. Second, we can develop a massive aid program to alleviate the causes of war. This plan would include the granting of funds to defense contractors to convert their efforts from military to civilian projects.

"I propose that seventy-five percent of next year's strategic budget be used to alleviate mass starvation and poverty among our less fortunate neighbors. I challenge our Soviet friends to match those funds dollar for dollar, ruble for ruble, to wipe out starvation from our planet in the next five years. Most of the funds will be channeled through international organizations, such as UNICEF, in order to strengthen those institutions and encourage other nations to join in our quest for a just and peaceful world."

The television screen fills with images—first of a poor child with a bloated stomach being handed something to eat, then with a chart that suggests the amount of money available for projects. The president goes into some detail on the plan, showing how effective the program would be, with both immediate famine relief and long-term health and development programs initiated at the local level in consultation with United Nations experts.

"A third priority would be the funding of a major international effort (under the auspices of the United Nations) to investigate and propose a broad range of international security measures: a crisis communications center, the elaboration of nonviolent defense and crisis resolution techniques, and the creation of international security forces. In consultation with our allies, we will reduce our global military commitments as alternative forms of security are put into place.

"Gone are the days when any great power can try to police the world or to impose its will on other people. I pledge myself to dialogue with the Soviets and others about ways to insure that foreign troops will not threaten the independence and self-determination of any peoples.

"An additional amount should be set aside for massive cross-cultural exchanges with the Soviet Union, and all communist countries, in an effort to demystify our images of one another and grow to appreciate our respective arts, literatures, and peoples.

"Funds should also be made available for extensive educational efforts around the globe to teach each new generation about the threat of nuclear weapons, and of war. Extensive courses in nonviolent action and peacemaking should be a central part of every curriculum in the public schools.

"Finally, several billion dollars should be earmarked for the rebuilding of our nation's cities and the industrial infrastructure of our economy. Henceforth, our security will be based on a strong economy, a confident people, and a safer world.

"The time has come for an end to petty politics and immature quarrels among nations. Although we have genuine differences, and will continue to be in conflict, we will fight only as brothers and sisters.

"We are living in a time of crisis, in a historic crossroads at which we will decide the fate of the earth. We are faced with decisions that call for the kind of courage shown by the men and women of conviction who founded this great country of ours.

"This task is not one we shall undertake alone, however; we must call on the statesmen and stateswomen of all the world's peoples to join us in taking a stand for life, and against nuclear annihilation.

"We must carry out our fondest hopes and dreams, and make them reality. I long for the day—and either it will come or we may destroy life on the planet—when we will burst forth from the nuclear cage.

The president paused, recalling the haunting faces of the night before. Could he make all the people of the world understand?

"We can achieve peace. This is my vision; this is my dream. Let it be yours.

"Only when we do this together, with all of humanity, can we join with Martin Luther King, Jr., in fulfilling that dream in which all of God's children join hands and sing, in the words of that great Afro-American spiritual, "Free at last! Free at last! Thank God almighty we're free at last!"

Even the camera operators had tears in their eyes when the president finished. Dan Rather felt a shiver run down his spine, and he sat in silence when the camera switched to him.

There was spontaneous, joyous celebration and dancing throughout the world at the news of the president's speech. People left their homes and poured into the streets to hug strangers.

That evening an emergency session of the UN passed a unanimous resolution applauding the president's proposal. The following morning, the Soviet general secretary came on television and announced that the Soviets, too, would immediately dismantle one-half of their arsenals. He thanked the president for his courage and proclaimed that his speech would go down in history as one of the most momentous of all times.

"The upward spiral of the arms race has been broken," the general secretary said. "Now we can get down to the business of working out the details that will usher in a new era of peace and prosperity."

At the Vatican, the pope appeared on the balcony to greet a cheering throng of millions of people. At his side stood leaders from the Russian Orthodox, Jewish, Buddhist, Moslem, Protestant, and Hindu faiths.

"Our prayers have been answered," the pope told the crowds. He read a joint declaration that the religious leaders had prepared.

"There is much work to be done, but we move forward into the future with hope. Henceforth, whatever our differences, we shall live in peace and justice. The nuclear cage will entrap us no more."

APPENDIX A

The Methods of Nonviolent Action

THE METHODS OF NONVIOLENT PROTEST AND PERSUASION

Formal Statements

1. Public speeches
2. Letters of opposition or support
3. Declarations by organizations and institutions
4. Signed public statements
5. Declarations of indictment and intention
6. Group or mass petitions

Communications with a Wider Audience

7. Slogans, caricatures and symbols
8. Banners, posters and displayed communications
9. Leaflets, pamphlets and books
10. Newspapers and journals
11. Records, radio and television
12. Skywriting and earthwriting

Group Representations

13. Deputations
14. Mock awards
15. Group lobbying
16. Picketing
17. Mock elections

Symbolic Public Acts

18. Displays of flags and symbolic colors
19. Wearing of symbols
20. Prayer and worship
21. Delivering symbolic objects
22. Protest disrobings
23. Destruction of own property
24. Symbolic lights
25. Displays of portraits
26. Paint as protest
27. New signs and names
28. Symbolic sounds
29. Symbolic reclamations
30. Rude gestures

Pressures on Individuals

31. "Haunting" officials
32. Taunting officials
33. Fraternization
34. Vigils

Drama and Music

35. Humorous skits and pranks
36. Performances of plays and music
37. Singing

Processions

38. Marches
39. Parades
40. Religious processions
41. Pilgrimages
42. Motorcades

Honoring the Dead

43. Political mourning
44. Mock funerals
45. Demonstrative funerals
46. Homage at burial places

Public Assemblies

47. Assemblies of protest or support
48. Protest meetings
49. Camouflaged meetings of protest
50. Teach-ins

Withdrawal and Renunciation

51. Walk-outs
52. Silence
53. Renouncing honors
54. Turning one's back

THE METHODS OF SOCIAL NONCOOPERATION

Ostracism of Persons

55. Social boycott
56. Selective social boycott
57. Lysistratic nonaction
58. Excommunication
59. Interdict

Noncooperation with Social Events, Customs and Institutions

60. Suspension of social and sports activities
61. Boycott of social affairs
62. Student strike
63. Social disobedience
64. Withdrawal from social institutions

Withdrawal from the Social System

65. Stay-at-home
66. Total personal noncooperation
67. "Flight" of workers
68. Sanctuary
69. Collective disappearance
70. Protest emigration (*hijrat*)

THE METHODS OF ECONOMIC NONCOOPERATION: (1) ECONOMIC BOYCOTTS

Action by Consumers

71. Consumers' boycott
72. Nonconsumption of boycotted goods
73. Policy of austerity
74. Rent withholding
75. Refusal to rent
76. National consumers' boycott
77. International consumers' boycott

Action by Workers and Producers

78. Workmen's boycott
79. Producers' boycott

Action by Middlemen

80. Suppliers' and handlers' boycott

Action by Owners and Management

81. Traders' boycott
82. Refusal to let or sell property
83. Lockout
84. Refusal of industrial assistance
85. Merchants' "general strike"

Action by Holders of Financial Resources

86. Withdrawal of bank deposits
87. Refusal to pay fees, dues, and assessments
88. Refusal to pay debts or interest
89. Severance of funds and credit
90. Revenue refusal
91. Refusal of a government's money

Action by Governments

92. Domestic embargo
93. Blacklisting of traders
94. International sellers' embargo
95. International buyers' embargo
96. International trade embargo

THE METHODS OF ECONOMIC NONCOOPERATION: (2) THE STRIKE

Symbolic Strikes

97. Protest strike
98. Quickie walkout (lightning strike)

Agricultural Strikes

99. Peasant strike
100. Farm workers' strike

Strikes by Special Groups

101. Refusal of impressed labor
102. Prisoners' strike
103. Craft strike
104. Professional strike

Ordinary Industrial Strikes

105. Establishment strike
106. Industry strike
107. Sympathetic strike

Restricted Strikes

108. Detailed strike
109. Bumper strike
110. Slowdown strike
111. Working-to-rule strike
112. Reporting "sick" (sick-in)

113. Strike by resignation
114. Limited strike
115. Selective strike

Multi-Industry Strikes

116. Generalized strike
117. General strike

Combination of Strikes and Economic Closures

118. Hartal
119. Economic shutdown

THE METHODS OF POLITICAL NONCOOPERATION

Rejection of Authority

120. Withholding or withdrawal of allegiance
121. Refusal of public support
122. Literature and speeches advocating resistance

Citizens' Noncooperation with Government

123. Boycott of legislative bodies
124. Boycott of elections
125. Boycott of government employment and positions
126. Boycott of government departments, agencies and other bodies
127. Withdrawal from government educational institutions
128. Boycott of government-supported organizations
129. Refusal of assistance to enforcement agents
130. Removal of own signs and placemarks
131. Refusal to accept appointed officials
132. Refusal to dissolve existing institutions

Citizens' Alternatives to Obedience

133. Reluctant and slow compliance

134. Nonobedience in absence of direct supervision
135. Popular nonobedience
136. Disguised disobedience
137. Refusal of an assemblage or meeting to disperse
138. Sitdown
139. Noncooperation with conscription and deportation
140. Hiding, escape and false identities
141. Civil disobedience of "illegitimate" laws

Action by Government Personnel

142. Selective refusal of assistance by government aides
143. Blocking of lines of command and information
144. Stalling and obstruction
145. General administrative noncooperation
146. Judicial noncooperation
147. Deliberate inefficiency and selective noncooperation by enforcement agents
148. Mutiny

Domestic Governmental Action

149. Quasi-legal evasions and delays
150. Noncooperation by constituent governmental units

International Governmental Action

151. Changes in diplomatic and other representation
152. Delay and cancellation of diplomatic events
153. Withholding of diplomatic recognition
154. Severance of diplomatic relations
155. Withdrawal from international organizations
156. Refusal of membership in international bodies
157. Expulsion from international organizations

THE METHODS OF NONVIOLENT INTERVENTION

Psychological Intervention

158. Self-exposure to the elements
159. The fast
    (a) Fast of moral pressure
    (b) Hunger strike
    (c) Satyagraphic fast
160. Reverse trial
161. Nonviolent harassment

Physical Intervention

162. Sit-in
163. Stand-in
164. Ride-in
165. Wade-in
166. Mill-in
167. Pray-in
168. Nonviolent raids
169. Nonviolent air raids
170. Nonviolent invasion
171. Nonviolent interjection
172. Nonviolent obstruction
173. Nonviolent occupation

Social Intervention

174. Establishing new social patterns
175. Overloading of facilities
176. Stall-in
177. Speak-in
178. Guerrilla theater
179. Alternative social institutions
180. Alternative communication system

Economic Intervention

181. Reverse strike
182. Stay-in strike
183. Nonviolent land seizure
184. Defiance of blockades
185. Politically motivated counterfeiting
186. Preclusive purchasing
187. Seizure of assets
188. Dumping
189. Selective patronage

190. Alternative markets
191. Alternative transportation systems
192. Alternative economic institutions

Political Intervention

193. Overloading of administrative systems

194. Disclosing identities of secret agents
195. Seeking imprisonment
196. Civil disobedience of "neutral" laws
197. Work-on without collaboration
198. Dual sovereignty and parallel government

Source: Gene Sharp, 1974, *The Politics of Nonviolent Action, Part Two: The Methods of Nonviolent Action*. Boston: Porter Sargent Publishers. Reprinted with permission of the author.

APPENDIX B

Nuclear Arms Control Treaties and Options

REVIEW OF SELECTED TREATIES

1959—Antarctic Treaty: Declares the Antarctic an area to be used exclusively for peaceful purposes.

1963—Limited Test Ban Treaty: Prohibits nuclear weapons tests in the atmosphere, in outer space, and underwater. Signed by the UK, USSR, and USA. (China and France have refused to adhere, although France stopped atmospheric tests in 1975.)

1963—"Hot Line" Agreement: Establishes a direct communications link between the U.S. and the USSR via telegraph-teleprinter equipment. Similar agreements concluded between the USSR and France (1966) and the UK (1967); improved with satellite circuits in 1971 agreement, and further technical improvements in 1984.

1967—Outer Space Treaty: Prohibits nuclear weapons and weapons of mass destruction in outer space; forbids military bases, testing of weapons, and military maneuvers on celestial bodies.

1967—Treaty of Tlatelolco (re. Latin America): Prohibits testing, use, manufacture, production, or acquisition by any means of any nuclear weapons by Latin American countries.

1968—Non-Proliferation Treaty: Prohibits transfer by nuclear weapon states, to any recipient whatsoever, of nuclear weapons or other nuclear explosive devices or of control over them. Commits nuclear powers to exchange information for peaceful uses of nuclear energy and to pursue measures relating to cessation of the nuclear arms race and to nuclear disarmament, and to pursue a treaty of general and complete disarmament.

1971—Sea-Bed Treaty: Prohibits nuclear weapons on the ocean floor.

1972—SALT I ABM Treaty: As modified, limits deployment of ABM systems to a single area in each country (U.S. and USSR).

1972—SALT I Interim Agreement (U.S. and USSR):   Provides a freeze for a period of five years of the aggregate number of ICBM launchers and ballistic missile launchers on modern submarines.

1979—SALT II (signed, but not ratified, by the U.S.):   Sets a limit on particular types of weapons systems and the number of MIRVs. Restricts testing and deployment of new types of ICBMs, bans the SS-16, and sets ceilings on launch-weight and throw-weight of strategic ballistic missiles.

MAJOR PROPOSALS

Nuclear Freeze: First discussed in 1964, recently proposed by Randall Forsberg as a "mutual freeze on the testing, production, and deployment of nuclear weapons and of missiles and new aircraft designed primarily to deliver nuclear weapons." A freeze resolution was passed by the U.S. House with some modification, but was postponed by the Senate. A bilateral freeze has been publicly endorsed by Yuri Andropov.

START: President Reagan's two-phased proposal introduced in the Geneva talks in 1982:

Phase I
1. reduce number of weapons on ICBMs, SLBMs, by ⅓ from 7,500 to 5,000 (same impact on both countries)
2. no more than 2,500 warheads on ICBMs (USSR would give up 2,500 warheads; U.S. could add 900)

Phase II
1. reduce number of ICBMs to 850 (U.S. would give up 204 ICBMs; USSR, 550)
2. reduce throw weight to equal level (lower than present U.S. levels)

Build-Down Proposal: The Reagan administration's plan to retire two existing missiles for each new missile deployed.

European Force Reduction Talks (INF):   *"Zero Option" U.S. Proposal:* The Reagan administration has proposed that the U.S. will not deploy cruise and Pershing II missiles if the Soviets remove their SS-20s from Europe. *Soviet Proposal:* Yuri Andropov has proposed a reduction of SS-20s to 140, an approximate equivalent to the French and British forces.

Comprehensive Test Ban: Considerable progress was made and agreement nearly reached in 1980, when talks were postponed indefinitely by the Reagan administration.

No First Use: Publicly stated policy of the USSR rejected by NATO allies, which reserve the option to initiate the use of nuclear weapons to turn back a conventional Soviet attack against Western Europe.

New Abolitionist Movement: Primarily a religious movement inspired by the nineteenth-century movement to abolish slavery. Proponents note, in response to claims of critics, that it was once idealistic to think that slavery could be abolished.

Nonviolent Civilian Defense: Involves a strengthened UN world court and police force combined with nonviolent noncooperation and nonviolent training for the civilian population as a means of resisting any enemy attempt to establish political control over a country.

Notes

CHAPTER 1

[1]The estimates in the discussion that follows are U.S. estimates as reported by the Center for Defense Information's publication *The Defense Monitor* 14 (1985, No. 6):5.

[2]Note: This number is changing because of the dismantling of the Titan missiles, which will continue until September 1987.

[3]There is a trade-off between accuracy and the size of the bomb a delivery system carries.

[4]They are designated as SS-N-6, SS-N-8, SS-N-17, and 32 of the SS-N-18s.

[5]*The Defense Monitor* 13 (1984, No. 2). The administration has been unable to get all of its military funding, however, and in the face of huge deficits, the Congress put a cap on the buildup in the fiscal year 1986 budget.

[6]From 1980 to 1985 there was a 92 percent increase (after inflation) for investment, which included weapons procurement, research, and military construction (Keller 1985a:11).

[7] See Aldridge's (1983a:26ff.) discussion of secret documents on the Strategic Air Command and on the Weapons System Evaluation Group, which discussed the ability to "crush Russia quickly by massive atomic bombing attacks."

[8]For example, cruise missiles have not been tested while flying over snow, and there are some questions about what such terrain would do to the computer guidance systems.

[9]There is some controversy about the actual range of the Pershing II; some experts argue that the actual range is much longer.

[10]*The Defense Monitor* 13 (1984, No. 4).

CHAPTER 2

[1]The primary strategic and theater weapons in the world's nuclear arsenals total about 12,000 megatons.

[2]By contrast, *The Journal of the American Medical Association*, for example, has published 268 articles dealing with nuclear war and atomic radiation since September 1945 (Lundberg 1985:660).

[3]A *Wall Street Journal* article in May 1983 (Alsop 1983) reported that nuclear war had become a hot topic in schools. Proponents argued that such education was an essential part of the curriculum, because the students were concerned about it. Schools in New York City, Milwaukee, Cambridge, Massachusetts, and California, as well as elsewhere, now require peace studies or nuclear-issues discussions. Critics, however, complain that students are not mature enough to deal with such complex issues, or that biased teachers may be producing a generation that is soft on communism.

[4]That is probably the problem Jesus was addressing when he warned against being judgmental. "Why do you see the speck that is in your brother's eye," he asked, "but not notice the log that is in your own eye?" (Matt. 7:3).

CHAPTER 3

[1]Between 1975 and 1980, for example, 45.1 percent of all American families changed residences (U.S. Bureau of the Census 1982:14).

[2]That is one scenario shown in "The War Game," an excellent cinéma vérité treatment of life after a limited nuclear war in Great Britain, produced for the BBC in 1966.

CHAPTER 4

[1]The exchange of completely identical items does occur sometimes, however (Sahlins 1965:48). For example, after one person buys another person lunch, the favor may be repeated in the opposite direction. These exchanges occur in certain marital transactions (see Reay 1959:99f.), friendship compacts (Seligman 1910:70), and peace agreements (Hogbin 1939:79; Loeb 1926:204; Williamson 1912:183).

[2]Some scholars have referred to generalized reciprocity as an univocal (rather than reciprocal) exchange (see Lévi-Strauss [1949] 1969:179; Malinowski 1926:22–23; Ekeh 1974:206–7).

[3]There is considerable evidence to suggest that a major reason for the bombing of Hiroshima and Nagasaki was to avoid an ongoing balanced reciprocal relationship with the Soviets as an ally (see Chapter Two).

[4]That may be part of the reason for the ambivalence about nuclear weapons among many in the military. There will be no congressional medals of honor in a nuclear war.

[5]The German term is *Stahlhardesgehause*, which is usually translated as "iron cage," although the exact translation is debated. His metaphor is the inspiration for the nuclear cage metaphor.

[6]There is some evidence to suggest, however, that the shift to the deterrent role of the military has weakened the distinction between military and civilian institutions (see Janowitz and Little 1974). We are tempted to speculate, however, that traditional military personnel, who miss some of the unique aspects of being in the military, may find that the best way to revive them is to encourage combat.

[7]In 1959, for example, the Navy proposed a finite deterrence that would rely on submarines. The Air Force opposed the plan—no doubt in part because it threatened the SAC monopoly on nuclear weapons (Pringle and Arkin 1983:119–20).

[8]See the more detailed explanation of this argument in Benford and Kurtz (forthcoming).

[9]Lifton refers to this phenomenon as "retirement wisdom."

[10]Rituals may well be an inherent (universal) aspect of human nature, and it may not be possible to live without rituals, any more than to live beyond culture. The choice is more between healthy rituals and unhealthy ones. For example, churches examine and change their rituals from time to time to maintain their deepest purpose.

CHAPTER 5

[1]Lorenz (1966); cf. Leahey and Lewin (1977). I am grateful to Lisa Davis for her comments and suggestions on this topic.

CHAPTER 6

[1]Boeing, General Dynamics, Grumman, Lockheed, and Rockwell International.

[2]The discussion here is based in large part on an interview I conducted with Eugene Zykov, information officer for the Soviet Embassy in Washington, D.C., on 27 August 1985. When I attempted to argue that the Soviets had their own military-industrial complex, Mr. Zykov claimed that I simply did not know much about the Soviet system.

[3]In the twentieth century, for example, the United States has used its military in Nicaragua in 1898–99, 1910, and 1912–33. Elsewhere in Central America and the Carribean, the U.S. military has invaded Cuba, Panama, the Dominican Republic, Honduras, Haiti, Guatemala, Costa Rica, and El Salvador.

[4]Klare (1981:128) concludes that the United States has a three to one advantage in manpower, at least twenty to one in carrier forces, and a five to one advantage in amphibious lift forces. Although the Soviets have a slight advantage in airlift capabilities (24,140 tons total compared to 21,135 for the United States), it is offset by "the superior range and in-flight refuel capacity of U.S. transports."

CHAPTER 7

[1]What I mean by the Arms Control movement is somewhat different from the arms control perspective that is not associated with the anti-nuclear weapons movement. The establishment arms control perspective has been a major part of the mainstream perspective and is closer to the Peace through Strength frame.

[2]The president admires a cartoon in which Brezhnev was "speaking to a general in his own army, and he said, 'I liked the arms race better when we were the only ones in it'" (Scheer 1982:158).

[3]See, for example, Weinraub (1984), who reports Walter Mondale's statement that "if elected, on his first day as President he would ask the Soviet leadership to meet with him within six months in Geneva for negotiations to freeze the arms race

and cut back stockpiles of nuclear weapons." A modified version of Forsberg's proposal was included in the 1984 Democratic party platform.

⁴The Lutheran Church in America embraced the concept in its "Social Statement on World Community" adopted in 1970 (see Donaghy 1981:17).

⁵At the time this book is going to press, the Soviet moratorium is still in effect, but the United States has failed to reciprocate.

⁶In fact, the logic of the deterrence argument could be applied to the UN as well, i.e., there has been no world war since the founding of the UN!

⁷Provisions for the commission are contained in Article XIII of the ABM treaty.

⁸Witness the recent refusal of the United States to accept the rulings of the World Court with reference to charges brought against the United States by Nicaragua.

⁹CBS News Special Report, "Two Voices of Poland," 2 November 1981, with Walter Cronkite. Reprinted in Zielonka (1983).

¹⁰Personal communication, 4 February 1986.

¹¹I am grateful to Kenneth Boulding for a conversation on this notion of the moving of taboo lines.

CHAPTER 8

¹The discussion that follows relies heavily on Freedman (1982) and Bobbitt (forthcoming), which should be consulted for more detailed discussions of these matters. Although Philip Bobbitt would disagree with many of my conclusions, I am indebted to him for teaching me a great deal about nuclear strategy.

²The discussion that follows draws considerably on the film's transcript, which is available along with the film from the American Security Council Foundation, Boston, Virginia 22713. Narrated by Charlton Heston, it features interviews with Defense Secretary Caspar Weinberger, Senator John Tower (then a Republican senator from Texas and chairman of the Senate Armed Services Committee) and includes excerpts of speeches by President Reagan, among others.

³*Countdown for America* (1982:9). General Larkin (U.S. Army, ret.) is a former deputy director of the Defense Intelligence Agency.

⁴The 12 June 1982 rally held in Central Park in New York, the largest peace demonstration in U.S. history.

⁵A game in which people race toward each other on a road; whoever turns aside first is the chicken.

⁶A similar miscalculation was made by Germany with regard to the bombing of London during the Second World War.

⁷See the discussion of Reagan's critique of deterrence as part of his rationale for SDI (Chapter Ten).

CHAPTER 9

¹Even more optimistic scenarios are developed in the Pentagon's Post Nuclear Attack Study II, which estimates a survival rate of 88.9 percent with an effective crisis relocation (Murphey 1982:200).

²Eric Alley, the county emergency planning officer for North Humberside.

³The information in this table and the discussion that follows are drawn from "Nuclear Civil Protection and Crisis Relocation Planning," a booklet published by the Division of Emergency Management of the Texas Department of Public Safety

in April 1983, and a presentation by Don Jones of the Texas Department of Public Safety, in October 1985.

[4] Several blast shelter proposals have been elaborated, including a tunnel-grid system that would accommodate nearly 1.5 million people (see Wigner 1966:36ff.). Despite the Department of Defense decision not to develop blast shelters, a current FEMA publication (FEMA 1980a) provides technical information for planners and architects on how to build protective shelters against a nuclear blast.

[5] These instructions were part of a four-page insert that appeared in the Austin, Texas, telephone directory in the early 1980s. In part because of the considerable furor the instructions caused, they were not included in subsequent editions of the directory.

[6] E.g., "close all window blinds, shades, and drapes to help prevent fires from the heat wave of a nuclear explosion."

[7] See, for example, the testimony of General Lyman L. Lemnitzer before a House subcommittee in 1961, reproduced in Brelis (1962:84–85).

[8] FEMA Office of Public Affairs, News Release No. 82-26, Washington, D.C., 30 March 1982, p. 2, quoted in Leaning (1982:94).

[9] The actual amount spent is a subject of much controversy. Although one estimate by FEMA is $2 billion annually, a 1978 CIA report points out that FEMA derived that figure from an estimate of the cost of undertaking the same program in the United States—75 percent of which represents labor costs if Soviet troops were paid on the same scale as U.S. wages, which they are not (Scheer 1982:115).

CHAPTER 10

[1] The conference, entitled "Star Wars: The Strategic Defense Initiative," was sponsored by the Southwestern Regional Program in National Security Affairs and the Military Studies Institute at Texas A&M University, 16–17 November 1984, College Station, Texas.

[2] The document is not dated but refers to the upcoming 1984 presidential elections. It appears to have been written before the president's March 1983 speech.

[3] In fact, the author points out the dangers of a high-visibility campaign by a group such as High Frontier, given the organization's "existing orientation [i.e., fundraising literature] to 'liberal bashing.' "

[4] Lehrman is chairman of Citizens for America, President Reagan's grass-roots citizens' lobby.

[5] At a speech sponsored by the Liberal Arts Committee of the University of Texas, Austin, 24 April 1985. Dr. Mark is now chancellor of the University of Texas.

[6] Colonel Myer, the presidential speechwriter who helped write the SDI section of that speech, claims that the president himself penned these words.

[7] See the discussion in Chapter One, above. The main argument against the window of vulnerability theory is that even if a large number of American weapons were destroyed, the United States would still have an overwhelming retaliatory capability, as shown by a Congressional Budget Office study.

[8] The section that follows relies heavily upon the cited newspaper accounts, Tsipis (1983), an interview with a staff member of the Lawrence Livermore Laboratories (in Livermore, California, 20 November 1984), and a presentation by Barry Daniel (a senior executive of Martin-Marietta Corporation) at the Star Wars conference cited in note 1.

[9] The UCS study, however, reports that "kill vehicles" (smart missiles) could also be used in the boost phase.

¹⁰The scientists and engineers working on SDI have to walk a fine line between frankness about the difficulties to be solved, which justifies the billions of dollars required to work out the bugs, and an ultimate optimism about the ability to do so.

¹¹In all fairness, the same argument could be made about the arms control alternative—even if 99 percent of all nuclear weapons were disarmed, it would not prevent a nuclear catastrophe. The hope of arms control proponents is that the agreements would also help to reduce the international tensions that might lead to a nuclear attack.

¹²Former head of the Defense Intelligence Agency and director of the High Frontier organization, which has lobbied for SDI.

¹³Some scientists have speculated that a satellite could simply dump sand or small pellets into orbit. Traveling at speeds of thousands of miles per hour, they would cause extensive damage to any object they hit, such as a battle station or mirror.

¹⁴Depressed-trajectory missiles do not go high into outer space like other ballistic missiles, and thus are more difficult to attack. Current research and development on SDI, furthermore, may not be aimed at defense against submarine-launched missiles, which have a lower trajectory than ICBMs and fly shorter distances, thereby striking their targets much more quickly and making their detection and destruction more difficult. There is some ambiguity about the extent to which SDI is directed at SLBMs.

¹⁵Sponsors of the campaign include former President Jimmy Carter; former Secretaries of State Dean Rusk, Cyrus R. Vance, and Edmund Muskie; former Secretary of Defense Robert S. McNamara; former Directors of the Central Intelligence Agency William E. Colby and Stansfield Turner; and chief U.S. negotiator for the treaty, Gerard Smith (see Johansen 1985:202).

¹⁶Johansen (1985:201) cites Major General Grayson D. Tate's testimony before Congress in 1983.

¹⁷Johansen (1985:202) points out that prohibitions against such tests were insisted upon by U.S. negotiators of the ABM treaty.

¹⁸As this document suggests, BMD generally has been a right-wing cause, and one of the key public relations tasks of its proponents has been to find ways of minimizing that aspect in the public discourse about SDI.

CHAPTER 11

¹Konstantin Simonov, "O proshlom vo imia budushchego," *Izvestiia*, 18 November 1962, quoted in Cohen (1985:93).

²See Cohen's (1985:192) discussion of sources of this information and Antonov-Ovseyenko's (1981) even higher estimates.

³The list that follows is excerpted from a more complete account in Scheer (1982:144–46).

⁴The declassified documents about Dropshot are collected in Brown (1978).

⁵The initiative grew out of the Parliamentarians for Global Action, with representatives from the national legislatures of thirty-one countries.

CHAPTER 12

¹Pointed out to me by A. M. Abraham, senior editor of the *Times* of India, in a personal interview, 21 October 1985.

²These agreements were the Threshold Test Ban (in 1974) and a 1976 treaty limiting peaceful nuclear explosions (which were allowed by the 1963 Limited Test Ban treaty).

³The ABM treaty is officially called the Treaty Between the United States of America and the Union of Soviet Socialist Republics on the Limitation of Antiballistic Missile Systems.

⁴For an extensive technical discussion of the verification issues and how they could be resolved with high reliability, see Sykes and Evernden (1982). Sykes is Higgins Professor of Geological Sciences at Columbia University and head of the earthquake studies group at Columbia's Lamont-Doherty Geological Observatory. Evernden is program manager of the U.S. Geological Survey's National Center for Earthquake Research. See also Allan Krass's (1985) excellent book, *Verification: How Much Is Enough?*

⁵This quotation, and those that follow, are taken from the pamphlet "To Enter the 21st Century without Nuclear Weapons: New Soviet Peace Proposals Outlined by Mikhail Gorbachev, General Secretary of the CPSU Central Committee, in his Statement of January 15, 1986" (Moscow: Novosti, 1986).

⁶I am thankful to Richard Kraemer for his comments on this topic.

⁷For an excellent discussion of these issues, see Union of Concerned Scientists (1983), on which I have relied in this section.

⁸The American Security Council is a nongovernmental, private organization that is critical of U.S. arms agreements with the Soviets.

CHAPTER 13

¹This phenomenon is not limited to the United States, despite the emphasis in this chapter. On religious attitudes toward nuclear weapons in England, for example, see Martin and Mullen (1983).

²See the excellent discussions in Bainton (1960), Wallis (1982), and the National Conference of Catholic Bishops' letter (1983:34ff.). Other readings suggested by the bishops include Yoder (1972); Merton (1968); Zahn (1967); Egan (1980); Fahey (1979); and Douglass (1966).

³Cyprian, *Collected Letters*; Letters to Cornelius; quoted by the National Conference of Catholic Bishops (1983:35).

⁴Sulpicius Severus, *The Life of Martin*, 4.3; quoted by the National Conference of Catholic Bishops (1983:35).

⁵Ca. A.D. 175; quoted by Origen in *Against Celsus*, VIII.68.

⁶One might question, for example, whether the celebrated defense of the Alamo met this criterion.

⁷A proposal to substitute the word "curb" for "halt" in the wording of the recommendation, so as not to appear in direct support of a particular political movement (the Freeze), was soundly rejected by the bishops.

CHAPTER 14

¹See Smith (1965:560–72) for the complete text of the Franck Report.

²For its first two years, CNVA was called Nonviolent Action Against Nuclear Weapons.

³Quoted material excerpted from a 1984 PSR pamphlet.

[4]See Boyer (1984), to whom we are indebted, for a more extensive analysis of the decline of nuclear pacifism.

[5]For example, see *The Gallup Report*, No. 188 (May 1981); No. 208 (Jan. 1983); No. 209 (Feb. 1983).

[6]The santuary movement is a wing of the peace movement that comprises pacifists and church groups who provide shelter or "sanctuary" for people who have fled Central America to avoid persecution and violence.

Bibliography

Abrams, H. 1981. "Medical Problems of Survivors in Nuclear War." *New England Journal of Medicine* 20 (12 November):1226–32.

Adams, Gordon. 1982. *The Politics of Defense Contracting: The Iron Triangle.* New Brunswick, N.J: Transaction Books.

————. 1984. "Moscow's Military Costs." *New York Times,* 10 January: A27.

Adams, Ruth, and Susan Cullen, eds. 1981. *The Final Epidemic: Physicians and Scientists on Nuclear War.* Chicago: Educational Foundation for Nuclear Science.

Adler, Les K., and Thomas G. Paterson. 1970. "Red Fascism: The Merger of Nazi Germany and Soviet Russia in the American Image of Totalitarianism, 1930s–1950s." *American Historical Review* (April):1046–64.

Aiken, Michael, and Jerald Hage. 1972. "Organizational Interdependence and Intraorganizational Structure." Pp. 367–94 in Brinkerhoff and Kunz (1973).

Aldridge, Robert C. 1983a. *First Strike! The Pentagon's Strategy for Nuclear War.* Boston: South End Press.

————. 1983b. "Wreaking Havoc." *Sojourners* 12 (August):14–17.

Alley, Eric. 1982. "Short-term Measures." Pp. 99–101 in Shaw et al. (1982).

Alperovitz, Gar. 1985a. *Atomic Diplomacy: Hiroshima and Potsdam.* New York: Penguin.

————. 1985b. "Hiroshima Remembered: The U.S. Was Wrong." *New York Times,* 4 August: E21.

Alsop, Ronald. 1983. " 'A' Is For Atom." *Wall Street Journal,* 24 May: 1, 20.

American Security Council Foundation. 1982. "Countdown for America." Boston, Va.: American Security Council Foundation. Photocopy transcript.

Andropov, Yuri. 1984. "Statement: September 28, 1983." Pp. 119–27 in Talbott (1984).

Antonov-Ovseyenko, Anton. 1981. *The Time of Stalin*. New York: Harper & Row.

Arendt, Hannah. 1951. *The Origins of Totalitarianism*. New York: Harcourt, Brace.

_____. 1977. *Eichmann in Jerusalem: A Report on the Banality of Evil*. Harmondsworth, England: Penguin Books.

Aron, Raymond. 1973. *Peace and War: A Theory of International Relations*. Abridged version. Translated by R. Howard and A. B. Fox. Garden City, N.Y.: Anchor.

Bainton, Roland. 1943. "Congregationalism: From the Just War to the Crusade in the Puritan Revolution." *Andover Newton Theological School Bulletin* 35 (April):1–20.

_____. 1960. *Christian Attitudes toward War and Peace*. Nashville, Tenn.: Abington.

Ball, George. 1985. "The War for Star Wars." *New York Review* 31 (11 April):38–44.

Barash, David P., and Judith Eve Lipton. 1982. *Stop Nuclear War!* New York: Grove Press.

Barkan, Steven E. 1979. "Strategic, Tactical and Organizational Dilemmas of the Protest Movement against Nuclear Power." *Social Problems* 27 (1):19–37.

Barnet, Richard J. 1977. *The Giants: Russia and America*. New York: Simon and Schuster, Touchstone.

_____. 1979. "Challenging the Myths of National Security." *New York Times Magazine* (1 April):25.

_____. 1984. "The Illusion of Security." Pp. 161–72 in Weston (1984).

_____, and Ronald E. Muller. 1974. *Global Reach: The Power of the Multinational Corporations*. New York: Simon and Schuster.

Barron, John. 1974. *KGB: The Secret Work of Soviet Secret Agents*. New York: Bantam Books.

_____. 1982. "The KGB's Magical War for Peace." *Reader's Digest* (October):205–59.

Baruch, Bernard. 1986. "The Baruch Plan." Pp. 60–69 in Gregory (1986).

Baskir, Lawrence M., and William A. Strauss. 1978. *Chance and Circumstance: The Draft, the War and the Vietnam Generation*. New York: Random House.

Bateson, Gregory. 1972. "A Theory of Play and Phantasy." Pp. 177–93 in *Steps to an Ecology of Mind*, by Gregory Bateson. New York: Ballantine Books.

Bean, Don. 1983. "U.N. Aide Says U.S. Could Easily Feed All." *Cleveland Plain Dealer*, 19 October.

Beardslee, William, and John Mack. 1982. "The Impact on Children and Adolescents of Nuclear Developments." Pp. 64–93 in Rogers et al. (1982).

_____. 1983. "Adolescents and the Threat of Nuclear War: The Evolution of a Perspective." *The Yale Journal of Biology and Medicine* 56:79–91.

Bell, Daniel. 1976. *The Cultural Contradictions of Capitalism*. New York: Basic Books.

Benford, Robert D. 1984. "The Interorganizational Dynamics of the Austin Peace Movement." Master's thesis, University of Texas at Austin.

Benford, Robert, and Lester R. Kurtz. Forthcoming. "Dancing in the Dark: Ritual Elements in the Nuclear Arms Race." *Journal of the Applied Behavioral Sciences*.

Beres, Louis Rene. 1979a. "*Hic Sunt Dracones*: The Nuclear Threat of International Terrorism." *Parameters: The Journal of the U.S. Army War College* 9 (June):11–19.

_____. 1979b. "The Porcupine Theory of Nuclear Proliferation: Shortening the Quills." *Parameters: The Journal of the U.S. Army War College* 9 (September):31–37.

_____. 1981. "Presidential Directive 59: A Critical Assessment." *Parameters: The Journal of the U.S. Army War College* 11 (March):19–28.

————. 1984. "Nuclear Strategy and World Order: The United States Imperative." Pp. 215–52 in Weston (1984).

Berger, Peter, and Thomas Luckmann. 1967. *The Social Construction of Reality: A Treatise in the Sociology of Knowledge.* New York: St. Martin's Press.

Bethe, Hans A., Richard L. Garwin, Kurt Gottfried, and Henry W. Kendall. 1984. "Space-based Ballistic-Missile Defense." *Scientific American* 251 (October):39–49.

Biddle, Wayne. 1985a. "Amending of 1972 ABM Pact Is Urged." *New York Times,* 31 May:3.

————. 1985b. "Star Wars' Technology: It's More Than a Fantasy." *New York Times,* 5 March:1, 6.

Blau, Peter M. 1963. *The Dynamics of Bureaucracy.* Rev. ed. Chicago: University of Chicago Press.

Blechman, Barry M., and Stephen S. Kaplan. 1978. *Force without War: U.S. Armed Forces as a Political Instrument.* Washington, D.C.: The Brookings Institute.

Boffey, Charles. 1985a. "Dark Side of 'Star Wars':System Could Also Attack." *New York Times,* 7 March:1.

————. 1985b. "Reagan, at a Lunch, Hails Scientists for 'Revolutionizing Our Lives.' " *New York Times,* 13 February 1985:10.

Boulding, Elise. 1984. "The Peace Movement over Two Decades." Paper presented to the Society for the Study of Social Problems, 25 August, San Antonio, Texas.

————. 1985. "Nongovernmental Organizations." *Bulletin of the Atomic Scientists* 41 (August):94–96.

Boulding, Kenneth. 1978. *Stable Peace.* Austin: University of Texas Press.

————. 1982. "The War Trap." Pp. 225–38 in Falk et al. (1982).

Bowman, Robert. 1986. *Star Wars: A Defense Insider's Case against the Strategic Defense Initiative.* Los Angeles: J.P. Tarcher.

Boyer, Paul. 1984. "From Activism to Apathy: The American People and Nuclear Weapons, 1963–1980." *Journal of American History* 70 (4):821–44.

Brelis, Dean. 1962. *Run, Dig or Stay? A Search for an Answer to the Shelter Question.* Boston: Beacon Press.

Brezhnev, Leonid I. 1981. *Peace Detente Cooperation.* New York: Consultants Bureau, Plenum.

Brinkerhoff, Merlin B., and Phillip R. Kunz. 1972. *Complex Organizations and Their Environments.* Dubuque, Iowa: William C. Brown.

Broad, William J. 1982. "A Fatal Flaw in the Concept of Space War." *Science* 215 (12 March):1372–74.

————. 1983. "X-Ray Laser Weapon Gains Favor." *New York Times,* 15 November:17, 20.

————. 1985a. "Science Showmanship: A Deep 'Star Wars' Rift." *New York Times,* 16 December:1, 10.

————. 1985b. *Star Warriors: A Penetrating Look Into the Lives of the Young Scientists Behind Our Space Age Weaponry.* New York: Simon and Schuster.

————. 1985c. " 'Star Wars' Research Forges Ahead." *New York Times,* 5 February:19–21.

Brodie, Bernard P. 1946. *The Absolute Weapon.* New York: Harcourt, Brace.

————. 1948. "The Atom Bomb as Policy-Maker." *Foreign Affairs* 27 (October):17–33.

————. 1957. "More about Limited War." *World Politics* 10 (October):112–22.

————. 1959. *Strategy in the Missile Age.* Princeton: Princeton University Press.

————. 1966. *Escalation and the Nuclear Option.* Princeton: Princeton University Press.

————. 1978. "The Development of Nuclear Strategy." *International Security* 2:65–83.

Bromley, David G., Anson D. Shupe, Jr., and J. C. Ventimiglia. 1979. "Atrocity Tales, the Unification Church, and the Social Construction of Evil." *Journal of Communication* 29 (Summer):42–53.

Brown, A. C., ed. 1978. *Dropshot: The United States Plan for War with the Soviet Union in 1957.* New York: Dial Press.

Brown, Dale W., ed. 1984. *What about the Russians?* Elgin, Ill.: The Brethren Press.

Brown, Harold. 1979. *Department of Defense Annual Report to the Congress, Fiscal Year 1980.* Washington, D.C.: U.S. Government Printing Office.

Brown, Wilton John. 1985. *Do Russian People Stand for War?* Moscow: Novosti Press.

Brzezinski, Zbigniew, Robert Jastrow, and Max M. Kampelman. 1985. "Defense in Space Is Not 'Star Wars.' " *New York Times Magazine* (27 January):28ff.

Bulletin of the Atomic Scientists. 1982. "Arms Control Advocates Protest Harassment of Soviet Peace Group." *Bulletin of the Atomic Scientists* 38 (November):62–63.

————, ed. 1983. "Onward and Upward with Space Defense." *Bulletin of the Atomic Scientists* 39 (June/July):4–8.

————. 1984. "Three Minutes to Midnight." *Bulletin of the Atomic Scientists* 40 (January):2.

Bundy, McGeorge F., George F. Kennan, Robert S. McNamara, and Gerard Smith. 1984. "Nuclear Weapons and the Atlantic Alliance." Pp. 374–84 in Weston (1984).

Burbank, Russ. 1982. "Educators Oppose Nuclear Arms Buildup." *MTA Today* (13 October):6–7.

Butterfield, Fox. 1984. "Experts Disagree on Children's Worries About Nuclear War." *New York Times*, 16 October:A16.

Cagan, Leslie. 1982. "June 12th: A Look Back, A Look Ahead." *The Mobilizer* 2 (1):9–10.

Caldicott, Helen. 1984. *Missile Envy.* New York: William Morrow and Company.

Canada Department of National Health and Welfare. 1957. *Civil Defense Notebook.* Ottawa: Edmond Cloutier.

Carnesale, Albert, Paul Doty, Stanley Hoffman, Samuel P. Huntington, Joseph S. Nye, Jr., and Scott D. Sagan. 1983a. *Living with Nuclear Weapons.* New York: Bantam Books.

————. 1983b. *What Is New about the Nuclear World?* Cambridge, Mass.: Harvard University Press.

Carson, Doyle I. 1982. "Nuclear Weapons and Secrecy." Pp. 34–41 in Rogers et al. (1982).

Cartwright, D. 1968. "The Nature of Group Cohesiveness." Pp. 91–109 in *Group Dynamics: Research and Theory*, edited by D. Cartwright and A. Zander. New York: Harper & Row.

Center for Defense Information. 1982. "Soviet Compliance with Salt I." Washington, D.C.: Center for Defense Information.

Cevoli, Cathy. 1983. "Colleges on the Right Course?" *Nuclear Times* 2 (October):33–36.

————. 1986. "Shedding Light on Burn-out: Advice for Activists." *Nuclear Times* 4 (January/February):20–22.

Chatfield, Charles. 1973. *Peace Movements in America.* New York: Schocken Books.

Chernenko, Konstantin. 1985a. "Konstantin Chernenko's Answers to Questions Put by U.S. Journalist Joseph Kingbury-Smith. June 12, 1984." Pp. 366–67 in Fedoseyev (1985b).

————. 1985b. "Konstantin Chernenko's Replies to an Appeal by U.S. Scientists." Pp. 360–62 in Fedoseyev (1985b).

Chivian, Eric, Susanna Chivian, Robert Jay Lifton, and John E. Mack, eds. 1982. *Last Aid: The Medical Dimensions of Nuclear War*. San Francisco: W. H. Freeman and Co.

Chivian, Eric S. et al. 1985. "Soviet Children and the Threat of Nuclear War: A Preliminary Study." *American Journal of Orthopsychiatry* (October):484–502.

Chomsky, Noam. 1981. *Radical Priorities*. Montreal: Black Rose Books.

————. 1982. *Towards a New Cold War*. New York: Pantheon.

Church of England General Synod. 1983. "Resolutions Passed by the General Synod of the Church of England concerning *The Church and the Bomb*." Pp. 181–82 in Martin and Mullen (1983).

"Civil Offense?" 1982. *Nation* 227 (16 December):660.

Clande, I. L. 1963. "United Nations' Use of Military Force." *Journal of Conflict Resolution* 7:117–29.

Clark, Gordon. 1984. "Centralization: Not a Dirty Word." *Nuclear Times* 3 (July):18.

Clausen, Peter A. 1985. "SDI in Search of a Mission." *Harvard International Review* (January/February).

Clausewitz, Carl von. [1832] 1968. *On War [Von Kriege]*. Baltimore: Penguin Books.

Clines, Francis X. 1983. "Reagan Denounces Ideology of Soviet as 'Focus of Evil.' " *New York Times* (9 March):A1, A18.

Clubb, Oliver. 1984. *KAL Flight 007: The Hidden Story*. Sag Harbor, N.Y.: Permanent Press.

Cockburn, Andrew. 1984. *The Threat: Inside the Soviet Military Machine*. New York: Vintage Books.

————, and Alexander Cockburn. 1980. "The Myth of Missile Accuracy." *The New York Review of Books* 28 (20 November):40–44.

Cohen, L. J., and J. P. Shapiro, eds. 1974. *Communist Systems in Comparative Perspective*. Garden City, N.Y.: Anchor.

Cohen, Stephen F. 1985. *Rethinking the Soviet Experience*. Oxford: Oxford University Press.

Coles, Robert. 1985. "Children and the Bomb." *Times Magazine* (8 December):44ff.

Collins, Randall. 1974. "Three Faces of Cruelty: Towards a Comparative Sociology of Violence." *Theory and Society* 1:425–40.

Combat Leader's Field Guide. 1980. Harrisburg, Penn.: Stackpole Books.

The Committee for the Compilation of Materials on Damage Caused by the Atomic Bombs in Hiroshima and Nagasaki. 1981. *Hiroshima and Nagasaki: The Physical, Medical, and Social Effects of the Atomic Bombings*. Trans. Eisei Ishikawa and David L. Swain. Tokyo: Iwanami Shoten; distributed in U.S. by Basic Books.

Committee on Foreign Relations, United States Senate. 1975. Subcommittee on Arms Control, International Organizations and Security Agreements, Analysis of Effects of Limited Nuclear War. *Sensitivity of Expected Fatalities and Attack Assumptions*. September:18.

————. 1979. *The Salt II Treaty*. Washington, D.C.: U.S. Government Printing Office.

"A Complex of Tricky Issues." 1982. *Newsweek* (26 April):26–29.

Cook, Alice, and Gwyn Kirk. 1983. *Greenham Women Everywhere: Dreams, Ideas and Actions from the Women's Peace Movement*. Boston: South End Press.

Corn, David. 1983a. "No More 'Easy Victories.'" *Nuclear Times* 1 (July):8–9.
————. 1983b. "Groups Rally around TV Movie." *Nuclear Times* 1 (August/September):6.
————. 1984. "Election Lessons to Build On." *Nuclear Times* 3 (December):12–15.
Cortright, David. 1984. "Coming Alive in '85: New Plans and Renewed Vision." *Nuclear Times* 3 (October/November):1, 18–20.
Coser, Lewis. 1963. "Peaceful Settlements and the Dysfunctions of Secrecy." *Journal of Conflict Resolution* 7:246–53.
Countdown for America. 1982. A film documentary produced by the American Security Council Foundation for the Coalition for Peace through Strength. Boston, Virginia.
Cronin, Bruce. 1984. "Celebrate Diversity." *Nuclear Times* 3 (December):18.
Crutzen, Paul, and John W. Birks. 1982. "The Atmosphere after a Nuclear War: Twilight at Noon." *Ambio* 11:114–25.
Dahl, Robert. 1985. *Controlling Nuclear Weapons: Democracy versus Guardianship.* Syracuse: Syracuse University Press.
Dallin, Alexander. 1984. *Black Box: KAL 007 and the Superpowers.* Berkeley: University of California Press.
Daniel, Barry. 1984. "Space Technologies—An Introduction." Address at symposium, Star Wars: The Strategic Defense Initiative, sponsored by the Southwestern Regional Program in National Security Affairs and the Military Studies Institute, Texas A&M University, 16–17 November, College Station, Texas.
Daniels, Marta, and Wendy Mogey. 1981. *Questions and Answers on the Soviet Threat and National Security.* Philadelphia: American Friends Service Committee.
Davidson, Donald L. 1983. *Nuclear Weapons and the American Churches: Ethical Positions on Modern Warfare.* Boulder, Colo.: Westview Press.
Davis, Horace B. 1980. *Toward a Marxist Theory of Nationalism.* New York: Monthly Review Press.
Day, Barbara, and Howard Waitzkin. 1985. "The Medical Profession and Nuclear War." *Journal of the American Medical Association* 254 (August):644–51.
Day, Samuel H., Jr. 1981. "Captain Coleman's Challenging Job and Why He Decided to Leave It." *The Progressive* 45 (August):27–31.
————. 1983a. "The New Resistance: Confronting the Nuclear War Machine." *The Progressive* 47 (April):22–30.
————. 1983b. *Nuclear Times* 1 (June):9.
DeBenedetti, Charles. 1980. *The Peace Reform in American History.* Bloomington: Indiana University Press.
————. 1983. "On the Significance of Citizen Peace Activism: America, 1961–1975." *Peace and Change* 9 (2/3):6–20.
"Defense Bucks Stop Here." 1983. *National Catholic Register.* 6 May:14.
DeGrasse, Robert, Jr., with Paul Murphy and William Ragen. 1982. *The Costs and Consequences of Reagan's Military Buildup.* A report to the International Association of Machinists and Aerospace Workers, AFL-CIO, and the Coalition for a New Foreign and Military Policy from the Council on Economic Priorities, 85 Fifth Ave., New York, N.Y. 10011.
"Delhi Declaration." 1985. Issued 28 January by Raul Alfonsin, Rajiv Gandhi Miguel de la Madrid, Julius Nyerere, Olaf Palme, and Andreas Papandreou. Pp. 13–14 in *Ending the Deadlock: The Political Challenge of the Nuclear Age.* New York: Parliamentarians for Global Action.
Department of Commerce, U.S. 1980. *Selected Acquisition Reports. Fourth Quarter 1980.* Washington, D.C.: U.S. Government Printing Office.

Dewey, John. 1929. *The Quest for Certainty.* The Gifford Lectures 1929. New York: Capricorn Books.

DeWitt, Hugh E. 1983. "Debate on a Comprehensive Nuclear Weapons Test Ban: Pro." *Physics Today* 36 (August):29–34.

Dillard, John. 1983. "Nuclear Potlatch." University of Texas, Austin. Photocopy.

Dimond, E. Grey. 1985. "The Logic of a University Student USSR-US Exchange Program." *Journal of the American Medical Association* 254 (August):658–59.

Divine, Robert A. 1978. *Blowing in the Wind: The Nuclear Test Ban Debate, 1954–1960.* New York: Oxford University Press.

Dombey, Norman. 1985. "International Agreements on Nuclear Weapons." *Bulletin of the Atomic Scientists* 38 (March):36–39.

Donaghy, John, ed. 1981. *To Proclaim Peace: Religious Statements on the Arms Race.* Nyack, N.Y.: Fellowship of Reconciliation.

Donnay, Albert. 1985. "Our Common Goal: A Nuclear Free World." *Disarmament Campaigns* 49 (November):3.

Donnelly, Chris. 1982. "Preparing to Survive—The Soviet Union." Pp. 252–74 in Shaw et al. (1982).

Dörfer, Ingemar. 1983. *The Selling of the F-16.* New York: Praeger.

Dorman, William A. 1983. "The Image of the Soviet Union in the American News Media: Coverage of Brezhnev, Andropov and MX." Paper presented at War, Peace and News Media Conference, 18–19 March, New York University.

Douglas, Mary. 1966. *Purity and Danger: An Analysis of Concepts of Pollution and Taboo.* London: Routledge & Kegan Paul.

————. 1982. *Natural Symbols: Explorations in Cosmology.* New York: Pantheon.

————, and Aaron Wildavsky. 1982. *Risk and Culture: An Essay on the Selection of Technical and Environmental Dangers.* Berkeley: University of California Press.

Douglass, James W. 1980. *Lightning East to West.* Portland, Ore.: Sunburst Press.

Drell, Sidney, and Frank von Hippel. 1976. "Limited Nuclear War." *Scientific American* 235 (November):34.

Drinan, Robert F., SJ. 1983. "Star Wars Leap Could Escalate Arms Race." *National Catholic Reporter* (6 May).

Driver, Christopher. 1964. *The Disarmers: A Study in Protest.* London: Hodder and Stoughton.

Drucker, Peter. 1969. *The Age of Discontinuity.* New York: Harper & Row.

Dugger, Ronnie. 1983. *On Reagan: The Man & His Presidency.* New York: McGraw-Hill Book Company.

Duke, David N. 1983. "Christians, Enemies, and Nuclear Weapons." *The Christian Century* (November):986–89.

Dulles, John Foster. 1954. "Policy for Security and Peace." *Foreign Affairs* 32 (April):353–64.

Dumas, Lloyd J. 1980. "Human Fallibility and Weapons." *Bulletin of the Atomic Scientists* 36 (September):15–20.

————. 1984. "Military Spending and Economic Decay." Pp. 172–94 in Weston (1984).

Dunn, Lewis A. 1986. "What Difference Will It Make?" Pp. 330–44 in Levine and Carlton (1986).

Durkheim, Emile. [1897] 1915. *The Elementary Forms of the Religious Life.* Translated by Joseph Ward Swain. New York: Free Press.

Dyer, Gwynne. 1985. *War.* New York: Crown Publishers Inc.

Egan, E. 1980. "The Beatitudes: Works of Mercy and Pacifism." Pp. 169–87 in *War or Peace: The Search for New Answers.* Edited by T. Shannon. New York.

Ehrlich, Paul R., Mark A. Harwell, Peter H. Raven, Carl Sagan, George M.

Woodwell, et al. 1983. "Long-term Biological Consequences of Nuclear War." *Science* 222 (23 December):1293–1300.

Ehrlich, Paul R., Carl Sagan, Donald Kennedy, and Walter Orr Roberts. 1984. *The Cold and the Dark: The World after Nuclear War.* New York: W. W. Norton.

Einstein, Albert. 1986. "Letter to President Roosevelt, August 2, 1939." Pp. 39–40 in Gregory (1986).

Eisenhower, Dwight D. 1953. "Peace in the World: Acts, Not Rhetoric Needed." *Vital Speeches of the Day* 19 (May):418–21.

Ekeh, Peter P. 1974. *Social Exchange Theory: The Two Traditions.* London: Heinemann.

Ellul, Jacques. 1969. *Violence.* New York: Seabury Press.

Epstein, William. 1975. *Last Chance: Nuclear Proliferation and Arms Control.* New York: Macmillan.

Erikson, Kai. 1966. *Wayward Puritans.* New York: Wiley.

Escalona, Sibylle. 1964. "Children and the Threat of Nuclear War." Pp. 3–24 in *Children and the Threat of Nuclear War,* by the Child Study Association of America. New York: Duell, Sloan and Pearce.

Etzioni, Amitai. 1967. "The Kennedy Experiment." *Western Political Quarterly* 20:361–80.

"Evangelicals Call for Moral Stand against Nuclear Arms Race." 1983. *Chicago Sun-Times* 18 June:13.

"Excerpts from Interview by Gromyko on Arms Talks." 1985. *New York Times,* 14 January:4.

Executive Office of the President, Office of Management and Budget. 1983. *Budget of the United States Government, Fiscal Year 1984.* Washington, D.C.: U.S. Government Printing Office.

Fabian, Larry. 1971. *Soldiers without Enemies: Preparing the United Nations for Peacekeeping.* Washington, D.C.: Brookings Institute.

Fainsod, Merle. 1963. *How Russia Is Ruled.* Cambridge, Mass.: Harvard University Press.

Falk, Richard A. 1963. *Law, Morality, and War in the Contemporary World.* New York: Praeger.

————. 1982. "Political Anatomy of Nuclearism." Pp. 128–265 in Lifton and Falk (1982).

————. 1984a. "Superpower Intervention in the Third World: The US Case." *International Foundation for Development Alternatives Dossier* 42 (July/August):45–55.

————. 1984b. "Nuclear Policy and World Order: Why Denuclearization?" Pp. 463–81 in Weston (1984).

————. 1984c. "Nuclear Weapons and the End of Democracy." Pp. 194–209 in Weston (1984).

————. 1985. "Liberation from Military Logic." *Bulletin of the Atomic Scientists* 41 (August):136–39.

Fallows, James. 1982. *National Defense.* New York: Vintage Books.

Farrell, Michael J. 1982. "War by Any Other Word Is Still Not Peace." *National Catholic Reporter* (14 May):9–11, 14.

Feagin, Joe R., ed. 1986. *Social Problems.* Englewood Cliffs, N.J.: Prentice-Hall.

————, and Lester R. Kurtz. 1986. "Problems of the Nuclear Age: Nuclear Power and Nuclear War." Pp. 377–98 in Feagin (1986).

Federal Emergency Management Agency. 1979. *Stockpile Report to the Congress.* Washington, D.C.: FEMA.

————. 1980a. *Above Ground Home Shelter.* Washington, D.C.: FEMA.

————. 1980b. *FEMA Attack Environmental Manual.* Washington, D.C.: FEMA.

————. 1980c. *Home Fallout Shelter: Lean-to Shelter Plan F.* Washington, D.C.: FEMA.

————. 1980d. *In Time of Emergency: A Citizen's Handbook on Emergency Management.* Washington, D.C.: Office of Public Affairs.

————. 1980e. *Home Fallout Shelter: Snack Bar–Basement Locale Plan D.* Washington, D.C.: FEMA.

————. 1980f. *Outside Concrete Shelter.* Washington, D.C.: FEMA.

————. 1980g. *Outdoor Warning Systems Guide.* Washington, D.C.: FEMA.

————. 1980h. *Questions and Answers in Crisis Relocation Planning.* Washington, D.C.: U.S. Government Printing Office.

Fedoseyev, P. N. 1985a. "Preventing Nuclear War Is the Prime Task of Humanity." Pp. 33–50 in Fedoseyev (1985b).

————. 1985b. *Peace and Disarmament: Academic Studies 1984.* Moscow: Progress Publishers.

Feld, Bernard T. 1971. *Impact of New Technologies on the Arms Race.* Cambridge: MIT Press.

————. 1982. "Pugwash 1982, Warsaw." *Bulletin of the Atomic Scientists* 38 (September):2–4.

Feoktistov, Lev. 1985. "Atomic Bomb as It Is." Pp. 71–83 in Fedoseyev (1985b).

Finch, Stuart. 1979. "The Study of Atomic Bomb Survivors in Japan." *The American Journal of Medicine* 66 (June):899–901.

————. 1981. "Occurrence of Cancer in Atomic Bomb Survivors." Pp. 151–65 in Adams and Cullen (1981).

Finn, James, ed. 1965. *Peace, the Churches, and the Bomb.* New York: Council on Religion and International Affairs.

Finsterbusch, Kurt. 1985. "Nuclear Issues in Social Research." *Society* 22 (January/February):2–3.

Fisher, Roger. 1981. "Preventing Nuclear War." Pp. 223–36 in Adams and Cullen (1981).

————, and William Ury. 1981. *Getting to Yes: Negotiating Agreement without Giving In.* Boston: Houghton Mifflin.

Ford, J. Massyngbaerde. 1984. *My Enemy Is My Guest.* Maryknoll, N.Y.: Orbis Books.

Forsberg, Randall. 1980. "Call to Halt the Nuclear Arms Race." Brookline, Mass.: Institute for Defense and Disarmament Studies.

————. 1982. "A Bilateral Nuclear-Weapon Freeze." *Scientific American* 247 (November):52–61.

Franck, James. 1986. "The Franck Report: A Report to the Secretary of War, June 11, 1945." Pp. 43–52 in Gregory (1986).

Frank, Andre Gunder. 1985. "Can the Debt (and Nuclear) Bomb(s) be Defused?" *International Foundation for Development Alternatives Dossier* 46 (March/April):67–72.

Frank, Jerome D. 1967. *Sanity and Survival: Psychological Aspects of War and Peace.* New York: Vintage Books.

————. 1982. "Sociopsychological Aspects of the Nuclear Arms Race." Pp. 1–10 in Rogers et al. (1982).

————. 1984. "Psychological Aspects of Disarmament and International Negotiations." Pp. 324–37 in Weston (1984).

Freedman, Lawrence. 1977. *U.S. Intelligence and the Soviet Strategic Threat.* London: Macmillan.

————. 1980. *Britain and Nuclear Weapons.* London: Macmillan.

————. 1982. *The Evolution of Nuclear Strategy.* New York: St. Martin's Press.

Freeman, Harold. 1984. "Imagine One Nuclear Bomb." Pp. 22–29 in Weston (1984).

Freud, Sigmund. [1921] 1959. *Group Psychology and the Analysis of the Ego.* Translated and edited by James Strachey. New York: W. W. Norton.

————. [1923] 1960. *The Ego and the Id.* Translated by Joan Riviere. Revised and newly edited by James Strachey. New York: W. W. Norton.

Fromm, Erich. 1961. *May Man Prevail? An Inquiry into the Facts and Fictions of Foreign Policy.* Garden City, N.Y.: Anchor.

————. 1973. *The Anatomy of Human Destructiveness.* New York: Holt, Rinehart and Winston.

————, and Michael Maccoby. 1962. "The Case Against Shelters." Pp. 71–92 in Melman (1962).

Galbraith, John Kenneth. 1981. "Economics of the Arms Race—And After." Pp. 48–57 in Adams and Cullen (1981).

————. 1984. "The Military Power." An address delivered at the University of Texas at Austin (27 March).

Gallagher, Jim. 1982. "How the Soviets Duped Billy Graham." *Chicago Sun Times.*

Gamson, William A. 1984. "Political Symbolism and Nuclear Arms Policy." Paper presented at the annual meeting of the American Sociological Association, August 1984, San Antonio, Texas.

Gandhi, M. K. 1957. *An Autobiography.* Boston: Beacon Press.

————. 1967. *Non-violent Resistance.* New York: Schocken Books.

Garrison, Jim. 1982. *The Darkness of God: Theology after Hiroshima.* Grand Rapids, Mich.: Eerdmans.

Garthoff, Raymond L. 1953. *Soviet Military Doctrine.* Glencoe, Ill.: The Free Press.

————. 1958. *Soviet Strategy in the Nuclear Age.* New York: Praeger.

Garwin, Richard L., and Kurt Gottfried. 1985. "Even Half Way Is Wrong." *New York Times,* 12 February:A19.

Gaylor, Noel. 1983. "Civil Defense Is No Defense." *Los Angeles Times,* 7 August: sec. 4, p. 5.

————. 1984. "How to Break the Momentum of the Nuclear Arms Race." Pp. 396–404 in Weston (1984).

Geertz, Clifford. 1973. *The Interpretation of Cultures: Selected Essays.* New York: Basic Books.

Geiger, H. Jack. 1981. "Illusion of Survival." Pp. 173–181 in Adams and Cullen (1981).

————. 1982. *The Medical Effects of Thermonuclear Weapons.* Hearing before the House Subcommittee on Investigations and Oversight of the Committee on Science and Technology, 97th Cong., 2d sess. Pp. 27–33.

Gelb, Leslie H. 1985a. "Arms Role Reversal: Two Sides Switch Disarmament Aims." *New York Times,* 6 January:1, 6.

————. 1985b. "Vision of Space Defense Posing New Challenges." *New York Times,* 3 March:1, 6.

Gennep, Arnold van. [1909] 1960. *Les rites de passage.* Paris: Nourry. Published in English as *The Rites of Passage,* translated by M. Visedon and G. Caffee. Chicago: University of Chicago Press.

Gerasimov, Gennadi. 1984. *Keep Space Weapon-Free.* Moscow: Novosti Press.

Gerth, Jeff. 1984. "U.S. Military Creates Secret Units." *New York Times,* 8 June:1, 4.

Gilpin, Robert. 1962. *American Scientists and Nuclear Weapons Policy.* Princeton: Princeton University Press.

Glaser, Barney, and Anselm Strauss. 1964. "Awareness Contexts and Social Interaction." *American Sociological Review* 29 (October):669–79.

Glasstone, Samuel, and Phillip J. Dolan, eds. 1977. *The Effects of Nuclear Weapons.* 3d ed. Washington, D.C.: U.S. Government Printing Office.

Gluckman, Max. 1962. "Les rites de passage." Pp. 1–53 in *Essays on the Ritual of Social Relations,* edited by Max Gluckman. Manchester: University of Manchester Press.

Goffman, Erving. 1959. *The Presentation of Self in Everyday Life.* Garden City, N.Y.: Anchor.

――――. 1967. *Interaction Ritual: Essays in Face-to-Face Behavior.* Chicago: Aldine.

――――. 1974. *Frame Analysis: An Essay on the Organization of Experience.* New York: Harper Colophon.

Goldblatt, J. 1982. *Agreements for Arms Control: A Critical Survey.* London: Taylor & Francis.

Goldfarb, Jeffrey C. 1982. *On Cultural Freedom: An Exploration of Public Life in Poland and America.* Chicago: The University of Chicago Press.

Goldman, Louis. 1984. "Is There a Soviet Bomb in Wichita?" *Bulletin of the Atomic Scientists* 40 (January):54–56.

Goldman, Ralph M. 1984. "Political Distrust as Generator of the Arms Race: Prisoners' and Security Dilemmas." Pp. 90–93 in Weston (1984).

Gollwitzer, Helmut. "A Biblical Call to Nuclear Non-Cooperation." 1982. Pp. 46–49 in Sojourners (1982).

Goodman, Terri. 1982. "Catholic Defense Workers Agonize." *National Catholic Register,* 7 May:1, 26–27.

Goodman, Walter. 1985. "Hiroshima at 40: Grappling with the Unthinkable." *New York Times,* 4 August:12.

Gorbachev, Mikhail. 1985a. "Mikhail Gorbachev's Answers to Questions from a Tass Correspondent." Press release from the Soviet Embassy Information Department, Washington, D.C., 14 August.

――――. 1985b. "Statement by Mikhail Gorbachev." Press release from the Soviet Embassy Information Department, Washington, D.C., 29 July.

――――. 1985c. *A Time for Peace.* New York: Richardson & Steirman.

Gordon, Suzanne. 1982. "The Ultimate Single Issue." *Working Papers* (May/June):21–25.

Goryunov, Felix. 1985. *East-West Business Ties: Two Approaches.* Moscow: Novosti Press.

Gottfried, Kurt, Henry W. Kendall, Hans A. Bethe, Peter A. Clausen, Richard L. Garwin, Noel Gayler, Richard Ned Lebow, Carl Sagan, and Victor Weisskopf. 1984. "Reagan's Star Wars." *The New York Review of Books* 31 (26 April):47–52.

Gottlieb, Sanford. 1982. *What about the Russians?.* Northfield, Mass.: Student/Teacher Organization to Prevent Nuclear War.

Gouldner, Alvin W. 1960. "The Norm of Reciprocity: A Preliminary Statement." *American Sociological Review* 25 (April):161–78.

Goure, Leon. 1962. *Civil Defense in the Soviet Union.* Berkeley: University of California Press.

――――. 1983. "The Soviet Civil Defense Program and the Present U.S. Civil Defense Debate." Pp. 223–29 in *Defense Department Authorization and Oversight. Part 8: Civil Defense.* Hearings before the House Committee on Armed Services, 98th Cong., 1st sess.

Gray, Colin. 1976. *The Soviet-American Arms Race.* Farnborough, Hants: Saxon House.

――――. 1977. *The Geopolitics of the Nuclear Era.* New York: Crane, Russak & Co.

――――. 1979. "Nuclear Strategy: The Case for a Theory of Victory." *International Security* 3 (Summer):54–87.

—————, and Keith Payne. 1986. "Victory Is Possible." Pp. 115–23 in Gregory (1986).

Gregory, Donna Uthus, ed. 1986. *The Nuclear Predicament.* New York: St. Martin's Press.

Gromyko, Andrei. 1980. *Lenin and the Soviet Peace Policy: Articles and Speeches, 1944–1980.* Moscow: Progress Publishers.

Grotius, Hugo. [1646] 1925. *De Jure Belli ac Pacis Libri Tres.* Vol. 2. Translated by Francis W. Kelsey et al. Oxford: Clarendon Press; London: Humphrey Milford.

Ground Zero. 1982. *Nuclear War: What's in It for You?* New York: Pocket Books.

—————. 1983. *What about the Russians—and Nuclear War?* New York: Pocket Books.

Groves, Leslie R. 1962. *Now It Can be Told: The Story of the Manhattan Project.* New York: Harper & Row.

Gwertzman, Bernard. 1984a. "2 Senators Press Reagan on Arms." *New York Times,* 4 December:A1.

—————. 1984b. " 'Star Wars' Is Not a Bargaining Chip, U.S. Says." *New York Times,* 24 December:7.

—————. 1985a. "Shultz Instructed to Spurn Russians on Space Weapons." *New York Times,* 3 January:1, 5.

—————. 1985b. "Minimum Goals Set on Space Weapons." *New York Times,* 21 February:1, 6.

Haberman, Clyde. 1984. "Japan's Anguish Lingers a Year after Flight 007." *New York Times,* 1 September:4.

—————. 1985. "40 Years after A-Bombs, Medical Burden Is Unclear." *New York Times,* 4 August:1, 12.

Halloran, Richard. 1984. "Bishop and Congressman Struggle over Nuclear Arms and Morality." *New York Times,* 28 June:A21.

—————. 1985. "U.S. Studies New Plan on Nuclear War." *New York Times,* 29 May:6.

The Harvard Nuclear Study Group. 1983. *Living with Nuclear Weapons.* New York: Bantam Books.

Harwell, Mark A. 1984. *Nuclear Winter: The Human and Environmental Consequences of Nuclear War.* New York: Springer-Verlag.

Healey, Richard. 1984. "Big Questions, Essential Steps." *Nuclear Times* 2 (July):16.

Hedemann, Ed. 1982. "Tax Resistance: An American Tradition." *Win* 18 (15 April):4–6.

Herrick, Robert L. 1980. "Review of *Secular Ritual,* edited by S. F. Moore and B. G. Myeroff, and *Rituals of the Kandyan State* by H. L. Seneviratne." *American Journal of Sociology* 86 (September):396–99.

Hersey, John. 1966. *Hiroshima.* New York: Bantam Books.

Hertsgaard, Mark. 1985. "What Became of the Freeze?" *Mother Jones* 10 (June):44–47.

Heyer, Robert, ed. 1982. *Nuclear Disarmament: Key Statements of Popes, Bishops, Councils and Chambers.* New York: Paulist Press.

Hilgartner, Stephen, Richard C. Bell, and Rory O'Connor. 1983. *Nukespeak: The Selling of Nuclear Technology in America.* New York: Penguin Books.

Hines, William. 1977. "Anti-nuclear Ferment in Europe." *The Progressive* 41 (September):19–21.

Hinson, E. Glenn. 1982. "Who Shall Suffer Injury at Our Hands?" Pp. 51–53 in Sojourners (1982).

Hirsch, Mike, Randy Hodson, and Lester Kurtz. 1986. "Bringing America Back:

An Inquiry into the Origins and Consequence of Resurgent Nationalism." Paper presented at the annual meeting of the American Sociological Association, September 1986, New York.

Hobsbawn, Eric. 1972. "Some Reflections on Nationalism." Pp. 385–407 in *Imagination and Precision in the Social Sciences*, edited by T. J. Nossiter, A. H. Hanson, and Stein Rokkan. London: Faber.

Hochschild, Adam. 1982. "The Eastern Front." *Mother Jones* 7 (September/October):30–37, 52–53.

Hogbin, Herbert Ian. 1939. *Experiments in Civilization: The Effects of European Culture on a Native Community of the Solomon Islands*. London: George Routledge and Sons.

Hogebrink, Laurens. 1985. "Political Pressures and Polarisation: Discussions in the Dutch Churches." *Disarmament Campaigns* 50 (December):3.

Hollenbach, David. 1983. *Nuclear Ethics*. New York: Paulist Press.

Hook, Sidney. 1963. *The Fail-Safe Fallacy*. New York: Stein & Day.

Horowitz, David. 1969. *Corporations and the Cold War*. New York: The Bertrand Russell Peace Foundation.

Horowitz, Irving Louis. 1972. "The Pentagon Papers and Social Science." Pp. 297–322 in *Beyond Conflict and Containment*, edited by Milton J. Rosenberg. New Brunswick, N.J.: Transaction Books.

———, and Ellen Kay Trimberger. 1976. "State Power and Military Nationalism in Latin America." *Comparative Politics* 8:223–44.

Hough, Jerry F. 1974. "The Soviet System: Petrification or Pluralism?" Pp. 449–86 in Cohen and Shapiro (1974).

Hubbel, J. G. 1978. "Soviet Civil Defense: The Grim Realities." *Reader's Digest* 112 (February):77–80.

Humanitas International. 1985. "Détente from Below." Pp. 4–6 in *Bridging the Atlantic: Special Report*. Menlo Park, Calif.: Humanitas International.

Humanitas International Human Rights Committee. 1984. "The Trials of Moscow's Independent Disarmament Activists." *Humanitas International* (Fall).

Hunthausen, Archbishop Raymond G. 1982. "Faith and Disarmament." Pp. 5–9 in Weigel (1982).

Independent Commission on Disarmament and Security Issues. 1984. "Elements of a Programme for Arms Control and Disarmament: Strengthening the United Nations Security System, Regional Approaches to Security, and Economic Security." Pp. 603–15 in Weston (1984).

Janis, Irving L. 1972. *Victims of Groupthink*. Boston: Houghton Mifflin Company.

Janowitz, Morris. 1970. "Sociological Research on Arms Control." Working Paper No. 169, Center for Social Organization Studies, Department of Sociology, University of Chicago.

———. 1978. *The Last Half-Century: Societal Change and Politics in America*. Chicago: University of Chicago Press.

———. 1983. *The Reconstruction of Patriotism: Education for Civic Consciousness*. Chicago: University of Chicago Press.

———, and R. W. Little. 1974. *Sociology and the Military Establishment*. Beverly Hills, Calif.: Sage Publications.

Jastrow, Robert. 1983a. *How to Make Nuclear Weapons Obsolete*. Boston: Little, Brown and Company.

———. 1983b. "Why Strategic Superiority Matters." *Commentary* (March):27–32.

———. 1984. "Reagan vs. the Scientists: Why the President Is Right about Missile Defense." *Commentary* (January):23–32.

Johansen, Robert C. 1984. "SALT II: A Symptom of the Arms Race." Pp. 94–105 in Weston (1984).

————. 1985. "The Future of Arms Control." *World Policy Journal* 2 (Spring):193–228.

Johnson, G. 1980. "Paradise Lost." *Bulletin of the Atomic Scientists* 36 (December):24–29.

Johnson, James Turner. 1973a. "Ideology and the *Jus ad Bellum.*" *Journal of the American Academy of Religion* 41 (June):212–28.

————. 1973b. "Toward Reconstructing the *Jus ad Bellum.*" *The Monist* 57 (October):461–88.

————. 1975. *Ideology, Reason, and the Limitation of War.* Princeton: Princeton University Press.

————. 1981. *Just War Tradition and the Restraint of War.* Princeton: Princeton University Press.

Joint Chiefs of Staff. 1978. *U.S. Military Posture FY1979.* Washington, D.C.: U.S. Government Printing Office.

————. 1979. *U.S. Military Posture FY1980.* Washington, D.C.: U.S. Government Printing Office.

————. 1980. *U.S. Military Posture FY1981.* Washington, D.C.: U.S. Government Printing Office.

————. 1981. *U.S. Military Posture FY1982.* Washington, D.C.: U.S. Government Printing Office.

Jones, Peter D. 1982. "A Complete Guide to European Disarmament." *Win* 18 (1 January):1–4.

Jordan, Amos A., and William J. Taylor. 1981. *American National Security: Policy and Process.* Baltimore: The Johns Hopkins University Press.

Kahn, Herman. 1960. *On Thermonuclear War.* Princeton: Princeton University Press.

————. 1962. *Thinking about the Unthinkable.* New York: Horizon Press.

————. 1965. *On Escalation: Metaphors and Scenarios.* New York: Praeger.

Kahneman, Daniel, and Amos Tversky. 1979. "Prospect Theory: An Analysis of Decision under Risk." *Econometrica* 47 (March):263–91.

Kaldor, Mary. 1986. "The Weapons System." Pp. 143–54 in Gregory (1986).

Kalven, Jamie. 1982. "Nuclear Weapons Freeze Campaign." *Bulletin of the Atomic Scientists* 38 (May):65.

Kaplan, Fred M. 1978. "Soviet Civil Defense Myth." *Bulletin of the Atomic Scientists* 34 (March-April):14–20.

————. 1980. *Dubious Spector: A Skeptical Look at the Soviet Nuclear Threat.* Washington, D.C.: The Institute for Policy Studies.

Katz, Arthur M. 1982. *Life after Nuclear War.* Cambridge: Ballinger Publishing Company.

Katz, Milton S. 1973. "Peace, Politics and Protest: SANE and the American Peace Movement, 1957–72." Ph.D. diss., St. Louis University.

Kavan, Jan, and Zdena Tomin. 1983. "Introduction." Pp. 3–9 in *Voices from Prague: Documents on Czechoslovakia and the Peace Movement,* edited by J. Kavan and Z. Tomin. London: Palach Press, Ltd.

Kehler, Randy. 1984. "We Need a Common Voice." *Nuclear Times* 2 (June):9–10.

Keju, Darlene. 1982. "Bikini: Where the Guinea Pigs Are People." *Win* 18 (1 August):20–21.

Keller, Bill. 1985a. "Pentagon Aide Calls Antimissile Plan Central to Military Outlook." *New York Times,* 22 February:11.

————. 1985b. "Pentagon Asserts 'Star Wars' Tests Won't Break Pact." *New York Times,* 21 April:1.

Kennan, George F. 1981. "A Modest Proposal." *The New York Review of Books* 28 (16 July):14–16.

————. 1982. *The Nuclear Delusion: Soviet-American Relations in the Atomic Age.* New York: Pantheon.

————. 1983. "Zero Options." *The New York Review of Books* 30 (12 May):3.

Kennedy, Edward. 1984. "Star Wars vs. the ABM Treaty." *Arms Control Today* (July/August):19.

Kennedy, John F. 1961. *Urgent National Needs: Address of the President of the United States, May 25, 1961.* H. Doc. 174, 87th Cong., 1st sess.

Kennedy, Robert F. 1969. *Thirteen Days.* New York: W. W. Norton.

Kerr, Thomas J. 1983. *Civil Defense in the U.S.: Bandaid for a Holocaust?* Boulder: Westview Press.

Kharkhardin, Oleg. 1985. "The Soviet Peace Committee." Pp. 275–81 in Fedoseyev (1985b).

Khrushchev: 1970. Ed. and trans. by Strobe Talbott. Boston: Little, Brown and Company.

Khrushchev, Nikita. 1971–74. *Khrushchev Remembers.* 2 vols. London: Andre Deutch.

Kissinger, Henry. 1957. *Nuclear Weapons and Foreign Policy.* New York: Harper & Row.

————. 1979. *The White House Years.* Boston: Little, Brown and Company.

Klare, Michael T. 1979. "The Power Projection Gap." *The Nation,* 228 (9 June):671–76.

————. 1981. *Beyond the "Vietnam Syndrome:" U.S. Intervention in the 1980s.* Washington, D.C.: Institute for Policy Studies.

————. 1984. *American Arms Supermarket.* Austin: University of Texas Press.

————. 1985. "Securing the Firebreak." *World Policy Journal* 2 (Spring):229–47.

Knightley, B. 1982. "Japan: The Movement Faces the 80s." *Win* 18 (14):12–13.

Kolkowicz, Roman. 1974. "Interest Groups in Soviet Politics: The Case of the Military." Pp. 317–34 in Cohen and Shapiro (1974).

Konrad, George. 1984. "Going beyond Yalta." *END Journal* 10 (June-July).

Krasnov, I. M. 1982. *The Soviet Union as Americans See It: 1917–1977.* Moscow: Progress Publishers.

Krass, Allan S. 1984. "Deterrence and Its Contradictions." Pp. 209–15 in Weston (1984).

————. 1985. *Verification: How Much Is Enough?* Lexington, Mass.: Lexington Books.

————, and Catherine Girrier. 1987. *Disproportionate Response: A Review of Alleged Soviet Treaty Violations.* Cambridge, Mass.: Union of Concerned Scientists.

Kriesberg, Louis. 1982. *Social Conflicts.* Englewood Cliffs, N.J.: Prentice-Hall.

Kull, Steven. 1985. "Nuclear Nonsense." *Foreign Policy* (Spring):28–52.

Kurtz, Jerry, and Pat Gilliam. 1983. *Nuclear War Manual for Dogs: An Illustrated Guide.* Baltimore: Zoo Press.

Kurtz, Lester R. 1986. *The Politics of Heresy.* Berkeley: University of California Press.

Kwitney, Jonathan. 1984. *Endless Enemies: The Making of an Unfriendly World.* New York: Congdon & Weed.

Labrie, Roger P., ed. 1980. *SALT Handbook: Key Documents and Issues, 1972–1979.* Washington, D.C.: American Enterprise Institute.

LaFeber, Walter. 1976. *America, Russia, and the Cold War: 1945–1975.* New York: Wiley.

Laird, Melvin R. 1982. "What Our Defense Really Needs." *The Washington Post,* 4 November:A15.

Lang, Kurt. 1972. *Military Institutions and the Sociology of War.* Beverly Hills: Sage Publications.

Laqueur, Walter Z., and Leopold Labedz, eds. 1965. *The State of Soviet Science.* Cambridge, Mass.: M.I.T. Press.

Lawyers Committee on Nuclear Policy. 1984. "Statement on the Illegality of Nuclear Weapons." Pp. 146–51 in Weston (1984).

Leadbeater, Marie. 1985. "The Ripple Effect: A Letter from New Zealand." *Disarmament Campaigns* 42 (March):3–4.

Leahey, Richard E., and Roger Lewin. 1977. "Is It Our Culture, Not Our Genes, that Makes Us Killers?" *Smithsonian* 8 (November):56–64.

Leaning, Jennifer. 1982. "Civil Defense in the Nuclear Age: Strategic, Medical, and Demographic Aspects." Pp. 93–111 in *United States and Soviet Civil Defense Programs.* Hearings before the Senate Subcommittee on Arms Control, Oceans, International Operations, and Environment of the Committee on Foreign Relations, 97th Cong., 2d sess.

————, and Langley Keyes, eds. 1984. *The Counterfeit Ark.* Cambridge: Ballinger Publishing Company.

Leavitt, Robert. 1983a. "Freezing the Arms Race: The Campaign in Washington." John F. Kennedy School of Government, Harvard University. Photocopy.

————. 1983b. "Freezing the Arms Race: The Genesis of a Mass Movement." John F. Kennedy School of Government, Harvard University. Photocopy.

Leebaert, Derek, ed. 1981. *Soviet Military Thinking.* Cambridge: Harvard Center for Science and International Affairs.

Lehrman, Lewis E. 1985. "A Moral Case for 'Star Wars.'" *New York Times*, 19 February:27.

Lemay, Curtis. 1972. "A Soldier's Duty." Pp. 109–16 in Gregory (1972).

Levine, Herbert M., and David Carlton, eds. 1986. *The Nuclear Arms Race Debated.* New York: McGraw-Hill.

Levine, Sol, and Paul E. White. 1972. "Exchange as a Conceptual Framework for the Study of Interorganizational Relationships." Pp. 341–55 in Brinkerhoff and Kunz (1972).

Lévi-Strauss, Claude. [1949] 1969. *The Elementary Structures of Kinship.* Revised edition, translated by J. H. Bell, J. R. von Sturmer, and R. Needham. Boston: Beacon Press.

Licklider, Roy E. 1971. *The Private Nuclear Strategists.* Columbus: Ohio State University Press.

Lifton, Robert Jay. 1964. "On Death and Death Symbolism: The Hiroshima Disaster." *Psychiatry* 27 (August):191–210.

————. 1968. *Death in Life: Survivors of Hiroshima.* New York: Basic Books.

————. 1982. "Imagining the Real." Pp. 3–125 in Lifton and Falk (1982).

————. 1984. "Beyond Psychic Numbing: A Call to Awareness." Pp. 111–122 in Weston (1984).

————. 1985a. "Hiroshima and Ourselves." *Journal of the American Medical Association* 254 (August):631–32.

————. 1985b. "Hiroshima Gives Substance to Our Terror, a Look into Abyss." *Los Angeles Times*, 6 August:5.

————. 1985c. "Toward a Nuclear-Age Ethos." *Bulletin of the Atomic Scientists* 41 (August):168–72.

————, and Kai Erikson. 1982. "Nuclear War's Effect on the Mind." pp. 274–78 in Lifton and Falk (1982).

————, and Richard Falk. 1982. *Indefensible Weapons: The Political and Psychological Case Against Nuclearism.* New York: Basic Books.

————, Eric Markusen, and Dorothy Austin. 1984. "The Second Death: Psychological Survival after Nuclear War." Pp. 285–300 in Leaning and Keyes (1984).

Likutov, Konstantin. 1985. *Soviet Foreign Policy: Questions and Answers*. Moscow: Novosti Press.
Lindop, Patricia J., and J. Rotblat. 1981. "Consequences of Radioactive Fallout." Pp. 117–50 in Adams and Cullen (1981).
Lipset, Seymour Martin. 1967. *The First New Nation: The United States in Historical and Comparative Perspective*. Garden City, N.Y.: Anchor.
Loeb, Edwin M. 1926. "Pomo Folkways." *University of California Publications in American Archeology and Ethnology*, 19:149–409.
Loeb, Paul. 1982. *Nuclear Culture*. New York: Coward, McCann, & Geoghegan, Inc.
⸺. 1983. "Teaching the Unthinkable." *Nuclear Times* 2 (October):26–28.
Lorenz, Konrad. 1966. *On Aggression*. New York: Harcourt Brace Jovanovich.
Lovins, Amory B., and L. Hunter Lovins. 1980. *Energy/War: Breaking the Nuclear Link*. New York: Harper Colophon.
Lown, Bernard, and Eugene Chazov. 1985. "Cooperation Not Confrontation: The Imperative of a Nuclear Age." *Journal of the American Medical Association* 254 (August):655–57.
Lowther, Mary P. 1973. "The Decline of Public Concern over the Bomb." *Kansas Journal of Sociology* 9 (Spring):77–88.
Lundberg, George D. 1985. "Editorial: Prescriptions for Peace in a Nuclear Age." *Journal of the American Medical Association* 254 (August):660–61.
Luttwak, Edward. 1983. *The Grand Strategy of the Soviet Union*. New York: St. Martin's Press.
⸺. 1984. *The Pentagon and the Art of War: The Question of Military Reform*. New York: Simon and Schuster.
MacDougall, John. 1984. "Ban Nuclear Testing, 1957–63: A Preliminary Research Report on a Popular Movement in America." University of Lowell, Lowell, Massachusetts. Photocopy.
MacGregor, G. H. C. 1954. *The New Testament Basis of Pacificism and the Relevance of an Impossible Ideal*. Nyack, N.Y.: Fellowship Publications.
McNamara, Robert S. 1963. *Defense Program and 1964 Defense Budget*. Washington, D.C.: U.S. Government Printing Office.
⸺. 1983. "The Military Role of Nuclear Weapons: Perceptions and Misperceptions." *Foreign Affairs* 62 (Fall):59–80.
⸺. 1987. *Blundering into Disaster: Surviving the First Century of the Nuclear Age*. New York: Pantheon.
McSorley, Richard. 1979. *The New Testament Basis of Peacemaking*. Washington, D.C.: Center for Peace Studies.
Malinowski, Bronislaw. 1926. *Crime and Custom in Savage Society*. London: Kegan Paul, Trench, Trubuer and Co.
Mandelbaum, Michael. 1981. *The Nuclear Revolution*. Cambridge: Cambridge University Press.
Mapes, Deb. 1985/86. "Taking the Initiative." *Defense & Disarmament News* 1 (December/January):7.
Markusen, Eric, and John B. Harris. 1985. "The Role of Education in Preventing Nuclear War." Pp. 33–54 in Zars et al. (1985).
Marshall, E. 1981. "New A-Bomb Studies Alter Radiation Estimates." *Science* 212 (May):900–903.
Martin, David. 1983. "The Christian Ethic and the Spirit of Security and Deterrence." Pp. 85-107 in Martin and Mullen (1983).
⸺, and Peter Mullen, eds. 1983. *Unholy Warfare: The Church and the Bomb*. Oxford: Basil Blackwell.
Martynov, Vladlen. 1985. "U.S. Imperialism—Enemy of Detente and Equitable International Economic Cooperation." Pp. 204–17 in Fedoseyev (1985).

Mauss, Marcel. [1925] 1954. *Essai sur le don: Forme et raison de l'echange dans les sociétés archaiques*. Published in English as *The Gift: Forms and Functions of Exchange in Archaic Societies*. Glencoe, Ill.: The Free Press.

Mavor, Air Marshal Sir Leslie. 1982. "Introduction." Pp. 3–13 in Shaw et al. (1982).

Mead, G. H. 1934. *Mind, Self, & Society: From the Standpoint of a Social Behaviorist*. Edited by Charles W. Morris. Chicago: University of Chicago Press.

Medreyev, Roy A. 1984. *An End to Silence: Uncensored Opinion in the Soviet Union*. New York: Norton.

Melko, Matthew. 1973. *Fifty-two Peaceful Societies*. Oakville, Ontario: Canadian Peace Research Institute.

Melman, Seymour. 1962. *No Place to Hide: Fact and Fiction about Fallout Shelters*. New York: Grove Press.

_____. 1972. "Pentagon Bourgeoisie." Pp. 184–97 in *Beyond Conflict and Containment*, edited by Milton J. Rosenberg. New Brunswick, N.J.: Transaction Books.

_____. 1983. *Profits without Production*. New York: Knopf.

Mendelsohn, Everett. 1985. "Disinventing Nuclear War." Pp. 72–76 in Zars et al. (1985).

Merton, Robert K., and Elinor Barber. 1976. "Sociological Ambivalence." Pp. 1–48 in *Sociological Ambivalence and Other Essays*, by Robert Merton. New York: Free Press.

Merton, Thomas. 1964. *Gandhi on Non-violence*. New York: New Directions Press.

_____. 1968. *Faith and Violence*. Notre Dame, Ind.: University of Notre Dame Press.

_____. 1980. *The Nonviolent Alternative*. New York: Farrar, Straus, Giroux.

Meyrowitz, Elliot L. 1983. "Are Nuclear Weapons Legal?" *Bulletin of the Atomic Scientists* 39 (October):49–52.

Michihiko, Hachiya. 1955. *Hiroshima Diary*. Chapel Hill: University of North Carolina Press.

Milgram, Stanley. 1974. *Obedience to Authority*. New York: Harper & Row.

Miller, Alex. 1986. "Peace Prize Boosts PSR." *Nuclear Times* 4 (January/February):11.

Miller, John. 1982. "June 14: Disobedience for Disarmament." *Win* (15 August):8–11.

Mills, C. Wright. [1958] 1976. *The Causes of World War III*. Westport, Conn.: Greenwood Press.

_____. 1959. *The Sociological Imagination*. London: Oxford University Press.

Mitchell, Greg. 1984. "Returning an Important 'Call.'" *Nuclear Times* 2 (August):12–13.

Mohr, Charles. 1984. "Repudiation of the '79 Arms Accord Is Urged." *New York Times*, 7 July.

_____. 1985a. "Former Military Aides Question Space-based Defense Plans." *New York Times*, 1 March:3.

_____. 1985b. "What Moscow Might Do in Replying to 'Star Wars.'" *New York Times*, 6 March:8.

_____. 1985c. "Study Says Space Arms Plan Imperials ABM Pact." *New York Times*, 26 March:A16.

_____. 1985d. "Science Advisor Optimistic about Missile Defense." *New York Times*, 22 May:9.

_____. 1985e. "Two Doubt Statements on A-Bombing of Japan." *New York Times*, 1 August:7.

_____. 1986. "Irate Carter Rebuts Reagan on Military and Security Policy." *New York Times*, 2 March:1, 18.

Mojtabai, A. G. 1986. *Blessed Assurance: At Home with the Bomb in Amarillo, Texas.* Boston: Houghton Mifflin.

Molander, Roger. 1982. "How I Learned to Start Worrying and Hate the Bomb." *The Washington Post*, 21 March:D1, D5.

————, and Robbie Nichols. 1985. *Who Will Stop the Bomb? A Primer on Nuclear Proliferation.* New York: Facts on File Publications.

Molotsky, Irvin. 1985. "Official Disputes an Article on Offensive Atom Weapons." *New York Times*, 1 June:7.

Montagu, Ashley, ed. 1978. *Learning Non-aggression.* New York: Oxford University Press.

Morgan, Patrick M. 1983. *Deterrence: A Conceptual Analysis.* Beverly Hills: Sage Publications.

Morgenthau, Hans J. 1977. "The Fallacy of Thinking Conventionally about Nuclear Weapons." Pp. 255–64 in *Arms Control and Technological Innovation*, edited by David Carlton and Carlo Schaerf. London: Croom H elm.

Morrison, Philip. 1983. "The Spiral of Peril: A Narrative of the Nuclear Arms Race." *Bulletin of the Atomic Scientists* 39 (January):10–17.

Morrow, James. 1986. *This Is the Way the World Ends.* New York: Henry Holt and Company.

Moskos, Charles C., Jr. 1967. *The Sociology of Political Independence.* Cambridge, Mass.: Schenkman Publishing Company.

Mowlan, Marjorie. 1983. "Peace Groups and Politics." *Bulletin of the Atomic Scientists* 39 (November):28–32.

Murphey, Walter. 1982. "The USA." Pp. 193-208 in Shaw et al. (1982).

Murphy, Paul. 1983. "Women Build the Peace Camp Movement." *Win* 19 (15 March):4–7.

Myer, Colonel Allan. 1984. "The Political and Strategic Context of the Strategic Defense Initiative." Address at symposium, Star Wars: The Strategic Defense Initiative, sponsored by the Southwestern Regional Program in National Security Affairs and the Military Studies Institute, Texas A&M University, 16–17 November, College Station, Texas.

Myers, Ched. 1983. "The Wind that Diverts the Storm: The Gospel and the Nuclear-Free and Independent Pacific Movement." *Sojourners* 12 (August):10–13.

Myrdal, Alva. 1982. *The Game of Disarmament: How the United States and Russia Run the Arms Race.* New York: Pantheon.

Nance, John. 1975. *The Gentle Tasaday: A Stone Age People in the Philippine Rain Forest.* New York: Harcourt, Brace.

Nash, Henry T. 1980. "The Bureaucratization of Homicide." *Bulletin of the Atomic Scientists* 36 (April):22–27.

Nathan, Otto, and Heinz Norden. 1981. *Einstein on Peace.* New York: Avenel Books.

National Conference of Catholic Bishops. 1983. *The Challenge of Peace: God's Promise and Our Response.* Washington, D.C.: United States Catholic Conference.

National Research Council. 1975. *Long-term Worldwide Effects of Multiple Nuclear Weapons Detonations.* Washington, D.C.: National Academy Press.

————. 1985. *The Effects on the Atmosphere of a Major Nuclear Exchange.* Washington, D.C.: National Academy Press.

Neill, W. H. 1976. *Plagues and Peoples.* Garden City, N.Y.: Anchor.

Nelkin, Dorothy, and Michael Pollak. 1981. *The Atom Besieged.* Cambridge: MIT Press.

Nieberg, Harold L. 1964. *Nuclear Secrecy and International Policy.* Washington, D.C.: Public Affairs Press.

Niedergang, Mark. 1982. "Freeze: Beginning Is Half." *Win* 18 (November):7–10.

Nitze, Paul. 1976. "Deterring Our Deterrent." *Foreign Policy* (Winter):195–210.

Nouwen, Henri. 1979. "Letting Go of All Things." *Sojourners* (May):1.
Novick, Aaron. 1946. "A Plea for Atomic Freedom." *New Republic* 114 (15 March):399–400.
O'Brien, Tim. 1985. *The Nuclear Age*. New York: Alfred A. Knopf.
Oestreicher, Paul. 1983. ". . . But I Say unto You." Pp. 197–205 in Martin and Mullen (1983).
Office of Civil Defense, Department of Defense. 1968. *Civil Defense, U.S.A.: A Programmed Orientation to Civil Defense*. Washington, D.C.: U.S. Government Printing Office.
Office of Technology Assessment, Congress of the United States. 1980. *The Effects of Nuclear War*. Totowa, N.J.: Allanhead, Osmun & Co.
Ogburn, William F. 1922. *Social Change: With Respect to Culture and Original Nature*. New York: B. W. Huebsch.
O'Keefe, Bernard J. 1983. *Nuclear Hostages*. Boston: Houghton Mifflin.
Oppenheimer, J. Robert. 1953. "Atomic Weapons and American Policy." *Foreign Affairs* 31 (July):525–35.
Osgood, Charles. 1962. *An Alternative to War or Surrender*. Urbana: University of Illinois Press.
————. 1984. "Disarmament Demands GRIT." Pp. 337–44 in Weston (1984).
Ostling, Richard N. 1982. "Bishops and the Bomb." *Time* (29 November):68–77.
Paine, Christopher. 1983. "Breakdown on the Build-down." *Bulletin of the Atomic Scientists* 39 (December):4–6.
Parkin, Frank. 1968. *Middle Class Radicalism: The British Campaign for Nuclear Disarmament*. Manchester: University of Manchester Press.
Parnas, David Lorge. 1985. "Software Aspects of Strategic Defense Systems." *Communications of ACM* 28 (December):1326–35.
Patterson, David S. 1973. "An Interpretation of the American Peace Movement, 1898–1914." Pp. 20–38 in Chatfield (1973).
Pauling, Linus. 1958. *No More War!* New York: Dodd, Mead & Company.
Payne, Keith. 1983. "Should the ABM Treaty Be Revised?" *Comparative Strategy* 4:1–20.
Peacock, Joe. 1983. "Politics of Whimsy at Greenham Common." *Sojourners* 12 (February):8–10.
————. 1985. "Peace: A Familiar, but Controversial Word—The Russian Orthodox Church." *Disarmament Campaigns* 50 (December):4–5.
Pearson, David. 1984. "K.A.L. 007: What the U.S. Knew and When We Knew It." *Nation* 239 (18–25 August):105–108, 110–24.
Peattie, Lisa. 1986. "Normalizing the Unthinkable." Pp. 155–62 in Gregory (1986).
Perrow, Charles. 1970. *Organizational Analysis: A Sociological View*. Belmont, Calif.: Wadsworth Publishing Company.
————. 1984. *Normal Accidents: Living with High Risk Technologies*. New York: Basic Books.
Peterson, Russell W. 1984. "Foreword." Pp. vii–xiii in Harwell (1984).
Petrovsky, Vladimir. 1985. *An Effective Instrument of Peace: 40th Anniversary of the United Nations*. Moscow: Novosti Press.
Pipes, Richard. 1976. "Detente: Moscow's View." In *Soviet Strategy in Europe*, edited by R. Pipes. New York: Crane, Russak & Co.
————. 1977. "Why the Soviet Union Thinks It Could Fight and Win a Nuclear War." *Commentary* 64 (July):21–34.
————. 1984. *Survival Is Not Enough: Soviet Realities and America's Future*. New York: Simon and Schuster.
Pitirim, Archbishop Konstantin Vladimirovich Nechayev. 1985. "To Preserve the Sacred Gift of Life." Pp. 160–69 in Fedoseyev (1985b).
Podhoretz, Norman. 1980. "The Present Danger." *Commentary* 69 (March):27–40.

Ponomarev, Boris. 1985. "The Role of Scientists in Strengthening International Security." Pp. 13–32 in Fedoseyev (1985b).

Pooley, Eric. 1983. "A Separate Peace." *The Progressive* 47 (March):28–32.

Porro, Jeffrey D. 1982. "The Policy War: Brodie vs. Kahn." *Bulletin of the Atomic Scientists* 38 (June):16–19.

Powers, Thomas. 1982a. "Choosing a Strategy for World War II." *The Atlantic Monthly* (November):82–110.

———. 1982b. "The Light of Armageddon." *Rolling Stone* (29 April):13–63.

———. 1984a. "Nuclear Winter and Nuclear Strategy." *The Atlantic Monthly* (November):53–64.

———. 1984b. *Thinking about the Next War*. New York: Mentor Books.

Price, Jerome. 1982. *The Antinuclear Movement*. Boston: Twayne Publishers.

Pringle, Peter, and William Arkin. 1983. *S.I.O.P.: The Secret U.S. Plan for Nuclear War*. New York: W. W. Norton.

Radcliffe-Brown, A. R. 1922. *The Andaman Islanders*. Cambridge: Cambridge University Press.

———. 1977. "Religion and Society." Pp. 103–28 in *The Social Anthropology of Radcliffe-Brown*, edited by Adam Kuper. London: Routledge & Kegan Paul.

Raloff, J. 1985. "Star Wars Defense: Is It Legal?" *Science News* 127 (19 January):39.

Ramsey, Paul. 1961. *War and the Christian Conscience: How Shall Modern War Be Conducted Justly?* Durham, N.C.: Duke University Press.

———. 1968. *The Just War: Force and Political Responsibility*. New York: Charles Scribner's Sons.

Rapaport, Anatol. 1964. *Fights, Games, and Debates*. New York: Harper & Row.

Raskin, Marcus. 1982. "Abolitionists & Prudentialists." *Nation* 235 (7–14 August):105–8.

Reagan, Ronald. 1982. "Transcript of Reagan's U.N. Speech on the Nuclear Arms Race." *New York Times*, 18 June:6.

———. 1984a. "Foreign Policy Address. January 16, 1984." Pp. 129–40 in Talbott (1984).

———. 1984b. "Remarks to the National Association of Evangelicals." Pp. 105–18 in Talbott (1984).

———. 1986. "National Security Address to the Nation, March 23, 1983." Pp. 206–14 in Gregory (1986).

Reay, Marie. 1959. *The Kuma: Freedom and Conformity in the New Guinea Highlands*. Melbourne: Melbourne University Press.

Reifel, Stuart. 1984. "Children Living with the Nuclear Threat." *Young Children* (July):74–80.

Rice, Jim, and Danny Collum. 1985. "A Challenge from the Churches: Nonviolent Resistance in the United States." *Disarmament Campaigns* 50 (December):10–11.

Richardson, Lewis. 1960. *Statistics of Deadly Quarrels*. Pittsburgh: Boxwood Press.

———, Nicholas Rashevski, and Ernest Trucco, eds. 1960. *Arms and Insecurity: A Mathematical Study of the Causes and Origins of War*. Pittsburgh: Boxwood Press.

Rickover, Hyman. 1982. "Advice from Admiral Rickover." *The New York Review of Books* 29 (18 March):12–14.

Rizzo, Renata. 1983a. "Professional Approach to Peace." *Nuclear Times* 1 (August/September):10–13.

———. 1983b. "Stop Fighting in Schools." *Nuclear Times* 2 (October):29–32.

———. 1985a. "Freeze Debates Direct Action." *Nuclear Times* 3 (January/February):9–10, 21.

————. 1985b. "The Media and the Movement: Bridging the Communications Gap." *Nuclear Times* 4 (November/December):16–19.

————. 1986. "The Freeze Carries On." *Nuclear Times* 4 (January/February):14–15.

Roberts, Geoffrey K. 1970. *Political Parties and Pressure Groups in Britain*. London: Weidenfeld and Nicolson.

Rogers, Rita R. 1982a. "On Emotional Responses to Nuclear Issues and Terrorism." Pp. 11–24 in Rogers et al. (1982).

————. 1982b. "Soviet-American Relationships under the Nuclear Umbrella." Pp. 25–33 in Rogers et al. (1982).

————, William Beardslee, Doyle I. Carson, Jerome Frank, John Mack, and Michael Mufson, eds. 1982. *Psychosocial Aspects of Nuclear Developments*. Report of the Task Force on Psychosocial Aspects of Nuclear Developments of the American Psychiatric Association. Washington, D.C.: American Psychiatric Association.

Rose, Peter I. 1963. "The Public and the Threat of War." *Social Problems* 11 (Summer):62–77.

Rosenberg, D. 1981–82. "A Smoking Radiation Ruin at the End of Two Hours." *International Security* 6 (Winter):3–38.

Rosenberg, Milton J. 1972. "Beyond the Cold War: The Pragmatic and Prophetic Modes in Policy Science." Pp. 1–27 in *Beyond Conflict and Containment*, edited by Milton J. Rosenberg. New Brunswick, N.J.: Transaction Books.

Rostow, Eugene. 1979. "The Case against Salt II." *Commentary* 67 (February):23–32.

Rothschild, Emma. 1983. "The Delusions of Deterrence." *The New York Review of Books* 29 (14 April):40–50.

Rothschild, Matthew, and Keenen Peck. 1985. "Star Wars: The Final Solution." *The Progressive* 49 (July):20–26.

Russell, Bertrand. 1959. *Common Sense and Nuclear Warfare*. New York: Simon and Schuster.

————. 1986. "The Russell-Einstein Manifesto." Pp. 70–73 in Gregory (1986).

Russett, Bruce, and Bruce G. Blair. 1978. "SALT II: Limited Negotiations." Pp. 114–21 in *Progress in Arms Control?* edited by B. Russett and B. Blair. San Francisco: W. H. Freeman and Co.

Sagan, Carl. 1983/84. "Nuclear War and Climatic Catastrophe: Some Policy Implications." *Foreign Affairs* 62 (Winter):257–92.

Sahlins, Marshall D. 1965. "On the Sociology of Primitive Exchange." Pp. 139–236 in *The Relevance of Models for Social Anthropology*, edited by Michael Banton. New York: Praeger.

Sanders, Jerry W. 1983. *Peddlers of Crisis: The Committee on the Present Danger and the Politics of Containment*. Boston: South End Press.

Santayana, George. 1972. "War." Pp. 117–20 in Gregory (1972).

Sarum, John, Sydney Bailey, John Elford, Paul Oestreicher, Barrie Paskins, Brendan Soane, and G. S. Ecclestone. 1982. *The Church and the Bomb: Nuclear Weapons and Christian Conscience*. Report of a working party under the chairmanship of the Bishop of Salisbury. London: Hodder and Stoughton.

Sayle, Murray. 1985. "KE007: A Conspiracy of Circumstance." *The New York Review of Books* 32 (25 April):44–54.

Scheer, Robert. 1982. *With Enough Shovels: Reagan, Bush and Nuclear War*. New York: Random House.

Schell, Jonathan. 1982. *The Fate of the Earth*. New York: Alfred A. Knopf.

Schelling, Thomas. 1965. *The Strategy of Conflict*. New York: Oxford University Press.

————, and Morton Halperin. 1961. *Strategy and Arms Control*. New York: Twentieth Century Fund.

Schlesinger, James. 1974. *1975 Defense Budget and FY 1975–79 Defense Program*. Washington, D.C.: U.S. Government Printing Office.

Schumpeter, Joseph A. [1942] 1962. *Capitalism, Socialism and Democracy*. New York: Harper Torchbooks.

Schwebel, Milton. 1964. "What Do They Think about War?" Pp. 25–33 in *Children and the Threat of Nuclear War*, by the Child Study Association of America. New York: Duell, Sloan and Pearce.

————. 1965. "Nuclear Cold War: Student Opinions and Professional Responsibility." Pp. 210–24 in *Behavioral Science and Human Survival*, edited by M. Schwebel. Palo Alto, Calif.: Science and Behavior Books.

Seligman, C. G. 1910. *The Melanesians of British New Guinea*. Cambridge: Cambridge University Press.

Sharp, Gene. 1973. *The Politics of Nonviolent Action, Part Two: The Methods of Nonviolent Action*. Boston: Porter Sargent Publishers.

————. 1985a. *Making Europe Unconquerable*. Cambridge: Ballinger Publishing Company.

————. 1985b. *National Security through Civilian-based Defense*. Omaha, Nebr.: Association for Transarmament Studies.

Shaw, Jennifer, Rear Admiral E. F. Gueritz, Henry Stanhope, Peter Evans, and John Buchanan-Brown. 1982. *Nuclear Attack: Civil Defense*. Compiled and edited by The Royal United Services Institute for Defence Studies. Oxford: Brassey's Publishers.

"The Shelter Fraud." 1982. *New York Times*, 3 April.

Shils, Edward 1956. *The Torment of Secrecy*. Glencoe, Ill.: Free Press.

Shokoff, James. 1972. *The Voices of War*. New York: Wiley.

Shore, Rima. 1984. "Citizens Back Detente from Below." *Nuclear Times* 2 (June):11–13.

Shute, Nevil. 1957. *On the Beach*. New York: William Morrow.

Sidel, Victor W., Jack Geiger, and Bernard Lown. 1962. "The Physician's Role in the Postattack Period." *New England Journal of Medicine* 266 (31 May):1137–44.

————. 1981. "Buying Death with Taxes." Pp. 35–47 in Adams and Cullen (1981).

Simmel, Georg. 1971. *On Individuality and Social Forms: Selected Writings*. Edited and with an introduction by Donald N. Levine. Chicago: University of Chicago Press.

Simon, Herbert A. 1955. "A Behavioral Model of Rational Choice." *Quarterly Journal of Economics* 99:99–118.

Sivard, Ruth Leger. 1983. *World Military and Social Expenditures 1983*. Washington, D.C.: World Priorities.

————. 1984. *World Military and Social Expenditures 1984*. Washington, D.C.: World Priorities.

————. 1985. *World Military and Social Expenditures 1985*. Washington, D.C.: World Priorities.

Smith, Alice Kimball. 1965. *A Peril and a Hope: The Scientists Movement in America, 1945–47*. Chicago: University of Chicago Press.

Smith, Hedrick. 1976. *The Russians*. New York: Ballantine Books.

————. 1983. "CIA Report Says Soviet Arms Spending Slowed." *New York Times*, 16 November:1.

Snitow, Ann. 1985. "Holding the Line at Greenham." *Mother Jones* 10 (February/March):30–34, 39–47.

Snow, David A., and Robert D. Benford. Forthcoming. "Ideology, Frame Resonance and Participant Mobilization." Chapter 7 in *From Structure to Action: Social Movement Participation Across Cultures*, edited by Bert Klandermans, Hanspeter Kresi, and Sidney Tarrow. Greenwich, Conn.: JAI Press.

_____. E. Burke Rochford, Jr., Steven K. Worden, and Robert D. Benford. 1987. "Frame Alignment Processes, Micromobilization, and Movement Participation." *American Sociological Review*. Forthcoming.

_____. Louis A. Zurcher, and Sheldon Ekland-Olson. 1980. "Social Networks and Social Movements: A Microstructural Approach to Recruitment." *American Sociological Review* 45:787–801.

Sojourners. 1982. *A Matter of Faith: A Study Guide for Churches on the Nuclear Arms Race*. Washington, D.C.: Sojourners.

Solo, Pam. 1984. "The Arms Race: Who's Ahead?" Pp. 73–89 in Brown (1984).

_____. 1985. "A New Atlantic Alliance: European and American Peace Movement Cooperation." *Disarmament Campaigns* 49 (November):10.

Solomon, Norman, and Ada Sanchez. 1983. "Doing Better than the Freeze." *Nuclear Times* 1 (July):16.

Solzhenitsyn, Alexander. 1980. "Misconceptions about Russia Are a Threat to America." *Foreign Affairs* 58 (Spring):797–834.

Starr, Mark. 1982. "Giving Peace a Chance." *Newsweek* (21 June):40–41.

"Star Wars": Delusions and Dangers. 1985. Translated from the Russian. Moscow: Military Publishing House.

Stinchcombe, Arthur L. 1972. "Social Structure and Organizations." Pp. 123–40 in Brinkerhoff and Kunz (1972).

Stockholm International Peace Research Institute. 1982. *The Arms Race and Arms Control*. London: Taylor and Francis Ltd.

Stoessinger, John G. 1985. *Why Nations Go to War*. New York: St. Martin's Press.

Stokes, Gale. 1978. "The Undeveloped Theory of Nationalism." *World Politics* 31 (October):150–60.

Stringfellow, William. 1973. *An Ethic for Christians and Other Aliens in a Strange Land*. Waco, Tex.: Word Books.

_____. 1984. "An Assault Upon Conscience: Violence in the Technocratic Society." *Sojourners* 13 (October):22–25.

Subcommittee on Arms Control, International and Security Agreements, Committee on Foreign Relations, United States Senate. 1975. *Analyses of Effects of Limited Nuclear War*. Washington, D.C.: U.S. Government Printing Office.

Subrahmanyam, K. 1986. "Regional Conflicts and Nuclear Fears." Pp. 344–49 in Levine and Carlton (1986).

Sumner, William Graham. [1906] 1940. *Folkways: A Study of the Sociological Importance of Usages, Manners, Customs, Mores, and Morals*. New York: Mentor Books.

Suzuki, Sunao. 1984. "Public Attitudes toward Peace." *Bulletin of the Atomic Scientists* 40 (February):27–31.

Swomley, John M., and George Kennan. 1984. "Are They Out to Bury Us?" Pp. 59–72 in Brown (1984).

Sykes, L. R., and T. F. Evernden. 1982. "The Verification of a Comprehensive Nuclear Test Ban." *Scientific American* 247 (October).

Symmons-Symonolewicz, Konstantin. 1965. "Nationalist Movements: An Attempt at a Comparative Typology." *Comparative Studies in Society and History* 7:221–30.

Szilard, Leo. 1955. "Disarmament and the Problem of Peace." *Bulletin of the Atomic Scientists* 11 (October):297–307.

"Taking Stock: The U.S. Military Buildup." 1984. *The Defense Monitor* 13 (4):1–12.

Talbott, S. 1984. *The Russians and Reagan*. New York: Vintage Books.

Taylor, Betsy. 1985. "Learning Electoral Lessons." *Nuclear Times* 4 (September/October):16–19.

Taylor, Richard, and Colin Pritchard. 1980. *The Protest Makers: The British Nuclear Disarmament Movement of 1958–1965, Twenty Years On.* Oxford: Pergamon Press.

Tempest, Rone. 1983a. "Kremlin System Looks Familiar." *Los Angeles Times,* 10 July: Part VI, 4.

————. 1983b. "U.S. Defense Establishment Wields a Pervasive Power." *Los Angeles Times,* 10 July: Part VI, 1–3.

Terkel, Studs. 1984. *The Good War.* New York: Pantheon.

Therese, Marie, Bengt Danielsson, and Cliff Johnson. 1982. "Polynesia—France's Sugar-coated Nuclear Fortress." *Win* 18 (1 August):14–16.

Thomas, William I. 1966. *On Social Organization and Social Personality.* Edited and with an introduction by Morris Janowitz. Chicago: University of Chicago Press.

Thompson, E. P. 1981. "A Letter to America." Pp. 3–52 in Thompson and Smith (1981).

————. 1982. *Beyond the Cold War.* New York: Pantheon.

————. 1985. *The Heavy Dancers: Writings on War, Past and Future.* New York: Pantheon.

————, and Dan Smith, eds. 1981. *Protest and Survive.* New York : Monthly Review Press.

Thompson, Henry, et al. 1985. "Star Wars Problems that Science Cannot Solve." *Manchester Guardian Weekly,* 14 July:2. Letter to the editor signed by Dr. Henry Thompson and seventy-nine others at the Department of Artificial Intelligence, University of Edinburgh.

Thompson, James. 1967. *Organizations in Action.* New York: McGraw-Hill Book Company.

Thucydides. 1954. *The Peloponnesian War.* Edited by Betty Radice and Robert Baldick. Translated by Rex Warner. Baltimore: Penguin Books.

Tilly, Charles. 1978. *From Mobilization to Revolution.* Reading, Mass.: Addison-Wesley.

Tilly, Charles, ed. 1975. *The Formation of National States in Western Europe.* Princeton: Princeton University Press.

Toyoda, Toshiyuki. 1984. "Scientists Look at Peace and Security." *Bulletin of the Atomic Scientists* 40 (February):16–19.

Trinkl, John. 1984. "Come Alive in '85: Post-election Assessments and Projections." *The Mobilizer* 4 (Fall/Winter):5–6.

Trocme, Andre. 1973. *Jesus and the Nonviolent Revolution.* Scottdale, Penn.: Herald Press.

Tsipis, Kosta. 1983. *Arsenal: Understanding Weapons in the Nuclear Age.* New York: Simon and Schuster.

Tucker, Robert C., ed. 1977. *Stalinism: Essays in Historical Interpretation.* New York: Norton.

Tucker, Robert W. 1960. *The Just War: A Study In Contemporary American Doctrine.* Baltimore: The Johns Hopkins University Press.

Turco, R. P., O. B. Toon, T. P. Ackerman, J. B. Pollack, and Carl Sagan. 1983. "Nuclear Winter: Global Atmospheric Consequences of Multiple Nuclear Explosions." *Science* 222 (23 December):1283–92.

Turner, Victor. 1967. *The Forest of Symbols.* Ithaca, N.Y.: Cornell University Press.

————. 1969. *The Ritual Process: Structure and Anti-Structure.* Ithaca, N.Y.: Cornell University Press.

Twain, Mark. 1972. "The War Prayer." Pp. 77–81 in Shokoff (1972).

Ulam, Adam. 1971. *The Rivals: America and Russia since World War II*. New York: Penguin Books.

Union of Concerned Scientists. 1983. *Briefing Manual: A Collection of Materials on Nuclear Weapons and Arms Control*. Cambridge, Mass.: Union of Concerned Scientists.

————. 1984. "Space-based Missile Defense." Briefing paper No. 8 (July 1984). Cambridge, Mass.: Union of Concerned Scientists.

————. 1985. "Arms Control Verification." Briefing paper (March 1985). Cambridge, Mass.: Union of Concerned Scientists.

United Campuses to Prevent Nuclear War. 1986. *"There's a Hand in Your Pocket . . ."* Washington, D.C.: United Campuses to Prevent Nuclear War.

United Methodist Bishops. 1986. *In Defense of Creation: The Nuclear Crisis and a Just Peace*. Nashville, Tenn.: Graded Press.

United Nations Department for Disarmament Affairs. 1985. *The United Nations and Disarmament: 1945–1985*. New York: United Nations.

United States Atomic Energy Commission. 1971. *In the Matter of J. Robert Oppenheimer: Transcripts before Personnel Security Board and Texts of Principal Documents and Letters*. Cambridge: MIT Press.

United States Bureau of the Census. 1982. *Statistical Abstract of the United States: 1982–1983*. 103d edition. Washington, D.C.: U.S. Bureau of the Census.

United States Department of Commerce. 1970. *Special Survey of U.S. Multinational Companies, 1970*. Washington, D.C.: U.S. Government Printing Office.

United States Department of State, Bureau of Public Affairs. 1982. "START Proposal." *GIST* (July).

Vaillancourt, Jean-Guy, and Ronald Babin, eds. 1984. *Le Mouvement Pour le Désarmement et la Paix*. Special Issue of *International Review of Community Development*.

Vanderzee, Joost. 1985. "Australia Refuses MX Tests." *Disarmament Campaigns* 42 (March):4.

Vatican Council II. [1965] 1982. *"Gaudium et Spes*, Constitution on the Church in the Modern World." Pp. 17–23 in Heyer (1982).

Ven, Willem van de. 1985. "3,743,455 Times No to Dutch Deployment." *Disarmament Campaigns* 50 (December):27–28.

Volpe, Maria R. 1985. "Dispute Resolution Gains Ground." *ASA Footnotes* (April):5.

Walker, Paul F. 1982. "Teach-ins on American Campuses." *Bulletin of the Atomic Scientists* 38 (February):10–11.

Wall, James M. 1983. "A Crusade that Exploits Deaths." *The Christian Century* 239 (28 September):835–36.

Wallerstein, Immanuel. 1974. *The Modern World System*. New York: Academic Press.

————. 1979. *The Capitalist World-Economy*. Cambridge: Cambridge University Press.

Wallis, Jim. 1982. *Waging Peace*. San Francisco: Harper & Row.

Walsh, Edwrd J. 1981. "Resource Mobilization and Citizen Protest in Communities around Three Mile Island." *Social Problems* 29 (1):1–21.

Walters, LeRoy. 1973. "The Just War and the Crusade: Antitheses or Analogies?" *The Monist* 57 (October):584–94.

Walzer, Michael. 1977. *Just and Unjust Wars: A Moral Argument with Historical Illustrations*. New York: Basic Books.

Weber, Max. 1946. *From Max Weber: Essays in Sociology*. Translated and edited by H. H. Gerth and C. Wright Mills. New York: Oxford University Press.

————. [1904–5] 1958. *The Protestant Ethic and the Spirit of Capitalism*. Translated by Talcott Parsons. New York: Charles Scribner's Sons.

————. 1968. *Economy and Society*. 3 vols. New York: Bedminster Press.

Weigel, George. 1982. *The Peace Bishops and the Arms Race: Can Religious Leadership Help in Preventing War?* Chicago: World Without War Publications.

Weinberger, Caspar W. 1982. *Department of Defense Annual Report to the Congress, Fiscal Year 1983.* Washington, D.C.: U.S. Government Printing Office.

————. 1983. *Department of Defense Annual Report to the Congress, Fiscal Year 1984.* Washington, D.C.: U.S. Government Printing Office.

Weinraub, Bernard. 1984. "Mondale Sees a Rise in Risk of War." *New York Times*, 4 January.

————. 1985. "Reagan Adamant on Space Defense Even after Talks." *New York Times*, 12 February:1.

Weinstein, John M. 1982. "Soviet Civil Defense: The Mine Shaft Gap Revisited." *Arms Control Today* 12 (July/August):1–3, 7–10.

Weissmann, Arnie. 1986. "Contract Warriors." *Third Coast* 5 (June):40–45, 76–83.

Weston, Burns H., ed. 1984. *Toward Nuclear Disarmament and Global Security: A Search for Alternatives.* Boulder, Colo.: Westview Press.

White House Paper. 1986. "The President's Strategic Defense Initiative." Pp. 215–24 in Gregory (1986).

Wicker, Tom. 1984. "A Damning Silence." *New York Times*, 7 September:29.

————. 1985. "Left Hand vs. Right Hand." *New York Times*, 26 February:27.

Wiesner, Jerome B., and Herbert F. York. 1964. "National Security and the Nuclear Test Ban." *Scientific American* 211 (October):27–35.

Wigner, Eugene P., ed. 1966. *Survival and the Bomb: Methods of Civil Defense.* Bloomington, Ind.: Indiana University Press.

Wilford, John Noble. 1983. "Influential Scientists Opposing President on Space Weapons." *New York Times*, 16 November:1, 8.

Wilkerson, David. 1985. *Set the Trumpet to Thy Mouth.* Lindale, Tex.: World Challenge.

Wilkinson, David. 1981. *Deadly Quarrels: Lewis F. Richardson and the Statistical Study of War.* Berkeley: University of California Press.

Will, George F. 1984. "Why Arms Control Is Harmful." *Newsweek* (18 June):104.

Willens, Harold. 1984. "Five Steps to Halt the Arms Race." *Newsweek* 104 (19 November):16.

Williams, William Appleman. 1980. *Empire as a Way of Life.* Oxford: Oxford University Press.

Williamson, Robert W. 1912. *The Matulu: Mountain People of British New Guinea.* London: Macmillan.

Winther, Judith. 1985. "Dialogue from the Grassroots: Twinning." *Disarmament Campaigns* 46 (July/August):12.

Wittner, Lawrence S. 1984. *Rebels against War: The American Peace Movement, 1933–1983.* Philadelphia: Temple University Press.

Woito, Robert. 1982. *To End War: A New Approach to International Conflict.* New York: The Pilgrim Press.

Wolfe, Alan. 1979. *The Rise and Fall of the 'Soviet Threat': Domestic Sources of the Cold War Consensus.* Washington, D.C.: The Institute for Policy Studies.

Wright, Quincy. 1965. *A Study of War.* Revised ed. Chicago: University of Chicago Press.

Yakovlev, Nikolai. 1984. *CIA Target—The USSR.* Moscow: Progress Publishers.

Yefremov, A. Y. 1979. *Nuclear Disarmament.* Moscow: Progress Publishers.

Yergin, Daniel. 1976. *Shattered Peace: The Origins of the Cold War and the National Security State.* Boston: Houghton Mifflin.

Yoder, John Howard. 1964. *The Christian Witness to the State.* Newton, Kans.: Faith and Life Press.

_____. 1971. *The Original Revolution*. Scottdale, Penn.: Herald Press.

_____. 1972. *The Politics of Jesus*. Grand Rapids, Mich.: Eerdmans.

_____. 1982. "Living the Disarmed Life." Pp. 40–43 in Sojourners (1982).

York, Herbert. 1970. *Race to Oblivion: A Participant's View of the Arms Race*. New York: Simon and Schuster.

Young, Nigel. 1983. "The Contemporary European Anti-nuclear Movement: Experiments in the Mobilization of Public Power." *Peace and Change* 9 (1):1–16.

Yudkin, Marcia. 1984. "When Kids Think the Unthinkable." *Psychology Today* (April):18–25.

Zagladin, Vadim. 1985. "Working-class Parties and the Anti-war Struggle." Pp. 131–47 in Fedoseyev (1985b).

Zahn, Gordon C. 1967. *War, Conscience, and Dissent*. New York: Hawthorn Books.

Zald, Mayer N., and John D. McCarthy. 1980. "Social Movement Industries: Competition and Cooperation among Social Movement Organizations." Pp. 1–20 in *Social Movements, Conflict and Change*, edited by Louis Kriesberg. Greenwich, Conn.: JAI Press.

Zarsky, Lyuba. 1982. "Creating a Nuclear Free Pacific." *Win* 18 (1 August):4–5.

Zhivkov, Todor, Gustav Husak, Erich Honecker, Janos Kadar, Wojciech Jaruzelski, Nicolae Ceausescu, and Yuri Andropov. 1985. "Political Declaration of the Warsaw Treaty Member States." Pp. 315–34 in Fedoseyev (1985b).

Zielonka, Jan. 1983. "Lessons from Poland." *Civilian-based Defense* 1 (December):1–3.

Zimmerman, William. 1969. *Soviet Perspectives on International Relations*. Princeton: Princeton University Press.

In addition to the source listed on page iv, the following are gratefully acknowledged:

page 55: George F. Kennan, 1982, *The Nuclear Delusion: Soviet-American Relations in the Atomic Age*, New York: Pantheon. Epigraph reprinted by permission of the publishers. Copyright © 1982 by Pantheon Books, a Division of Random House, Inc.

page 58: Nikita Khrushchev, 1970, *Khrushchev Remembers*, vol. 1, Strobe Talbott, ed. and trans., Boston: Little, Brown. Excerpt reprinted by permission of the publisher.

page 77: Erich Fromm, 1961, *May Man Prevail? An Inquiry into the Facts and Fictions of Foreign Policy*, Garden City, N.Y.: Anchor Books, pp. 29–30. Epigraph reprinted by permission of the Annis Fromm Royalty Trust.

page 101: John Kenneth Galbraith, 1984, "The Military Power," an address delivered at the University of Texas at Austin, March 27, 1984. Excerpt reprinted by permission of the author.

pages 107, 108, and 109: William A. Gamson, 1984, "Political Symbolism and Nuclear Arms Policy," unpublished paper presented at the annual meeting of the American Sociological Association, San Antonio, Texas. Excerpts reprinted by permission of the author.

page 112: Konstantin Likutov, 1985, *Soviet Foreign Policy: Questions and Answers*, Moscow: Novosti Press, p. 28. Reprinted by permission of the publisher.

page 119: Epigraph reprinted from *Matthew* 26:50-52, the *Revised Standard Version Bible*, copyright 1946, 1952, 1971 by the Division of Christian Education of the National Council of the Churches of Christ in the USA, and used by permission.

page 127: James Morrow, 1986, *This Is the Way the World Ends*, New York: Henry Holt and Company. Epigraph reprinted by permission of the publisher.

pages 145, 180, and 251: Robert Scheer, 1982, *With Enough Shovels: Reagan, Bush and Nuclear War*. New York: Random House. Epigraphs reprinted by permission of the publisher.

page 184: Thomas Powers, 1976, *Thinking About the Next War*. New York and Scarborough: Mentor Books. Epigraph reprinted by permission of Alfred A. Knopf.

page 186: Noam Chomsky, 1982, *Towards a New Cold War*, New York: Pantheon. Epigraph reprinted by permission of the publisher. Copyright © 1982 by Pantheon Books, a Division of Random House, Inc.

page 188: Nikolai Yakovlev, 1984, *CIA Target—the USSR*, Moscow: Progress Publishers. Epigraph reprinted by permission of the publisher.

pages 189 and 191: Wilton John Brown, 1985, *Do Russian People Stand for War?* Moscow: Novosti Press. Epigraphs reprinted by permission of the publisher.

pages 220, 223, 224, 225, 227, 229, and 230: National Conference of Catholic Bishops, 1983, *The Challenge of Peace: God's Promise, Our Response*. Washington, D.C.: United States Catholic Conference. Reprinted by permission of the publisher.

Index

ABM. *See* Treaty: ABM
Abraham, A. M., 291
Abrahamson, James, 171
Abrams, H., 44, 155
Accidents, nuclear, 17, 49
Acheson, Dean, 206
Acheson-Lilienthal Report, 206, 241
ACORN, 257
Activism, peace, 199, 237–39
  and feminism, 256
  See also Disobedience, civil; Pacifism;
    Peace movements
Adams, Gordon, 98,99
Adelman, Kenneth, 187, 211
Adler, Les K., 182
Afghanistan, 118, 119, 251
Agape, 222
Agape Community, 256
Aggression, 79
Aiken, Michael, 64
Air Force (U.S.), 288
Air-launched cruise missiles (ALCMs). *See*
  Cruise missiles
Alamogordo, New Mexico, 25, 54
Aldridge, Robert G., 18
Alfonsin, Raul, 199
Algonquin Indians, 239
Alley, Eric, 146, 289
Alperovitz, Gar, 21, 22
Alsop, Ronald, 287
American Friends Service Committee
  (AFSC), 232, 238, 259, 261
American Public Health Association, 29
American Security Council, 217, 292
American Security Council Foundation,
  131, 289
Andropov, Yuri, 87, 172
Antarctic treaty. *See* Treaty: Antarctic
Anti-Ballistic Missile treaty (ABM). *See*
  Treaty: ABM
Antisatellite weapons (ASAT), 18, 116,
  172, 174
Antiwar movements, American. *See* Peace
  movements
Antonov-Ovseyenko, Anton, 291
Apocalypse, 1
Apollo, 165
Ardrey, Robert, 79
Arendt, Hannah, 88
Arkin, William, 135, 136, 288
Armageddon, 37, 219, 226, 250
Armed Services Committees, 99, 171
  House Defense Appropriations
    Subcommittee, 99

Senate Defense Appropriations
    Subcommittee, 99
Arms control, 20, 108, 111–12, 125–26,
  131, 160, 162, 171–74, 185, 201, 204,
  288
Arms Control and Disarmament Agency,
  187, 217, 248
Arms limitation agreements. *See* Treaty
Arms race, nuclear, 10–13, 19, 29, 37,
  110–11, 236
  beneficiaries of, 100
  and the church, 219, 220, 221
  defense expenditures in, 13. *See also*
    Budgets, military
  diversification of American and Soviet
    arsenals in, 11
  evolution of, 59–61
  political implications of, 29, 37
  responsibility for, 191
  rituals of, 71–74
  second, 49
  social psychology of, 77–89
  superpower relations in, 180, 191–92
  third, 50
  weapons development in, 11
Arms reduction, 200–1
Aron, Raymond, 181
Arsenals, nuclear
  balance of, 11, 12, 13
  justifications for, 34, 103, 106, 109, 110,
    111, 115, 133, 177
  Soviet, 9, 10, 11, 163, 183, 191, 287
  U.S., 7, 12, 34, 38, 103, 106, 112, 115,
    133, 163, 182
  See also Weapons
ASAT system. *See* Antisatellite weapons
Asher, Sarah Beth, xvi
Asroc antisubmarine weapon missile, 7
Assured destruction, 129, 130, 159, 161,
  248. *See also* Mutual Assured
    Destruction
Aurand, Captain, 135
Aurelius, Marcus, 223
Auschwitz, 68

B-1B bomber, 15, 98
B-52 Stratofortress (U.S.), 8
Backfire bomber (Soviet), 10
Bainton, Roland, 222, 292
Balance of payments (U.S.), 31
Balance of power, 153, 157, 191
Balance of terror, 60, 87
Balance of trade, 31
Ball, George, 161

Ball-Kilbourne, Gary, L., 232
Ballistic Missile Defense, 159, 160, 163–65
  phases of, 165
Bandy, John, xvi, 238
Barash, David, 239
Barber, Elinor, 178
Barnet, Richard, 102, 109, 196
Barron, John, 132, 233
Baruch Plan, 206, 241
Bateson, Gregory, 108
Bear bomber (Soviet Tu-95), 10
Beardslee, William, 32
Bell, Daniel, 198
Benford, Robert D., xvi, 249, 258, 288
Beres, Louis René, 17
Berger, Peter, L., 108
Berks, John, 27
Bethe, Hans, 165
Biddle, Wayne, 174, 178
Bids and Proposals program, 98
Biological effects of nuclear war. *See*
  Effects of nuclear weapons
Bishops, Catholic. *See* Catholic bishops
Bishops, United Methodist. *See* United
  Methodist bishops
Bison bomber (Soviet Mya-4), 10
Blair, Bruce G., 210
Blau, Peter, 69
Blechman, Barry, 102, 103, 197
BMD. *See* Ballistic Missile Defense
Bobbitt, Philip, 289
Boeing, 288
Bolsheviks, 183, 189
Bomber, intercontinental, 7, 60
Bombers, Soviet. *See also* Backfire bomber;
  Bear bomber, Bison bomber
  long-range, 10
  medium-range, 10
  number of, 10
  as percentage of Soviet nuclear arsenal,
  11
Bombers, U.S. *See also* Strategic triad, U.S.
  advanced technology (ATB), 8
  as percentage of U.S. arsenal, 11
  strategic, 8
Bombing Encyclopedia, 68
Bombs
  aerial, 7
  atomic, 2, 21–24, 60. *See also* Weapons
  cluster, 118
  gravity, 8
  hydrogen. *See* Weapons
  neutron, 60
  1-megaton (MT), 3–5, 43. *See also*
    Weapons
  plutonium, 3
Boulding, Elise, 239
Boulding, Kenneth, 123, 199, 225, 268,
  289
Bowman, Robert, 170, 175

Boyer, Paul, 244, 249, 293
Bradlee, Benjamin, 187
Bravo test, 25, 207
Brethren, the, 239
Brezhnev, Leonid, 151, 208, 288
Broad, William J., 165, 166, 171
Brodie, Bernard, 135, 136
Brookings Institution, 196
Brown, A. C., 291
Brown, Harold, 216
Brown, Wilton John, 113, 193, 195
Bryan, Wayne, xvi
Brzezinski, Zbigniew, 163
Buchheim, Robert, 217
Buckley, James, 187
Budgets, military, 12–15, 19, 29, 30, 31,
  32, 40, 63, 92, 94, 95, 102, 159, 190,
  191, 193, 286
  buildup of, 14
  calculations of, 12, 13, 190, 191
  effects of, 15, 29, 30, 31, 32, 94, 95, 193
  justifications of, 13, 34, 63, 181, 193,
  291
  as percentage of GNP, 13
  projections of, U.S., 14, 15, 19
  projections of, Soviet, 19
  total outlay for, U.S. and Soviet, 13, 40
Build-down proposal, 212, 284
Bundy, McGeorge, 74, 213
Burbank, Russ, 258
Bureau of the Census, U.S., 287
Bureaucracy, xiii, 37, 60, 61, 62–70, 75,
  92, 100, 117, 141, 142, 143, 177
  career structure in, 65
  diversification of, 63–65
  and impersonal violence, 80
  stability of, 62, 63
Bush, George, 187
Butterfield, Fox, 33
Byrnes, James F., 22

C³ I, 138, 167, 168
Cagan, Leslie, 260
Caldicott, Helen, 255
Camp David, 121
Campaign for Nuclear Disarmament
  (CND), 251, 259
Canadian Broadcasting Corporation, 175
Capitalism, 34, 189, 192, 193, 194, 198,
  215
Carter, Jimmy, 142, 143, 186, 196, 291
  administration of, 136, 250
Cartwright, D., 83
Catholic bishops (U.S.), 161, 220, 223–25,
  227, 229, 231, 234–35, 256, 292
  National Conference of, 161
Catholic Church, Roman, 220. *See also*
  Catholic bishops; Popes, Roman
  Catholic
Carnesdale, Albert, 238

Carson, Doyle, 37, 38
Celsius, 222
Center for Defense Information, 15, 217, 286
Center for Electromechanics at the University of Texas, 167
Central Intelligence Agency (CIA), 12–14, 36, 190, 191, 196, 217
Cevoli, Cathy, 254, 258, 263
Chain reaction, 2, 3, 6, 19, 47, 60
  in hydrogen bombs, 3
  of social consequences, 47
Chakravarty, Burenda N., 207
Chatfield, Charles, 239
Chayes, Anram, 173
Chernenko, Konstantin, 192, 193
Chernobyl, 6, 42
Chernus, Ira, xvi
Chicago Metallurgical Laboratory (Met Lab), 240, 241
Children
  attitudes of, on nuclear war, 40
  effects of war on, 32, 33, 40
Children's Campaign for Nuclear Disarmament, 256–57
Chivian, Eric, 32
Chomsky, Noam, 58, 105, 186
Christian church, 219–36, 233
  and peace movement, 220, 221, 233
  and traditions on war, 221–27
Christian Science Monitor, 220
CIA. *See* Central Intelligence Agency
Circular Error Probable (CEP), 16, 17
Citizen Exchange Corps, 261
Citizens for America, 290
Civil defense programs, 43, 66, 67, 75, 86, 132, 145–57, 248, 290
  Soviet, 151, 152, 157
  See also Crisis relocation planning
Clande, I. L., 121
Clark, Tina, xvi
Clark, William, 229
Clausewitz, Carlvon, 135
Clubb, Oliver, 36
Cohen, Stephen F., 183, 198
Colby, William E., 74, 291
Cold War, 243
  and academia, 198
Coleman, Ronald, 69
Coles, Robert, 33
Collins, Randall, 80
Cominos, Joan, xvi
Cominos, Nick, xvi
Command, control, communications, and intelligence, 138, 167, 168
Committee on the Compilation of Materials on Damage Caused by the Atomic Bombs in Hiroshima and Nagasaki, 22
Committee on Foreign Relations, 216

Committee on Nonviolent Action (CNVA), 245
Committee on the Present Danger (CPD), 186, 187, 202, 210
Committee on the Social and Political Implications, 240
Communism, 34, 73, 181–83, 186, 187, 195, 196, 197, 198, 231, 287. *See also* Socialism
Compliance, arms control, 117, 212
Conflict Clinic, 121
Conflict resolution, 121
Congress, U.S., 96–99, 105
  lobbying, 15, 98, 245, 253.
  See also Armed Services Committees
Congressional Budget Office, 10, 290
Connally, John B., 187
Constantine, Emperor, 223
Constitution of the USSR (1977), 194
Contractors, military. *See* Military-industrial complex
Controlled response, 129, 130, 136. *See also* Flexible response
Conventional forces, 103, 118
Cooke, Terence, 229
Corn, David, 253
Coser, Louis, 121
Counterfeit nurturance, 46
Countervailing strategy. *See* Strategy: countervailing
Cousins, Norman, 244
Crisis Communication Center, 121
Crisis Management, 121
Crisis relocation planning (CRP), 43, 86, 145, 146, 147–49, 153, 156, 157, 258.
  See also Civil defense programs
Cronkite, Walter, 289
Cruise missiles, 7, 15, 16, 17, 18, 20, 60, 118, 169, 172, 212, 250
  air-launched (ALCMs), 8, 18, 19
  design of, 16, 60
  ground-launched (GLCMs), 7, 15, 16, 18
  mobility of, 18
  sea-launched (SLCMs), 18
  TERCOM guidance system in, 16
Crusades, Christian, 222, 225, 226
Crutzen, Paul, 27
Cultural lag, 72, 139
Cyprian of Carthage, 222

Dallin, Alexander, 36
Damage limitation, 129
Daniel, Barry, 165, 290
Daniels, Marta, 196
Davis, Lisa, 288
Day, Samuel H., 69
Dayan, Moshe, 36
Death imprint, 46
DeBenedetti, Charles, 242, 245, 246, 247, 248

Defense, ballistic missile, 159, 160, 163–65.
    See also Strategic Defense Initiative
Defense, civilian-based nonviolent, 119,
    120–23, 213
Defense Department, U.S., 17, 58, 96, 97,
    169, 173, 175, 217, 290. *See also*
    Pentagon
Defense Intelligence Agency, 289, 291
Defense, point, 165
Defense Science Board, 93
Delivery systems, weapon, 7, 12, 15, 133
Delta class submarines (Soviet), 10
Democracy, 1, 37–40, 49, 182, 187
Democratic party, U.S., 111
Depressed-trajectory missiles, 291
Destruction without detonation, 37, 39
Detente, 173, 194, 199, 202, 209, 210, 250
    from below, 199, 200, 261
Deterrence
    central, 101
    and civil defense, 149, 150
    extended, 101
    nuclear, 37, 74, 78, 101, 110, 111, 114,
        115, 125, 127, 128, 134, 135, 137,
        141–44, 149, 150, 153, 156, 159, 160,
        161, 164, 172, 174, 177, 188, 193,
        220, 227, 229, 231, 235, 287–89
    and rationality, 137
    UN role in, 289
Deuterium, 3, 166
Dewey, John, 138
Dewitt, Hugh, 63
Dillard, John, xv
Disarmament, nuclear, 109–11, 193, 232,
    233, 235, 238, 259
    bilateral, 232
    radical pacifists and, 233
    unilateral, 233
Disobedience, civil
    and active pacifism, 245, 253, 259, 260
    and the church, 233, 234
    in the Philippines, 120
    in Poland, 120
Dirksen, Edward, 90
Divine, Robert, 244, 246
DOD. *See* Defense Department, U.S.
Dodd, Thomas, 246
Donaghy, John, 234, 289
Donnay, Albert, 260
Donnelly, Chris, 152
Douglas, Mary, 81
Douglass, James, 292
Drift and thrust, 91, 104, 105
Driver, Christopher, 248
Dropshot, 190, 291
Drucker, Peter, 101
Dubin, Steven, xvi
Dulles, John Foster, 129
Dumas, Lloyd, 17, 30, 31

Dunn, Louis, 51
Dutch Inter-Church Peace Council (IKV),
    251, 259

East, John P., 209
Economy
    and distribution of resources, 29–32
    global, 101, 106
    military. *See* military-industrial complex
Educators for Social Responsibility (ESR),
    258
Effects of nuclear weapons, 3, 4, 5, 6, 7,
    19, 22, 23
    blast, 4, 5, 19, 25, 39, 155, 171. *See* also
        Weapons
    on children, 32, 33, 40
    electromagnetic pulse, 6, 19, 26, 39, 172
    firestorms, 6
    on human life, 22, 23, 28, 29, 39
    psychological, and limited nuclear war,
        33, 45–47
    radiation. *See* Radiation
    thermal, 4, 10, 25
    See also Nuclear winter.
Egan, 292
Ehrlich, Paul, 7, 28, 52
Einstein, Albert, 242
Eisenhower, Dwight D., 22, 29, 58, 90,
    135, 237, 244
Elective affinity, 53, 100
Electromagnetic pulse (EMP), 6, 19, 26,
    39, 172
Engels, Frederick, 195
Enlightenment, 221
Enola Gay, 21
Epstein, William, 207
Erikson, Kai, 86
Escalona, Sibylle, 32
Etzioni, Amitai, 115
European Force Reduction Talks (INF),
    212, 284
Evangelicals for Social Action, 226
Evernden, T. F., 292
Evil, social construction of, 22, 34–37, 40,
    72, 73, 75, 80, 81, 84, 85, 87–89, 104,
    112, 180, 181, 194, 201, 202
Expansionism, Soviet, 181, 182

Fahey, 292
Falk, Richard, A., 37, 38, 144, 266
Falwell, Jerry, 219, 226
Fascism, 240
FB-111A (U.S. bomber), 8
Feagin, Joe R., xvi, 91
Federal Emergency Management Agency
    (FEMA), 66, 133, 147, 156, 290
Federation of American Scientists (FAS),
    241, 255
Fedoseyev, Pyotr, 95, 112, 190, 193

Feld, Bernard, 242
Fellowship of Reconciliation (FOR), 243
FEMA. *See* Federal Emergency
    Management Agency
Feoktistov, Lev, 192
Finch, Stuart, 44
Finsterbusch, Kurt, 28
Firestorms, 6
First-strike capability, 8, 15, 16, 73, 111,
    172, 192. *See also* Strategy:
    counterforce
Fisher, Roger, 121
Fission, nuclear, 2, 19
Five Continents Peace Initiative, 199
Flexible response, 130, 136, 138, 142, 220,
    250. *See also* Controlled response
Fluorine, 166
Ford, J. M., 230
Forrestal, James, 109
Forsberg, Randall, 60, 111, 112, 119, 210,
    252, 289
Foster, John S., Jr., 187
Frames of thought, 108, 184–85, 186, 188,
    199, 258
Franck Report, 240
Frank, A. G., 137
Frank, Jerome, 34, 35, 79, 80, 81, 123
Freedman, Lawrence, 248, 250, 289
Freedom, 197, 198
Freedom of Information Act, 50
Freeze, nuclear, 73, 111, 112, 116, 125,
    131, 132, 160, 176, 209, 214, 232,
    252, 256, 259, 260, 261, 288
    bilateral, 210, 213, 232, 253
    and 1984 campaign, 253
Freud, Sigmund, 79
Fromm, Erich, 34, 77, 153
Fusion, nuclear, 2, 3, 19

Galosh missiles, 172
Galbraith, John Kenneth, 30
Gamson, William, 107, 108, 109
Gandhi, Mohandas K., 233, 245
Gandhi, Rajiv, 199
Garwin, Richard L., 170, 172
Gayler, Noel, 138
Gedi Gun, 167
Geiger, H. Jack, 43
Gelb, Leslie, 161, 174
General Advisory Committee on Arms
    Control and Disarmament, 187
Gilliam, Pat, 153
Gilpin, Robert, 241, 242
Glaser, Barney, 108
Goffman, Erving, 82, 108, 258, 266
Goldblatt, 212
Goldfarb, Jeffrey, 197
Goldman, Louis, 64
Gollwitzer, Helmut, 233

Goodman, Walter, 33
Gorbachev, Mikhail, 125, 189, 190, 193,
    214
Gordon, Suzanne, 252
Gottfried, Kurt, 172
Gottlieb, Sanford, xvi, 188
Gourè, Lèon, 150
Graduated and reciprocated initiatives in
    tension reduction (GRIT), 115–16
Graham, Billy, 220
Graham, Daniel O., 169
Graham, William, 187
Gray, Colin, 140, 182, 187
Gray Panthers, 257
Grazhdanskaya Oborona, 151
Great Patriotic War. *See* World War II
Greenham Common, 251, 257
GRIT, 115–16
Grob, 151
Gromyko, Andrei A., 174, 208
Gronlund, Lisbeth, xvi
Gross national product (GNP), 183
    Soviet, 13, 100
    U.S., 94, 100
Ground-launched cruise missiles (GLCMs).
    See Cruise missiles
Ground zero, 5
Ground Zero (organization), 60, 254
Group dynamics, 82–85
Group to Establish Trust Between the
    USSR and the USA, 113, 261
Group of Good Will, 114
Groupthink, 84, 85, 89, 108, 129
Groves, Leslie, 22
Guidance systems, 16, 133
Guiffrida, Louis, 150
Gwertzman, Bernard, 169, 171, 174, 209

Haeber, Amoretta, 187
Haeber, Francis, 187
Haig, Alexander, 220
Halloran, Richard, 175, 229
Hardened-point targets, 163, 164
Harvard Negotiation Project, 121
Harvard Russian Research Center, 198
Haverman, Clyde, 36
Hawk missile, 174
Hedemann, Ed, 239
Heimer, Carol, xvi
Hertsgaard, Mark, 264
Heston, Charlton, 289
Hibakusha, 46, 47. *See also* Hiroshima
High Frontier, 290, 291
Hilgartner, Stephen, 248
Hinson, E. Glenn, 222
Hippolytus, Canons of, 222
Hiroshima, 3, 6, 9, 21, 22, 23, 24, 25, 26,
    37, 39, 43, 47, 49, 86, 155, 213, 241,
    242, 249, 287

Hitler, Adolf, 180, 181, 182, 184
Hodson, Randy, xvi, 104
Hogbin, Herbert, 287
Holocaust, nuclear, 1, 40, 114, 220, 226, 248, 249
  predictions of, 1, 40, 220, 248
Hoover, J. Edgar, 187
Hotline, 208, 283
Howard, Michael, 196
Human rights, 183–84
Humanitus International, 114
Hunthausen, Raymond, 220, 233, 234
Hyde, Henry J., 229
Hydrogen, 3, 166

Ikle, Fred C., 171, 175, 187
Illusions, nuclear, 85, 86, 89
  of foreknowledge, 86, 89
  of limit and control, 86, 89
  of preparation and protection, 86, 89.
    See also Civil defense programs
  of rationality, 86, 89
  of recovery, 86, 89
Imperialism (U.S.) and Third World
    exploitation, 189, 193–94
Independent Research and Development
    program, 97
INF. *See* European Force Reduction Talks
Initiatives, peace, 114, 115, 116, 206, 233
  and nuclear free zones, 260
  See also Peace movements
Inspections, on-site, 212, 213, 214
Institute for Defense and Disarmament
    Studies, 252
Institute for Strategic Studies, 134
Institutionalization of nonmilitary
    establishments, 117, 176. *See also*
    Bureaucracy
Intercontinental ballistic missiles (ICBMs)
  location of, 45, 208, 209
  as percentage of U.S. and Soviet
    arsenals, 11, 19
  Soviet, 9, 10, 11, 19, 131, 163, 209, 211
  U.S., 4, 7, 8, 11, 15, 19, 60, 131, 158,
    163, 169, 209, 211. *See also* MX
    missiles; Titan missiles
Inter-faith Task Force, 221
Interim Committee, 240
Intermediate-range ballistic missiles, 7, 11.
  See also European Force Reduction
  Talks
International Court of Justice, 121
International Monetary Fund, 117
International peacekeeping forces, 121
International Physicians for the Prevention
    of Nuclear War (IPPNW), 255
Iron cage, bureaucracy as, xiii, 61, 76, 287
Iron triangle, 70, 97, 105, 177

Janis, Irving, 84
Janowitz, Morris, 287
Japan, 21, 22–25, 49. *See also* Hiroshima;
  Nagasaki
Japanese Committee, 23
Jastrow, Robert, 162, 163, 169, 172, 175
Jesus of Nazareth, 220, 222, 226, 230, 233,
    239, 256, 287
Johansen, Robert C., 174, 291
Johnson, G., 25
Johnson Island, 26
Johnson, James Turner, 222, 223, 225
Johnson, Lyndon B., 149, 249
Joint Chiefs of Staff (U.S.), 13, 22, 26, 64,
    197, 214, 217
Joint War Planning Board, 190
Jones, Charles G., 226
Jones, David, 150
Jones, Don, 290
Jones, Peter, 250
Jones, Thomas K., 42, 66, 152
Judaism, 230
Jus ad Bellum, 223
Jus in Bello, 223
Just-war Theory, 221, 223, 235

Kahn, Herman, 135
Kahneman, Daniel, 81
Kalven, Jamie, 252
Kant, Immanuel, xiv
Kaplan, Fred M., 152, 197
Kaplan, Stephen S., 102
Katz, Arthur M., 28, 42, 43, 44, 45, 48, 49
Kavan, Jan, 199
Kehler, Randy, 253
Keju, Darlene, 261
Keller, Bill, 173
Keller, Jack A., Jr., 232
Kemp, Geoffrey, 187
Kendall, Henry W., 175
Kennan, George, 55, 185, 213
Kennedy, Edward, 174, 252
Kennedy, John F., 1, 135, 146, 208, 215,
    248
Kerr, Thomas J., 164
Keyes, Langley, 147
Keyworth, George, 166, 169
KGB, 233
Kharkhardin, Oleg, 113
Khrushchev, Nikita, 34, 58, 151, 195, 215,
    248
Kill vehicles. *See* Missiles: "smart"
King, Martin Luther, Jr., 144, 233
Kirkpatrick, Jeane, 187
Kissinger, Henry, 160, 249
Kistiakowsky, George, 25, 39, 54
Klare, Michael, 288
Knelman, F. H., 226

Knightly, B., 244
Korean Air Lines Flight 007, 36
Kraemer, Richard, 292
Krass, Allan, 292
Kriesberg, Louis, xvi, 121
Kurtz, Jerry, 153
Kurtz, Lester R., 73, 74, 77, 91, 104, 238, 288

"Ladder of escalation," 129
Lamberson, Donald L., 169
Lance missiles, 7
Land-based nuclear weapons, 7. *See also* Intercontinental ballistic missiles, Lance missiles, Land mines; Short-range artillery round
Land mines, atomic, 7
Lang, Kurt, 62
Larkin, Richard X., 289
La Rocque, Gene R., 59, 74
Lasers, 164, 165, 166, 170
  chemical, 166
  ground-based, 166
  X-ray, 3, 19, 166
Laue, James, 121
Launch-weight, 209
Lawrence Livermore Laboratory, 166, 290
Lawyers Alliance for Nuclear Arms Control (LANAC), 257
Lawyers Committee on Nuclear Policy (LCNP), 257
Leadbeater, Marie, 261
Leahey, Richard, 288
Leahy, William D., 22
Leaning, Jennifer, 44, 45, 47, 66, 147, 150, 154, 155, 156, 290
Leavitt, Robert, 252, 253
Leebaert, Derek, 152
Lehman, John, 187
Lehrman, Lewis E., 161, 290
Lenin, V. I., 183, 194
Le Suer, Beverly, xvi
Levi-Strauss, Claude, 287
Lewin, Roger, 288
Lifton, Robert Jay, 28, 33, 45, 46, 68, 80, 86, 134, 139, 239
Likutov, Konstantin, 112, 140, 173, 188, 193, 194
Lilienthal, David, 206
Limited Test Ban Treaty. *See* Treaty: Test Ban, limited
Lindop, Patricia, 44
Little Boy bomb, 21, 23
Little, R. W., 287
Loeb, Paul, 254, 287
Lorenz, Konrad, 79, 288
Lown, Bernard, 255
"Low-option attack," 142

Luce, Clare Boothe, 187
Luckmann, Thomas, 108
Lutheran Church, 289
Luttwak, Edward, 70

Maccoby, Michael, 153
MacDougall, John, 238
Mack, John, 32
M.A.D. *See* Mutual Assured Destruction
Madrid, Miguel de la, 199
Malinowski, Bronislaw, 287
Managerialism, 186
Mandelbaum, Michael, 38
Manhattan Project, 22, 25, 38, 54, 165, 240, 241
Mapes, Deb, 260
Mariner 9, 27
Mark-500, 17
Mark, Hans, 161, 290
Marshall, Charles Burton, 187
Marshall, E., 155
Martin, David, 292
Martin of Tours, 222
Martyndv, Vladlen, 195
Marullo, Sam, xvi, 238
MARV (maneuvering reentry vehicle), 17
Marx, Karl, 195
Matthew, 119
Matthiesen, Leroy, 69
McCarthy, Joseph, 198, 215
McDonald, Dwight, 243
McFarland, Sam, xvi
McNamara, Robert, 74, 129, 177, 213, 291
Mead, George, H., 82
Meese, Edward III, 150
Meir, Golda, 36
Melman, Seymour, 30, 31, 92, 94–95
Mennonites, 239
Merton, Robert, 52, 178
Merton, Thomas, 292
Met Lab, 240, 241
Meyrowitz, Elliot L., 257
Michihiko, Hachiya, 23
Midgetman missiles, 212
Milgram, Stanley, 81
Militarism
  and containment, 186
  and expansion, 15
  imperialist, 192
Militarization, 100, 101, 103, 105, 178, 181, 193, 204
  of space, 18, 178
Military-industrial complex, 30, 64, 69, 70, 76, 90, 91, 92–95, 96, 97, 98, 99, 103, 104, 105, 143, 189, 192, 288
Military spending. *See* Budgets, military
Miller, John, 260

Mills, C. Wright, 30, 70, 80, 91, 92, 104, 117, 267
Milstein, Mikhail, 188, 191
Minuteman missiles, 8
Missiles. *See also* Cruise missiles; Depressed-trajectory missiles; Intercontinental ballistic missiles
 accuracy of, 8
 computer guidance systems in, 286
 intermediate-range, 7, 11. *See also* European Force Reduction Talks
 short-range, 164
 "smart," 163, 164, 167, 170, 290
 warhead explosives of, 4
 yield of, 8
Mobilization Committees to End the War in Vietnam (MOBE), 249, 259
Mogey, Wendy, 196
Mohr, Charles, 21, 171, 172, 173, 196
Mojtabai, A. G., 79, 226
Molander, Roger, 49, 67
Mondale, Walter, 288
Monroe Doctrine, 102
Moore, April, xvi
Morris, Desmond, 79
Morrison, Philip, 60
Morrow, James, 127
Moscow, 152, 208, 225, 247
Mullen, Peter, 292
Muller, Ronald E., 102
Multiple independently targetable reentry vehicles (MIRVs), 8, 9, 60, 209, 212
Murphey, Walter, 146, 286
Murphy, George, 187
Mushroom cloud, 5
Muskie, Edmund, 291
Mutual Assured Destruction (M.A.D.), 129, 150, 159, 162, 168, 188, 199
Mutual Assured Security, 169
MX missiles, 4, 8, 15, 16, 17, 18, 209, 253
Myer, Allan, 159, 161, 162, 290
Myers, Beverlee A., 153
Myers, Ched, 261
Myrdal, Alva, 205, 206, 217
"Mystification of technique," 70, 76

Nagasaki, 21, 22, 23, 24, 25, 39, 43, 243, 249, 287
Nash, Henry T., 68, 88
National Academy of Sciences, 26
National Campaign to Save the ABM treaty, 173
National Committee for a Sane Nuclear Policy (SANE), 244–46, 249, 253, 259, 260
National Council of Churches, 231
National Federation of Temple Youth, 232
National Institute for Dispute Resolution, 121

National Institute of Justice, 121
National Research Council, 25, 155
National Security Council, 217
National Security Decision Directive (Jan. 1984), 174
National Technical Means, 216
Nationalism, 104–5, 106, 215, 219
NATO. *See* North Atlantic Treaty Organization
NAVSTAR, 17
Navy (U.S.), 288
Nazis, 68, 80, 189, 190
Nelkin, Dorothy, 251
Netherlands Reformed Church, 233
Neutrons, 2, 5
New Abolitionist movement, 213, 214, 284
New Deal, 187
New Economic Policy (NEP), 183
Nicols, Robbie, 49
Nieberg, Harold, 38
Niedergang, Mark, 252
Nitze, Paul H., 170, 171, 174, 186, 187, 188, 211
Nixon, Richard, 139, 208, 215
No First Use Policy, 285
Non-proliferation treaty (NPT). *See* Treaty: Non-Proliferation of Nuclear Weapons
Nonviolent action
 direct, 245, 256, 260
 methods of, 278–82
 Nonviolent civil defense, 285
Nonviolent sanctions, Harvard program on, 119
North Atlantic Treaty Organization (NATO), 13, 19, 101, 128, 192, 207, 212, 213, 250
Nouwen, Henri, 234
Novick, Aaron, 240
NPT. *See* Treaty: Non-Proliferation of Nuclear Weapons
Nuclear cage, xii–xiv, 1, 2, 18, 20, 40, 52, 66, 77, 86, 88, 91, 104, 105, 115, 162, 178, 184, 195, 213, 237, 238, 287
 social psychology of, 77, 78
Nuclear Free Pacific movement, 261
Nuclear free zones, 193, 260
Nuclear Non-Proliferation treaty. *See* Treaty: Non-Proliferation of Nuclear Weapons
Nuclear power, 2, 6, 50, 51
Nuclear Supreme Council, 70
Nuclear train, 256
Nuclear umbrella, 102–3
Nuclear Weapons Freeze Campaign, 238, 245, 253
Nuclear winter, 7, 19, 26, 27, 28, 29, 39, 45, 52, 154, 155, 199. *See also* Effects of nuclear weapons

Nuclearism, 39
"Nukespeak," 249
Nyerere, Julius, 199

O'Donnell, Peter, Jr., 187
Office of Civilian Defense, 146
Office of Technology Assessment (OTA),
44
Ogburn, William F., 72, 139
Origen, 222
Osgood, Charles, 115, 137

Pacifism, 221, 222, 223, 231, 232, 235. *See
also* Disobedience, civil
active, 245–47
and the church, 221, 222, 223, 231, 235
decline of, 247–49
history of, 239, 240–65
Palme, Olof, 199
Panel on Computing in Support of Battle
Management, 170
Pantex nuclear weapons plant, 69, 79, 256
Papandreou, Andreas, 199
Parliamentarians for Global Action, 121,
291
Parnas, David, 170
Particle-beam weapons, 164, 167, 170
Paterson, Thomas G., 182
Patriot missiles, 174
Pauling, Linus, 244
Pax Christi, 221, 251
Payne, Keith, 163, 164, 169
Peace education, 15, 255
Peace initiatives. *See* Initiatives, peace
Peacekeeper missiles. *See* MX missiles
Peace Links, 257
Peace movements, 122, 195, 210, 220,
237–65
American, 251–54
antinuclear, 240, 244
and the church, 220, 221
European, 250, 251
New Abolitionist, 213, 214, 284
nonaligned, 122
nonviolent direct action in, 245
religious, 239
scientists', 240–43
secular, 239
Soviet, 113, 114, 261
strategies of, 260
Peace through Strength ideology, 1, 100,
108, 109, 111, 112, 114, 125, 126,
131–33, 150, 159, 176, 178, 185, 188,
210, 211, 226, 288
Pearl Harbor, 240
Peattie, Lisa, 67
Peck, Keenen, 265
Pentagon, 18, 64, 97, 99, 105, 196, 213.
See also Defense Department, U.S.

People to People International, 261
People's Test Ban, 253
Perle, Richard, 187
Perrow, Charles, 64
Pershing II missiles, 16, 17, 20, 213, 250,
286
Peterson, Russell W., 28
Physicians for Social Responsibility (PSR),
247, 255
Picket, Clarence, 244
Pipes, Richard, 140, 182, 187
Pisar, Samuel, 100
Plowshares Eight, 256
Podhoretz, Norman, 181
Policy, nuclear, 1, 11, 13, 21, 22, 38, 43,
70, 81, 83, 85, 88, 108, 112, 128, 129,
135, 141, 143, 177, 182, 185, 191,
194, 213, 220
Political action committees (PACs), 98, 99,
253
Pollak, Michael, 251
Ponomarev, Boris, 191, 192, 193
Popes, Roman Catholic, 220
John Paul II, 227
John XXIII, 224
Pius XII, 224
Porro, Jeffrey D., 129
Poseidon submarines. *See* Submarine-
launched ballistic missiles
Posner, Vladimir, 187
Post Nuclear Attack Study, 289. *See also*
Survivability; Crisis relocation
planning
Powers, Thomas, 22, 28, 54, 136, 139, 141,
142
Presidential Directive (PD) 59, 250
Presidential prerogative, 38, 196
Presidential power, 38, 129
President's Foreign Intelligence Advisory
Board, 187
Pringle, Peter, 135, 136, 288
Pritchard, Colin, 248
Program on Nonviolent Sanctions in
Conflict and Defense, 119
Proliferation, nuclear, 49, 51, 207
horizontal and vertical, 51, 207
Psychic numbing, 46, 53, 86, 264, 265
Pugwash Conference on Science and
World Affairs, 242

Quakers. *See* Society of Friends

Radar, phased-array, 162
Radcliffe-Brown, A. R., 71
Radiation, 3, 5, 6, 19, 25, 26, 39, 44, 48,
49, 154–55, 287
effects of, 5, 6, 25, 26, 39, 44, 48, 49
and fallout, 5, 6, 43, 48, 149, 208, 244
gamma, 4, 5, 6

Radio Free Europe, 190
Radio Liberty, 190
Railgun, electromagnetic, 167
Ramsey, Paul, 225
RAND Corporation, 197
Rather, John D. G., 175
Rationality, 137, 138, 143–44
  bounded, 81
Razmerov, Vladimir, 113, 193, 195
Reagan, Ronald, 14, 84, 87, 111, 125, 132,
    150, 158, 161, 162, 164, 180, 182,
    186, 187, 188, 196, 209, 210, 214,
    219, 251, 289
  administration of, 13, 16, 35, 84, 102,
    108, 111, 118, 160, 161, 190, 191,
    210, 226
Reality construction, 123
Reay, Marie, 287
Reciprocity, 34, 58, 59, 60, 61, 75, 82, 85,
    91, 104, 105, 108, 115, 123, 126, 139,
    141, 143, 168, 176, 177, 181, 194,
    201, 212, 287
  escalation of, 58
  in weapons development, 60, 61
  and logic of deterrence, 127
  types of, 168
Reifel, Stuart, 32
Reification, 73
Religion, 33, 79, 124, 141, 190, 219
  and superpower relations, 190
Resources, economic, 29–32
Revolutionary War, 239
Reykjavik summit meeting, 116, 175, 214
Richardson, Lewis, 144
Risk, 82, 84, 143
Ritual, 71, 74, 75, 109, 122–25, 126, 136,
    142, 143, 176, 201, 234, 288
Rizzo, Renata, 254, 257, 258, 260, 264
Roche, John, 187
Rogers, Rita, 78
Roman Catholic Church. *See* Catholic
    Church, Roman
Roosevelt, Franklin, 187
Rose, Peter I., 154
Rostow, Eugene, 186, 187
Rotblat, J., 44
Rothschild, Emma, 138
Rothschild, Matthew, 265
Rumsfeld, Donald, 187
Rusk, Dean, 291
Russell, Bertrand, 242
Russett, Bruce, 210
Rutland, Peter, xvi

Sakharov, Andrei, 183
SALT. *See* Treaty: Strategic Arms
    Limitation Talks
Sanchez, Ada, 253
Sanctuary movement, 263

Sanders, Jerry, 186
SANE. *See* National Committee for a Sane
    Nuclear Policy
Satellites, navigational, 17
Saturn V, 168
Sayle, Murray, 36
Scenarios
  best-case, 156
  winning, 66, 76, 141, 192
  worst-case, 68, 69, 169, 215, 216
Scharansky, Anatoly, 183
Scheer, Robert, 43, 145, 150, 152, 180,
    196, 204, 211, 288, 290, 291
Schell, Jonathan, 28, 59, 104, 254, 268
Schlesinger, James R., 171
Schweitzer, Albert, 244
Scoville, Herbert, 74
Screen Actors Guild, 187
SDI. *See* Strategic Defense Initiative
Seabury, Paul, 187
Secrecy, governmental, 37, 38, 40
Seligman, C. G., 287
Shalom, concept of, 230
Sharp, Gene, 119, 120, 124, 282
Sherzer, Joel, xvi
Shils, Edward, 37
Shore, Rima, 261
Short-range artillery rounds, 7
Short-range attack missiles (SAMs), 8
Shultz, George, 174, 187
Shute, Nevil, 244
Sidel, Victor, 29
Silberman, Laurence, 187
Simmel, Georg, 71
Simon, Herbert A., 81
Simonov, Konstantin, 291
Sivard, Ruth Leger, 7, 13, 29, 51, 60
Skinner, B. F., 79
Smith, Alice Kimball, 292
Smith, Gerard C., 174, 213, 291
Smith, Hedrick, 100
Snitow, Ann, 257
Snow, David, 258
Social systems, 41, 42
  effects of nuclear threat on, 42
Socialism, 189, 190, 194, 198. *See also*
    Communism
Socialization, 82
Society of Friends, 239. *See also* American
    Friends Service Committee
Society of Professionals in Dispute
    Resolution, 121
Sociological ambivalence, 178
Sociology of knowledge, 52. *See also*
    Frames of thought
Solidarity (Polish union), 120
Solo, Pam, 259, 261
Solomon, Norman, 253
Solzhenitsyn, Alexander, 184

Soviet Peace Council, 113
Space mines, 172
Special Committee on Dispute Resolution (American Bar Association), 121
SS-9 (Soviet ICBM), 9
SS-18 (Soviet ICBM), 10
Stalin, Joseph, 183, 184
Standing Consultative Commission (SCC), 117, 126, 217
Star Wars. *See* Strategic Defense Initiative
START. *See* Strategic Arms Reduction Talks
State Department (U.S.), 187
Stealth bomber, 15
Stein, Peter, xvi
Stilwell, R. G., 187
Stimson, Henry L., 240
Stinchcombe, Arthur, xvi, 62
Stockholm Peace Institute, 134
Stockwell, John, xvi
Strategic Air Command (SAC), 43, 286, 288
Strategic Arms Reduction Talks (START), 211, 212, 284
Strategic Defense Initiative (SDI), 15, 111, 158–79, 192, 249, 264, 289, 290, 291
Strategic Integrated Operation Plan (SIOP), 135
Strategic nuclear weapons, 7, 8
Strategic triad, U.S., 8, 9, 11. *See also* Bombers, intercontinental; Intercontinental ballistic missiles; Submarine-launched ballistic missiles
Strategy
  of city withholding, 25, 129
  cost-imposing, 130
  counterforce, 15, 19, 43, 48, 129, 136
  countervailing, 109, 129, 130, 131, 136, 138, 220
  countervalue, 15, 16, 129
  of massive retaliations, 129
  U.S., 174, 177, 191
Strauss, Anselm, 108
Stringfellow, William, 64, 66
Student Peace Union, 246
Student/Teacher Organization to Prevent Nuclear War, 258
Submarine-launched ballistic missiles (SLBMs), 7, 8, 9, 10, 11, 12, 17, 19, 59, 60, 131, 172
  as percentage of arsenals, 11
  warning time for, 17
  See also Arsenals, nuclear
Subrahmanyan, K., 51
Subroc antisubmarine missiles, 7
Superpower relations (U.S. and USSR), 180–203
  Soviet threat model in, 181–88, 202
  U.S. threat model in, 188–95, 202

Survivability, 11, 16, 18, 33, 42, 43, 141, 150, 152, 156, 157, 179
  of ICBMs, 11, 19
Suzuki, Sunao, 244
Swaggart, Jimmie, 226
Swords into Plowshares, 231, 234
Sykes, L. R., 292
Symms, Steven D., 209
Szilard, Leo, 241

Taboo lines, 289
Tate, Grayson D., 291
Taylor, Betsy, 253
Taylor, Richard, 248
Teller, Edward, 166
Tempest, Rone, 95, 98, 100
Terrain contour matching (TERCOM), 8, 16
Terrier missiles, 7
Tertullian, 222
Theater nuclear forces, 7
Thermonuclear weapons, 1, 2, 3, 4, 5, 6, 7, 19, 22, 23, 26, 27, 50. *See also* Effects of nuclear weapons
Thomas, Lewis, 28
Thomas, Norman, 243
Thomas, William I., 53, 82, 134
Thompson, James, 63
Throw-weight, 11, 19, 73, 209, 211
Tilly, Charles, 251
Titan missiles, 286
Tomin, Zdena, 121, 199
Toon, Owen, 27
Totalitarianism, 182, 183
Tovish, Aaron, 121
Tower, John, 188, 211, 289
Toyoda, Toshiyuki, 244
Treaty
  ABM (Treaty Between the United States of America and the Union of Soviet Socialist Republics on the Limitation of Anti-Ballistic Missile Systems, 1972), 162, 173, 174, 208, 209, 217, 289, 291, 292
  Antarctic (1959), 206, 283
  "Hot Line" (Memorandum of Understanding Between the United States and the USSR Regarding the Establishment of a Direct Communication Link), 208, 283
  Law of the Sea, 121
  Non-Proliferation of Nuclear Weapons (1968), 50, 205, 206, 207, 283
  Outer Space (1967), 206, 283
  Sea-Bed (1971), 206, 284
  Strategic Arms Limitation Talks (SALT), 8, 182, 186, 191, 208–210, 211, 212, 216, 217, 250, 284

Treaty, (*cont.*)
  Test Ban, comprehensive, 116, 118, 212, 213, 217, 284
  Test Ban, limited, 115, 205, 207, 212, 247, 248, 283, 292
  Test Ban, threshold, 292
  of Tlatelolco (1967), 206, 283
Trident II missile program, 15, 16
Trident submarine. *See* Submarine-launched ballistic missiles
Trinity test site, 25, 54
Tritium, 3
Truman, Harry S., 21, 22, 190, 241
Trust Group. *See* Group to Establish Trust Between the USSR and the USA
Tsipis, Kosta, 5, 165, 167, 290
TTAPS, 27, 28, 39
Turco, Richard P., 7, 27, 28, 39, 52
Turner, Stansfield, 291
Turpin, Jennifer, xv, 77, 200
Tversky, Amos, 81

Union of Concerned Scientists, 169, 170, 292
United Campuses to Prevent Nuclear War (UCAM), xvi, 15, 123, 253, 258
United Methodist bishops, 223, 225, 229, 230, 235
United Nations, 32, 117, 206, 289
  General Assembly, 193
  International Children's Emergency Fund (UNICEF), 32, 122
United States Arms Control and Disarmament Agency, 117
University Research Institute, xvi
Uranium 2, 3, 235
Urban, Gregory, xvi
Ury, William, 121

Van Slyck, DeForrest, 184
Vance, Cyrus R., 291
Vatican Council, Second, 225
Verification, 201, 212, 214, 217
  agreements on, 208,
Vietnam War, 14, 31, 139, 196, 249, 250, 252
Violence, instinctive and learned, 79–80
Vittachi, Tarzie, 32
Volpe, Maria, 121

Walesa, Lech, 120
Walker, Paul F., 252
Wall, James, 36
Wallis, Jim, 292
Wallis, W. Allen, 187
Walters, LeRoy, 222
Walzer, Michael, 225
War, Department of (U.S.), 58
War, limited nuclear, 43–48, 128, 139, 140–43

and Catholic bishops, 227
  in deterrence policy, 128, 139
  medical and biological effects of, 43–45
  psychological effects of, 45–47
  social consequences of, 47–48
  social psychology of, 77–80
Warfare, psychological, 190
War Resisters League (WRL), 243, 249, 251, 259
Warning systems, 17
Warnke, Paul, 204
Warsaw Pact, 192, 207
  military expenditures of, 13, 19
Weapons
  counterforce, 15, 16, 18, 19, 43, 135, 163, 173, 178, 212
  effects of. *See* Effects of nuclear weapons
  systems, 7, 19
  testing of, 25, 26, 207
  three generations of, 3, 16.
  See also entries under specific weapons
Weapons System Evaluation Group, 286
Webber, Bill, xvi
Weber, Max, xiii, 53, 55, 61, 68, 76, 99, 137
Weinberger, Caspar, 103, 139, 142, 161, 164, 169, 220, 289
Weinraub, Bernard, 288
Weinstein, John M., 151
Weinraub, Bernard, 169, 288
Weiss, Seymour, 187
Weissmann, Arnie, 94
Wicker, Tom, 175
Wikinson, David, 144
Wildavsky, Aaron, 81
Wilford, John Noble, 170
Wilkerson, David, 226
Willens, Harold, 117
Williams, Edward Bennett, 187
Williamson, Robert, 287
Window of vulnerability, 10, 11, 74, 163, .290
Winpisinger, William W., 30
Wittner, Lawrence, 241, 244, 245, 246, 249
Women Strike for Peace, 246
Women's Action for Nuclear Disarmament (WAND), 253, 257
Women's Pentagon Action, 257
World Court, 117, 289
World Meteorological Organization, 217
World Peace Council, 132
World War I, 239
World War II, xi, 4, 6, 30, 92, 105, 112, 146, 151, 181

X-ray laser, 3, 19, 166

Yakovlev, Nikolai, 188, 189, 190
Yankee class submarines (Soviet), 10

Yefremov, A. Y., 189, 191, 209, 213
Yoder, John Howard, 292
York, Herbert, 60
Young, Nigel, 259
Yudkin, Marcia, 32

Zagladin, Vadim, 194, 195
Zahn, Gordon, 292

Zarsky, Lyuba, 261
Zen Buddhism, 266
Zero option, 212
Zhivkov, Todor, 192
Zimmerman, William, 195
Zumwalt, E. R., Jr., 187
Zurcher, Louis, xvi, 67
Zykov, Eugene, 288